Android Studio
Development Essentials

Android Studio Development Essentials – Second Edition

ISBN-13: 978-1500613860

Rev 2.0c

 eBookFrenzy

Table of Contents

1. Introduction

The goal of this book is to teach the skills necessary to develop Android based applications using the Android Studio Integrated Development Environment (IDE) and the Android 5 Software Development Kit (SDK).

Beginning with the basics, this book provides an outline of the steps necessary to set up an Android development and testing environment. An overview of Android Studio is included covering areas such as tool windows, the code editor and the Designer tool. An introduction to the architecture of Android is followed by an in-depth look at the design of Android applications and user interfaces using the Android Studio environment. More advanced topics such as database management, content providers and intents are also covered, as are touch screen handling, gesture recognition, camera access and the playback and recording of both video and audio. This edition of the book also covers printing, transitions and cloud-based file storage.

In addition to covering general Android development techniques, the book also includes Google Play specific topics such as implementing maps using the Google Maps Android API, in-app billing and submitting apps to the Google Play Developer Console.

Chapters also cover advanced features of Android Studio such as Gradle build configuration and the implementation of build variants to target multiple Android device types from a single project code base.

Assuming you already have some Java programming experience, are ready to download Android Studio and the Android SDK, have access to a Windows, Mac or Linux system and ideas for some apps to develop, you are ready to get started.

1.1 Downloading the Code Samples

The source code and Android Studio project files for the examples contained in this book are available for download at:

http://www.ebookfrenzy.com/print/androidstudio/index.php

The steps to load a project from the code samples into Android Studio are as follows:

1. From the *Welcome to Android Studio* dialog, select the *Import project* option.
2. In the project selection dialog, navigate to and select the folder containing the project to be imported and click on OK.
3. Click on OK in the *Sync Android SDKs* dialog.
4. Click Yes in the *Language Level Changed* dialog if it appears.

1.2 **Download the eBook**

Thank you for purchasing the print edition of this book. If you would like to download the eBook version of this book, please email proof of purchase to *feedback@ebookfrenzy.com* and we will provide you with a download link for the book in PDF, ePub and MOBI formats.

1.3 **Feedback**

We want you to be satisfied with your purchase of this book. If you find any errors in the book, or have any comments, questions or concerns please contact us at *feedback@ebookfrenzy.com*.

1.4 **Errata**

Whilst we make every effort to ensure the accuracy of the content of this book, it is inevitable that a book covering a subject area of this size and complexity may include some errors and oversights. Any known issues with the book will be outlined, together with solutions, at the following URL:

http://www.ebookfrenzy.com/errata/androidstudio.html

In the event that you find an error not listed in the errata, please let us know by emailing our technical support team at *feedback@ebookfrenzy.com*. They are there to help you and will work to resolve any problems you may encounter.

2. Setting up an Android Studio Development Environment

Before any work can begin on the development of an Android application, the first step is to configure a computer system to act as the development platform. This involves a number of steps consisting of installing the Java Development Kit (JDK) and the Android Studio Integrated Development Environment (IDE) which also includes the Android Software Development Kit (SDK).

This chapter will cover the steps necessary to install the requisite components for Android application development on Windows, Mac OS X and Linux based systems.

2.1 System Requirements

Android application development may be performed on any of the following system types:

* Windows 2003 (32-bit or 64-bit)
* Windows Vista (32-bit or 64-bit)
* Windows 7 (32-bit or 64-bit)
* Windows 8 / Windows 8.1
* Mac OS X 10.8.5 or later (Intel based systems only)
* Linux systems with version 2.11 or later of GNU C Library (glibc)
* Minimum of 2GB of RAM (4GB is preferred)
* 1.5GB of available disk space

2.2 Installing the Java Development Kit (JDK)

The Android SDK was developed using the Java programming language. Similarly, Android applications are also developed using Java. As a result, the Java Development Kit (JDK) is the first component that must be installed.

Android development requires the installation of either version 6 or 7 of the Standard Edition of the Java Platform Development Kit. Java is provided in both development (JDK) and runtime (JRE) packages. For the purposes of Android development, the JDK must be installed.

2.2.1 Windows JDK Installation

For Windows systems, the JDK may be obtained from Oracle Corporation's website using the following URL:

http://www.oracle.com/technetwork/java/javase/downloads/index.html

Assuming that a suitable JDK is not already installed on your system, download the latest JDK package that matches the destination computer system. Once downloaded, launch the installation executable and follow the on screen instructions to complete the installation process.

2.2.2 Mac OS X JDK Installation

Java is not installed by default on recent versions of Mac OS X. To confirm the presence or otherwise of Java, open a Terminal window and enter the following command:

```
java -version
```

Assuming that Java is currently installed, output similar to the following will appear in the terminal window:

```
java version "1.7.0_71"
Java(TM) SE Runtime Environment (build 1.7.0_71-b14)
Java HotSpot(TM) 64-Bit Server VM (build 24.71-b01, mixed mode)
```

In the event that Java is not installed, issuing the "java" command in the terminal window will result in the appearance of a message which reads as follows together with a dialog on the desktop providing a More Info button which, when clicked will display the Oracle Java web page:

```
No Java runtime present, requesting install
```

On the Oracle Java web page, locate and download the Java SE 7 JDK installation package for Mac OS X.

Open the downloaded disk image (.dmg file) and double-click on the icon to install the Java package (Figure 2-1):

Figure 2-1

The Java for OS X installer window will appear and take you through the steps involved in installing the JDK. Once the installation is complete, return to the Terminal window and run the following command, at which point the previously outlined Java version information should appear:

```
java -version
```

2.3 Linux JDK Installation

Firstly, if the chosen development system is running the 64-bit version of Ubuntu then it is essential that the 32-bit library support packages be installed:

```
sudo apt-get install lib32z1 lib32ncurses5 lib32bz2-1.0 lib32stdc++6
```

As with Windows based JDK installation, it is possible to install the JDK on Linux by downloading the appropriate package from the Oracle web site, the URL for which is as follows:

http://www.oracle.com/technetwork/java/javase/downloads/index.html

Packages are provided by Oracle in RPM format (for installation on Red Hat Linux based systems such as Red Hat Enterprise Linux, Fedora and CentOS) and as a tar archive for other Linux distributions such as Ubuntu.

On Red Hat based Linux systems, download the .rpm JDK file from the Oracle web site and perform the installation using the *rpm* command in a terminal window. Assuming, for example, that the downloaded JDK file was named *jdk-7u71-linux-x64.rpm*, the commands to perform the installation would read as follows:

```
su
rpm -ihv jdk-7u71-linux-x64.rpm
```

To install using the compressed tar package (tar.gz) perform the following steps:

1. Create the directory into which the JDK is to be installed (for the purposes of this example we will assume */home/demo/java*).

2. Download the appropriate tar.gz package from the Oracle web site into the directory.

3. Execute the following command (where *<jdk-file>* is replaced by the name of the downloaded JDK file):

```
tar xvfz   <jdk-file>.tar.gz
```

4. Remove the downloaded tar.gz file.

5. Add the path to the *bin* directory of the JDK installation to your $PATH variable. For example, assuming that the JDK ultimately installed into */home/demo/java/jdk1.7.0_71* the following would need to be added to your $PATH environment variable:

```
/home/demo/java/jdk1.7.0_71/bin
```

This can typically be achieved by adding a command to the *.bashrc* file in your home directory (specifics may differ depending on the particular Linux distribution in use). For example, change directory to your home directory, edit the *.bashrc* file contained therein and add the following line at the end of the file (modifying the path to match the location of the JDK on your system):

```
export PATH=/home/demo/java/jdk1.7.0_71/bin:$PATH
```

Having saved the change, future terminal sessions will include the JDK in the $PATH environment variable.

2.4 **Downloading the Android Studio Package**

Most of the work involved in developing applications for Android will be performed using the Android Studio environment. Android Studio may be downloaded from the following web page:

http://developer.android.com/sdk/index.html

From this page, either click on the download button if it lists the correct platform (for example on a Windows based web browser the button will read "Download Android Studio for Windows"), or select the "Other Download Options" link to manually select the appropriate package for your platform and operating system. On the subsequent screen, accept the terms and conditions to initiate the download.

2.5 **Installing Android Studio**

Once downloaded, the exact steps to install Android Studio differ depending on the operating system on which the installation is being performed.

2.5.1 Installation on Windows

Locate the downloaded Android Studio installation executable file (named *android-studio-bundle-<version>*.exe) in a Windows Explorer window and double click on it to start the installation process, clicking the *Yes* button in the User Account Control dialog if it appears.

Once the Android Studio setup wizard appears, work through the various screens to configure the installation to meet your requirements in terms of the file system location into which Android Studio should be installed and whether or not it should be made available to other users of the system. Although there are no strict rules on where Android Studio should be installed on the system, the remainder of this book will assume that the installation was performed into a sub-folder of the user's home directory named *android-studio*. Once the options have been configured, click on the *Install* button to begin the installation process.

On versions of Windows with a Start menu, the newly installed Android Studio can be launched from the entry added to that menu during the installation. On Windows 8, the executable can be pinned to the task bar for easy access by navigating to the *android-studio\bin* directory, right-clicking on the executable and selecting the *Pin to Taskbar* menu option. Note that the executable is provided in 32-bit (*studio*) and 64-bit (*studio64*) executable versions. If you are running a 32-bit system be sure to use the *studio* executable.

2.5.2 Installation on Mac OS X

Android Studio for Mac OS X is downloaded in the form of a disk image (.dmg) file. Once the *android-studio-ide-<version>*.dmg file has been downloaded, locate it in a Finder window and double click on it to open it as shown in Figure 2-2:

Figure 2-2

To install the package, simply drag the Android Studio icon and drop it onto the Applications folder. The Android Studio package will then be installed into the Applications folder of the system, a process which will typically take a few minutes to complete.

To launch Android Studio, locate the executable in the Applications folder using a Finder window and double click on it. When attempting to launch Android Studio, an error dialog may appear indicating that the JVM cannot be found. If this error occurs, it will be necessary to download and install the Mac OS X Java 6 JRE package on the system. This can be downloaded from Apple using the following link:

http://support.apple.com/kb/DL1572

Once the Java for OS X package has been installed, Android Studio should launch without any problems.

For future easier access to the tool, drag the Android Studio icon from the Finder window and drop it onto the dock.

2.5.3 Installation on Linux

Having downloaded the Linux Android Studio package, open a terminal window, change directory to the location where Android Studio is to be installed and execute the following command:

```
unzip /<path to package>/android-studio-ide-<version>-linux.zip
```

Note that the Android Studio bundle will be installed into a sub-directory named *android-studio*. Assuming, therefore, that the above command was executed in */home/demo*, the software packages will be unpacked into */home/demo/android-studio*.

To launch Android Studio, open a terminal window, change directory to the *android-studio/bin* sub-directory and execute the following command:

```
./studio.sh
```

On Linux it may also necessary to specify the location of the Java Development Kit using the following steps:

1. Launch Android Studio and create a new project.
2. Select the *File -> Other Settings -> Default Project Structure...* menu option.
3. Enter the full path to the directory containing the JDK into the *JDK Location* field.
4. Click *Apply* followed by *OK*.

2.6 **The Android Studio Setup Wizard**

The first time that Android Studio is launched after being installed, a dialog will appear providing the option to import settings from a previous Android Studio version. If you have settings from a previous version and would like to import them into the latest installation, select the appropriate option and location. Alternatively, indicate that you do not need to import any previous settings and click on the OK button to proceed.

After Android Studio has finished loading, the setup wizard will appear as shown in Figure 2-3.

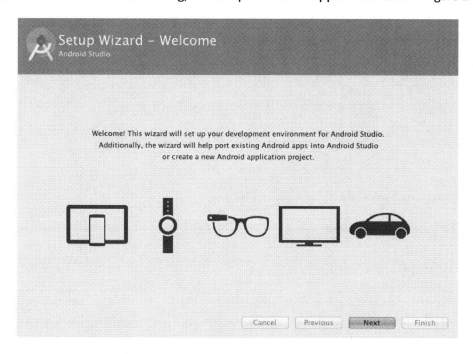

Figure 2-3

Click on the Next button, choose the Standard installation option and click on Next once again. On the license agreement screen, select and accept each of the licenses listed before clicking on Finish to complete the setup process. The Welcome to Android Studio screen should then appear:

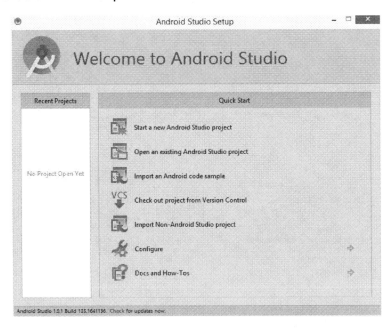

Figure 2-4

2.7 Installing the Latest Android SDK Packages

The steps performed so far have installed Java, the Android Studio IDE and the current set of default Android SDK packages. Before proceeding, it is worth taking some time to verify which packages are installed and to install any missing packages.

This task can be performed using the *Android SDK Manager*, which may be launched from within the Android Studio tool by selecting the *Configure -> SDK Manager* option from within the Android Studio welcome dialog. Once invoked, the SDK Manager tool will appear as illustrated in Figure 2-5:

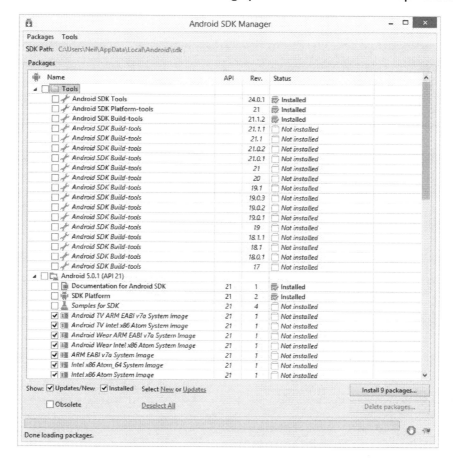

Figure 2-5

Within the Android SDK Manager, make sure that the following packages are listed as *Installed* in the Status column:

- Tools > Android SDK Tools
- Tools > Android SDK Platform-tools
- Tools > Android SDK Build-tools
- SDK Platform (most recent version) > SDK Platform
- SDK Platform (most recent version) > ARM EABI v7a System Image
- Extras > Android Support Repository
- Extras > Android Support Library
- Extras > Google Repository
- Extras > Google USB Driver (Required on Windows systems only)
- Extras > Intel x86 Emulator Accelerator (HAXM installer)

In the event that any of the above packages are listed as *Not Installed*, simply select the checkboxes next to those packages and click on the *Install packages* button to initiate the installation process. In the resulting dialog, accept the license agreements before clicking on the *Install* button. The SDK Manager will then begin to download and install the designated packages. As the installation proceeds, a progress bar will appear at the bottom of the manager window indicating the status of the installation.

Once the installation is complete, review the package list and make sure that the selected packages are now listed as *Installed* in the *Status* column. If any are listed as *Not installed,* make sure they are selected and click on the *Install packages...* button again.

2.8 **Making the Android SDK Tools Command-line Accessible**

Most of the time, the underlying tools of the Android SDK will be accessed from within the Android Studio environment. That being said, however, there will also be instances where it will be useful to be able to invoke those tools from a command prompt or terminal window. In order for the operating system on which you are developing to be able to find these tools, it will be necessary to add them to the system's *PATH* environment variable.

Regardless of operating system, the PATH variable needs to be configured to include the following paths (where *<path_to_android_sdk_installation>* represents the file system location into which the Android SDK was installed):

```
<path_to_android_sdk_installation>/sdk/tools
<path_to_android_sdk_installation>/sdk/platform-tools
```

The location of the SDK on your system can be identified by launching the SDK Manager and referring to the *SDK Path:* field located at the top of the manager window as highlighted in Figure 2-6:

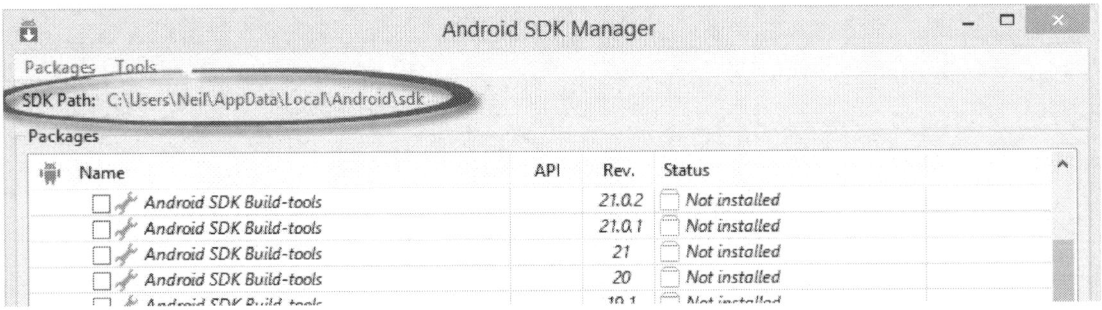

Figure 2-6

Once the location of the SDK has been identified, the steps to add this to the PATH variable are operating system dependent:

2.8.1 Windows 7

1. Right-click on *Computer* in the desktop start menu and select *Properties* from the resulting menu.
2. In the properties panel, select the *Advanced System Settings* link and, in the resulting dialog, click on the *Environment Variables...* button.
3. In the Environment Variables dialog, locate the *Path* variable in the *System variables* list, select it and click on *Edit....* Locate the end of the current variable value string and append the path to the android platform tools to the end, using a semicolon to separate the path from the preceding values. For example, assuming Android Studio was installed into *C:\Users\demo\AppData\Local\Android\sdk*, the following would be appended to the end of the current Path value:

```
;C:\Users\demo\AppData\Local\Android\sdk\platform-
tools;C:\Users\demo\AppData\Local\Android\sdk\tools
```

4. Click on OK in each dialog box and close the system properties control panel.

Once the above steps are complete, verify that the path is correctly set by opening a *Command Prompt* window (*Start -> All Programs -> Accessories -> Command Prompt*) and at the prompt enter:

```
echo %Path%
```

The returned path variable value should include the paths to the Android SDK platform tools folders. Verify that the *platform-tools* value is correct by attempting to run the *adb* tool as follows:

```
adb
```

The tool should output a list of command line options when executed.

Similarly, check the *tools* path setting by attempting to launch the Android SDK Manager:

```
android
```

In the event that a message similar to the following message appears for one or both of the commands, it is most likely that an incorrect path was appended to the Path environment variable:

```
'adb' is not recognized as an internal or external command,
operable program or batch file.
```

2.8.2 Windows 8.1

1. On the start screen, move the mouse to the bottom right hand corner of the screen and select *Search* from the resulting menu. In the search box, enter *Control Panel*. When the Control Panel icon appears in the results area, click on it to launch the tool on the desktop.

2. Within the Control Panel, use the *Category* menu to change the display to *Large Icons.* From the list of icons select the one labeled *System*.

3. Follow the steps outlined for Windows 7 starting from step 2 through to step 4.

Open the command prompt window (move the mouse to the bottom right hand corner of the screen, select the Search option and enter *cmd* into the search box). Select *Command Prompt* from the search results.

Within the Command Prompt window, enter:

```
echo %Path%
```

The returned path variable value should include the paths to the Android SDK platform tools folders. Verify that the *platform-tools* value is correct by attempting to run the *adb* tool as follows:

```
adb
```

The tool should output a list of command line options when executed.

Similarly, check the *tools* path setting by attempting to launch the Android SDK Manager:

```
android
```

In the event that a message similar to the following message appears for one or both of the commands, it is most likely that an incorrect path was appended to the Path environment variable:

```
'adb' is not recognized as an internal or external command,
operable program or batch file.
```

2.8.3 Linux

On Linux this will involve once again editing the *.bashrc* file. Assuming that the Android SDK bundle package was installed into */home/demo/Android/sdk*, the export line in the *.bashrc* file would now read as follows:

```
export
PATH=/home/demo/java/jdk1.7.0_10/bin:/home/demo/Android/sdk/platform-
tools:/home/demo/Android/sdk/tools:/home/demo/android-studio/bin:$PATH
```

Note also that the above command adds the *android-studio/bin* directory to the PATH variable. This will enable the *studio.sh* script to be executed regardless of the current directory within a terminal window.

2.8.4 Mac OS X

A number of techniques may be employed to modify the $PATH environment variable on Mac OS X. Arguably the cleanest method is to add a new file in the */etc/paths.d* directory containing the paths to be added to $PATH. Assuming an Android SDK installation location of */Users/demo/Library/Android/sdk*, the path may be configured by creating a new file named *android-sdk* in the */etc/paths.d* directory containing the following lines:

```
/Users/demo/Library/Android/sdk/tools
/Users/demo/Library/Android/sdk/platform-tools
```

Note that since this is a system directory it will be necessary to use the *sudo* command when creating the file. For example:

```
sudo vi /etc/paths.d/android-sdk
```

2.9 **Updating the Android Studio and the SDK**

From time to time new versions of Android Studio and the Android SDK are released. New versions of the SDK are installed using the Android SDK Manager. Android Studio will typically notify you when an update is ready to be installed.

To manually check for Android Studio updates, click on the *Check for updates now* link located at the bottom of the Android Studio welcome screen, or use the *Help -> Check for Update...* menu option accessible from within the Android Studio main window.

2.10 **Summary**

Prior to beginning the development of Android based applications, the first step is to set up a suitable development environment. This consists of the Java Development Kit (JDK), Android SDKs, and Android Studio IDE. In this chapter, we have covered the steps necessary to install these packages on Windows, Mac OS X and Linux.

3. Creating an Example Android App in Android Studio

The preceding chapters of this book have covered the steps necessary to configure an environment suitable for the development of Android applications using the Android Studio IDE. Before moving on to slightly more advanced topics, now is a good time to validate that all of the required development packages are installed and functioning correctly. The best way to achieve this goal is to create an Android application and compile and run it. This chapter will cover the creation of a simple Android application project using Android Studio. Once the project has been created, a later chapter will explore the use of the Android emulator environment to perform a test run of the application.

3.1 Creating a New Android Project

The first step in the application development process is to create a new project within the Android Studio environment. Begin, therefore, by launching Android Studio so that the "Welcome to Android Studio" screen appears as illustrated in Figure 3-1:

Figure 3-1

Once this window appears, Android Studio is ready for a new project to be created. To create the new project, simply click on the *Start a new Android Studio project* option to display the first screen of the *New Project* wizard as shown in Figure 3-2:

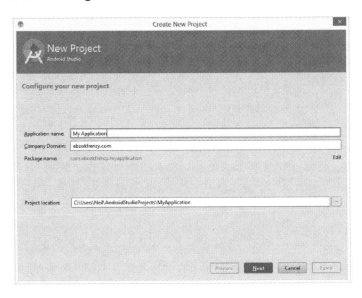

Figure 3-2

3.2 Defining the Project and SDK Settings

In the *New Project* window, set the *Application name* field to *AndroidSample*. The application name is the name by which the application will be referenced and identified within Android Studio and is also the name that will be used when the completed application goes on sale in the Google Play store.

The *Package Name* is used to uniquely identify the application within the Android application ecosystem. It should be based on the reversed URL of your domain name followed by the name of the application. For example, if your domain is *www.mycompany.com*, and the application has been named *AndroidSample*, then the package name might be specified as follows:

```
com.mycompany.androidsample
```

If you do not have a domain name, you may also use *ebookfrenzy.com* for the purposes of testing, though this will need to be changed before an application can be published:

```
com.ebookfrenzy.androidsample
```

The *Project location* setting will default to a location in the folder named *AndroidStudioProjects* located in your home directory and may be changed by clicking on the button to the right of the text field containing the current path setting.

Click Next to proceed. On the form factors screen, enable the *Phone and Tablet* option and set the minimum SDK setting to API 8: Android 2.2 (Froyo). The reason for selecting an older SDK release is that this ensures that the finished application will be able to run on the widest possible range of Android devices. The higher the minimum SDK selection, the more the application will be restricted to newer Android devices. A useful chart (Figure 3-3) can be viewed by clicking on the *Help me choose* link. This outlines the various SDK versions and API levels available for use and the percentage of Android devices in the marketplace on which the application will run if that SDK is used as the minimum level. In general it should only be necessary to select a more recent SDK when that release contains a specific feature that is required for your application. To help in the decision process, selecting an API level from the chart will display the features that are supported at that level.

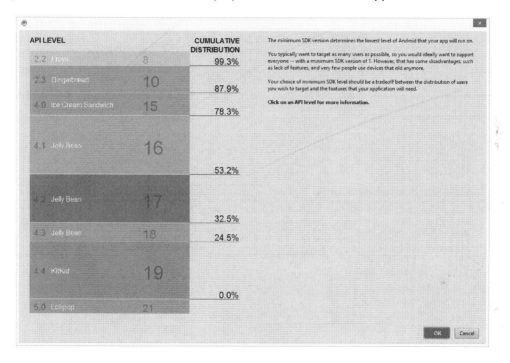

Figure 3-3

Since the project is not intended for Google TV, Google Glass or wearable devices, leave the remaining options disabled before clicking *Next*.

3.3 Creating an Activity

The next step is to define the type of initial activity that is to be created for the application. A range of different activity types is available when developing Android applications. The *Master/Detail Flow* option will be covered in a later chapter. For the purposes of this example, however, simply select the option to create a *Blank Activity*.

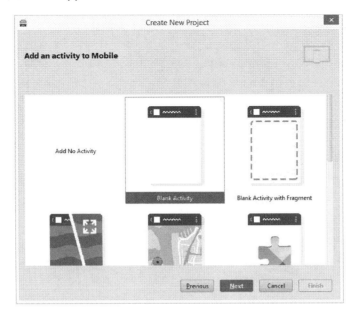

Figure 3-4

With the Blank Activity option selected, click *Next.* On the final screen (Figure 3-5) name the activity and title *AndroidSampleActivity*. The activity will consist of a single user interface screen layout which, for the purposes of this example, should be named *activity_android_sample* as shown in Figure 3-5 and with a menu resource named *menu_android_sample*:

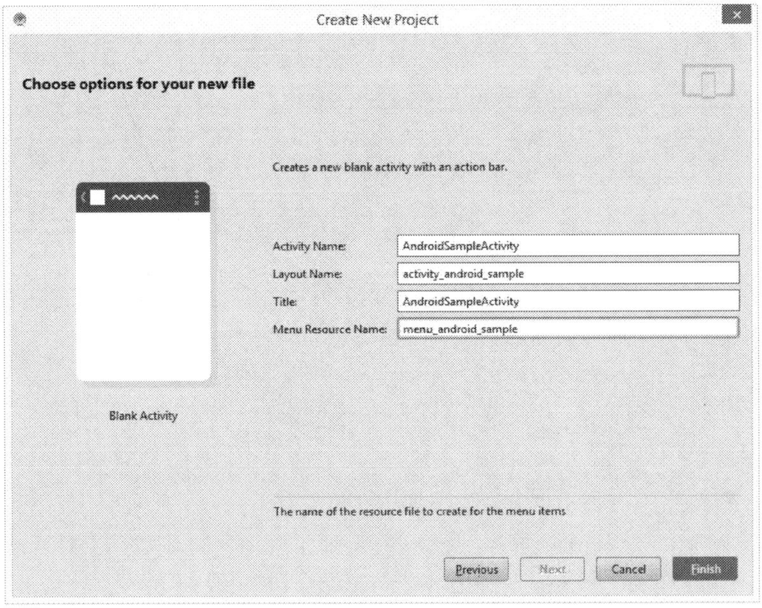

Figure 3-5

Finally, click on *Finish* to initiate the project creation process.

3.4 **Modifying the Example Application**

At this point, Android Studio has created a minimal example application project and opened the main window.

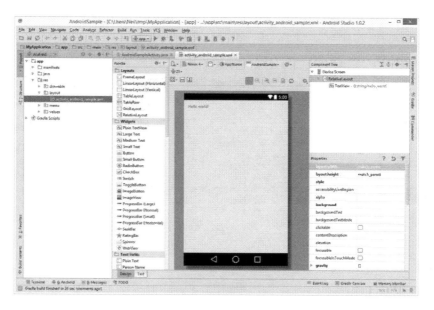

Figure 3-6

The newly created project and references to associated files are listed in the *Project* tool window located on the left hand side of the main project window. The Project tool window has a number of modes in which information can be displayed. By default, this panel will be in *Android* mode. This setting is controlled by the drop down menu at the top of the panel as highlighted in Figure 3-6. If the panel is not currently in Android mode, click on this menu and switch to Android mode:

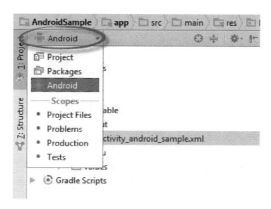

Figure 3-7

Creating an Example Android App in Android Studio

The example project created for us when we selected the option to create an activity consists of a user interface containing a label that will read "Hello World" when the application is executed.

The next step in this tutorial is to modify the user interface of our application so that it displays a larger text view object with a different message to the one provided for us by Android Studio.

The user interface design for our activity is stored in a file named *activity_android_sample.xml* which, in turn, is located under *app -> res -> layout* in the project file hierarchy. Using the Project tool window, locate this file as illustrated in Figure 3-8:

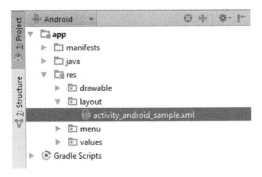

Figure 3-8

Once located, double click on the file to load it into the User Interface Designer tool which will appear in the center panel of the Android Studio main window:

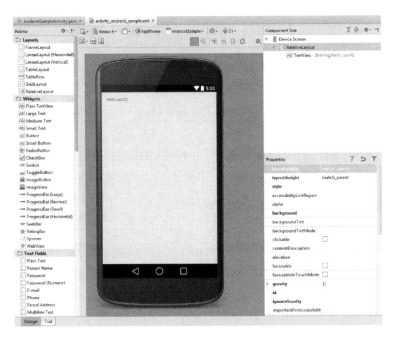

Figure 3-9

In the toolbar across the top of Designer window is a menu currently set to *Nexus 4* which is reflected in the visual representation of the device within the Designer panel. A wide range of other device options are available for selection by clicking on this menu.

To change the orientation of the device representation between landscape and portrait simply use the

drop down menu immediately to the right of the device selection menu showing the  icon.

As can be seen in the device screen, the layout already includes a label that displays a Hello World! message. Running down the left hand side of the panel is a palette containing different categories of user interface components that may be used to construct a user interface, such as buttons, labels and text fields. It should be noted, however, that not all user interface components are obviously visible to the user. One such category consists of *layouts*. Android supports a variety of different layouts that provide different levels of control over how visual user interface components are positioned and managed on the screen. Though it is difficult to tell from looking at the visual representation of the user interface, the current design has been created using a RelativeLayout. This can be confirmed by reviewing the information in the *Component Tree* panel which, by default, is located in the upper right hand corner of the Designer panel and is shown in Figure 3-10:

Figure 3-10

As we can see from the component tree hierarchy, the user interface consists of a RelativeLayout parent with a single child in the form of a TextView object.

The first step in modifying the application is to delete the TextView component from the design. Begin by clicking on the TextView object within the user interface view so that it appears with a blue border around it. Once selected, press the Delete key on the keyboard to remove the object from the layout.

In the Palette panel, locate the *Widgets* category. Click and drag the *Large Text* object and drop it in the center of the user interface design when the green marker lines appear to indicate the center of the display:

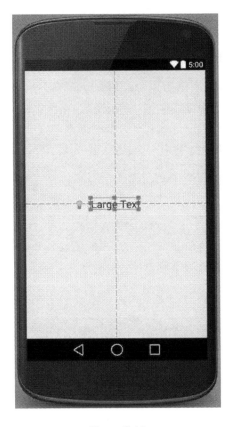

Figure 3-11

The Android Studio Designer tool also provides an alternative to dragging and dropping components from the palette on to the design layout. Components may also be added by selecting the required object from the palette and then simply clicking on the layout at the location where the component is to be placed.

The next step is to change the text that is currently displayed by the TextView component. Double click on the object in the design layout to display the text and id editing panel as illustrated in Figure 3-12. Within the panel, change the text property from "Large Text" to "Welcome to Android Studio".

Figure 3-12

At this point it is important to explain the light bulb next to the TextView object in the layout. This indicates a possible problem and provides some recommended solutions. Clicking on the icon in this instance informs us that the problem is as follows:

```
[I18N] Hardcoded string "Welcome to Android Studio", should use
@string resource
```

This I18N message is informing us that a potential issue exists with regard to the future internationalization of the project ("I18N" comes from the fact that the word "internationalization" begins with an "I", ends with an "N" and has 18 letters in between). The warning is reminding us that when developing Android applications, attributes and values such as text strings should be stored in the form of *resources* wherever possible. Doing so enables changes to the appearance of the application to be made by modifying resource files instead of changing the application source code. This can be especially valuable when translating a user interface to a different spoken language. If all of the text in a user interface is contained in a single resource file, for example, that file can be given to a translator who will then perform the translation work and return the translated file for inclusion in the application. This enables multiple languages to be targeted without the necessity for any source code changes to be made. In this instance, we are going to create a new resource named *welcomestring* and assign to it the string "Welcome to Android Studio".

Click on the arrow to the right of the warning message to display the menu of possible solutions (Figure 3-13).

Figure 3-13

From the menu, select the *Extract string resource* option to display the *Extract Resource* dialog. In this dialog, enter *welcomestring* into the *Resource name:* field before clicking on *OK.* The string is now stored as a resource in the *app -> res -> values -> strings.xml* file.

3.5 Reviewing the Layout and Resource Files

Before moving on to the next chapter, we are going to look at some of the internal aspects of user interface design and resource handling. In the previous section, we made some changes to the user interface by modifying the *activity_android_sample.xml* file using the UI Designer tool. In fact, all that the Designer was doing was providing a user-friendly way to edit the underlying XML content of the file. In practice, there is no reason why you cannot modify the XML directly in order to make user interface changes and, in some instances, this may actually be quicker than using the Designer tool. At the bottom of the Designer panel are two tabs labeled *Design* and *Text* respectively. To switch to the XML view simply select the *Text* tab as shown in Figure 3-14:

Figure 3-14

As can be seen from the structure of the XML file, the user interface consists of the RelativeLayout component, which in turn, is the parent of the TextView object. We can also see that the *text* property of the TextView is set to our *welcomestring* resource. Although varying in complexity and content, all user interface layouts are structured in this hierarchical, XML based way.

One of the more powerful features of Android Studio can be found to the right hand side of the XML editing panel. This is the Preview panel and shows the current visual state of the layout. As changes are made to the XML layout, these will be reflected in the preview panel. To see this in action, modify the XML layout to change the background color of the RelativeLayout to a shade of red as follows:

```
<RelativeLayout
xmlns:android="http://schemas.android.com/apk/res/android"
    xmlns:tools="http://schemas.android.com/tools"
    android:layout_width="match_parent"
    android:layout_height="match_parent"
    android:paddingLeft="16dp"
    android:paddingRight="16dp"
    android:paddingTop="16dp"
    android:paddingBottom="16dp"
    tools:context=".AndroidSampleActivity"
    android:background="#ff2438">

    <TextView
        android:layout_width="wrap_content"
        android:layout_height="wrap_content"
        android:textAppearance="?android:attr/textAppearanceLarge"
        android:text="@string/welcomestring"
        android:id="@+id/textView"
        android:layout_centerVertical="true"
        android:layout_centerHorizontal="true" />

</RelativeLayout>
```

Note that the color of the preview changes in real-time to match the new setting in the XML file. Note also that a small red square appears in the left hand margin (also referred to as the *gutter*) of the XML editor next to the line containing the color setting. This is a visual cue to the fact that the color red has been set on a property. Change the color value to #a0ff28 and note that both the small square in the margin and the preview change to green.

Finally, use the Project view to locate the *app -> res -> values -> strings.xml* file and double click on it to load it into the editor. Currently the XML should read as follows:

```
<?xml version="1.0" encoding="utf-8"?>
<resources>
```

```
<string name="app_name">AndroidSample</string>
<string name="hello_world">Hello world!</string>
<string name="action_settings">Settings</string>
<string name="welcomestring">Welcome to Android Studio</string>

</resources>
```

As a demonstration of resources in action, change the string value currently assigned to the *welcomestring* resource and then return to the Designer by selecting the tab for the layout file in the editor panel. Note that the layout has picked up the new resource value for the welcome string.

There is also a quick way to access the value of a resource referenced in an XML file. With the Designer tool in Text mode, click on the "@string/welcomestring" property setting so that it highlights and then press Ctrl+B on the keyboard. Android Studio will subsequently open the *strings.xml* file and take you to the line in that file where this resource is declared. Use this opportunity to revert the string resource back to the original "Welcome to Android Studio" text.

3.6 **Previewing the Layout**

So far in this chapter, the layout has only been previewed on a representation of the Nexus 4 device. As previously discussed, the layout can be tested for other devices by making selections from the device menu in the toolbar across the top edge of the Designer panel. Another useful option provided by this menu is *Preview All Screen Sizes* which, when selected, shows the layout in all currently configured device configurations as demonstrated in Figure 3-15:

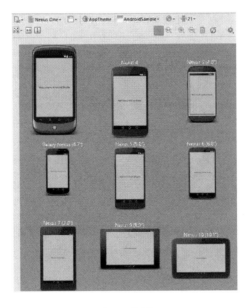

Figure 3-15

To revert to a single preview layout, select the device menu once again, this time choosing the *Remove Previews* option.

3.7 **Summary**

Whilst not excessively complex, a number of steps are involved in setting up an Android development environment. Having performed those steps, it is worth working through a simple example to make sure the environment is correctly installed and configured. In this chapter, we have created a simple application and then used the Android Studio UI Designer to modify the user interface layout. In doing so, we explored the importance of using resources wherever possible, particularly in the case of string values, and briefly touched on the topic of layouts. Finally, we looked at the underlying XML that is used to store the user interface designs of Android applications.

Whilst it is useful to be able to preview a layout from within the Android Studio Designer tool, there is no substitute for testing an application by compiling and running it. In a later chapter entitled *Creating an Android Virtual Device (AVD) in Android Studio*, the steps necessary to set up an emulator for testing purposes will be covered in detail. Before running the application, however, the next chapter will take a small detour to provide a guided tour of the Android Studio user interface.

4. A Tour of the Android Studio User Interface

Whilst it is tempting to plunge into running the example application created in the previous chapter, doing so involves using aspects of the Android Studio user interface which are best described in advance.

Android Studio is a powerful and feature rich development environment that is, to a large extent, intuitive to use. That being said, taking the time now to gain familiarity with the layout and organization of the Android Studio user interface will considerably shorten the learning curve in later chapters of the book. With this in mind, this chapter will provide an initial overview of the various areas and components that make up the Android Studio environment.

4.1 The Welcome Screen

The welcome screen (Figure 4-1) is displayed any time that Android Studio is running with no projects currently open (open projects can be closed at any time by selecting the *File -> Close Project* menu option). If Android Studio was previously exited while a project was still open, the tool will by-pass the welcome screen next time it is launched, automatically opening the previously active project.

Figure 4-1

A Tour of the Android Studio User Interface

In addition to a list of recent projects, the Quick Start menu provides a range of options for performing tasks such as opening, creating and importing projects along with access to projects currently under version control. In addition, the *Configure* option provides access to the SDK Manager along with a vast array of settings and configuration options. A review of these options will quickly reveal that there is almost no aspect of Android Studio that cannot be configured and tailored to your specific needs.

Finally, the status bar along the bottom edge of the window provides information about the version of Android Studio currently running, along with a link to check if updates are available for download.

4.2 **The Main Window**

When a new project is created, or an existing one opened, the Android Studio *main window* will appear. When multiple projects are open simultaneously, each will be assigned its own main window. The precise configuration of the window will vary depending on which tools and panels were displayed the last time the project was open, but will typically resemble that of Figure 4-2.

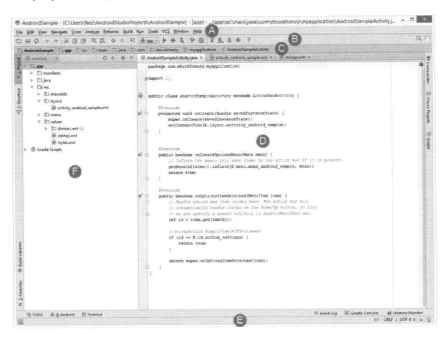

Figure 4-2

The various elements of the main window can be summarized as follows:

A – Menu Bar – Contains a range of menus for performing tasks within the Android Studio environment.

B – Toolbar – A selection of shortcuts to frequently performed actions. The toolbar buttons provide quicker access to a select group of menu bar actions. The toolbar can be customized by right-clicking on the bar and selecting the *Customize Menus and Toolbars...* menu option.

C – Navigation Bar – The navigation bar provides a convenient way to move around the files and folders that make up the project. Clicking on an element in the navigation bar will drop down a menu listing the subfolders and files at that location ready for selection. This provides an alternative to the Project tool window.

D – Editor Window – The editor window displays the content of the file on which the developer is currently working. What gets displayed in this location, however, is subject to context. When editing code, for example, the code editor will appear. When working on a user interface layout file, on the other hand, the user interface Designer tool will appear. When multiple files are open, each file is represented by a tab located along the top edge of the editor as shown in Figure 4-3.

Figure 4-3

E – Status Bar – The status bar displays informational messages about the project and the activities of Android Studio together with the tools menu button located in the far left corner. Hovering over items in the status bar will provide a description of that field. Many fields are interactive, allowing the user to click to perform tasks or obtain more detailed status information.

F – Project Tool Window – The project tool window provides a hierarchical overview of the project file structure allowing navigation to specific files and folders to be performed. The drop-down menu in the toolbar can be used to display the project in a number of different ways. The default setting is the *Android* view which is the mode primarily used in the remainder of this book.

The project tool window is just one of a number of tool windows available within the Android Studio environment.

4.3 The Tool Windows

In addition to the project view tool window, Android Studio also includes a number of other windows which, when enabled, are displayed along the bottom and sides of the main window. The tool window quick access menu can be accessed by hovering the mouse pointer over the button located in the far left hand corner of the status bar (Figure 4-4) without clicking the mouse button.

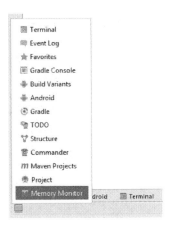

Figure 4-4

Selecting an item from the quick access menu will cause the corresponding tool window to appear within the main window.

Alternatively, a set of *tool window bars* can be displayed by clicking on the quick access menu icon in the status bar. These bars appear along the left, right and bottom edges of the main window (as indicated by the arrows in Figure 4-5) and contain buttons for showing and hiding each of the tool windows. When the tool window bars are displayed, a second click on the button in the status bar will hide them.

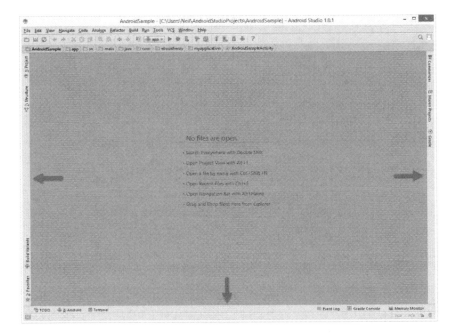

Figure 4-5

Clicking on a button will display the corresponding tool window whilst a second click will hide the window. Buttons prefixed with a number (for example 1: Project) indicate that the tool window may also be displayed by pressing the Alt key on the keyboard (or the Command key for Mac OS X) together with the corresponding number.

The location of a button in a tool window bar indicates the side of the window against which the window will appear when displayed. These positions can be changed by clicking and dragging the buttons to different locations in other window tool bars.

Each tool window has its own toolbar along the top edge. The buttons within these toolbars vary from one tool to the next, though all tool windows contain a settings option, represented by the cog icon, which allows various aspects of the window to be changed. Figure 4-6 shows the settings menu for the project view tool window. Options are available, for example, to undock a window and to allow it to float outside of the boundaries of the Android Studio main window.

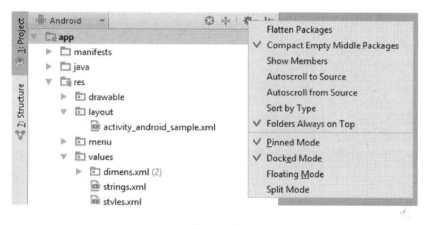

Figure 4-6

All of the windows also include a far right button on the toolbar providing an additional way to hide the tool window from view. A search of the items within a tool window can be performed simply by giving that window focus by clicking in it and then typing the search term (for example the name of a file in the Project tool window). A search box will appear in the window's tool bar and items matching the search highlighted.

Android Studio offers a wide range of window tool windows, the most commonly used of which are as follows:

Project – The project view provides an overview of the file structure that makes up the project allowing for quick navigation between files. Generally, double clicking on a file in the project view will cause that file to be loaded into the appropriate editing tool.

Structure – The structure tool provides a high level view of the structure of the source file currently displayed in the editor. This information includes a list of items such as classes, methods and variables in the file. Selecting an item from the structure list will take you to that location in the source file in the editor window.

Favorites – A variety of project items can be added to the favorites list. Right-clicking on a file in the project view, for example, provides access to an *Add to Favorites* menu option. Similarly, a method in a source file can be added as a favorite by right-clicking on it in the Structure tool window. Anything added to a Favorites list can be accessed through this Favorites tool window.

Build Variants – The build variants tool window provides a quick way to configure different build targets for the current application project (for example different builds for debugging and release versions of the application, or multiple builds to target different device categories).

TODO – As the name suggests, this tool provides a place to review items that have yet to be completed on the project. Android Studio compiles this list by scanning the source files that make up the project to look for comments that match specified TODO patterns. These patterns can be reviewed and changed by selecting the *File -> Settings...* menu option and navigating to the *TODO* page listed under *IDE Settings*.

Messages – The messages tool window records output from the Gradle build system (Gradle is the underlying system used by Android Studio for building the various parts of projects into runnable applications) and can be useful for identifying the causes of build problems when compiling application projects.

Android – The Android tool window provides access to the Android debugging system. Within this window tasks such as monitoring log output from a running application, taking screenshots and videos of the application, stopping a process and performing basic debugging tasks can be performed.

Terminal – Provides access to a terminal window on the system on which Android Studio is running. On Windows systems this is the Command Prompt interface, whilst on Linux and Mac OS X systems this takes the form of a Terminal prompt.

Run – The run tool window becomes available when an application is currently running and provides a view of the results of the run together with options to stop or restart a running process. If an application is failing to install and run on a device or emulator, this window will typically provide diagnostic information relating to the problem.

Event Log – The event log window displays messages relating to events and activities performed within Android Studio. The successful build of a project, for example, or the fact that an application is now running will be reported within this window tool.

Gradle Console – The Gradle console is used to display all output from the Gradle system as projects are built from within Android Studio. This will include information about the success or otherwise of the build process together with details of any errors or warnings.

Maven Projects – Maven is a project management and build system designed to ease the development of complex Java based projects and overlaps in many areas with the functionality provided by Gradle. Google has chosen Gradle as the underlying build system for Android development, so unless you are already familiar with Maven or have existing Maven projects to import, your time will be better spent learning and adopting Gradle for your projects. The Maven projects tool window can be used to add, manage and import Maven based projects within Android Studio.

Gradle – The Gradle tool window provides a view onto the Gradle tasks that make up the project build configuration. The window lists the tasks that are involved in compiling the various elements of the project into an executable application. Right-click on a top level Gradle task and select the *Open Gradle Config* menu option to load the Gradle build file for the current project into the editor. Gradle will be covered in greater detail later in this book.

Commander – The Commander window tool can best be described as a combination of the Project and Structure tool windows, allowing the file hierarchy of the project to be traversed and for the various elements that make up classes to be inspected and loaded into the editor or designer windows.

Memory Monitor – Connects to running Android applications and monitors memory usage statistics in the form of a real-time graph.

Designer – Available when the UI Designer is active, this tool window provides access to the designer's Component Tree and Properties panels.

4.4 **Android Studio Keyboard Shortcuts**

Android Studio includes an abundance of keyboard shortcuts designed to save time when performing common tasks. A full keyboard shortcut keymap listing can be viewed and printed from within the Android Studio project window by selecting the *Help -> Default Keymap Reference* menu option.

4.5 **Switcher and Recent Files Navigation**

Another useful mechanism for navigating within the Android Studio main window involves the use of the *Switcher*. Accessed via the *Ctrl-Tab* keyboard shortcut, the switcher appears as a panel listing both the tool windows and currently open files (Figure 4-7).

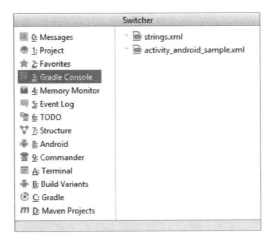

Figure 4-7

Once displayed, the switcher will remain visible for as long as the Ctrl key remains depressed. Repeatedly tapping the Tab key whilst holding down the Ctrl key will cycle through the various selection options, whilst releasing the Ctrl key causes the currently highlighted item to be selected and displayed within the main window.

In addition to the switcher, navigation to recently opened files is provided by the Recent Files panel (Figure 4-8). This can be accessed using the Ctrl-E keyboard shortcut (Cmd-E on Mac OS X). Once displayed, either the mouse pointer can be used to select an option or, alternatively, the keyboard arrow keys can be used to scroll through the file name and tool window options. Pressing the Enter key will select the currently highlighted item.

Figure 4-8

4.6 **Changing the Android Studio Theme**

The overall theme of the Android Studio environment may be changed either from the welcome screen using the *Configure -> Settings* option, or via the *File -> Settings…* menu option of the main window.

Once the settings dialog is displayed, select the *Appearance* option in the left hand panel and then change the setting of the *Theme* menu before clicking on the *Apply* button. The themes currently available consist of IntelliJ, Windows and Darcula. Figure 4-9 shows an example of the main window with the Darcula theme selected:

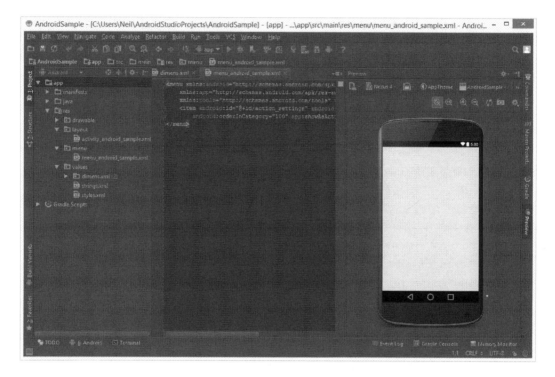

Figure 4-9

4.7 **Summary**

The primary elements of the Android Studio environment consist of the welcome screen and main window. Each open project is assigned its own main window which, in turn, consists of a menu bar, toolbar, editing and design area, status bar and a collection of tool windows. Tool windows appear on the sides and bottom edges of the main window and can be accessed either using the quick access menu located in the status bar, or via the optional tool window bars.

There are very few actions within Android Studio which cannot be triggered via a keyboard shortcut. A keymap of default keyboard shortcuts can be accessed at any time from within the Android Studio main window.

5. Creating an Android Virtual Device (AVD) in Android Studio

In the course of developing Android apps in Android Studio it will be necessary to compile and run an application multiple times. An Android application may be tested by installing and running it either on a physical device or in an *Android Virtual Device (AVD)* emulator environment. Before an AVD can be used, it must first be created and configured to match the specification of a particular device model. The goal of this chapter, therefore, is to work through the steps involved in creating such a virtual device using the Nexus 7 tablet as a reference example.

5.1 About Android Virtual Devices

AVDs are essentially emulators that allow Android applications to be tested without the necessity to install the application on a physical Android based device. An AVD may be configured to emulate a variety of hardware features including options such as screen size, memory capacity and the presence or otherwise of features such as a camera, GPS navigation support or an accelerometer. As part of the standard Android Studio installation, a number of emulator templates are installed allowing AVDs to be configured for a range of different devices. Additional templates may be loaded or custom configurations created to match any physical Android device by specifying properties such as processor type, memory capacity and the size and pixel density of the screen. Check the online developer documentation for your device to find out if emulator definitions are available for download and installation into the AVD environment.

When launched, an AVD will appear as a window containing an emulated Android device environment. Figure 5-1, for example, shows an AVD session configured to emulate the Google Nexus 7 device.

New AVDs are created and managed using the Android Virtual Device Manager, which may be used either in command-line mode or with a more user-friendly graphical user interface.

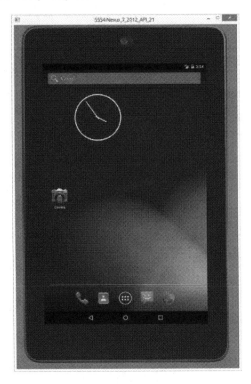

Figure 5-1

5.2 Creating a New AVD

In order to test the behavior of an application, it will be necessary to create an AVD for a specific Android device configuration.

To create a new AVD, the first step is to launch the AVD Manager. This can be achieved from within the Android Studio environment by selecting the *Tools -> Android -> AVD Manager* menu option from within the main window. Alternatively, the tool may be launched from a terminal or command-line prompt using the following command:

```
android avd
```

Once launched, the tool will appear as outlined in Figure 5-2. Assuming a new Android SDK installation, no AVDs will currently be listed:

22. Jul. 2016:
   Your CPU does not support
   sequired features.
      (VT-X or SVM).

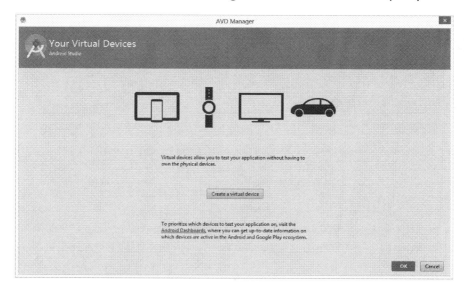

Figure 5-2

Begin the AVD creation process by clicking on the *Create a virtual device* button in order to invoke the *Virtual Device Configuration* dialog:

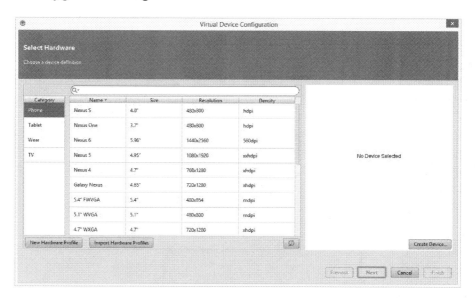

Figure 5-3

Within the dialog, perform the following steps to create a first generation Nexus 7 compatible emulator:

1. From the *Category* panel, select the *Tablet* option to display the list of available Android tablet AVD templates.

2. Select the *Nexus 7 (2012)* device option and click *Next*.
3. On the System Image screen, select the latest version of Android (at time of writing this is Android 5.0.1, Lollipop API level 21) for the *armeabi-v7a* ABI. Click *Next* to proceed.
4. Enter a descriptive name (for example *Nexus 7*) into the name field.
5. Click *Finish* to create the AVD.

With the AVD created, the AVD Manager may now be closed. If future modifications to the AVD are necessary, simply re-open the AVD Manager, select the AVD from the list and click on the pencil icon in the *Actions* column of the device row in the AVD Manager.

5.3 **Starting the Emulator**

To perform a test run of the newly created AVD emulator, simply select the emulator from the AVD Manager and click on the launch button (the green triangle in the Actions column) followed by *Launch* in the resulting *Launch Options* dialog. The emulator will appear in a new window and, after a short period of time, the "android" logo will appear in the center of the screen. The first time the emulator is run, it can take up to 10 minutes for the emulator to fully load and start. On subsequent invocations, this will typically reduce to a few minutes. In the event that the startup time on your system is considerable, do not hesitate to leave the emulator running. The system will detect that it is already running and attach to it when applications are launched, thereby saving considerable amounts of startup time.

Another option when using the emulator is to enable the *Snapshot* option in the AVD settings screen. This option, which can only be used when the *Use Host GPU* option is disabled, enables the state of an AVD instance to be saved and reloaded next time it is launched. This can result in an emulator startup time of just a few seconds.

To enable snapshots, edit the settings for the AVD configuration and click on the *Show Advanced Settings* button. In the *Emulated Performance* section of the advanced settings panel, disable the *Use Host GPU* option and enable the *Store a snapshot for faster startup* as outlined in Figure 5-4:

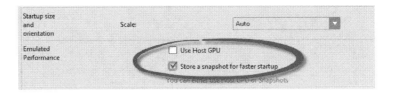

Figure 5-4

To save time in the next section of this chapter, leave the emulator running before proceeding.

5.4 **Running the Application in the AVD**

With an AVD emulator configured, the example AndroidSample application created in the earlier chapter now can be compiled and run. With the AndroidSample project loaded into Android Studio, simply click on the run button represented by a green triangle located in the Android Studio toolbar as shown in Figure 5-5 below, select the *Run -> Run...* menu option or use the Shift+F10 keyboard shortcut:

Figure 5-5

By default, Android Studio will respond to the run request by displaying the *Choose Device* dialog. This provides the option to execute the application on an AVD instance that is already running, or to launch a new AVD session specifically for this application. Figure 5-6 lists the previously created Nexus7 AVD as a running device as a result of the steps performed in the preceding section. With this device selected in the dialog, click on *OK* to install and run the application on the emulator.

Figure 5-6

Once the application is installed and running, the user interface for the AndroidSampleActivity class will appear within the emulator:

Figure 5-7

In the event that the activity does not automatically launch, check to see if the launch icon has appeared among the apps on the emulator. If it has, simply click on it to launch the application. Once the run process begins, the Run and Android tool windows will become available. The Run tool window will display diagnostic information as the application package is installed and launched. Figure 5-8 shows the Run tool window output from a successful application launch:

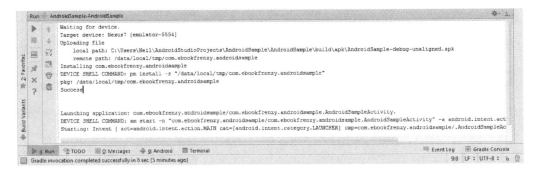

Figure 5-8

If problems are encountered during the launch process, the Run tool will provide information that will hopefully help to isolate the cause of the problem.

Assuming that the application loads into the emulator and runs as expected, we have safely verified that the Android development environment is correctly installed and configured.

5.5 Run/Debug Configurations

A particular project can be configured such that a specific device or emulator is used automatically each time it is run from within Android Studio. This avoids the necessity to make a selection from the device chooser each time the application is executed. To review and modify the Run/Debug configuration, click on the button to the left of the run button in the Android Studio toolbar and select the *Edit Configurations...* option from the resulting menu:

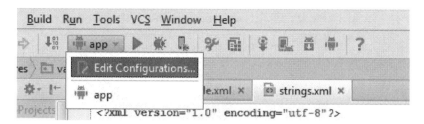

Figure 5-9

In the *Run/Debug Configurations* dialog, the application may be configured to always use a preferred emulator by enabling the *Emulator* option listed in the *Target Device* section and selecting the emulator from the drop down menu. Figure 5-10, for example, shows the AndroidSample application configured to run by default on the previously created Nexus 7 emulator:

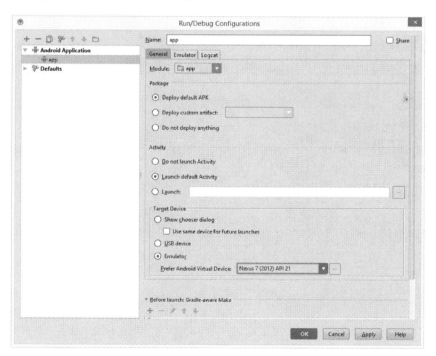

Figure 5-10

Be sure to switch the Target Device setting back to "Show chooser dialog" mode before moving on to the next chapter of the book.

5.6 **Stopping a Running Application**

When building and running an application for testing purposes, each time a new revision of the application is compiled and run, the previous instance of the application running on the device or emulator will be terminated automatically and replaced with the new version. It is also possible, however, to manually stop a running application from within Android Studio.

To stop a running application, begin by displaying the *Android* tool window either using the window bar button, or via the quick access menu (invoked by moving the mouse pointer over the button in the left hand corner of the status bar as shown in Figure 5-11).

Figure 5-11

Once the Android tool window appears, make sure that the *Devices | ADB Logs* tab is selected, and that the Nexus 7 emulator entry is selected in the Devices panel. From the list of processes located beneath the device name, find and select the *androidsample* process as outlined in Figure 5-12:

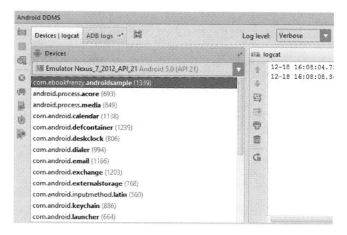

Figure 5-12

With the process selected, stop it by clicking on the red *Terminate Application* button in the vertical toolbar to the left of the process list:

Figure 5-13

An alternative to using the Android tool window is to open the Android Debug Monitor. This can be launched via the *Tools -> Android -> Android Device Monitor* menu option. Once launched, the process may be selected from the list (Figure 5-14) and terminated by clicking on the red *Stop* button located in the toolbar above the list.

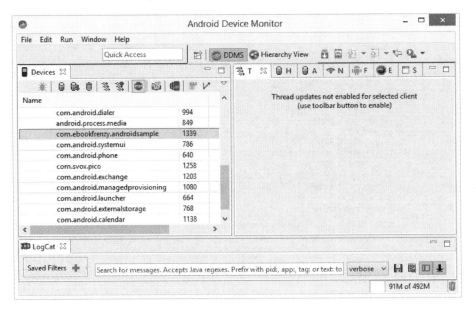

Figure 5-14

5.7 AVD Command-line Creation

As previously discussed, in addition to the graphical user interface it is also possible to create a new AVD directly from the command-line. This is achieved using the *android* tool in conjunction with some command-line options. Once initiated, the tool will prompt for additional information before creating the new AVD.

Assuming that the system has been configured such that the Android SDK *tools* directory is included in the PATH environment variable, a list of available targets for the new AVD may be obtained by issuing the following command in a terminal or command window:

```
android list targets
```

The resulting output from the above command will contain a list of Android SDK versions that are available on the system. For example:

```
Available Android targets:
----------
id: 1 or "android-21"
     Name: Android 5.0.1
     Type: Platform
     API level: 21
     Revision: 2
     Skins: HVGA, QVGA, WQVGA400, WQVGA432, WSVGA, WVGA800 (default),
WVGA854, WXGA720, WXGA800, WXGA800-7in
```

```
Tag/ABIs : default/armeabi-v7a
```

The syntax for AVD creation is as follows:

```
android create avd -n <name> -t <targetID> [-<option> <value>]
```

For example, to create a new AVD named *Nexus7* using the target id for the Android 5.0.1 API level 21 device (in this case id 1), the following command may be used:

```
android create avd -n Nexus7 -t 1
```

The android tool will create the new AVD to the specifications required for a basic Android 5.0.1 device, also providing the option to create a custom configuration to match the specification of a specific device if required. Once a new AVD has been created from the command line, it may not show up in the Android Device Manager tool until the *Refresh* button is clicked.

In addition to the creation of new AVDs, a number of other tasks may be performed from the command line. For example, a list of currently available AVDs may be obtained using the *list avd* command line arguments:

```
android list avd

Available Android Virtual Devices:
    Name: GenericAVD
    Path: C:\Users\Neil\.android\avd\GenericAVD.avd
  Target: Android 5.0.1 (API level 21)
 Tag/ABI: default/armeabi-v7a
    Skin: WVGA800
---------
    Name: Nexus_7_2012_API_21
  Device: Nexus 7 (Google)
    Path: C:\Users\Neil\.android\avd\Nexus_7_2012_API_21.avd
  Target: Android 5.0.1 (API level 21)
 Tag/ABI: default/armeabi-v7a
    Skin: nexus_7
  Sdcard:
C:\Users\Neil\.android\avd\Nexus_7_2012_API_21.avd\sdcard.img
Snapshot: yes
```

Similarly, to delete an existing AVD, simply use the *delete* option as follows:

```
android delete avd -n <avd name>
```

5.8 **Android Virtual Device Configuration Files**

By default, the files associated with an AVD are stored in the .*android/avd* sub-directory of the user's home directory, the structure of which is as follows (where *<avd name>* is replaced by the name assigned to the AVD):

```
<avd name>.avd/config.ini
<avd name>.avd/userdata.img
<avd name>.ini
```

The *config.ini* file contains the device configuration settings such as display dimensions and memory specified during the AVD creation process. These settings may be changed directly within the configuration file and will be adopted by the AVD when it is next invoked.

The *<avd name>.ini* file contains a reference to the target Android SDK and the path to the AVD files. Note that a change to the *image.sysdir* value in the *config.ini* file will also need to be reflected in the *target* value of this file.

5.9 **Moving and Renaming an Android Virtual Device**

The current name or the location of the AVD files may be altered from the command line using the *android* tool's *move avd* argument. For example, to rename an AVD named Nexus7 to Nexus7B, the following command may be executed:

```
android move avd -n Nexus7 -r Nexus7B
```

To physically relocate the files associated with the AVD, the following command syntax should be used:

```
android move avd -n <avd name> -p <path to new location>
```

For example, to move an AVD from its current file system location to /tmp/Nexus7Test:

```
android move avd -n Nexus7 -p /tmp/Nexus7Test
```

Note that the destination directory must not already exist prior to executing the command to move an AVD.

5.10 **Summary**

A typical application development process follows a cycle of coding, compiling and running in a test environment. Android applications may be tested on either a physical Android device or using an Android Virtual Device (AVD) emulator. AVDs are created and managed using the Android AVD Manager tool which may be used either as a command line tool or using a graphical user interface.

When creating an AVD to simulate a specific Android device model it is important that the virtual device be configured with a hardware specification that matches that of the physical device.

6. Testing Android Studio Apps on a Physical Android Device

Whilst much can be achieved by testing applications using an Android Virtual Device (AVD), there is no substitute for performing real world application testing on a physical Android device and there are a number of Android features that are only available on physical Android devices.

Communication with both AVD instances and connected Android devices is handled by the *Android Debug Bridge (ADB)*. In this chapter we will work through the steps to configure the adb environment to enable application testing on a physical Android device with Mac OS X, Windows and Linux based systems.

6.1 An Overview of the Android Debug Bridge (ADB)

The primary purpose of the ADB is to facilitate interaction between a development system, in this case Android Studio, and both AVD emulators and physical Android devices for the purposes of running and debugging applications.

The ADB consists of a client, a server process running in the background on the development system and a daemon background process running in either AVDs or real Android devices such as phones and tablets.

The ADB client can take a variety of forms. For example, a client is provided in the form of a command-line tool named *adb* located in the Android SDK *platform-tools* sub-directory. Similarly, Android Studio also has a built-in client.

A variety of tasks may be performed using the *adb* command-line tool. For example, a listing of currently active virtual or physical devices may be obtained using the *devices* command-line argument. The following command output indicates the presence of an AVD on the system but no physical devices:

```
$ adb devices
List of devices attached
emulator-5554    device
```

6.2 **Enabling ADB on Android 5.0 based Devices**

Before ADB can connect to an Android device, that device must first be configured to allow the connection. On phone and tablet devices running Android 5.0 or later, the steps to achieve this are as follows:

1. Open the Settings app on the device and select the *About tablet* or *About phone* option.
2. On the *About* screen, scroll down to the *Build number* field (Figure 6-1) and tap on it seven times until a message appears indicating that developer mode has been enabled.

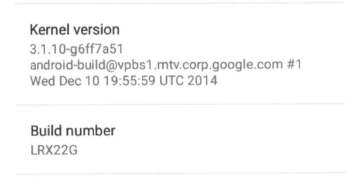

Figure 6-1

3. Return to the main Settings screen and note the appearance of a new option titled *Developer options*. Select this option and locate the setting on the developer screen entitled *USB debugging*. Enable the checkbox next to this item as illustrated in Figure 6-2 to enable the adb debugging connection.

Debugging

USB debugging
Debug mode when USB is connected

Figure 6-2

4. Swipe downward from the top of the screen to display the notifications panel (Figure 6-3) and note that the device is currently connected as a *media device*.

Figure 6-3

At this point, the device is now configured to accept debugging connections from adb on the development system. All that remains is to configure the development system to detect the device when it is attached. Whilst this is a relatively straightforward process, the steps involved differ depending on whether the development system is running Windows, Mac OS X or Linux. Note that the following steps assume that the Android SDK *platform-tools* directory is included in the operating system PATH environment variable as described in the chapter entitled *Setting up an Android Studio Development Environment*.

6.2.1 Mac OS X ADB Configuration

In order to configure the ADB environment on a Mac OS X system, connect the device to the computer system using a USB cable, open a terminal window and execute the following command:

```
android update adb
```

Next, restart the adb server by issuing the following commands in the terminal window:

```
$ adb kill-server
$ adb start-server
* daemon not running. starting it now on port 5037 *
* daemon started successfully *
```

Once the server is successfully running, execute the following command to verify that the device has been detected:

```
$ adb devices
List of devices attached
74CE000600000001        offline
```

If the device is listed as *offline*, go to the Android device and check for the presence of the dialog shown in Figure 6-8 seeking permission to *Allow USB debugging.* Enable the checkbox next to the option that reads *Always allow from this computer*, before clicking on *OK*. Repeating the *adb devices* command should now list the device as being available:

```
List of devices attached
015d41d4454bf80c        device
```

In the event that the device is not listed, try logging out and then back in to the Mac OS X desktop and, if the problem persists, rebooting the system.

6.2.2 Windows ADB Configuration

The first step in configuring a Windows based development system to connect to an Android device using ADB is to install the appropriate USB drivers on the system. In the case of some devices, the

Google USB Driver must be installed (a full listing of devices supported by the Google USB driver can be found online at http://developer.android.com/sdk/win-usb.html).

To install this driver, perform the following steps:

1. Launch Android Studio and open the Android SDK Manager, either by selecting *Configure -> SDK Manager* from the Welcome screen, or using the *Tools -> Android -> SDK Manager* menu option when working on an existing project.
2. Scroll down to the *Extras* section and check the status of the *Google USB Driver* package to make sure that it is listed as *Installed.*
3. If the driver is not installed, select it and click on the *Install packages* button to initiate the installation.
4. Once installation is complete, close the Android SDK Manager.

For Android devices not supported by the Google USB driver, it will be necessary to download the drivers provided by the device manufacturer. A listing of drivers and download information can be obtained online at http://developer.android.com/tools/extras/oem-usb.html.

When an Android device is attached to a Windows system it is configured as a *Portable Device*. In order for the device to connect to ADB it must be configured as an *Android ADB Composite Device*.

First, connect the Android device to the computer system if it is not currently connected. Next, display the Control Panel and select Device Manager. In the resulting dialog, check for a category entitled *Other Devices*. Unfold this category and check to see if the Android device is listed (in the case of Figure 6-4, a Nexus 7 has been detected):

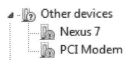

Figure 6-4

Right-click on the device name and select *Update Driver Software* from the menu. Select the option to *Browse my computer for driver software* and in the next dialog, keep the *Include subfolder* option selected and click on the *Browse…* button. Navigate to the location into which the USB drivers were installed. In the case of the Google USB driver, this will be in the *sdk\extras\google\usb_driver* subfolder of the Android Studio installation directory (the location of which can be found in the SDK Manager). Once located, click on *OK* to select the driver folder followed by *Next* to initiate the installation.

During the installation, a Windows Security prompt will appear seeking permission to install the driver as illustrated in Figure 6-5. When this dialog appears, click on the *Install* button to proceed.

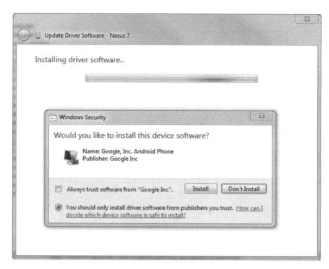

Figure 6-5

Once the installation completes, the Windows driver update screen will refresh to display a message indicating that the driver has been installed and that the device is now recognized as an Android Composite ADB Interface:

Figure 6-6

Return to the Device Manager and note that the device is no longer listed under *Other Devices* and is now categorized as an Android Composite ADB Interface. Figure 6-7, for example, shows the device entry for a Nexus 7 tablet using the Google USB driver.

Figure 6-7

With the drivers installed and the device now being recognized as the correct device type, open a Command Prompt window and execute the following command:

```
adb devices
```

This command should output information about the connected device similar to the following:

```
List of devices attached
015d41d4454bf80c          offline
```

If the device is listed as *offline* or *unauthorized*, go to the device display and check for the dialog shown in Figure 6-8 seeking permission to *Allow USB debugging.*

Figure 6-8

Enable the checkbox next to the option that reads *Always allow from this computer*, before clicking on *OK*. Repeating the *adb devices* command should now list the device as being ready:

```
List of devices attached
015d41d4454bf80c          device
```

In the event that the device is not listed, execute the following commands to restart the ADB server:

```
adb kill-server
adb start-server
```

If the device is still not listed, try executing the following command:

```
android update adb
```

Note that it may also be necessary to reboot the system.

6.2.3 Linux adb Configuration

For the purposes of this chapter, we will once again use Ubuntu Linux as a reference example in terms of configuring adb on Linux to connect to a physical Android device for application testing.

Begin by attaching the Android device to a USB port on the Ubuntu Linux system. Once connected, open a Terminal window and execute the Linux *lsusb* command to list currently available USB devices:

```
~$ lsusb
Bus 001 Device 003: ID 18d1:4e44 asus Nexus 7 [9999]
```

```
Bus 001 Device 001: ID 1d6b:0001 Linux Foundation 1.1 root hub
```

Each USB device detected on the system will be listed along with a vendor ID and product ID. A list of vendor IDs can be found online at *http://developer.android.com/tools/device.html#VendorIds*. The above output shows that a Google Nexus 7 device has been detected. Make a note of the vendor and product ID numbers displayed for your particular device (in the above case these are 18D1 and 4E44 respectively).

Use the *sudo* command to edit the *51-android.rules* file located in the */etc/udev/rules.d* directory. For example:

```
sudo gedit  /etc/udev/rules.d/51-android.rules
```

Within the editor, add the appropriate entry for the Android device, replacing <vendor_id> and <product_id> with the vendor and product IDs returned previously by the *lsusb* command:

```
SUBSYSTEM=="usb", ATTR{idVendor}=="<vendor_id>",
ATTRS{idProduct}=="<product_id>", MODE="0660", OWNER="root",
GROUP="androidadb", SYMLINK+="android%n"
```

Once the entry has been added, save the file and exit from the editor.

Next, use an editor to modify (or create if it does not yet exist) the adb_usb.ini file:

```
gedit  ~/.android/adb_usb.ini
```

Once the file is loaded into the editor, add the following lines (once again replacing <vendor_id> and <product_id> with the vendor and product IDs returned previously by the *lsusb* command) before saving the file and exiting:

```
0x<vendor_id>
0x<product_id>
```

Using the above syntax, the entries for the Nexus 7 would, for example, read:

```
0x18d1
0x4e44
```

The final task is to create the *androidadb* user group and add your user account to it. To achieve this, execute the following commands making sure to replace <user name> with your Ubuntu user account name:

```
sudo addgroup --system androidadb
sudo adduser <username> androidadb
```

Once the above changes have been made, reboot the Ubuntu system. Once the system has restarted, open a Terminal window, start the adb server and check the list of attached devices:

```
$ adb start-server
* daemon not running. starting it now on port 5037 *
* daemon started successfully *
$ adb devices
List of devices attached
015d41d4454bf80c        offline
```

If the device is listed as *offline*, go to the Android device and check for the dialog shown in Figure 6-8 seeking permission to *Allow USB debugging*.

6.3 **Testing the adb Connection**

Assuming that the adb configuration has been successful on your chosen development platform, the next step is to try running the test application created in the chapter entitled *Creating an Example Android App in Android Studio* on the device.

Launch Android Studio, open the AndroidSample project and, once the project has loaded, click on the run button located in the Android Studio toolbar (Figure 6-9).

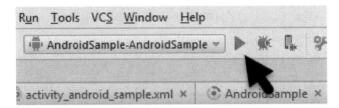

Figure 6-9

Assuming that the project has not previously been configured to run automatically in an emulator environment, the *Choose Device* dialog will appear with the connected Android device listed as a currently running device. Figure 6-10, for example, lists a Nexus 7 device as a suitable target for installing and executing the application.

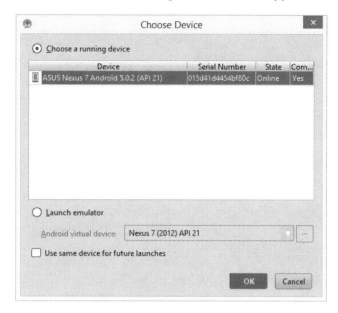

Figure 6-10

To make this the default device for testing, enable the *Use same device for future launches* option. With the device selected, click on the *OK* button to install and run the application on the device. As with the emulator environment, diagnostic output relating to the installation and launch of the application on the device will be logged in the Run tool window.

6.4 **Summary**

Whilst the Android Virtual Device emulator provides an excellent testing environment, it is important to keep in mind that there is no real substitute for making sure an application functions correctly on a physical Android device. This, after all, is where the application will be used in the real world.

By default, however, the Android Studio environment is not configured to detect Android devices as a target testing device. It is necessary, therefore, to perform some steps in order to be able to load applications directly onto an Android device from within the Android Studio development environment. The exact steps to achieve this goal differ depending on the development platform being used. In this chapter, we have covered those steps for Linux, Mac OS X and Windows based platforms.

7. The Basics of the Android Studio Code Editor

Developing applications for Android involves a considerable amount of programming work which, by definition, involves typing, reviewing and modifying lines of code. It should come as no surprise that the majority of a developer's time spent using Android Studio will typically involve editing code within the editor window.

The modern code editor needs to go far beyond the original basics of typing, deleting, cutting and pasting. Today the usefulness of a code editor is generally gauged by factors such as the amount by which it reduces the typing required by the programmer, ease of navigation through large source code files and the editor's ability to detect and highlight programming errors in real-time as the code is being written. As will become evident in this chapter, these are just a few of the areas in which the Android Studio editor excels.

Whilst not an exhaustive overview of the features of the Android Studio editor, this chapter aims to provide a guide to the key features of the tool. Experienced programmers will find that some of these features are common to most code editors available today, whilst a number are unique to this particular editing environment.

7.1 The Android Studio Editor

The Android Studio editor appears in the center of the main window when a Java, XML or other text based file is selected for editing. Figure 7-1, for example, shows a typical editor session with a Java source code file loaded:

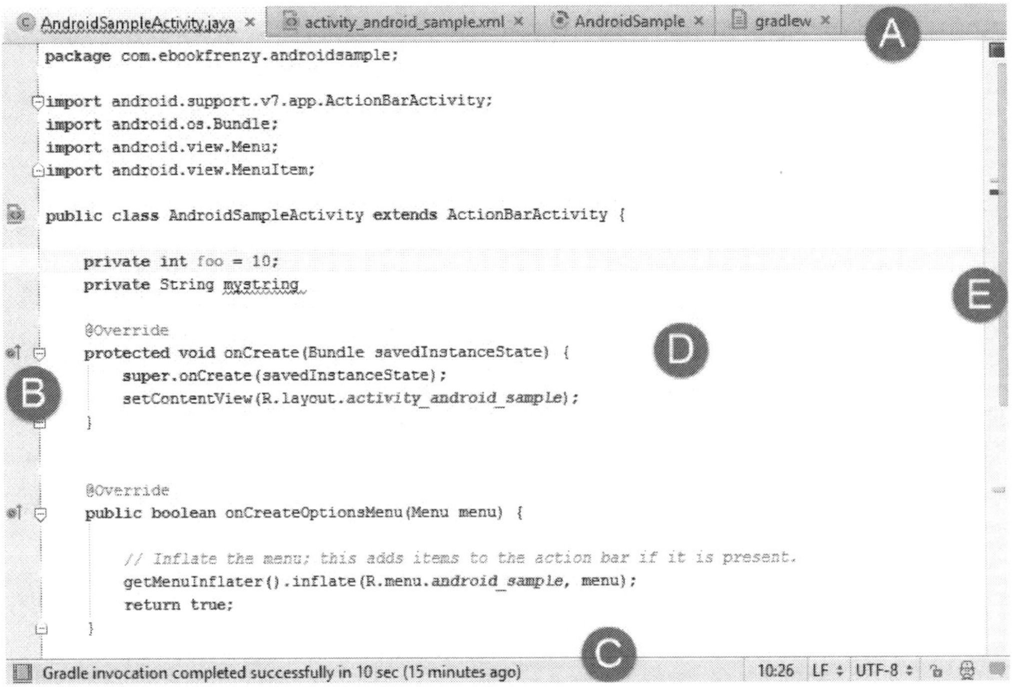

Figure 7-1

The elements that comprise the editor window can be summarized as follows:

A – Document Tabs – Android Studio is capable of holding multiple files open for editing at any one time. As each file is opened, it is assigned a document tab displaying the file name in the tab bar located along the top edge of the editor window. A small dropdown menu will appear in the far right hand corner of the tab bar when there is insufficient room to display all of the tabs. Clicking on this menu will drop down a list of additional open files. A wavy red line underneath a file name in a tab indicates that the code in the file contains one or more errors that need to be addressed before the project can be compiled and run.

Switching between files is simply a matter of clicking on the corresponding tab or using the *Alt-Left* and *Alt-Right* keyboard shortcuts. Navigation between files may also be performed using the Switcher mechanism (accessible via the *Ctrl-Tab* keyboard shortcut).

To detach an editor panel from the Android Studio main window so that it appears in a separate window, click on the tab and drag it to an area on the desktop outside of the main window. To return the editor to the main window, click on the file tab in the separated editor window and drag and drop it onto the original editor tab bar in the main window.

B – The Editor Gutter Area - The gutter area is used by the editor to display informational icons and controls. Some typical items, among others, which appear in this gutter area are debugging breakpoint markers, controls to fold and unfold blocks of code, bookmarks, change markers and line numbers. Line numbers are switched off by default but may be enabled by right-clicking in the gutter and selecting the *Show Line Numbers* menu option.

C – The Status Bar – Though the status bar is actually part of the main window, as opposed to the editor, it does contain some information about the currently active editing session. This information includes the current position of the cursor in terms of lines and characters and the encoding format of the file (UTF-8, ASCII etc.). Clicking on these values in the status bar allows the corresponding setting to be changed. Clicking on the line number, for example, displays the *Go to Line* dialog.

D – The Editor Area – This is the main area where the code is displayed, entered and edited by the user. Later sections of this chapter will cover the key features of the editing area in detail.

E – The Validation and Marker Sidebar – Android Studio incorporates a feature referred to as "on-the-fly code analysis". What this essentially means is that as you are typing code, the editor is analyzing the code to check for warnings and syntax errors. The colored square at the top of the validation sidebar will change color from green (no warnings or errors detected) to yellow (warnings detected) and red (errors have been detected). Clicking on this square will display a popup containing a summary of the issues found with the code in the editor as illustrated in Figure 7-2:

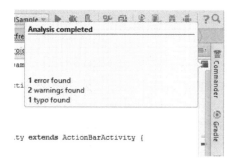

Figure 7-2

The sidebar also displays markers at the locations where issues have been detected using the same color coding. Hovering the mouse pointer over a marker when the line of code is visible in the editor area will display a popup containing a description of the issue (Figure 7-3):

Figure 7-3

Hovering the mouse pointer over a marker for a line of code which is currently scrolled out of the viewing area of the editor will display a "lens" overlay containing the block of code where the problem is located (Figure 7-4) allowing it to be viewed without the necessity to scroll to that location in the editor:

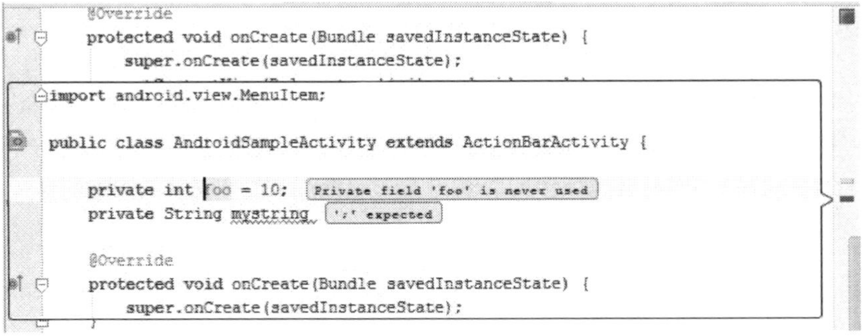

Figure 7-4

It is also worth noting that the lens overlay is not limited to warnings and errors in the sidebar. Hovering over any part of the sidebar will result in a lens appearing containing the code present at that location within the source file.

Having provided an overview of the elements that comprise the Android Studio editor, the remainder of this chapter will explore the key features of the editing environment in more detail.

7.2 Splitting the Editor Window

By default, the editor will display a single panel showing the content of the currently selected file. A particularly useful feature when working simultaneously with multiple source code files is the ability to split the editor into multiple panes. To split the editor, right-click on a file tab within the editor window and select either the *Split Vertically* or *Split Horizontally* menu option. Figure 7-5, for example, shows the splitter in action with the editor split into three panels:

Figure 7-5

The orientation of a split panel may be changed at any time by right-clicking on the corresponding tab and selecting the *Change Splitter Orientation* menu option. Repeat these steps to unsplit a single panel, this time selecting the *Unsplit* option from the menu. All of the split panels may be removed by right-clicking on any tab and selecting the *Unsplit All* menu option.

Window splitting may be used to display different files, or to provide multiple windows onto the same file, allowing different areas of the same file to be viewed and edited concurrently.

7.3 **Code Completion**

The Android Studio editor has a considerable amount of built-in knowledge of Java programming syntax and the classes and methods that make up the Android SDK, as well as knowledge of your own code base. As code is typed, the editor scans what is being typed and, where appropriate, makes suggestions with regard to what might be needed to complete a statement or reference. When a completion suggestion is detected by the editor, a panel will appear containing a list of suggestions. In Figure 7-6, for example, the editor is suggesting possibilities for the beginning of a String declaration:

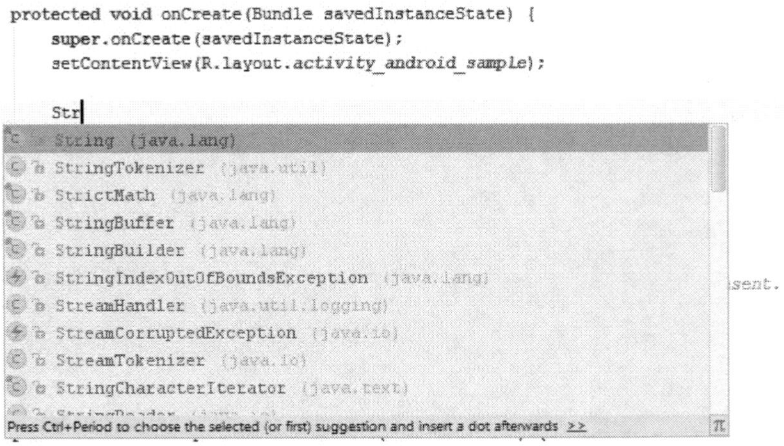

```
protected void onCreate(Bundle savedInstanceState) {
    super.onCreate(savedInstanceState);
    setContentView(R.layout.activity_android_sample);

    Str
```

Figure 7-6

If none of the auto completion suggestions are correct, simply keep typing and the editor will continue to refine the suggestions where appropriate. To accept the top most suggestion, simply press the Enter or Tab key on the keyboard. To select a different suggestion, use the arrow keys to move up and down the list, once again using the Enter or Tab key to select the highlighted item.

Completion suggestions can be manually invoked using the *Ctrl-Space* keyboard sequence. This can be useful when changing a word or declaration in the editor. When the cursor is positioned over a word in the editor, that word will automatically highlight. Pressing *Ctrl-Space* will display a list of alternate suggestions. To replace the current word with the currently highlighted item in the suggestion list, simply press the Tab key.

In addition to the real-time auto completion feature, the Android Studio editor also offers a system referred to as *Smart Completion*. Smart completion is invoked using the *Shift-Ctrl-Space* keyboard sequence and, when selected, will provide more detailed suggestions based on the current context of the code. Pressing the *Shift-Ctrl-Space* shortcut sequence a second time will provide more suggestions from a wider range of possibilities.

Code completion can be a matter of personal preference for many programmers. In recognition of this fact, Android Studio provides a high level of control over the auto completion settings. These can be viewed and modified by selecting the *File -> Settings...* menu option and choosing *Editor -> Code Completion* from the *IDE Settings* section of the settings panel as shown in Figure 7-7:

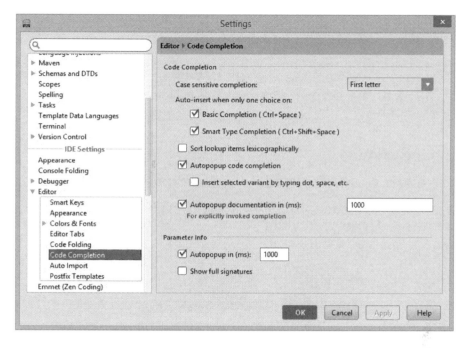

Figure 7-7

7.4 Statement Completion

Another form of auto completion provided by the Android Studio editor is statement completion. This can be used to automatically fill out the parentheses and braces for items such as methods and loop statements. Statement completion is invoked using the *Shift-Ctrl-Enter* (*Shift-Cmd-Enter* on Mac OS X) keyboard sequence. Consider for example the following code:

```
protected void myMethod()
```

Having typed this code into the editor, triggering statement completion will cause the editor to automatically add the braces to the method:

```
protected void myMethod() {

}
```

7.5 Parameter Information

It is also possible to ask the editor to provide information about the argument parameters accepted by a method. With the cursor positioned between the brackets of a method call, the *Ctrl-P* (*Cmd-P* on Mac OS X) keyboard sequence will display the parameters known to be accepted by that method, with the most likely suggestion highlighted in bold:

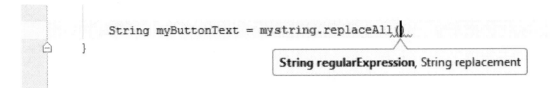

```
String myButtonText = mystring.replaceAll(
```

```
                                    String regularExpression, String replacement
```

Figure 7-8

7.6 Code Generation

In addition to completing code as it is typed the editor can, under certain conditions, also generate code for you. The list of available code generation options shown in Figure 7-9 can be accessed using the *Alt-Insert* keyboard shortcut when the cursor is at the location in the file where the code is to be generated.

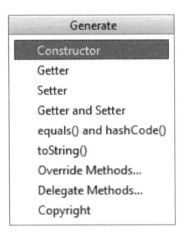

Figure 7-9

For the purposes of an example, consider a situation where we want to be notified when an Activity in our project is about to be destroyed by the operating system. As will be outlined in a later chapter of this book, this can be achieved by overriding the *onStop()* lifecycle method of the Activity superclass. To have Android Studio generate a stub method for this, simply select the *Override Methods...* option from the code generation list and select the *onStop()* method from the resulting list of available methods:

Figure 7-10

Having selected the method to override, clicking on *OK* will generate the stub method at the current cursor location in the Java source file as follows:

```
@Override
protected void onStop() {
      super.onStop();
}
```

7.7 Code Folding

Once a source code file reaches a certain size, even the most carefully formatted and well organized code can become overwhelming and difficult to navigate. Android Studio takes the view that it is not always necessary to have the content of every code block visible at all times. Code navigation can be made easier through the use of the *code folding* feature of the Android Studio editor. Code folding is controlled using markers appearing in the editor gutter at the beginning and end of each block of code in a source file. Figure 7-11, for example, highlights the start and end markers for a method declaration which is not currently folded:

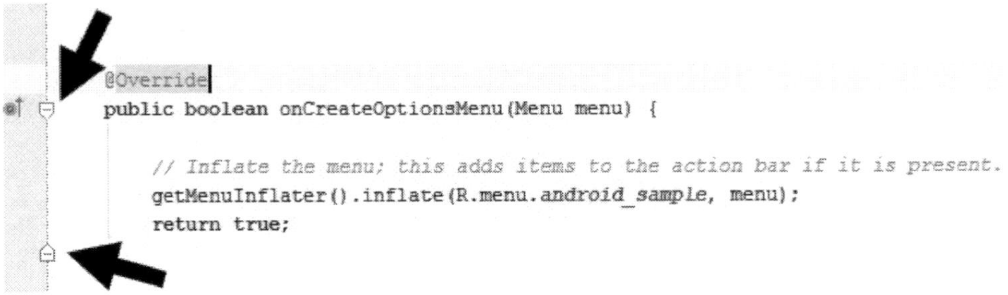

```
@Override
public boolean onCreateOptionsMenu(Menu menu) {

    // Inflate the menu; this adds items to the action bar if it is present.
    getMenuInflater().inflate(R.menu.android_sample, menu);
    return true;
```

Figure 7-11

Clicking on either of these markers will fold the statement such that only the signature line is visible as shown in Figure 7-12:

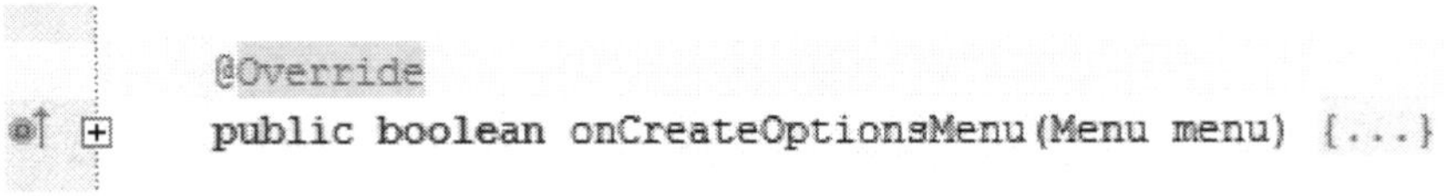

```
@Override
public boolean onCreateOptionsMenu(Menu menu) {...}
```

Figure 7-12

To unfold a collapsed section of code, simply click on the '+' marker in the editor gutter. To see the hidden code without unfolding it, hover the mouse pointer over the "{...}" indicator as shown in Figure 7-13. The editor will then display the lens overlay containing the folded code block:

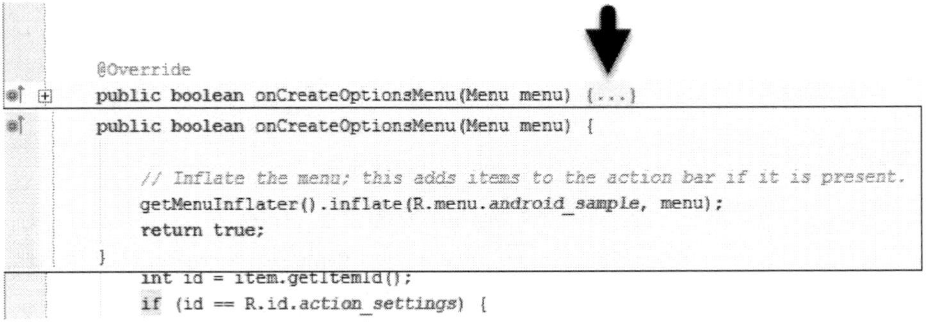

```
@Override
public boolean onCreateOptionsMenu(Menu menu) {...}
public boolean onCreateOptionsMenu(Menu menu) {

    // Inflate the menu; this adds items to the action bar if it is present.
    getMenuInflater().inflate(R.menu.android_sample, menu);
    return true;
}
    int id = item.getItemId();
    if (id == R.id.action_settings) {
```

Figure 7-13

All of the code blocks in a file may be folded or unfolded using the *Ctrl-Shift-Plus* and *Ctrl-Shift-Minus* keyboard sequences.

By default, the Android Studio editor will automatically fold some code when a source file is opened. To configure the conditions under which this happens, select *File -> Settings...* and choose the *Editor -> Code Folding* entry listed under *IDE Settings* in the resulting settings panel (Figure 7-14):

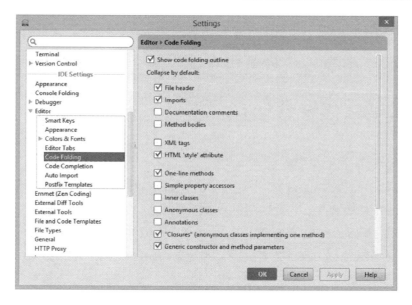

Figure 7-14

7.8 Quick Documentation Lookup

Context sensitive Java and Android documentation can be accessed by placing the cursor over the declaration for which documentation is required and pressing the *Ctrl-Q* keyboard shortcut (*Ctrl-J* on Mac OS X). This will display a popup containing the relevant reference documentation for the item. Figure 7-15, for example, shows the documentation for the Android Menu class.

Figure 7-15

Once displayed, the documentation popup can be moved around the screen as needed. Clicking on the push pin icon located in the right hand corner of the popup title bar will ensure that the popup remains visible once focus moves back to the editor, leaving the documentation visible as a reference while typing code.

7.9 **Code Reformatting**

In general, the Android Studio editor will automatically format code in terms of indenting, spacing and nesting of statements and code blocks as they are added. In situations where lines of code need to be reformatted (a common occurrence, for example, when cutting and pasting sample code from a web site), the editor provides a source code reformatting feature which, when selected, will automatically reformat code to match the prevailing code style.

To reformat source code, press the *Ctrl-Alt-L* keyboard shortcut sequence to display the *Reformat Code* dialog (Figure 7-16). This dialog provides the option to reformat only the currently selected code, the entire source file currently active in the editor or all files in a given project folder.

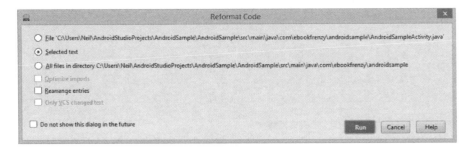

Figure 7-16

The full range of code style preferences can be changed from within the project settings dialog. Select the *File -> Settings* menu option and choose *Code Style* listed under *Project Settings* in the left hand panel to access a list of supported programming and markup languages. Selecting a language will provide access to a vast array of formatting style options, all which may be modified from the Android Studio default to match your preferred code style.

7.10 **Summary**

The Android Studio editor goes to great length to reduce the amount of typing needed to write code and to make that code easier to read and navigate. In this chapter we have covered a number of the key editor features including code completion, code generation, editor window splitting, code folding, reformatting and documentation lookup.

8. An Overview of the Android Architecture

So far in this book, steps have been taken to set up an environment suitable for the development of Android applications using Android Studio. An initial step has also been taken into the process of application development through the creation of a simple Android Studio application project.

Before delving further into the practical matters of Android application development, however, it is important to gain an understanding of some of the more abstract concepts of both the Android SDK and Android development in general. Gaining a clear understanding of these concepts now will provide a sound foundation on which to build further knowledge.

Starting with an overview of the Android architecture in this chapter, and continuing in the next few chapters of this book, the goal is to provide a detailed overview of the fundamentals of Android development.

8.1 The Android Software Stack

Android is structured in the form of a software stack comprising applications, an operating system, run-time environment, middleware, services and libraries. This architecture can, perhaps, best be represented visually as outlined in Figure 8-1. Each layer of the stack, and the corresponding elements within each layer, are tightly integrated and carefully tuned to provide the optimal application development and execution environment for mobile devices.

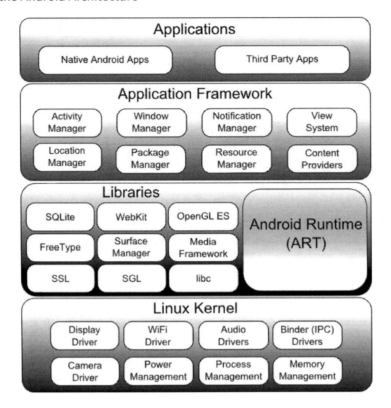

Figure 8-1

The remainder of this chapter will work through the different layers of the Android stack, starting at the bottom with the Linux Kernel.

8.2 The Linux Kernel

Positioned at the bottom of the Android software stack, the Linux Kernel provides a level of abstraction between the device hardware and the upper layers of the Android software stack. Based on Linux version 2.6, the kernel provides preemptive multitasking, low-level core system services such as memory, process and power management in addition to providing a network stack and device drivers for hardware such as the device display, Wi-Fi and audio.

The original Linux kernel was developed in 1991 by Linus Torvalds and was combined with a set of tools, utilities and compilers developed by Richard Stallman at the Free Software Foundation to create a full operating system referred to as GNU/Linux. Various Linux distributions have been derived from these basic underpinnings such as Ubuntu and Red Hat Enterprise Linux.

It is important to note, however, that Android uses only the Linux kernel. That said, it is worth noting that the Linux kernel was originally developed for use in traditional computers in the form of desktops and servers. In fact, Linux is now most widely deployed in mission critical enterprise server environments. It is a testament to both the power of today's mobile devices and the efficiency and performance of the Linux kernel that we find this software at the heart of the Android software stack.

8.3 **Android Runtime – ART**

When an Android app is built within Android Studio it is compiled into an intermediate bytecode format (referred to as DEX format). When the application is subsequently loaded onto the device, the Android Runtime (ART) uses a process referred to as Ahead-of-Time (AOT) compilation to translate the bytecode down to the native instructions required by the device processor. This format is known as Executable and Linkable Format (ELF).

Each time the application is subsequently launched, the ELF executable version is run, resulting in faster application performance and improved battery life.

This contrasts with the Just-in-Time (JIT) compilation approach used in older Android implementations whereby the bytecode was translated within a virtual machine (VM) each time the application was launched.

8.4 **Android Libraries**

In addition to a set of standard Java development libraries (providing support for such general purpose tasks as string handling, networking and file manipulation), the Android development environment also includes the Android Libraries. These are a set of Java-based libraries that are specific to Android development. Examples of libraries in this category include the application framework libraries in addition to those that facilitate user interface building, graphics drawing and database access.

A summary of some key core Android libraries available to the Android developer is as follows:

- **android.app** – Provides access to the application model and is the cornerstone of all Android applications.
- **android.content** – Facilitates content access, publishing and messaging between applications and application components.
- **android.database** – Used to access data published by content providers and includes SQLite database management classes.
- **android.graphics** – A low-level 2D graphics drawing API including colors, points, filters, rectangles and canvases.
- **android.hardware** – Presents an API providing access to hardware such as the accelerometer and light sensor.
- **android.opengl** – A Java interface to the OpenGL ES 3D graphics rendering API.
- **android.os** – Provides applications with access to standard operating system services including messages, system services and inter-process communication.

- **android.media** – Provides classes to enable playback of audio and video.
- **android.net** – A set of APIs providing access to the network stack. Includes *android.net.wifi*, which provides access to the device's wireless stack.
- **android.print** – Includes a set of classes that enable content to be sent to configured printers from within Android applications.
- **android.provider** – A set of convenience classes that provide access to standard Android content provider databases such as those maintained by the calendar and contact applications.
- **android.text** – Used to render and manipulate text on a device display.
- **android.util** – A set of utility classes for performing tasks such as string and number conversion, XML handling and date and time manipulation.
- **android.view** – The fundamental building blocks of application user interfaces.
- **android.widget** - A rich collection of pre-built user interface components such as buttons, labels, list views, layout managers, radio buttons etc.
- **android.webkit** – A set of classes intended to allow web-browsing capabilities to be built into applications.

Having covered the Java-based libraries in the Android runtime, it is now time to turn our attention to the C/C++ based libraries contained in this layer of the Android software stack.

8.4.1 C/C++ Libraries

The Android runtime core libraries outlined in the preceding section are Java-based and provide the primary APIs for developers writing Android applications. It is important to note, however, that the core libraries do not actually perform much of the actual work and are, in fact, essentially Java "wrappers" around a set of C/C++ based libraries. When making calls, for example, to the *android.opengl* library to draw 3D graphics on the device display, the library actually ultimately makes calls to the *OpenGL ES* C++ library which, in turn, works with the underlying Linux kernel to perform the drawing tasks.

C/C++ libraries are included to fulfill a wide and diverse range of functions including 2D and 3D graphics drawing, Secure Sockets Layer (SSL) communication, SQLite database management, audio and video playback, bitmap and vector font rendering, display subsystem and graphic layer management and an implementation of the standard C system library (libc).

In practice, the typical Android application developer will access these libraries solely through the Java based Android core library APIs. In the event that direct access to these libraries is needed, this can be achieved using the Android Native Development Kit (NDK), the purpose of which is to call the native methods of non-Java programming languages (such as C and C++) from within Java code using the Java Native Interface (JNI).

8.5 **Application Framework**

The Application Framework is a set of services that collectively form the environment in which Android applications run and are managed. This framework implements the concept that Android applications are constructed from reusable, interchangeable and replaceable components. This concept is taken a step further in that an application is also able to *publish* its capabilities along with any corresponding data so that they can be found and reused by other applications.

The Android framework includes the following key services:

- **Activity Manager** – Controls all aspects of the application lifecycle and activity stack.
- **Content Providers** – Allows applications to publish and share data with other applications.
- **Resource Manager** – Provides access to non-code embedded resources such as strings, color settings and user interface layouts.
- **Notifications Manager** – Allows applications to display alerts and notifications to the user.
- **View System** – An extensible set of views used to create application user interfaces.
- **Package Manager** – The system by which applications are able to find out information about other applications currently installed on the device.
- **Telephony Manager** – Provides information to the application about the telephony services available on the device such as status and subscriber information.
- **Location Manager** – Provides access to the location services allowing an application to receive updates about location changes.

8.6 **Applications**

Located at the top of the Android software stack are the applications. These comprise both the native applications provided with the particular Android implementation (for example web browser and email applications) and the third party applications installed by the user after purchasing the device.

8.7 **Summary**

A good Android development knowledge foundation requires an understanding of the overall architecture of Android. Android is implemented in the form of a software stack architecture consisting of a Linux kernel, a runtime environment and corresponding libraries, an application framework and a set of applications. Applications are predominantly written in Java and compiled down to bytecode format within the Android Studio build environment. When the application is subsequently installed on a device, this bytecode is compiled down by the Android Runtime (ART) to the native format used by the CPU. The key goals of the Android architecture are performance and efficiency, both in application execution and in the implementation of reuse in application design.

9. The Anatomy of an Android Application

Regardless of your prior programming experiences, be it Windows, Mac OS X, Linux or even iOS based, the chances are good that Android development is quite unlike anything you have encountered before.

The objective of this chapter, therefore, is to provide an understanding of the high-level concepts behind the architecture of Android applications. In doing so, we will explore in detail both the various components that can be used to construct an application and the mechanisms that allow these to work together to create a cohesive application.

9.1 Android Activities

Those familiar with object-oriented programming languages such as Java, C++ or C# will be familiar with the concept of encapsulating elements of application functionality into classes that are then instantiated as objects and manipulated to create an application. Since Android applications are written in Java, this is still very much the case. Android, however, also takes the concept of re-usable components to a higher level.

Android applications are created by bringing together one or more components known as *Activities*. An activity is a single, standalone module of application functionality that usually correlates directly to a single user interface screen and its corresponding functionality. An appointments application might, for example, have an activity screen that displays appointments set up for the current day. The application might also utilize a second activity consisting of a screen where new appointments may be entered by the user.

Activities are intended as fully reusable and interchangeable building blocks that can be shared amongst different applications. An existing email application, for example, might contain an activity specifically for composing and sending an email message. A developer might be writing an application that also has a requirement to send an email message. Rather than develop an email composition activity specifically for the new application, the developer can simply use the activity from the existing email application.

Activities are created as subclasses of the Android *Activity* class and must be implemented so as to be entirely independent of other activities in the application. In other words, a shared activity cannot rely on being called at a known point in a program flow (since other applications may make use of the activity in unanticipated ways) and one activity cannot directly call methods or access instance data of another activity. This, instead, is achieved using *Intents* and *Content Providers*.

By default, an activity cannot return results to the activity from which it was invoked. If this functionality is required, the activity must be specifically started as a *sub-activity* of the originating activity.

9.2 **Android Intents**

Intents are the mechanism by which one activity is able to launch another and implement the flow through the activities that make up an application. Intents consist of a description of the operation to be performed and, optionally, the data on which it is to be performed.

Intents can be *explicit*, in that they request the launch of a specific activity by referencing the activity by class name, or *implicit* by stating either the type of action to be performed or providing data of a specific type on which the action is to be performed. In the case of implicit intents, the Android runtime will select the activity to launch that most closely matches the criteria specified by the Intent using a process referred to as *Intent Resolution*.

9.3 **Broadcast Intents**

Another type of Intent, the *Broadcast Intent*, is a system wide intent that is sent out to all applications that have registered an "interested" *Broadcast Receiver*. The Android system, for example, will typically send out Broadcast Intents to indicate changes in device status such as the completion of system start up, connection of an external power source to the device or the screen being turned on or off.

A Broadcast Intent can be *normal* (asynchronous) in that it is sent to all interested Broadcast Receivers at more or less the same time, or *ordered* in that it is sent to one receiver at a time where it can be processed and then either aborted or allowed to be passed to the next Broadcast Receiver.

9.4 **Broadcast Receivers**

Broadcast Receivers are the mechanism by which applications are able to respond to Broadcast Intents. A Broadcast Receiver must be registered by an application and configured with an *Intent Filter* to indicate the types of broadcast in which it is interested. When a matching intent is broadcast, the receiver will be invoked by the Android runtime regardless of whether the application that registered the receiver is currently running. The receiver then has 5 seconds in which to complete any tasks required of it (such as launching a Service, making data updates or issuing a notification to the user) before returning. Broadcast Receivers operate in the background and do not have a user interface.

9.5 **Android Services**

Android Services are processes that run in the background and do not have a user interface. They can be started and subsequently managed from activities, Broadcast Receivers or other Services. Android Services are ideal for situations where an application needs to continue performing tasks but does not necessarily need a user interface to be visible to the user. Although Services lack a user interface, they can still notify the user of events using notifications and *toasts* (small notification messages that appear on the screen without interrupting the currently visible activity) and are also able to issue Intents.

Services are given a higher priority by the Android runtime than many other processes and will only be terminated as a last resort by the system in order to free up resources. In the event that the runtime does need to kill a Service, however, it will be automatically restarted as soon as adequate resources once again become available. A Service can reduce the risk of termination by declaring itself as needing to run in the *foreground*. This is achieved by making a call to *startForeground()*. This is only recommended for situations where termination would be detrimental to the user experience (for example, if the user is listening to audio being streamed by the Service).

Example situations where a Service might be a practical solution include, as previously mentioned, the streaming of audio that should continue when the application is no longer active, or a stock market tracking application that needs to notify the user when a share hits a specified price.

9.6 **Content Providers**

Content Providers implement a mechanism for the sharing of data between applications. Any application can provide other applications with access to its underlying data through the implementation of a Content Provider including the ability to add, remove and query the data (subject to permissions). Access to the data is provided via a Universal Resource Identifier (URI) defined by the Content Provider. Data can be shared in the form of a file or an entire SQLite database.

The native Android applications include a number of standard Content Providers allowing applications to access data such as contacts and media files.

The Content Providers currently available on an Android system may be located using a *Content Resolver*.

9.7 **The Application Manifest**

The glue that pulls together the various elements that comprise an application is the Application Manifest file. It is within this XML based file that the application outlines the activities, services, broadcast receivers, data providers and permissions that make up the complete application.

9.8 **Application Resources**

In addition to the manifest file and the Dex files that contain the byte code, an Android application package will also typically contain a collection of *resource files*. These files contain resources such as the strings, images, fonts and colors that appear in the user interface together with the XML representation of the user interface layouts. By default, these files are stored in the */res* sub-directory of the application project's hierarchy.

9.9 **Application Context**

When an application is compiled, a class named *R* is created that contains references to the application resources. The application manifest file and these resources combine to create what is known as the *Application Context*. This context, represented by the Android *Context* class, may be used in the application code to gain access to the application resources at runtime. In addition, a wide range of methods may be called on an application's context to gather information and make changes to the application's environment at runtime.

9.10 **Summary**

A number of different elements can be brought together in order to create an Android application. In this chapter, we have provided a high-level overview of activities, Services, Intents and Broadcast Receivers together with an overview of the manifest file and application resources.

Maximum reuse and interoperability are promoted through the creation of individual, standalone modules of functionality in the form of activities and intents, whilst data sharing between applications is achieved by the implementation of content providers.

Whilst activities are focused on areas where the user interacts with the application (an activity essentially equating to a single user interface screen), background processing is typically handled by Services and Broadcast Receivers.

The components that make up the application are outlined for the Android runtime system in a manifest file which, combined with the application's resources, represents the application's context.

Much has been covered in this chapter that is most likely new to the average developer. Rest assured, however, that extensive exploration and practical use of these concepts will be made in subsequent chapters to ensure a solid knowledge foundation on which to build your own applications.

10. Understanding Android Application and Activity Lifecycles

In the preceding few chapters we have learned that Android applications run within processes and that they are comprised of multiple components in the form of activities, Services and Broadcast Receivers. The goal of this chapter is to expand on this knowledge by looking at the lifecycle of applications and activities within the Android runtime system.

Regardless of the fanfare about how much memory and computing power resides in the mobile devices of today compared to the desktop systems of yesterday, it is important to keep in mind that these devices are still considered to be "resource constrained" by the standards of modern desktop and laptop based systems, particularly in terms of memory. As such, a key responsibility of the Android system is to ensure that these limited resources are managed effectively and that both the operating system and the applications running on it remain responsive to the user at all times. In order to achieve this, Android is given full control over the lifecycle and state of both the processes in which the applications run, and the individual components that comprise those applications.

An important factor in developing Android applications, therefore, is to gain an understanding of both the application and activity lifecycle management models of Android, and the ways in which an application can react to the state changes that are likely to be imposed upon it during its execution lifetime.

10.1 Android Applications and Resource Management

Each running Android application is viewed by the operating system as a separate process. If the system identifies that resources on the device are reaching capacity it will take steps to terminate processes to free up memory.

When making a determination as to which process to terminate in order to free up memory, the system takes into consideration both the *priority* and *state* of all currently running processes, combining these factors to create what is referred to by Google as an *importance hierarchy*. Processes are then terminated starting with the lowest priority and working up the hierarchy until sufficient resources have been liberated for the system to function.

10.2 **Android Process States**

Processes host applications and applications are made up of components. Within an Android system, the current state of a process is defined by the highest-ranking active component within the application that it hosts. As outlined in Figure 10-1, a process can be in one of the following five states at any given time:

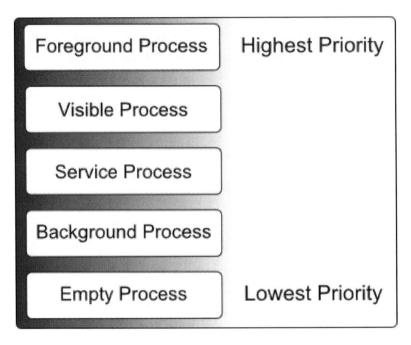

Figure 10-1

10.2.1 Foreground Process

These processes are assigned the highest level of priority. At any one time, there are unlikely to be more than one or two foreground processes active and these are usually the last to be terminated by the system. A process must meet one or more of the following criteria to qualify for foreground status:

- Hosts an activity with which the user is currently interacting.
- Hosts a Service connected to the activity with which the user is interacting.
- Hosts a Service that has indicated, via a call to *startForeground()*, that termination would be disruptive to the user experience.
- Hosts a Service executing either its *onCreate()*, *onResume()* or *onStart()* callbacks.
- Hosts a Broadcast Receiver that is currently executing its *onReceive()* method.

10.2.2 Visible Process

A process containing an activity that is visible to the user but is not the activity with which the user is interacting is classified as a "visible process". This is typically the case when an activity in the process is visible to the user but another activity, such as a partial screen or dialog, is in the foreground. A process is also eligible for visible status if it hosts a Service that is, itself, bound to a visible or foreground activity.

10.2.3 Service Process

Processes that contain a Service that has already been started and is currently executing.

10.2.4 Background Process

A process that contains one or more activities that are not currently visible to the user, and does not host a Service that qualifies for *Service Process* status. Processes that fall into this category are at high risk of termination in the event that additional memory needs to be freed for higher priority processes. Android maintains a dynamic list of background processes, terminating processes in chronological order such that processes that were the least recently in the foreground are killed first.

10.2.5 Empty Process

Empty processes no longer contain any active applications and are held in memory ready to serve as hosts for newly launched applications. This is somewhat analogous to keeping the doors open and the engine running on a bus in anticipation of passengers arriving. Such processes are, obviously, considered the lowest priority and are the first to be killed to free up resources.

10.3 Inter-Process Dependencies

The situation with regard to determining the highest priority process is slightly more complex than outlined in the preceding section for the simple reason that processes can often be inter-dependent. As such, when making a determination as to the priority of a process, the Android system will also take into consideration whether the process is in some way serving another process of higher priority (for example, a service process acting as the content provider for a foreground process). As a basic rule, the Android documentation states that a process can never be ranked lower than another process that it is currently serving.

10.4 The Activity Lifecycle

As we have previously determined, the state of an Android process is determined largely by the status of the activities and components that make up the application that it hosts. It is important to understand, therefore, that these activities also transition through different states during the execution lifetime of an application. The current state of an activity is determined, in part, by its position in something called the *Activity Stack*.

10.5 **The Activity Stack**

For each application that is running on an Android device, the runtime system maintains an *Activity Stack*. When an application is launched, the first of the application's activities to be started is placed onto the stack. When a second activity is started, it is placed on the top of the stack and the previous activity is *pushed* down. The activity at the top of the stack is referred to as the *active* (or *running*) activity. When the active activity exits, it is *popped* off the stack by the runtime and the activity located immediately beneath it in the stack becomes the current active activity. The activity at the top of the stack might, for example, simply exit because the task for which it is responsible has been completed. Alternatively, the user may have selected a "Back" button on the screen to return to the previous activity, causing the current activity to be popped off the stack by the runtime system and therefore destroyed. A visual representation of the Android Activity Stack is illustrated in Figure 10-2:

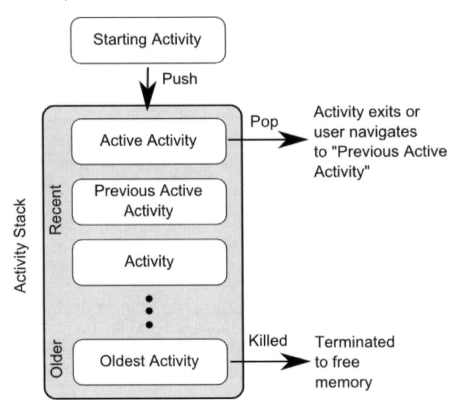

Figure 10-2

As shown in the diagram, new activities are pushed on to the top of the stack when they are started. The current active activity is located at the top of the stack until it is either pushed down the stack by a new activity, or popped off the stack when it exits or the user navigates to the previous activity. In the event that resources become constrained, the runtime will kill activities, starting with those at the bottom of the stack.

The Activity Stack is what is referred to in programming terminology as a Last-In-First-Out (LIFO) stack in that the last item to be pushed onto the stack is the first to be popped off.

10.6 **Activity States**

An activity can be in one of a number of different states during the course of its execution within an application:

- **Active / Running** – The activity is at the top of the Activity Stack, is the foreground task visible on the device screen, has focus and is currently interacting with the user. This is the least likely activity to be terminated in the event of a resource shortage.
- **Paused** – The activity is visible to the user but does not currently have focus (typically because this activity is partially obscured by the current *active* activity). Paused activities are held in memory, remain attached to the window manager, retain all state information and can quickly be restored to active status when moved to the top of the Activity Stack.
- **Stopped** – The activity is currently not visible to the user (in other words it is totally obscured on the device display by other activities). As with paused activities, it retains all state and member information, but is at higher risk of termination in low memory situations.
- **Killed** – The Activity has been terminated by the runtime system in order to free up memory and is no longer present on the Activity Stack. Such activities must be restarted if required by the application.

10.7 **Configuration Changes**

So far in this chapter, we have looked at two of the causes for the change in state of an Android activity, namely the movement of an activity between the foreground and background, and termination of an activity by the runtime system in order to free up memory. In fact, there is a third scenario in which the state of an activity can dramatically change and this involves a change to the device configuration.

By default, any configuration change that impacts the appearance of an activity (such as rotating the orientation of the device between portrait and landscape, or changing a system font setting) will cause the activity to be destroyed and recreated. The reasoning behind this is that such changes affect resources such as the layout of the user interface and simply destroying and recreating impacted activities is the quickest way for an activity to respond to the configuration change.

10.8 **Handling State Change**

If nothing else, it should be clear from this chapter that an application and, by definition, the components contained therein will transition through many states during the course of its lifespan. Of particular importance is the fact that these state changes (up to and including complete termination) are imposed upon the application by the Android runtime subject to the actions of the user and the availability of resources on the device.

In practice, however, these state changes are not imposed entirely without notice and an application will, in most circumstances, be notified by the runtime system of the changes and given the opportunity to react accordingly. This will typically involve saving or restoring both internal data structures and user interface state, thereby allowing the user to switch seamlessly between applications and providing at least the appearance of multiple, concurrently running applications. The steps involved in gracefully handling state changes will be covered in detail in the next chapter entitled *Handling Android Activity State Changes*.

10.9 **Summary**

Mobile devices are typically considered to be resource constrained, particularly in terms of onboard memory capacity. Consequently, a prime responsibility of the Android operating system is to ensure that applications, and the operating system in general, remain responsive to the user.

Applications are hosted on Android within processes. Each application, in turn, is made up of components in the form of activities and Services.

The Android runtime system has the power to terminate both processes and individual activities in order to free up memory. Process state is taken into consideration by the runtime system when deciding whether a process is a suitable candidate for termination. The state of a process is largely dependent upon the status of the activities hosted by that process.

The key message of this chapter is that an application moves through a variety of states during its execution lifespan and has very little control over its destiny within the Android runtime environment. Those processes and activities that are not directly interacting with the user run a higher risk of termination by the runtime system. An essential element of Android application development, therefore, involves the ability of an application to respond to state change notifications from the operating system, a topic that is covered in the next chapter.

11. Handling Android Activity State Changes

Based on the information outlined in the chapter entitled *Understanding Android Application and Activity Lifecycles* it is now evident that the activities that make up an application pass through a variety of different states during the course of the application's lifespan. The change from one state to the other is imposed by the Android runtime system and is, therefore, largely beyond the control of the activity itself. That said, in most instances the runtime will provide the activity in question with a notification of the impending state change, thereby giving it time to react accordingly. In most cases, this will involve saving or restoring data relating to the state of the activity and its user interface.

The primary objective of this chapter is to provide a high-level overview of the ways in which an activity may be notified of a state change and to outline the areas where it is advisable to save or restore state information. Having covered this information, the chapter will then touch briefly on the subject of *activity lifetimes*.

11.1 The Activity Class

With few exceptions, activities in an application are created as subclasses of either the Android *Activity* class, or another class that is, itself, subclassed from the Activity class (for example the *ActionBarActivity* or *FragmentActivity* classes).

Consider, for example, the simple *AndroidSample* project created in *Creating an Example Android App in Android Studio*. Load this project in the Android Studio environment and locate the *AndroidSampleActvity.java* file (located in *app -> java -> com.ebookfrenzy.androidsample*). Having located the file, double click on it to load it into the editor where it should read as follows:

```
package com.ebookfrenzy.androidsample;

import android.support.v7.app.ActionBarActivity;
import android.os.Bundle;
import android.view.Menu;
import android.view.MenuItem;
```

```java
public class AndroidSampleActivity extends ActionBarActivity {

    @Override
    protected void onCreate(Bundle savedInstanceState) {
        super.onCreate(savedInstanceState);
        setContentView(R.layout.activity_android_sample);
    }

    @Override
    public boolean onCreateOptionsMenu(Menu menu) {

        // Inflate the menu; this adds items to the action bar if it
is present.
        getMenuInflater().inflate(R.menu.android_sample, menu);
        return true;
    }

    @Override
    public boolean onOptionsItemSelected(MenuItem item) {
        // Handle action bar item clicks here. The action bar will
        // automatically handle clicks on the Home/Up button, so long
        // as you specify a parent activity in AndroidManifest.xml.
        int id = item.getItemId();
        if (id == R.id.action_settings) {
            return true;
        }
        return super.onOptionsItemSelected(item);
    }
}
```

When the project was created, we instructed Android Studio also to create an initial activity named *AndroidSampleActivity*. As is evident from the above code, the AndroidSampleActivity class *extends,* and is therefore a subclass of, the *ActionBarActivity* class.

A review of the reference documentation for the ActionBarActivity class would reveal that it is itself a subclass of the Activity class. This can be verified within the Android Studio editor using the *Hierarchy* tool window. With the *AndroidSampleActivity.java* file loaded into the editor, click on ActionBarActivity in the *public class* declaration line and press the *Ctrl-H* keyboard shortcut. The hierarchy tool window will subsequently appear displaying the class hierarchy for the selected class. As illustrated in Figure 11-1, ActionBarActivity is clearly subclassed from the FragmentActivity class which is itself a subclass of the Activity class:

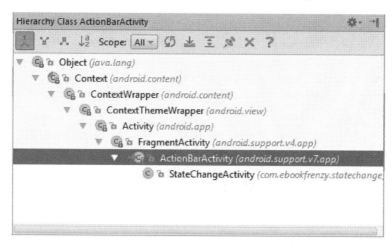

Figure 11-1

This raises the question as to why ActionBarActivity was used instead of the Activity class. The reason for this can be traced back to the selections made when the project was first created. When choosing the SDK version targets for the project in the chapter entitled *Creating an Example Android App in Android Studio*, the project was configured to target a minimum SDK level of API 8: Android 2.2. Since the introduction of Android 3.0, however, applications have included an ActionBar view across the top of the screen which provides menu options and information to the user. The purpose of the ActionBarActivity class is to make this ActionBar available to applications that are required to run on older versions of Android and is included as part of the *android.support.v7* support library. Had we specified API 11: Android 3.0 or later as the minimum SDK for the AndroidSample project, however, the activity would have been declared as a subclass of the Activity class instead of ActionBarActivity since backwards compatibility for the ActionBar would not have been required.

The Activity class and its subclasses contain a range of methods that are intended to be called by the Android runtime to notify an activity that its state is changing. For the purposes of this chapter, we will refer to these as the *activity lifecycle methods.* An activity class simply needs to *override* these methods and implement the necessary functionality within them in order to react accordingly to state changes.

One such method is named *onCreate()* and, turning once again to the above code fragment, we can see that this method has already been overridden and implemented for us in the *AndroidSampleActivity* class. In a later section we will explore in detail both *onCreate()* and the other relevant lifecycle methods of the Activity class.

11.2 Dynamic State vs. Persistent State

A key objective of Activity lifecycle management is ensuring that the state of the activity is saved and restored at appropriate times. When talking about *state* in this context we mean the data that is currently being held within the activity and the appearance of the user interface. The activity might, for example, maintain a data model in memory that needs to be saved to a database, content provider or file. Such state information, because it persists from one invocation of the application to another, is referred to as the *persistent state.*

The appearance of the user interface (such as text entered into a text field but not yet committed to the application's internal data model) is referred to as the *dynamic state*, since it is typically only retained during a single invocation of the application (and also referred to as *user interface state* or *instance state*).

Understanding the differences between these two states is important because both the ways they are saved, and the reasons for doing so, differ.

The purpose of saving the persistent state is to avoid the loss of data that may result from an activity being killed by the runtime system while in the background. The dynamic state, on the other hand, is saved and restored for reasons that are slightly more complex.

Consider, for the sake of an example, that an application contains an activity (which we will refer to as *Activity A*) containing a text field and some radio buttons. During the course of using the application, the user enters some text into the text field and makes a selection from the radio buttons. Before performing an action to save these changes, however, the user then switches to another activity causing *Activity A* to be pushed down the Activity Stack and placed into the background. After some time, the runtime system ascertains that memory is low and consequently kills *Activity A* to free up resources. As far as the user is concerned, however, *Activity A* was simply placed into the background and is ready to be moved to the foreground at any time. On returning *Activity A* to the foreground the user would, quite reasonably, expect the entered text and radio button selections to have been retained. In this scenario, however, a new instance of *Activity A* will have been created and, if the dynamic state was not saved and restored, the previous user input lost.

The main purpose of saving dynamic state, therefore, is to give the perception of seamless switching between foreground and background activities, regardless of the fact that activities may actually have been killed and restarted without the user's knowledge.

The mechanisms for saving persistent and dynamic state will become clearer in the following sections of this chapter.

11.3 The Android Activity Lifecycle Methods

As previously explained, the Activity class contains a number of lifecycle methods which act as event handlers when the state of an Activity changes. The primary methods supported by the Android Activity class are as follows:

- **onCreate(Bundle savedInstanceState)** – The method that is called when the activity is first created and the ideal location for most initialization tasks to be performed. The method is passed an argument in the form of a *Bundle* object that may contain dynamic state information (typically relating to the state of the user interface) from a prior invocation of the activity.
- **onRestart()** – Called when the activity is about to restart after having previously been stopped by the runtime system.
- **onStart()** – Always called immediately after the call to the *onCreate()* or *onRestart()* methods, this method indicates to the activity that it is about to become visible to the user. This call will be followed by a call to *onResume()* if the activity moves to the top of the activity stack, or *onStop()* in the event that it is pushed down the stack by another activity.
- **onResume()** – Indicates that the activity is now at the top of the activity stack and is the activity with which the user is currently interacting.
- **onPause()** – Indicates that a previous activity is about to become the foreground activity. This call will be followed by a call to either the *onResume()* or *onStop()* method depending on whether the activity moves back to the foreground or becomes invisible to the user. Steps should be taken within this method to store any *persistent data* required by the activity (such as data stored to a content provider, database or file). This method should also ensure that any CPU intensive tasks such as animation are stopped.
- **onStop()** – The activity is now no longer visible to the user. The two possible scenarios that may follow this call are a call to *onRestart()* in the event that the activity moves to the foreground again, or *onDestroy()* if the activity is being terminated.
- **onDestroy()** – The activity is about to be destroyed, either voluntarily because the activity has completed its tasks and has called the *finish()* method or because the runtime is terminating it either to release memory or due to a configuration change (such as the orientation of the device changing). It is important to note that a call will not always be made to *onDestroy()* when an activity is terminated.

In addition to the lifecycle methods outlined above, there are two methods intended specifically for saving and restoring the *dynamic state* of an activity:

- **onRestoreInstanceState(Bundle savedInstanceState)** – This method is called immediately after a call to the *onStart()* method in the event that the activity is restarting from a previous invocation in which state was saved. As with *onCreate()*, this method is passed a Bundle object containing the previous state data. This method is typically used in situations where it makes more sense to restore a previous state after the initialization of the activity has been performed in *onCreate()* and *onStart()*.
- **onSaveInstanceState(Bundle outState)** – Called before an activity is destroyed so that the current *dynamic state* (usually relating to the user interface) can be saved. The method is passed the Bundle object into which the state should be saved and which is subsequently passed through to the *onCreate()* and *onRestoreInstanceState()* methods when the activity is restarted.

Note that this method is only called in situations where the runtime ascertains that dynamic state needs to be saved.

When overriding the above methods in an activity, it is important to remember that with the exception of *onRestoreInstanceState()* and *onSaveInstanceState()*, the method implementation must include a call to the corresponding method in the *Activity* super class. For example, the following method overrides the *onRestart()* method but also includes a call to the super class instance of the method:

```
protected void onRestart() {
        super.onRestart();
        Log.i(TAG, "onRestart");
}
```

Failure to make this super class call in method overrides will result in the runtime throwing an exception during execution of the activity. Whilst calls to the super class in the *onRestoreInstanceState()* and *onSaveInstanceState()* are optional there are considerable benefits in doing so, a subject that will be covered in the chapter entitled *Saving and Restoring the User Interface State of an Android Activity*.

11.4 Activity Lifetimes

The final topic to be covered involves an outline of the *entire*, *visible* and *foreground* lifetimes through which an activity will transition during execution:

- **Entire Lifetime** –The term "entire lifetime" is used to describe everything that takes place within an activity between the initial call to the *onCreate()* method and the call to *onDestroy()* prior to the activity terminating.
- **Visible Lifetime** – Covers the periods of execution of an activity between the call to *onStart()* and *onStop()*. During this period the activity is visible to the user though may not be the activity with which the user is currently interacting.
- **Foreground Lifetime** – Refers to the periods of execution between calls to the *onResume()*and *onPause()* methods.

It is important to note that an activity may pass through the *foreground* and *visible* lifetimes multiple times during the course of the *entire* lifetime.

The concepts of lifetimes and lifecycle methods are illustrated in Figure 11-2:

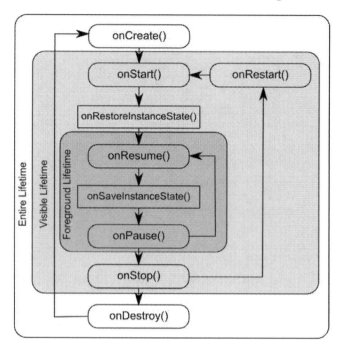

Figure 11-2

11.5 **Summary**

All activities are derived from the Android *Activity* class which, in turn, contains a number of event methods that are designed to be called by the runtime system when the state of an activity changes. By overriding these methods, an activity can respond to state changes and, where necessary, take steps to save and restore the current state of both the activity and the application. Activity state can be thought of as taking two forms. The persistent state refers to data that needs to be stored between application invocations (for example to a file or database). Dynamic state, on the other hand, relates instead to the current appearance of the user interface.

In this chapter, we have highlighted the lifecycle methods available to activities and covered the concept of activity lifetimes. In the next chapter, entitled *Android Activity State Changes – An Example Application*, we will implement an example application that puts much of this theory into practice.

12. Android Activity State Changes by Example

The previous chapters have discussed in some detail the different states and lifecycles of the activities that comprise an Android application. In this chapter, we will put the theory of handling activity state changes into practice through the creation of an example application. The purpose of this example application is to provide a real world demonstration of an activity as it passes through a variety of different states within the Android runtime.

In the next chapter, entitled *Saving and Restoring the State of an Android Activity*, the example project constructed in this chapter will be extended to demonstrate the saving and restoration of dynamic activity state.

12.1 Creating the State Change Example Project

The first step in this exercise is to create the new project. Begin by launching Android Studio and, if necessary, closing any currently open projects using the *File -> Close Project* menu option so that the Welcome screen appears.

Select the *Start a new Android Studio project* quick start option from the welcome screen and, within the resulting new project dialog, enter *StateChange* into the Application name field and *ebookfrenzy.com* as the Company Domain setting before clicking on the *Next* button.

On the form factors screen, enable the *Phone and Tablet* option and set the minimum SDK setting to API 8: Android 2.2 (Froyo). Continue to proceed through the screens, requesting the creation of a blank activity named *StateChangeActivity*, a corresponding layout named *activity_state_change* and a menu resource named *menu_state_change*.

Upon completion of the project creation process, the *StateChange* project should be listed in the Project tool window located along the left-hand edge of the Android Studio main window with the *activity_state_change.xml* layout file pre-loaded into the Designer as illustrated in Figure 12-1:

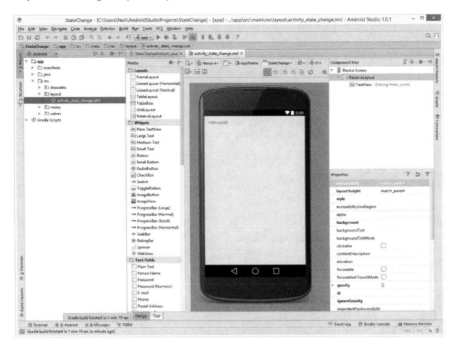

Figure 12-1

The next action to take involves the design of the user interface for the activity. This is stored in a file named *activity_state_change.xml* which should already be loaded into the Designer tool. If it is not, one way to access this file is to navigate to it in the project tool window where it can be found in the *app -> res -> layout* folder. Once located, double clicking on the file will load it into the Android Studio Designer tool. A quicker option, however, is to use the *Go to declaration* editor shortcut, the purpose of which is to take you directly to the file and location where the currently selected item in the editor window is declared.

In this case, the *activity_state_change* layout is referenced in the *onCreate()* method of the *StateChangeActivity.java* file (located in the project panel under *app -> java -> com.ebookfrenzy.statechange*):

```
@Override
protected void onCreate(Bundle savedInstanceState) {
    super.onCreate(savedInstanceState);
    setContentView(R.layout.activity_state_change);
}
```

To open the file in the Designer, click on the *activity_state_change* reference so that it highlights and press the Ctrl-B keyboard shortcut sequence. Android Studio will then open the *activity_state_change.xml* file in the Designer tool ready for the layout work to begin.

12.2 Designing the User Interface

With the user interface layout loaded into the Designer tool, it is now time to design the user interface for the example application. Instead of the "Hello world!" TextView currently present in the user interface design, the activity actually requires an EditText view. Select the TextView object in the Designer canvas and press the Delete key on the keyboard to remove it from the design.

From the Palette located on the left side of the Designer, locate the *Text Fields* category and click and drag a *Plain Text* component over to the visual representation of the device screen. Move the component to the center of the display so that the center guidelines appear and drop it into place so that the layout resembles that of Figure 12-2.

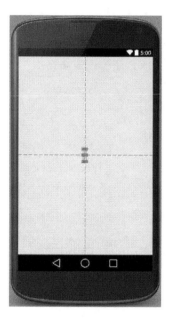

Figure 12-2

Note that the light bulb icon has appeared next to the view indicating that assistance is available to us in configuring this component. When working with EditText views in an Android user interface it is necessary to declare the *input type* for the view. This simply defines the type of text or data that will be entered by the user. For example, if the input type is set to *Phone*, the user will be restricted to entering numerical digits into the view. Alternatively, if the input type is set to *TextCapCharacters,* the input will default to upper case characters. Input type settings may also be combined.

For the purposes of this example, we will set the input type to support general text input. To do so, click on the light bulb icon followed by the right facing arrow at the end of the message describing the problem. From the list of potential solutions (Figure 12-3) click on the *Add inputType attribute* option:

Figure 12-3

From the resulting *Set Attribute Value* dialog, select the *text* option from the drop down menu.

The final step in the user interface design process is to increase the width of the TextView component. With the component selected in the layout, scroll down the list of attributes in the *Properties* panel until the *width* attribute comes into view and enter a value of 200dp as outlined in Figure 12-4:

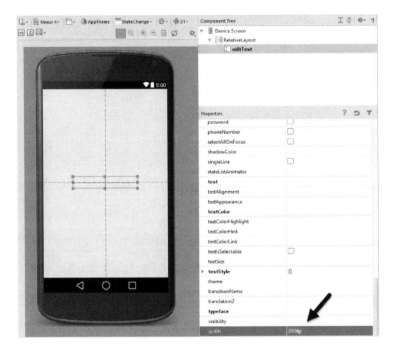

Figure 12-4

12.3 **Overriding the Activity Lifecycle Methods**

At this point, the project contains a single activity named *StateChangeActivity*, which is derived from the Android *ActionBarActivity* class. The source code for this activity is contained within the *StateChangeActivity.java* file which should already be open in an editor session and represented by a tab in the editor tab bar. In the event that the file is no longer open, navigate to it in the Project tool window panel (*app -> java -> com.ebookfrenzy.statechange -> StateChangeActivity*) and double click on it to load the file into the editor. Once loaded the code should read as follows:

```
package com.ebookfrenzy.statechange;

import android.support.v7.app.ActionBarActivity;
import android.os.Bundle;
import android.view.Menu;
import android.view.MenuItem;


public class StateChangeActivity extends ActionBarActivity {

    @Override
    protected void onCreate(Bundle savedInstanceState) {
        super.onCreate(savedInstanceState);
        setContentView(R.layout.activity_state_change);
    }



    @Override
    public boolean onCreateOptionsMenu(Menu menu) {

        // Inflate the menu; this adds items to the action bar if it
is present.
        getMenuInflater().inflate(R.menu.menu_state_change, menu);
        return true;
    }

    @Override
    public boolean onOptionsItemSelected(MenuItem item) {
        // Handle action bar item clicks here. The action bar will
        // automatically handle clicks on the Home/Up button, so long
        // as you specify a parent activity in AndroidManifest.xml.
        int id = item.getItemId();
        if (id == R.id.action_settings) {
            return true;
        }
        return super.onOptionsItemSelected(item);
    }

}
```

So far the only lifecycle method overridden by the activity is the *onCreate()* method which has been implemented to call the super class instance of the method before setting up the user interface for the activity. We will now modify this method so that it outputs a diagnostic message in the Android

Studio LogCat panel each time it executes. For this, we will use the *Log* class, which requires that we import *android.util.Log* and declare a tag that will enable us to filter these messages in the log output:

```
package com.ebookfrenzy.statechange;

import android.support.v7.app.ActionBarActivity;
import android.os.Bundle;
import android.view.Menu;
import android.view.MenuItem;
import android.util.Log;

public class StateChangeActivity extends ActionBarActivity {

    private static final String TAG = "StateChange";

    @Override
    protected void onCreate(Bundle savedInstanceState) {
        super.onCreate(savedInstanceState);
        setContentView(R.layout.activity_state_change);
        Log.i(TAG, "onCreate");
    }
    .
    .
    .
}
```

The next task is to override some more methods, with each one containing a corresponding log call. These override methods may be added manually or generated using the *Alt-Insert* keyboard shortcut as outlined in the chapter entitled *The Basics of the Android Studio Code Editor*. Note that the Log calls will still need to be added manually if the methods are being auto-generated:

```
    @Override
    protected void onStart() {
        super.onStart();
        Log.i(TAG, "onStart");
    }

    @Override
    protected void onResume() {
        super.onResume();
        Log.i(TAG, "onResume");
    }
```

```java
    @Override
    protected void onPause() {
        super.onPause();
        Log.i(TAG, "onPause");
    }

    @Override
    protected void onStop() {
        super.onStop();
        Log.i(TAG, "onStop");
    }

    @Override
    protected void onRestart() {
        super.onRestart();
        Log.i(TAG, "onRestart");
    }

    @Override
    protected void onDestroy() {
        super.onDestroy();
        Log.i(TAG, "onDestroy");
    }

    @Override
    protected void onSaveInstanceState(Bundle outState) {
        super.onSaveInstanceState(outState);
        Log.i(TAG, "onSaveInstanceState");
    }

    @Override
    protected void onRestoreInstanceState(Bundle savedInstanceState) {
        super.onRestoreInstanceState(savedInstanceState);
        Log.i(TAG, "onRestoreInstanceState");
    }
```

12.4 Filtering the LogCat Panel

The purpose of the code added to the overridden methods in *StateChangeActivity.java* is to output logging information to the *LogCat* panel within the Android tool window. With no filters defined, the log will list every event that takes place within the device or emulator making it difficult to find the log messages for our overridden methods. Before running the application, therefore, it is recommended to create a filter which, when selected, will ensure that only those log messages containing the tag declared in our activity are displayed.

Begin by displaying the Android tool window using either the tools menu button located in the far left corner of the status bar or the *Alt-6* keyboard shortcut. Within the tool window, make sure that the *Devices/logcat* tab is selected before accessing the menu in the upper right hand corner of the panel (which will probably currently read *No Filters*). From this menu, select the *Edit Filter Configuration* menu option as shown in Figure 12-5:

Figure 12-5

In the *Create New Logcat Filter* dialog (Figure 12-6), name the filter *Lifecycle* and, in the *by Log Tag (regex)* field, enter the Tag value declared in *StateChangeActivity.java* (in the above code example this was *StateChange*).

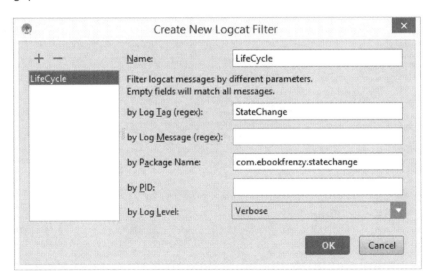

Figure 12-6

When the changes are complete, click on the *OK* button to create the filter and dismiss the dialog. Instead of listing *No Filters,* the newly created filter should now be selected in the Android tool window.

12.5 **Running the Application**

For optimal results, the application should be run on a physical Android device, details of which can be found in the chapter entitled *Testing Android Studio Apps on a Physical Android Device*. With the device configured and connected to the development computer, click on the run button represented by a green triangle located in the Android Studio toolbar as shown in Figure 12-7 below, select the *Run -> Run...* menu option or use the Shift+F10 keyboard shortcut:

Figure 12-7

Select the physical Android device from the *Choose Device* dialog if it appears (assuming that you have not already configured it to be the default target). After Android Studio has built the application and installed it on the device it should start up and be running in the foreground.

A review of the LogCat panel should indicate which methods have so far been triggered (taking care to ensure that the *Lifecycle* filter created in the preceding section is selected to filter out log events that are not currently of interest to us):

Figure 12-8

12.6 **Experimenting with the Activity**

With the diagnostics working, it is now time to exercise the application with a view to gaining an understanding of the activity lifecycle state changes. To begin with, consider the initial sequence of log events in the LogCat panel:

```
onCreate
onStart
onResume
```

Clearly, the initial state changes are exactly as outlined in Figure 11-2. Note, however, that a call was not made to *onRestoreInstanceState()* since the Android runtime detected that there was no state to restore in this situation.

Tap on the Home icon in the bottom status bar on the device display and note the sequence of method calls reported in the log as follows:

```
onPause
onSaveInstanceState
onStop
```

In this case, the runtime has noticed that the activity is no longer in the foreground, is not visible to the user and has stopped the activity, but not without providing an opportunity for the activity to save the dynamic state. Depending on whether the runtime ultimately destroyed the activity or simply restarted it, the activity will either be notified it has been restarted via a call to *onRestart()* or will go through the creation sequence again when the user returns to the activity.

As outlined in *Understanding Android Application and Activity Lifecycles*, the destruction and recreation of an activity can be triggered by making a configuration change to the device, such as rotating from portrait to landscape. To see this in action, simply rotate the device while the *StateChange* application is in the foreground. When using the emulator, device rotation may be simulated using the Ctrl-F12 keyboard shortcut or by pressing the number 7 on the keyboard keypad while Num Lock is off. The resulting sequence of method calls in the log should read as follows:

```
onPause
onSaveInstanceState
onStop
onDestroy
onCreate
onStart
onRestoreInstanceState
onResume
```

Clearly, the runtime system has given the activity an opportunity to save state before being destroyed and restarted.

12.7 **Summary**

The old adage that a picture is worth a thousand words holds just as true for examples when learning a new programming paradigm. In this chapter, we have created an example Android application for the purpose of demonstrating the different lifecycle states through which an activity is likely to pass. In the course of developing the project in this chapter, we also looked at a mechanism for generating diagnostic logging information from within an activity.

In the next chapter, we will extend the *StateChange* example project to demonstrate how to save and restore an activity's dynamic state.

13. Saving and Restoring the State of an Android Activity

If the previous few chapters have achieved their objective, it should now be a little clearer as to the importance of saving and restoring the state of a user interface at particular points in the lifetime of an activity.

In this chapter, we will extend the example application created in *Android Activity State Changes – An Example Application* to demonstrate the steps involved in saving and restoring state when an activity is destroyed and recreated by the runtime system.

A key component of saving and restoring dynamic state involves the use of the Android SDK *Bundle* class, a topic that will also be covered in this chapter.

13.1 Saving Dynamic State

An activity, as we have already learned, is given the opportunity to save dynamic state information via a call from the runtime system to the activity's implementation of the *onSaveInstanceState()* method. Passed through as an argument to the method is a reference to a Bundle object into which the method will need to store any dynamic data that needs to be saved. The Bundle object is then stored by the runtime system on behalf of the activity and subsequently passed through as an argument to the activity's *onCreate()* and *onRestoreInstanceState()* methods if and when they are called. The data can then be retrieved from the Bundle object within these methods and used to restore the state of the activity.

13.2 Default Saving of User Interface State

In the previous chapter, the diagnostic output from the *StateChange* example application showed that an activity goes through a number of state changes when the device on which it is running is rotated sufficiently to trigger an orientation change.

Launch the *StateChange* application once again, this time entering some text into the EditText field prior to performing the device rotation. Having rotated the device, the following state change sequence should appear in the LogCat window:

```
onPause
onSaveInstanceState
onStop
onDestroy
onCreate
onStart
onRestoreInstanceState
onResume
```

Clearly this has resulted in the activity being destroyed and re-created. A review of the user interface of the running application, however, should show that the text entered into the EditText field has been preserved. Given that the activity was destroyed and recreated, and that we did not add any specific code to make sure the text was saved and restored, this behavior requires some explanation.

In actual fact most of the view widgets included with the Android SDK already implement the behavior necessary to automatically save and restore state when an activity is restarted. The only requirement to enable this behavior is for the *onSaveInstanceState()* and *onRestoreInstanceState()* override methods in the activity to include calls to the equivalent methods of the super class:

```
@Override
protected void onSaveInstanceState(Bundle outState) {
    super.onSaveInstanceState(outState);
}

@Override
protected void onRestoreInstanceState(Bundle savedInstanceState) {
    super.onRestoreInstanceState(savedInstanceState);
}
```

The automatic saving of state for a user interface view can be disabled in the XML layout file by setting the *android:saveEnabled* property to *false*. For the purposes of an example, we will disable the automatic state saving mechanism for the EditText view in the user interface layout and then add code to the application to manually save and restore the state of the view.

To configure the EditText view such that state will not be saved and restored in the event that the activity is restarted, edit the *activity_state_change.xml* file so that the entry for the view reads as follows (note that the XML can be edited directly by clicking on the *Text* tab on the bottom edge of the Designer panel):

```
<EditText
    android:layout_width="wrap_content"
    android:layout_height="wrap_content"
    android:id="@+id/editText"
```

```
android:saveEnabled="false"
android:inputType="text"
android:layout_centerVertical="true"
android:layout_centerHorizontal="true"
android:width="200dp" />
```

After making the change, run the application, enter text and rotate the device to verify that the text is no longer saved and restored before proceeding.

13.3 **The Bundle Class**

For situations where state needs to be saved beyond the default functionality provided by the user interface view components, the Bundle class provides a container for storing data using a *key-value pair* mechanism. The *keys* take the form of string values, whilst the *values* associated with those *keys* can be in the form of a primitive value or any object that implements the Android *Parcelable* interface. A wide range of classes already implements the Parcelable interface. Custom classes may be made "parcelable" by implementing the set of methods defined in the Parcelable interface details of which can be found in the Android documentation at:

http://developer.android.com/reference/android/os/Parcelable.html

The Bundle class also contains a set of methods that can be used to get and set key-value pairs for a variety of data types including both primitive types (including Boolean, char, double and float values) and objects (such as Strings and CharSequences).

For the purposes of this example, and having disabled the automatic saving of text for the EditText view, we need to make sure that the text entered into the EditText field by the user is saved into the Bundle object and subsequently restored. This will serve as a demonstration of how to manually save and restore state within an Android application and will be achieved using the *putCharSequence()* and *getCharSequence()* methods of the Bundle class respectively.

13.4 **Saving the State**

The first step in extending the *StateChange* application is to make sure that the text entered by the user is extracted from the EditText component within the *onSaveInstanceState()* method of the *StateChangeActivity* activity, and then saved as a key-value pair into the Bundle object.

In order to extract the text from the EditText object we first need to identify that object in the user interface. Clearly, this involves bridging the gap between the Java code for the activity (contained in the *StateChangeActivity.java* source code file) and the XML representation of the user interface (contained within the *activity_state_change.xml* resource file). In order to extract the text entered into the EditText component we need to gain access to that user interface object.

Each component within a user interface has associated with it a unique identifier. By default, the Designer tool constructs the ID for a newly added component from the object type. If more than one view of the same type is contained in the layout the type name is followed by a sequential number (though this can, and should, be changed to something more meaningful by the developer). As can be seen by checking the *Component* panel within the Android Studio main window when the *activity_state_change.xml* file is selected and the Designer tool displayed, the EditText component has been assigned the ID *editText*:

Figure 13-1

As outlined in the chapter entitled *The Anatomy of an Android Application*, all of the resources that make up an application are compiled into a class named *R*. Amongst those resources are those that define layouts, including the layout for our current activity. Within the R class is a subclass named *layout*, which contains the layout resources, and within that subclass is our *activity_state_change* layout. With this knowledge, we can make a call to the *findViewById()* method of our activity object to get a reference to the editText object as follows:

```
final EditText textBox = (EditText) findViewById(R.id.editText);
```

Having obtained a reference to the EditText object and assigned it to *textBox,* we can now obtain the text that it contains by calling the object's *getText()* method, which, in turn, returns the current text in the form of a *CharSequence* object:

```
CharSequence userText = textBox.getText();
```

Finally, we can save the text using the Bundle object's *putCharSequence()* method, passing through the key (this can be any string value but in this instance, we will declare it as "savedText") and the *userText* object as arguments:

```
outState.putCharSequence("savedText", userText);
```

Bringing this all together gives us a modified *onSaveInstanceState()* method in the *StateChangeActivity.java* file that reads as follows (noting also the additional import directive for *android.widget.EditText*):

```
package com.ebookfrenzy.statechange;

import android.support.v7.app.ActionBarActivity;
import android.os.Bundle;
import android.util.Log;
import android.view.Menu;
import android.view.MenuItem;
import android.widget.EditText;

public class StateChangeActivity extends ActionBarActivity {
.
.
.
    protected void onSaveInstanceState(Bundle outState) {
        super.onSaveInstanceState(outState);
        Log.i(TAG, "onSaveInstanceState");

        final EditText textBox =
          (EditText) findViewById(R.id.editText);
        CharSequence userText = textBox.getText();
        outState.putCharSequence("savedText", userText);

    }
.
.
.
```

Now that steps have been taken to save the state, the next phase is to ensure that it is restored when needed.

13.5 Restoring the State

The saved dynamic state can be restored in those lifecycle methods that are passed the Bundle object as an argument. This leaves the developer with the choice of using either *onCreate()* or *onRestoreInstanceState()*. The method to use will depend on the nature of the activity. In instances where state is best restored after the activity's initialization tasks have been performed, the *onRestoreInstanceState()* method is generally more suitable. For the purposes of this example we will add code to the *onRestoreInstanceState()* method to extract the saved state from the Bundle using the "savedText" key. We can then display the text on the editText component using the object's *setText()* method:

```
@Override
protected void onRestoreInstanceState(Bundle savedInstanceState) {
```

```
        super.onRestoreInstanceState(savedInstanceState);
        Log.i(TAG, "onRestoreInstanceState");

        final EditText textBox =
                (EditText) findViewById(R.id.editText);

        CharSequence userText =
                        savedInstanceState.getCharSequence("savedText");

        textBox.setText(userText);
}
```

13.6 Testing the Application

All that remains is once again to build and run the *StateChange* application. Once running and in the foreground, touch the EditText component and enter some text before rotating the device to another orientation. Whereas the text changes were previously lost, the new text is retained within the editText component thanks to the code we have added to the activity in this chapter.

13.7 Summary

The saving and restoration of dynamic state in an Android application is simply a matter of implementing the appropriate code in the appropriate lifecycle methods. For most user interface views, this is handled automatically by the Activity super class. In other instances, this typically consists of extracting values and settings within the *onSaveInstanceState()* method and saving the data as key-value pairs within the Bundle object passed through to the activity by the runtime system.

State can be restored in either the *onCreate()* or the *onRestoreInstanceState()* methods of the activity by extracting values from the Bundle object and updating the activity based on the stored values.

In this chapter, we have used these techniques to update the *StateChange* project so that the Activity retains changes through the destruction and subsequent recreation of an activity.

14. Understanding Android Views, View Groups and Layouts

With the possible exception of listening to streaming audio, a user's interaction with an Android device is primarily visual and tactile in nature. All of this interaction takes place through the user interfaces of the applications installed on the device, including both the built-in applications and any third party applications installed by the user. It should come as no surprise, therefore, that a key element of developing Android applications involves the design and creation of user interfaces.

Within this chapter, the topic of Android user interface structure will be covered, together with an overview of the different elements that can be brought together to make up a user interface; namely Views, View Groups and Layouts.

14.1 Designing for Different Android Devices

The term "Android device" covers a vast array of tablet and smartphone products with different screen sizes and resolutions. As a result, application user interfaces must now be carefully designed to ensure correct presentation on as wide a range of display sizes as possible. A key part of this is ensuring that the user interface layouts resize correctly when run on different devices. This can largely be achieved through careful planning and the use of the layout managers outlined in this chapter.

It is also important to keep in mind that the majority of Android based smartphones and tablets can be held by the user in both portrait and landscape orientations. A well-designed user interface should be able to adapt to such changes and make sensible layout adjustments to utilize the available screen space in each orientation.

14.2 Views and View Groups

Every item in a user interface is a subclass of the Android *View* class (to be precise *android.view.View*). The Android SDK provides a set of pre-built views that can be used to construct a user interface. Typical examples include standard items such as the Button, CheckBox, ProgressBar and TextView classes. Such views are also referred to as *widgets* or *components*. For requirements that are not met by the widgets supplied with the SDK, new views may be created either by subclassing and extending an existing class, or creating an entirely new component by building directly on top of the View class.

A view can also be comprised of multiple other views (otherwise known as a *composite view*). Such views are subclassed from the Android *ViewGroup* class (*android.view.ViewGroup*) which is itself a subclass of *View*. An example of such a view is the RadioGroup, which is intended to contain multiple RadioButton objects such that only one can be in the "on" position at any one time. In terms of structure, composite views consist of a single parent view (derived from the ViewGroup class and otherwise known as a *container view* or *root element)* that is capable of containing other views (known as *child views*).

Another category of ViewGroup based container view is that of the layout manager.

14.3 **Android Layout Managers**

In addition to the widget style views discussed in the previous section, the SDK also includes a set of views referred to as *layouts*. Layouts are container views (and, therefore, subclassed from ViewGroup) designed for the sole purpose of controlling how child views are positioned on the screen.

The Android SDK includes the following layout views that may be used within an Android user interface design:

- **LinearLayout** – Positions child views in a single row or column depending on the orientation selected. A *weight* value can be set on each child to specify how much of the layout space that child should occupy relative to other children.
- **TableLayout** – Arranges child views into a grid format of rows and columns. Each row within a table is represented by a *TableRow* object child, which, in turn, contains a view object for each cell.
- **FrameLayout** – The purpose of the FrameLayout is to allocate an area of screen, typically for the purposes of displaying a single view. If multiple child views are added they will, by default, appear on top of each other positioned in the top left hand corner of the layout area. Alternate positioning of individual child views can be achieved by setting gravity values on each child. For example, setting a *center_vertical* gravity on a child will cause it to be positioned in the vertical center of the containing FrameLayout view.
- **RelativeLayout** – Probably the most powerful and flexible of the layout managers, this allows child views to be positioned relative both to each other and the containing layout view through the specification of alignments and margins on child views. For example, child *View A* may be configured to be positioned in the vertical and horizontal center of the containing RelativeLayout view. *View B*, on the other hand, might also be configured to be centered horizontally within the layout view, but positioned 30 pixels above the top edge of *View A*, thereby making the vertical position *relative* to that of *View A*. The RelativeLayout manager can be of particular use when designing a user interface that must work on a variety of screen sizes and orientations.

- **AbsoluteLayout** – Allows child views to be positioned at specific X and Y coordinates within the containing layout view. Use of this layout is discouraged since it lacks the flexibility to respond to changes in screen size and orientation.

- **GridLayout** – The GridLayout is a relatively new layout manager that was introduced as part of Android 4.0. A GridLayout instance is divided by invisible lines that form a grid containing rows and columns of cells. Child views are then placed in cells and may be configured to cover multiple cells both horizontally and vertically allowing a wide range of layout options to be quickly and easily implemented. Gaps between components in a GridLayout may be implemented by placing a special type of view called a *Space* view into adjacent cells, or by setting margin parameters.

When considering the use of layouts in the user interface for an Android application it is worth keeping in mind that, as will be outlined in the next section, these can be nested within each other to create a user interface design of just about any necessary level of complexity.

14.4 **The View Hierarchy**

Each view in a user interface represents a rectangular area of the display. A view is responsible for what is drawn in that rectangle and for responding to events that occur within that part of the screen (such as a touch event).

A user interface screen is comprised of a view hierarchy with a *root view* positioned at the top of the tree and child views positioned on branches below. The child of a container view appears on top of its parent view and is constrained to appear within the bounds of the parent view's display area. Consider, for example, the user interface illustrated in Figure 14-1:

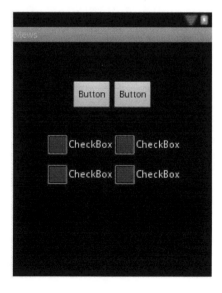

Figure 14-1

Understanding Android Views, View Groups and Layouts

In addition to the visible button and checkbox views, the user interface actually includes a number of layout views that control how the visible views are positioned. Figure 14-2 shows an alternative view of the user interface, this time highlighting the presence of the layout views in relation to the child views:

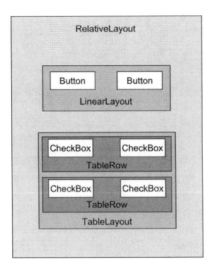

Figure 14-2

As was previously discussed, user interfaces are constructed in the form of a view hierarchy with a root view at the top. This being the case, we can also visualize the above user interface example in the form of the view tree illustrated in Figure 14-3:

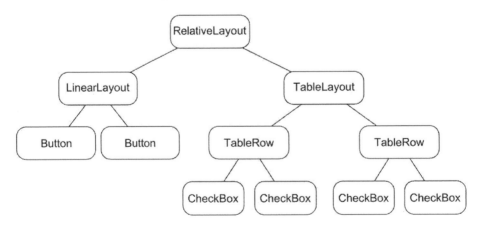

Figure 14-3

The view hierarchy diagram gives probably the clearest overview of the relationship between the various views that make up the user interface shown in Figure 14-1. When a user interface is displayed to the user, the Android runtime walks the view hierarchy, starting at the root view and working down the tree as it renders each view.

14.5 **Creating User Interfaces**

With a clearer understanding of the concepts of views, layouts and the view hierarchy, the following few chapters will focus on the steps involved in creating user interfaces for Android activities. In fact, there are three different approaches to user interface design: using the Android Studio Designer tool, handwriting XML layout resource files or writing Java code, each of which will be covered.

14.6 **Summary**

Each element within a user interface screen of an Android application is a view that is ultimately subclassed from the *android.view.View* class. Each view represents a rectangular area of the device display and is responsible both for what appears in that rectangle and for handling events that take place within the view's bounds. Multiple views may be combined to create a single *composite view*. The views within a composite view are children of a *container view* which is generally a subclass of *android.view.ViewGroup* (which is itself a subclass of *android.view.View*). A user interface is comprised of views constructed in the form of a view hierarchy.

The Android SDK includes a range of pre-built views that can be used to create a user interface. These include basic components such as text fields and buttons, in addition to a range of layout managers that can be used to control the positioning of child views. In the event that the supplied views do not meet a specific requirement, custom views may be created, either by extending or combining existing views, or by subclassing *android.view.View* and creating an entirely new class of view.

User interfaces may be created using the Android Studio Designer tool, handwriting XML layout resource files or by writing Java code. Each of these approaches will be covered in the chapters that follow.

Chapter 15

15. A Guide to the Android Studio Designer Tool

It is difficult to think of an Android application concept that does not require some form of user interface. Most Android devices come equipped with a touch screen and keyboard (either virtual or physical) and taps and swipes are the primary form of interaction between the user and application. Invariably these interactions take place through the application's user interface.

A well designed and implemented user interface, an important factor in creating a successful and popular Android application, can vary from simple to extremely complex, depending on the design requirements of the individual application. Regardless of the level of complexity, the Android Studio Designer tool significantly simplifies the task of designing and implementing Android user interfaces.

15.1 The Android Studio Designer

As has been demonstrated in previous chapters, the Designer tool provides a "what you see is what you get" (WYSIWYG) environment in which views can be selected from a palette and then placed onto a canvas representing the display of an Android device. Once a view has been placed on the canvas, it can be moved, deleted and resized (subject to the constraints of the parent view). Further, a wide variety of properties relating to the selected view may be modified using the Properties panel.

Under the surface, the Designer tool actually constructs an XML resource file containing the definition of the user interface that is being designed. As such, the Designer tool operates in two distinct modes referred to as *Design mode* and *Text mode*.

15.2 Design Mode

In design mode, the user interface can be visually manipulated by directly working with the view palette and the graphical representation of the layout.

Figure 15-1 highlights the key areas of the Android Studio Designer tool in design mode:

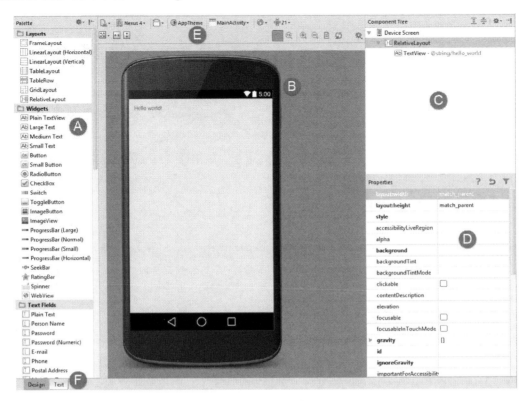

Figure 15-1

A – Palette – The palette provides access to the range of view components provided by the Android SDK. These are grouped into categories for easy navigation. Items may be added to the layout either by dragging a view component from the palette and dropping it at the desired position on the layout, or by clicking on a widget in the palette and then clicking at the location on the layout where it is to be positioned.

B – Device Screen – The device screen provides a visual "what you see is what you get" representation of the user interface layout as it is being designed. This layout allows for direct manipulation of the design in terms of allowing views to be selected, deleted, moved and resized. The device model represented by the layout can be changed at any time using a menu located in the toolbar.

Note that if you find the image of the device frame surrounding the display layout distracting, it can be turned off by selecting the settings menu in the toolbar (represented by the gear icon) and toggling off the *Include Device Frames (if available)* option.

C – Component Tree – As outlined in the previous chapter (*Understanding Android Views, View Groups and Layouts*) user interfaces are constructed using a hierarchical structure. The component tree provides a visual overview of the hierarchy of the user interface design. Selecting an element from the component tree will cause the corresponding view in the layout to be selected. Similarly, selecting a view from the device screen layout will select that view in the component tree hierarchy.

D – Properties – All of the component views listed in the palette have associated with them a set of properties that can be used to adjust the behavior and appearance of that view. The Designer's properties panel provides access to the properties of the currently selected view in the layout allowing changes to be made.

E – Toolbar – The Designer toolbar provides quick access to a wide range of options including, amongst other options, the ability to zoom in and out of the device screen layout, change the device model currently displayed, rotate the layout between portrait and landscape and switch to a different Android SDK API level. The toolbar also has a set of context sensitive buttons which will appear when relevant view types are selected in the device screen layout.

F – Mode Switching Tabs – The tabs located along the lower edge of the Designer provide a way to switch back and forth between the Designer tool's text and design modes.

15.3 **Text Mode**

It is important to keep in mind when using the Android Studio Designer tool that all it is really doing is providing a user friendly approach to creating XML layout resource files. At any time during the design process, the underlying XML can be viewed and directly edited simply by clicking on the *Text* tab located at the bottom of the Designer tool panel. To return to design mode, simply click on the *Design* tab.

Figure 15-2 highlights the key areas of the Android Studio Designer tool in text mode:

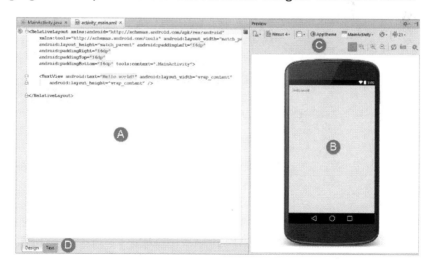

Figure 15-2

A – Editor – The editor panel displays the XML that makes up the current user interface layout design. This is the full Android Studio editor environment containing all of the features previously outlined in the *The Basics of the Android Studio Code Editor* chapter of this book.

B – Preview – As changes are made to the XML in the editor, these changes are visually reflected in the preview window. This provides instant visual feedback on the XML changes as they are made in the editor, thereby avoiding the need to switch back and forth between text and design mode to see changes. Whilst the preview does not allow direct manipulation of the views, double clicking on a view in the preview will automatically switch to design mode and preselect the corresponding view in the device screen layout.

C – Toolbar – The toolbar in text mode provides a subset of those functions available in design mode with the addition of a button to take a screenshot of the current device screen layout.

D - Mode Switching Tabs – The tabs located along the lower edge of the Designer provide a way to switch back and forth between the Designer tool's text and design modes.

15.4 Setting Properties

The properties panel provides access to all of the available settings for the currently selected component. Clicking in the panel and typing characters will begin a search process to highlight and select the closest match to the typed characters.

Whilst the properties panel provides access to the full list of properties for the currently selected component, quick access to a subset of common properties can be gained by double clicking on the component view in the layout. Double clicking on a TextView component, for example, provides quick access to the text and id properties for the view as shown in Figure 15-3:

Figure 15-3

Some properties, both in the main properties and quick access panels contain a button displaying three dots. This indicates that a settings dialog is available to assist in selecting a suitable property value. To display the dialog, simply click on the button. Properties for which a finite number of valid options are available will present a drop down menu (Figure 15-4) from which a selection may be made.

Figure 15-4

By default, the properties panel only lists the most commonly used properties. Access to the full range of properties for the currently selected component type is available by switching the panel into *expert mode.* This mode can be toggled on and off by clicking on the funnel button in the toolbar as indicated by the arrow in Figure 15-5:

Figure 15-5

In most instances, access to the expert mode properties will not be needed, though it is useful to be aware of this mode in the event that the property you are looking for is not listed in standard mode.

15.5 Type Morphing

The morphing feature of the Designer tool allows a component view that is already part of the user interface layout to be changed from one type to another. Morphing can, for example, be used to change a TextView component into an EditText view component. Whilst morphing is limited in terms of the types of conversion that can be performed (it is not possible, for example, to morph a TextView into a ProgressBar), this does provide a quicker alternative to deleting and adding components in many cases.

To morph a component, simply right-click on the view in the layout and select the *Morphing* menu option followed by the type to which the view is to be changed. Figure 15-6, for example, shows the morphing options available for an ImageButton component:

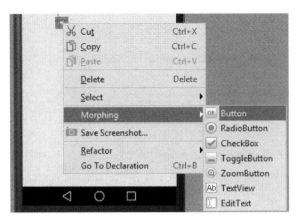

Figure 15-6

15.6 **Creating a Custom Device Definition**

The device menu in the Designer toolbar provides a list of preconfigured device types which, when selected, will appear as the device screen canvas. In addition to the pre-configured device types, any AVD instances that have previously been configured within the Android Studio environment will also be listed within the menu. To add additional device configurations, display the device menu, select the *Add Device Definition...* option and follow the steps outlined in the chapter entitled *Creating an Android Virtual Device (AVD) in Android Studio*.

15.7 **Summary**

A key part of developing Android applications involves the creation of the user interface. Within the Android Studio environment, this is performed using the Designer tool which operates in two modes. In design mode, view components are selected from a palette and positioned on a layout representing an Android device screen and configured using a list of properties. In text mode, the underlying XML that represents the user interface layout can be directly edited, with changes reflected in a preview screen. These modes combine to provide an extensive and intuitive user interface design environment.

16. Designing a User Interface using the Android Studio Designer Tool

By far the easiest and most productive mechanism for designing a user interface for an Android application is to make use of the Android Studio Designer tool. The goal of this chapter is to provide an overview of how to create a user interface using this tool. The exercise included in this chapter will also be used as an opportunity to outline the creation of an activity starting with a "bare-bones" Android Studio project.

Having covered the use of the Android Studio Designer, the chapter will also provide an overview of the concepts behind manually writing and editing XML layout resource files before introducing the Hierarchy Viewer tool.

16.1 An Android Studio Designer Tool Example

The first step in this phase of the example is to create a new Android Studio project. Begin, therefore, by launching Android Studio and closing any previously opened projects by selecting the *File -> Close Project* menu option. Within the Android Studio welcome screen click on the *Start a new Android Studio project* quick start option to display the first screen of the new project dialog.

Enter *LayoutSample* into the Application name field and *ebookfrenzy.com* as the Company Domain setting before clicking on the *Next* button.

In previous examples, we have requested that Android Studio create a template activity for the project. We will, however, be using this tutorial to learn how to create an entirely new activity and corresponding layout resource file manually, so make sure that the *Add No Activity* option is selected before clicking on *Finish* to create the new project.

16.2 Creating a New Activity

Once the project creation process is complete, the Android Studio main window should appear with a blank background containing a message that reads "No files are open".

Designing a User Interface using the Android Studio Designer Tool

The next step in the project is to create a new activity. This will be a valuable learning exercise since there are many instances in the course of developing Android applications where new activities need to be created from the ground up.

Begin by displaying the Project tool window using the Alt-1 keyboard shortcut. Once displayed, unfold the hierarchy by clicking on the right facing arrows next to the entries in the Project window. The objective here is to gain access to the *app -> java -> com.ebookfrenzy.layoutsample* folder in the project hierarchy. Once the package name is visible, right-click on it and select the *New -> Activity -> Blank Activity* menu option as illustrated in Figure 16-1:

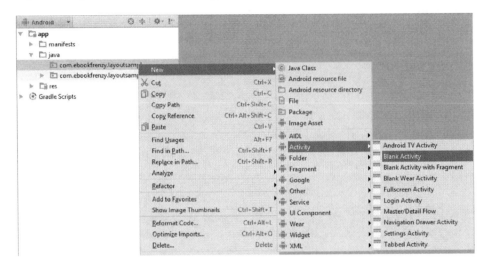

Figure 16-1

In the resulting *New Activity* dialog, name the new activity *LayoutSampleActivity*, the layout *activity_layout_sample* and the menu resource *menu_layout_sample*.

In order for an application to be able to run on a device it needs to have an activity designated as the *launcher activity*. Without a launcher activity, the operating system will not know which activity to start up when the application first launches and, as such, the application will fail to start. Since this example only has one activity, it needs to be designated as the launcher activity for the application so make sure that the *Launcher Activity* option is selected before clicking on the *Finish* button.

At this point Android Studio should have added two files to the project. The Java source code file for the activity should be located in the *app -> java -> com.ebookfrenzy.layoutsample* folder.

In addition, the XML layout file for the user interface should have been created in the *app -> res -> layout* folder and should also have been preloaded into the Designer tool.

Finally, the new activity should have been added to the *AndroidManifest.xml* file and designated as the launcher activity. The manifest file can be found in the project window under the *app -> manifests* folder and should contain the following XML:

```xml
<?xml version="1.0" encoding="utf-8"?>
<manifest xmlns:android="http://schemas.android.com/apk/res/android"
    package="com.ebookfrenzy.layoutsample" >

    <application
        android:allowBackup="true"
        android:icon="@mipmap/ic_launcher"
        android:label="@string/app_name"
        android:theme="@style/AppTheme" >
        <activity
            android:name=".LayoutSampleActivity"
            android:label="@string/title_activity_layout_sample" >
            <intent-filter>
                <action android:name="android.intent.action.MAIN" />

                <category
                    android:name="android.intent.category.LAUNCHER" />
            </intent-filter>
        </activity>
    </application>

</manifest>
```

16.3 **Designing the User Interface**

Locate and double click on the *activity_layout_sample.xml* layout file located in the *app -> res -> layout* folder to load it into the Designer tool.

By default the layout should contain a single component view in the form of the TextView displaying the "Hello World!" message. Select this component and remove it by pressing the keyboard delete key.

From within the *Widgets* palette category, drag a Button view object into the center of the display view. Note that green horizontal and vertical dashed lines appear to indicate the center axes of the display. Once centered, release the mouse button to drop the view into position. Click and drag a Plain Text object from the Text Fields section of the palette and position it so that it appears above the button as illustrated in Figure 16-2:

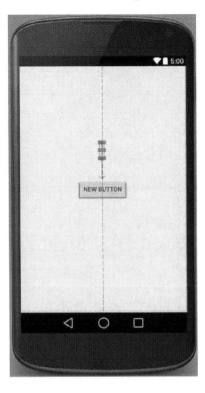

Figure 16-2

Click on the light bulb icon to display the hints menu and click on the message that reads "This text field does not specify an inputType or a hint" and select *text* as the input type in the *Set Attribute* dialog. Click on OK to dismiss the dialog and set the attribute.

16.4 Editing View Properties

Once a view object has been placed into the user interface, the properties of that view may also be modified from within the Designer tool. In the first instance, the width of the EditText object may be inadequate for allowing the user to enter text. In order to change this, select the EditText object and locate and select the *Width* property in the *Properties* panel. In the value field, enter a value for the desired width of the field. The value must include a unit of measurement from the following list:

- **in** – Inches
- **mm** – Millimeters
- **pt** – Points (1/72 of an inch)
- **dp** – Density-independent pixels. An abstract unit of measurement based on the physical density of the device display relative to a 160dpi display baseline.
- **sp** – Scale-independent pixels. Similar to dp but scaled based on the user's font preference.

- **px** – Actual screen pixels. Use is not recommended since different displays will have different pixels per inch. Use *dp* in preference to this unit.

For the purposes of this example, we will use density independent pixels as our unit of measurement, so enter 350dp into the dialog and click on the *OK* button. The width of the EditText view should change accordingly.

Next, double click on the Button view and in the resulting panel, change the text property from "New Button" to "Press Me". Click on the light bulb icon followed by the I18N message to display the *Extract Resource* dialog. Name the resource *button_string* and click on *OK* to create a string resource for the button.

The very simple user interface design is now complete. Designing a more complex user interface layout is a continuation of the steps outlined above. Simply drag and drop views onto the display, position and set properties as needed and nest layouts as required.

16.5 **Running the Application**

All that remains is to test that the application runs. Click on the run button in the main window toolbar. Select either the simulator or a physical Android device and wait for the application to start. Assuming the absence of errors, the application and activity should launch and appear exactly as designed using the Designer tool.

16.6 **Manually Creating an XML Layout**

Whilst the design of layouts using the layout tool greatly improves productivity, it is still possible to create XML layouts by manually editing the XML. The structure of an XML layout file is actually quite straightforward and follows the hierarchical approach of the view tree. The first line of an XML resource file should ideally include the following standard declaration:

```
<?xml version="1.0" encoding="utf-8"?>
```

This declaration should be followed by the root element of the layout, typically a container view such as a layout manager. This is represented by both opening and closing tags and any properties that need to be set on the view. The following XML, for example, declares a RelativeLayout view as the root element and sets *match_parent* properties such that it fills all the available space of the device display with padding on each side of 64 density independent pixels:

```
<RelativeLayout
    xmlns:android="http://schemas.android.com/apk/res/android"
    xmlns:tools="http://schemas.android.com/tools"
    android:layout_width="match_parent"
    android:layout_height="match_parent"
```

```
        android:paddingLeft="64dp"
        android:paddingRight="64dp"
        android:paddingTop="64dp"
        android:paddingBottom="64dp"
        tools:context=
          "com.ebookfrenzy.layoutsample.layoutsample.LayoutSampleActivity">

</RelativeLayout>
```

Any children that need to be added to the RelativeLayout parent must be *nested* within the opening and closing tags. In the following example, a Button and an EditText field have been added as children of the RelativeLayout view:

```
<RelativeLayout
    xmlns:android="http://schemas.android.com/apk/res/android"
    xmlns:tools="http://schemas.android.com/tools"
    android:layout_width="match_parent"
    android:layout_height="match_parent"
    android:paddingLeft="64dp"
    android:paddingRight="64dp"
    android:paddingTop="64dp"
    android:paddingBottom="64dp"
    tools:context=
      "com.ebookfrenzy.layoutsample.layoutsample.LayoutSampleActivity">

    <Button
        android:layout_width="wrap_content"
        android:layout_height="wrap_content"
        android:text="@string/button_string"
        android:id="@+id/button"
        android:layout_centerVertical="true"
        android:layout_centerHorizontal="true" />

    <EditText
        android:layout_width="wrap_content"
        android:layout_height="wrap_content"
        android:id="@+id/editText"
        android:layout_above="@+id/button"
        android:layout_centerHorizontal="true"
        android:layout_marginBottom="51dp"
        android:inputType="text"
        android:width="350dp" />
```

```
</RelativeLayout>
```

Also, note that the two child views have a number of properties declared. In the case of the Button view, it has been assigned ID "button" and configured to display the text that is represented by a string resource named *button_string*. Additionally, it has been centered vertically and horizontally within the parent view and *wrap_content* height and width properties have been declared so that the button is sized to accommodate the content (in this case the text shown on the button).

The EditText view, on the other hand, has a width declared as 350dp, is centered horizontally within the parent and positioned 51dp above the button view.

This XML file is, of course, the layout that was created using the Designer tool in this chapter.

When to write XML manually as opposed to using the Designer tool in design mode is a matter of personal preference. There are, however, advantages to using design mode.

Firstly, design mode will generally be quicker given that it avoids the necessity to type lines of XML. Additionally, design mode avoids the necessity to learn the intricacies of the various property values of the Android SDK view classes. Rather than continually refer to the Android documentation to find the correct keywords and values, most properties can be located by referring to the Properties panel.

All the advantages of design mode aside, it is important to keep in mind that the two approaches to user interface design are in no way mutually exclusive. As an application developer, it is quite likely that you will end up creating user interfaces within design mode whilst performing fine-tuning and layout tweaks of the design by directly editing the generated XML resources. Both views of the interface design are, after all, a single mouse click apart within the Android Studio environment making it easy to switch back and forth as needed. In fact, a useful tip to remember is that selecting a view in the display layout and pressing the Ctrl-B keyboard shortcut will automatically jump to and highlight the XML for that view in the resource file.

16.7 Using the Hierarchy Viewer

A useful tool for closely inspecting the view hierarchy of an activity is the Hierarchy Viewer. The main purpose of the tool is to provide a detailed overview of the entire view tree for activities within currently running applications and to provide some insight into the layout rendering performance.

The hierarchy viewer can only be used to inspect applications that are either running within an Android emulator, or on a device running a *development* version of Android. To run the tool on the *LayoutSample* application created in this chapter, launch the application on an Android Virtual Device emulator and wait until it has loaded and is visible on the emulator display. Once running, select the *Tools -> Android -> Android Device Monitor* menu option. In the DDMS window, select the *Window ->*

Designing a User Interface using the Android Studio Designer Tool

Open Perspective... menu option and choose *Hierarchy View* from the resulting dialog before clicking on the *OK* button.

When the Hierarchy Viewer appears, it will consist of a number of different panels. The left hand panel, illustrated in Figure 16-3, lists all the windows currently active on the device or emulator such as the navigation bar, status bar and launcher. The window listed in bold is the current foreground window, which should, in this case, be *LayoutSampleActivity*.

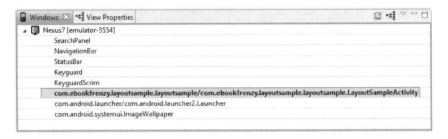

Figure 16-3

Selecting the layout sample window will cause the hierarchy to load into the Tree View panel as shown in Figure 16-4 (note that there may be a short delay between selection of the window and the hierarchy diagram appearing):

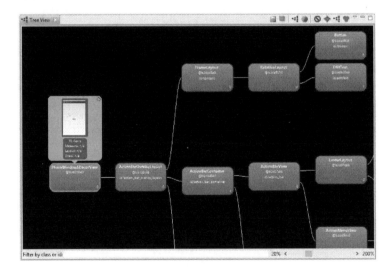

Figure 16-4

Whilst it is possible to zoom in and out of the tree view using the scale at the bottom of the panel or by spinning the mouse wheel, in most cases the tree will be too large to view entirely within the Tree View panel. To move the view window around the tree simply click and drag in the Tree View panel, or move the lens within the Tree Overview panel (Figure 16-5):

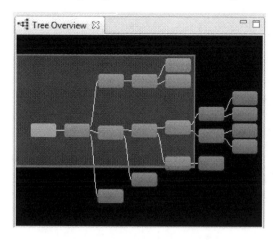

Figure 16-5

When reviewing the tree view, keep in mind that some views in addition to those included in the activity layout will be displayed. These are the views and layouts that, for example, display the action bar across the top of the screen and provide an area for the activity to be displayed.

Selecting a node in the Tree View will cause the corresponding element in the user interface representation to be highlighted in red in the Layout View. In Figure 16-6 the RelativeLayout view is currently selected:

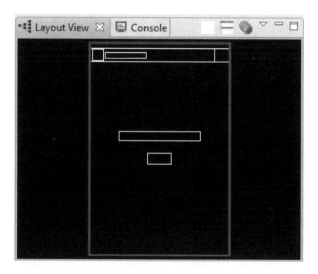

Figure 16-6

Similarly, selecting views from the Layout View will cause the corresponding node in the Tree View to highlight and move into view.

Additional information about a view can be obtained by selecting the node within the Tree View. A panel will then popup next to the node and can be dismissed by performing a right-click on the node. Double clicking on a node will display a dialog containing a rendering of how the view appears within the application user interface. Figure 16-7, for example, shows the button from the LayoutSample application:

Figure 16-7

Options are also available within the tool to perform tasks such as invalidating a selected layout view (thereby forcing it to be redrawn) and to save the tree view as a PNG image file. The hierarchy viewer can also be used to display information about the speed with which the child views of a selected node are rendered when the user interface is created. To display this performance information, select the node to act as the root view and click on the toolbar button indicated in Figure 16-8. When enabled, the colored dots within the nodes indicate the performance in each category (measure, layout and draw) with red indicating slower performance for the view relative to other views in the activity. Container views with larger numbers of child views may display red status simply because the view has to wait for each child to render. This is not necessarily an indication of a performance problem with that view.

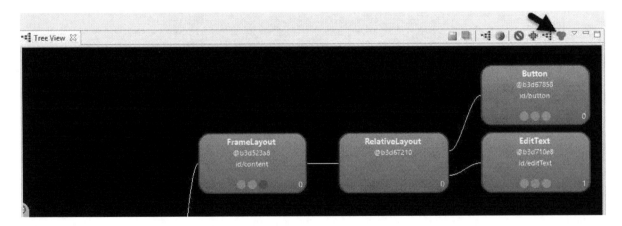

Figure 16-8

16.8 Summary

The Android Studio Designer tool provides a visually intuitive method for designing user interfaces. Using a drag and drop paradigm combined with a set of property editors, the tool provides considerable productivity benefits to the application developer.

User interface designs may also be implemented by manually writing the XML layout resource files, the format of which is well structured and easily understood.

The fact that the Designer tool generates XML resource files means that these two approaches to interface design can be combined to provide a "best of both worlds" approach to user interface development.

Finally, a detailed overview of the view tree for an activity and an indication of the performance of each view within that activity can be obtained using the Hierarchy Viewer tool.

Chapter 17

17. Creating an Android User Interface in Java Code

Up until this point in the book, all user interface design tasks have been performed using the Android Studio Designer tool, either in text or design mode. An alternative to writing XML resource files or using Android Studio Designer is to write Java code to directly create, configure and manipulate the view objects that comprise the user interface of an Android activity. Within the context of this chapter, we will explore some of the advantages and disadvantages of writing Java code to create a user interface before describing some of the key concepts such as view properties, layout parameters and rules. Finally, an example project will be created and used to demonstrate some of the typical steps involved in this approach to Android user interface creation.

17.1 Java Code vs. XML Layout Files

There are a number of key advantages to using XML resource files to design a user interface as opposed to writing Java code. In fact, Google goes to considerable lengths in the Android documentation to extol the virtues of XML resources over Java code. As discussed in the previous chapter, one key advantage to the XML approach includes the ability to use the Android Studio Designer tool, which, itself, generates XML resources. A second advantage is that once an application has been created, changes to user interface screens can be made by simply modifying the XML file, thereby avoiding the necessity to recompile the application. Also, even when hand writing XML layouts, it is possible to get instant feedback on the appearance of the user interface using the preview feature of the Android Studio Designer tool. In order to test the appearance of a Java created user interface the developer will, inevitably, repeatedly cycle through a loop of writing code, compiling and testing in order to complete the design work.

In terms of the strengths of the Java coding approach to layout creation, perhaps the most significant advantage that Java has over XML resource files comes into play when dealing with dynamic user interfaces. XML resource files are inherently most useful when defining static layouts, in other words layouts that are unlikely to change significantly from one invocation of an activity to the next. Java code, on the other hand, is ideal for creating user interfaces dynamically at run-time. This is particularly useful in situations where the user interface may appear differently each time the activity executes subject to external factors.

A knowledge of working with user interface components in Java code can also be useful when dynamic changes to a static XML resource based layout need to be performed in real-time as the activity is running.

Finally, some developers simply prefer to write Java code than to use layout tools and XML, regardless of the advantages offered by the latter approaches.

17.2 Creating Views

As previously established, the Android SDK includes a toolbox of view classes designed to meet most of the basic user interface design needs. The creation of a view in Java is simply a matter of creating instances of these classes, passing through as an argument a reference to the activity with which that view is to be associated.

The first view (typically a container view to which additional child views can be added) is displayed to the user via a call to the *setContentView()* method of the activity. Additional views may be added to the root view via calls to the object's *addView()* method.

When working with Java code to manipulate views contained in XML layout resource files, it is necessary to obtain the ID of the view. The same rule holds true for views created in Java. As such, it is necessary to assign an ID to any view for which certain types of access will be required in subsequent Java code. This is achieved via a call to the *setId()* method of the view object in question. In later code, the ID for a view may be obtained via a subsequent call to the object's *getId()* method.

17.3 Properties and Layout Parameters

Each view class has associated with it a range of *properties*. These property settings are set directly on the view instances and generally define how the view object will appear or behave. Examples of properties are the text that appears on a Button object, or the background color of a RelativeLayout view. Each view class within the Android SDK has a pre-defined set of methods that allow the user to *set* and *get* these property values. The Button class, for example, has a *setText()* method which can be called from within Java code to set the text displayed on the button to a specific string value. The background color of a *RelativeLayout* object, on the other hand, can be set with a call to the object's *setBackgroundColor()* method.

Whilst property settings are internal to view objects and dictate how a view appears and behaves, *Layout Parameters* are used to control how a view appears relative to its parent view and other sibling views. Layout parameters are not set in quite the same way as properties, but rather stored in a *ViewGroup.LayoutParams* instance (or a subclass thereof) which is then either passed through as an argument when the view is added to the parent view, or assigned to the child view via a call to the view's *setLayoutParams()* method.

A LayoutParams object for a view is typically created by declaring how the view should be sized in relation to the parent view (i.e. whether it should fill the parent or be sized to fit the content it needs to display). Once the LayoutParams object exists, additional *rules*, such as whether the view should be aligned with another view, can be added via calls to the *addRule()* method of the LayoutParams object.

There are subclasses of *ViewGroup.LayoutParams* for each of the layout types (AbsoluteLayout.LayoutParams, RelativeLayout.LayoutParams and so on).

Having covered the theory of user interface creation from within Java code, the remainder of this chapter will work methodically through the creation of an example application with the objective of putting this theory into practice.

17.4 Creating the Example Project in Android Studio

Launch Android Studio and select the *Start a new Android Studio project* option from the quick start list in the welcome screen. If any existing projects are already open, close them first using the *File -> Close* menu option.

In the new project configuration dialog, enter *JavaLayout* into the Application name field and *ebookfrenzy.com* as the Company Domain setting before clicking on the *Next* button.

On the form factors screen, enable the *Phone and Tablet* option and set the minimum SDK setting to API 8: Android 2.2 (Froyo). Continue to proceed through the screens, requesting the creation of a blank activity named *JavaLayoutActivity* with a corresponding layout named *activity_java_layout* and with the menu resource name set to *menu_java_layout*.

Once the project has been created, the *JavaLayoutActivity.java* file should automatically load into the editing panel. As we have come to expect, Android Studio has created a template activity and overridden the *onCreate()* method, providing an ideal location for Java code to be added to create a user interface.

17.5 Adding Views to an Activity

The *onCreate()* method is currently designed to use a resource layout file for the user interface. Begin, therefore, by deleting this line from the method:

```
@Override
protected void onCreate(Bundle savedInstanceState) {
        super.onCreate(savedInstanceState);
        setContentView(R.layout.activity_java_layout);
}
```

Creating an Android User Interface in Java Code

The next modification to the *onCreate()* method is to write some Java code to add a RelativeLayout object with a single Button view child to the activity. This involves the creation of new instances of the RelativeLayout and Button classes. The Button view then needs to be added as a child to the RelativeLayout view which, in turn, is displayed via a call to the *setContentView()* method of the activity instance:

```
package com.ebookfrenzy.javalayout;

import android.support.v7.app.ActionBarActivity;
import android.os.Bundle;
import android.view.Menu;
import android.view.MenuItem;
import android.widget.Button;
import android.widget.RelativeLayout;


public class JavaLayoutActivity extends ActionBarActivity {

    @Override
    protected void onCreate(Bundle savedInstanceState) {
        super.onCreate(savedInstanceState);
        Button myButton = new Button(this);
        RelativeLayout myLayout = new RelativeLayout(this);
        myLayout.addView(myButton);
        setContentView(myLayout);
    }
    .
    .
    .
}
```

Once the above additions have been made, compile and run the application (either on a physical device or an emulator). Once launched, the visible result will be a button containing no text appearing in the top left hand corner of the RelativeLayout view as shown in Figure 17-1:

Figure 17-1

17.6 **Setting View Properties**

For the purposes of this exercise, we need the background of the RelativeLayout view to be blue and the Button view to display text that reads "Press Me". Both of these tasks can be achieved by setting properties on the views in the Java code as outlined in the following code fragment:

```java
package com.ebookfrenzy.javalayout;

import android.support.v7.app.ActionBarActivity;
import android.os.Bundle;
import android.view.Menu;
import android.view.MenuItem;
import android.widget.Button;
import android.widget.RelativeLayout;
import android.graphics.Color;

public class JavaLayoutActivity extends ActionBarActivity {

    @Override
    protected void onCreate(Bundle savedInstanceState) {
        super.onCreate(savedInstanceState);
        Button myButton = new Button(this);
        myButton.setText("Press Me");
        myButton.setBackgroundColor(Color.YELLOW);

        RelativeLayout myLayout = new RelativeLayout(this);
        myLayout.setBackgroundColor(Color.BLUE);

        myLayout.addView(myButton);
        setContentView(myLayout);
    }
.
.
```

```
      .
    }
```

When the application is now compiled and run, the layout will reflect the property settings such that the layout will appear with a blue background and the button will display the assigned text on a yellow background.

17.7 Adding Layout Parameters and Rules

By default, the RelativeLayout view has placed the button view in the top left corner of the display. In order to instruct the layout view to place the button in a different location, in this case centered both horizontally and vertically, it will be necessary to create a LayoutParams object and initialize it with the appropriate values.

Typically, a new LayoutParams instance is created by passing through the height and width values for the view. These values should be set to either *MATCH_PARENT, WRAP_CONTENT* or specific size values. The MATCH_PARENT setting instructs the parent layout to expand the child view so that it matches the size of the parent. WRAP_CONTENT, on the other hand, instructs the parent to size the child view so that it is only large enough to display any content it may be configured to show to the user.

The code to create a LayoutParams object for our button would read as follows:

```
RelativeLayout.LayoutParams buttonParams =
             new RelativeLayout.LayoutParams(
                 RelativeLayout.LayoutParams.WRAP_CONTENT,
                 RelativeLayout.LayoutParams.WRAP_CONTENT);
```

The above code creates a new RelativeLayout LayoutParams object named *buttonParams* and sets the height and width such that the button will only be large enough to display the "Press Me" text previously configured via the property setting.

Now that the LayoutParams object has been created, the next step is to add some additional rules to the parameters to instruct the layout parent to center the button vertically and horizontally. This is achieved by calling the *addRule()* method of the *buttonParams* object, passing through the appropriate values as arguments:

```
buttonParams.addRule(RelativeLayout.CENTER_HORIZONTAL);
buttonParams.addRule(RelativeLayout.CENTER_VERTICAL);
```

Simply creating a new LayoutParams object and configuring it is only useful if that object is then assigned to the child view. One way to achieve this is to pass the LayoutParams object through as an argument when the child view is added to the parent:

```
myLayout.addView(myButton, buttonParams);
```

Alternatively, the parameters can be assigned to the child via a call to the *setLayoutParams()* method of the view:

```
myButton.setLayoutParams(buttonParams);
```

Bringing these together results in a modified *onCreate()* method that reads as follows:

```
@Override
protected void onCreate(Bundle savedInstanceState) {
    super.onCreate(savedInstanceState);
    Button myButton = new Button(this);
    myButton.setText("Press me");
    myButton.setBackgroundColor(Color.YELLOW);

    RelativeLayout myLayout = new RelativeLayout(this);
    myLayout.setBackgroundColor(Color.BLUE);

    RelativeLayout.LayoutParams buttonParams =
            new RelativeLayout.LayoutParams(
                RelativeLayout.LayoutParams.WRAP_CONTENT,
                RelativeLayout.LayoutParams.WRAP_CONTENT);

    buttonParams.addRule(RelativeLayout.CENTER_HORIZONTAL);
    buttonParams.addRule(RelativeLayout.CENTER_VERTICAL);

    myLayout.addView(myButton, buttonParams);
    setContentView(myLayout);
}
```

Having made the above changes, compile and run the application once again, this time noting that the button is now centered within the RelativeLayout view as illustrated in Figure 17-2:

Figure 17-2

In order to gain a clearer understanding of the height and width layout parameter settings, temporarily modify the *buttonParams* creation code to read as follows, then re-compile and run the application:

```
RelativeLayout.LayoutParams buttonParams =
            new RelativeLayout.LayoutParams(
                RelativeLayout.LayoutParams.MATCH_PARENT,
                RelativeLayout.LayoutParams.MATCH_PARENT);
```

With both the height and width parameters set to *MATCH_PARENT,* the button is now sized to match the parent view and consequently fills the entire display.

Before continuing, revert the height and width settings to *WRAP_CONTENT.*

17.8 Using View IDs

So far in this tutorial it has not been necessary to use view IDs. In order to demonstrate the use of IDs in Java code, the example will now be extended to add another view in the form of an EditText view that will be configured to be aligned 80 pixels above the existing button and centered horizontally. The following code modifications add the new view to the activity and then set IDs of *myButtonId* and *myEditTextId* on the Button and EditText views respectively. Layout parameters are then created for the EditText view so that it is aligned with the button (note the call to *getId()* on the button to get the view ID) and centered horizontally within the layout. Finally, the *margins* property of the EditText field is configured to set the bottom margin to 80 pixels before adding the new view to parent layout.

The view IDs first need to be declared as value resources. Right click on the *app -> res -> values* folder, select the *New -> Values resource file* menu option and name the new resource file *id.xml*. With the resource file created, edit it so that it reads as follows:

```xml
<?xml version="1.0" encoding="utf-8"?>
<resources>
    <item name="myButtonId" type="id" />
    <item name="myEditTextId" type="id" />
</resources>
```

Next, edit the *JavaLayoutActivity.java* file and add the code to create the EditText view and assign the view IDs:

```java
package com.ebookfrenzy.javalayout;

import android.support.v7.app.ActionBarActivity;
import android.os.Bundle;
import android.view.Menu;
import android.view.MenuItem;
import android.widget.Button;
import android.widget.RelativeLayout;
import android.graphics.Color;
import android.widget.EditText;

public class JavaLayoutActivity extends ActionBarActivity {

    @Override
    protected void onCreate(Bundle savedInstanceState) {
        super.onCreate(savedInstanceState);
        Button myButton = new Button(this);
        myButton.setText("Press me");
        myButton.setBackgroundColor(Color.YELLOW);

        RelativeLayout myLayout = new RelativeLayout(this);
        myLayout.setBackgroundColor(Color.BLUE);

        EditText myEditText = new EditText(this);

        myButton.setId(R.id.myButtonId);
        myEditText.setId(R.id.myEditTextId);

        RelativeLayout.LayoutParams buttonParams =
                new RelativeLayout.LayoutParams(
```

```
                      RelativeLayout.LayoutParams.WRAP_CONTENT,
                      RelativeLayout.LayoutParams.WRAP_CONTENT);


        RelativeLayout.LayoutParams textParams =
             new RelativeLayout.LayoutParams(
                RelativeLayout.LayoutParams.WRAP_CONTENT,
                RelativeLayout.LayoutParams.WRAP_CONTENT);

        textParams.addRule(RelativeLayout.ABOVE, myButton.getId());
        textParams.addRule(RelativeLayout.CENTER_HORIZONTAL);
        textParams.setMargins(0, 0, 0, 80);

        buttonParams.addRule(RelativeLayout.CENTER_HORIZONTAL);
        buttonParams.addRule(RelativeLayout.CENTER_VERTICAL);

        myLayout.addView(myButton, buttonParams);
        myLayout.addView(myEditText, textParams);
        setContentView(myLayout);
    }
  .
  .
  .
}
```

A test run of the application should show the EditText field centered above the button with a margin of 80 pixels.

17.9 Converting Density Independent Pixels (dp) to Pixels (px)

The final task in this exercise is to set the width of the EditText view to 200dp. As outlined in the chapter entitled *Designing an Android User Interface using the Graphical Layout Tool*, when setting sizes and positions in user interface layouts it is better to use density independent pixels (dp) rather than pixels (px). When the margin was set in the above section, the value was declared in px instead of dp. The reason for this was that such method calls only accept values in pixels. In order to set a position using dp, therefore, it is necessary to convert a dp value to a px value at runtime, taking into consideration the density of the device display. In order, therefore, to set the width of the EditText view to 350dp, the following code needs to be added to the *onCreate()* method:

```
package com.ebookfrenzy.javalayout;

import android.app.Activity;
import android.os.Bundle;
import android.widget.RelativeLayout;
```

```
import android.widget.Button;
import android.widget.RelativeLayout;
import android.graphics.Color;
import android.widget.EditText;
import android.content.res.Resources;
import android.util.TypedValue;

public class JavaLayoutActivity extends ActionBarActivity {

    @Override
    public void onCreate(Bundle savedInstanceState) {
        super.onCreate(savedInstanceState);

        Button myButton = new Button(this);
        myButton.setText("Press me");

        EditText myEditText = new EditText(this);

        myButton.setId(R.id.myButtonId);
        myEditText.setId(R.id.myEditTextId);

        RelativeLayout myLayout = new RelativeLayout(this);
        myLayout.setBackgroundColor(Color.BLUE);

        RelativeLayout.LayoutParams buttonParams =
                new RelativeLayout.LayoutParams(
                    RelativeLayout.LayoutParams.WRAP_CONTENT,
                    RelativeLayout.LayoutParams.WRAP_CONTENT);

        buttonParams.addRule(RelativeLayout.CENTER_HORIZONTAL);
        buttonParams.addRule(RelativeLayout.CENTER_VERTICAL);

        RelativeLayout.LayoutParams textParams =
                new RelativeLayout.LayoutParams(
                    RelativeLayout.LayoutParams.WRAP_CONTENT,
                    RelativeLayout.LayoutParams.WRAP_CONTENT);

        textParams.addRule(RelativeLayout.ABOVE, myButton.getId());
        textParams.addRule(RelativeLayout.CENTER_HORIZONTAL);
        textParams.setMargins(0, 0, 0, 80);

        Resources r = getResources();
        int px = (int) TypedValue.applyDimension(
```

```
                    TypedValue.COMPLEX_UNIT_DIP, 200,
                         r.getDisplayMetrics());

        myEditText.setWidth(px);

        myLayout.addView(myButton, buttonParams);
        myLayout.addView(myEditText, textParams);
        setContentView(myLayout);
    }
}
```

Compile and run the application one more time and note that the width of the EditText view has changed as illustrated in Figure 17-3:

Figure 17-3

17.10 Summary

As an alternative to writing XML layout resource files or using the Android Studio Designer tool, Android user interfaces may also be dynamically created in Java code.

Creating layouts in Java code consists of creating instances of view classes and setting properties on those objects to define required appearance and behavior.

How a view is positioned and sized relative to its parent view and any sibling views is defined using layout parameters, which are stored in LayoutParams objects. Once a LayoutParams object has been created and initialized with height and width behavior settings, additional rules may then be added to configure the parameters further.

The example activity created in this chapter has, of course, created the same user interface (the change in background color notwithstanding) as that created in the previous chapter using the Graphical Layout tool and XML resources. If nothing else, this chapter should have provided an appreciation of the level to which the Android Studio Designer tool and XML resources shield the developer from many of the complexities of creating Android user interface layouts.

There are, however, instances where it makes sense to create a user interface in Java. This approach is most useful, for example, when creating dynamic user interface layouts.

18. Using the Android GridLayout Manager in Android Studio Designer

A useful layout manager that was introduced as part of the Android 4.0 SDK is the GridLayout manager class. As the name suggests, this class allows child views to be arranged in a grid layout. There are a number of ways to implement the GridLayout within the user interface of an Android application, including through the use of layout resources and Java code. Perhaps the easiest approach, however, is to make use of some GridLayout specific features built into the Android Studio Designer tool.

This chapter will introduce the basics of the GridLayout class before exploring the creation of a GridLayout-based user interface using Android Studio Designer. Directly creating GridLayout user interface designs using XML layout resources as an alternative to using the Designer tool will be covered in the next chapter, entitled *Working with the Android GridLayout using XML Layout Resources*.

18.1 Introducing the Android GridLayout and Space Classes

The purpose of the GridLayout is to allow child views to be positioned in a grid arrangement. The GridLayout essentially consists of a number of invisible horizontal and vertical *grid lines* that serve to divide the layout view into a series of *rows* and *columns*, with each intersecting row and column forming a *cell* which can, in turn, contain one or more views. The grid lines are referred to as *indices*, which are numbered starting at 0 for the line at the leading edge of the layout. Row and column numbering also starts at 0 beginning in the top left hand corner of the grid.

The positioning of a view within a cell can be defined through the use of *gravity* settings on that child view. The gravity of a child view can, for example, be configured such that the view appears centered, fills the entire cell or is positioned in a specific corner of the cell within which it resides.

In addition, a child view of a GridLayout parent may also be configured to span multiple rows and columns through the use of the *rowSpan* and *columnSpan* properties of the child.

Another useful class that can be used in conjunction with the GridLayout is the Space class. This is a very simple class, the sole purpose of which is to create gaps within layouts. In the case of the GridLayout class, a Space view can be placed in any cell much like any other view object.

In addition to using the Space class to create gaps, the spacing around views in cells can be controlled via the various margin layout properties (top, bottom, left and right) of each child.

18.2 **The GridLayout Example**

Given the visual nature of both the GridLayout class and the Android Studio Designer tool, the best way to gain a level of familiarity with the concepts involved is to work through an example. The remainder of this chapter, therefore, will create an example application that demonstrates some of the key features of the GridLayout class within the context of the Designer tool.

18.3 **Creating the GridLayout Project**

Begin by launching Android Studio and creating a new project. Within the *New Project* dialog, enter *GridLayoutSample* into the Application name field and *ebookfrenzy.com* as the Company Domain setting before clicking on the *Next* button.

On the form factors screen, enable the *Phone and Tablet* option and set the minimum SDK setting to API 14: Android 4.0 (IceCreamSandwich). Continue to proceed through the screens, requesting the creation of a blank activity named *GridLayoutSampleActivity* with a corresponding layout named *activity_grid_layout_sample* and the menu resource name set to *menu_grid_layout_sample*.

Click on the *Finish* button to initiate the project creation process.

18.4 **Creating the GridLayout Instance**

Within the project tool window, navigate to the *app -> res -> layout* folder and double click on the *activity_grid_layout_sample.xml* file to load it into the Android Studio Designer.

With the layout displayed, select the *Hello World!* Text View object and press the keyboard Delete key to remove it from the layout.

The layout design currently consists solely of a RelativeLayout manager to which we can now add a GridLayout manager instance. From the *Layouts* section of the Designer palette, select a GridLayout manager and drag and drop it on the device screen. The layout should fill the screen with padding margins on each side as shown in Figure 18-1:

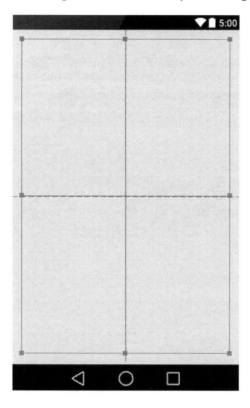

Figure 18-1

For the purposes of this tutorial, the GridLayout is only required to be large enough to accommodate the child views contained therein. As such, the height and width parameters of the GridLayout view need to be changed from *fill_parent* to *wrap_content*. One way to make this change is to locate the properties in the Designer tool's Properties panel. A quicker option is to select the GridLayout instance and use the two buttons in the Designer toolbar. Set the width property by clicking on the layout width button as highlighted in Figure 18-2:

Figure 18-2

Having set the width property to wrap_content, click on the adjacent toolbar button to similarly set the layout_height property. These settings will have the effect of shrinking the layout down to a small square ready to accommodate some child views. If the GridLayout instance is still positioned in the center of the screen, click and drag it to the upper left hand corner.

18.5 **Adding Views to GridLayout Cells**

To place view objects into the cells of a GridLayout, simply click on the required view in the palette and drag it to the GridLayout instance in the device screen layout canvas. As the view passes over the GridLayout, information will appear indicating the placement of the view if it is dropped at that point. Begin by clicking and dragging a Button view from the palette over to the top left hand corner of the GridLayout as illustrated in Figure 18-3:

Figure 18-3

As is evident from the message displayed by the tool, releasing the view at this point will position it in the cell referenced by the co-ordinates of 0,0.

Release the view at this point and note that the Button is placed in the cell as shown in Figure 18-4:

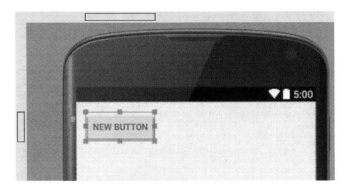

Figure 18-4

Note also that green bars have appeared in the margins on the upper and right-hand sides of the main Designer area. These bars represent the rows and columns present in the GridLayout (currently the layout has one row and one column).

Repeat the above steps to place a second button into the GridLayout so that it is positioned in row zero and after column 0 such that it appears immediately to the right of the first button.

Drag a third Button view to a position to the left of the first Button view until the message shown in Figure 18-5 appears providing the option to shift column 0 right and insert the new view into the cell at 0,0:

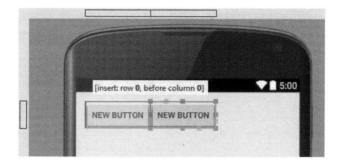

Figure 18-5

When the view is dropped at this position, the existing columns will be shifted one place to the right, a new column will be inserted at the left hand edge of the GridLayout and the new button placed into the cell.

Following the same sequence of steps, add one Button view on the second row of the grid positioned *after* row 0 in column 0 so that the layout resembles that of Figure 18-6:

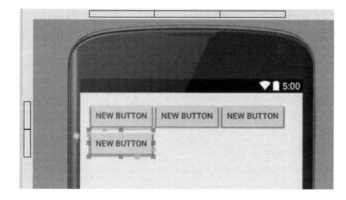

Figure 18-6

18.6 Moving and Deleting Rows and Columns

Note that as additional rows and columns have been added, additional green bars have appeared in the margins to represent those rows and columns. These bars are not purely informational. Entire rows and columns can be moved by clicking and dragging the corresponding green block to a new position within the same axis. Right-clicking on a block and selecting *Delete* from the resulting menu will remove the entire row or column from the GridLayout.

18.7 **Implementing Cell Row and Column Spanning**

For the next phase of this tutorial, two of the Button views will be modified to span multiple cells. To begin with, the far right hand button in the top row will be modified to span both rows. To achieve this, select the button from the layout and locate the *layout:rowSpan* property listed in the Properties panel. Once located, enter the value of 2 into the field as highlighted in Figure 18-7:

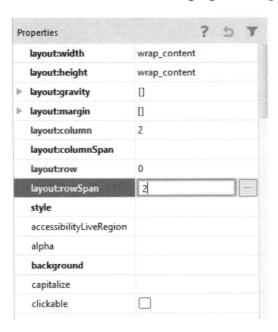

Figure 18-7

Next, select the sole Button view on the second row, this time changing the corresponding *layout:columnSpan* value in the Properties panel to 2.

These two views are now configured to span multiple cells. A review of the layout canvas, however, shows that the views have remained the same size even though the cells in which they reside now span multiple rows or columns. The reason for this is that the gravity settings for these views need to be changed.

18.8 **Changing the Gravity of a GridLayout Child**

The gravity properties of the child views of a GridLayout dictate the size and positioning of those views relative to the cell in which those views are contained. By default, the views added so far in this chapter have been set up to be aligned with the top left hand corner of the containing cells. In order to make the above cell spanning visible, the gravity of the two Button views need to be changed so that the views occupy the space available.

One option is to center the child view within the cell. Begin by selecting the top right hand Button view. In the Properties panel, locate the *layout:gravity* line and click on the *center* value field to drop down a list of available options. From the list, select the *vertical* value as shown in Figure 18-8:

Figure 18-8

A subset of gravity properties may also be configured using the Designer toolbar Gravity button as illustrated in Figure 18-9:

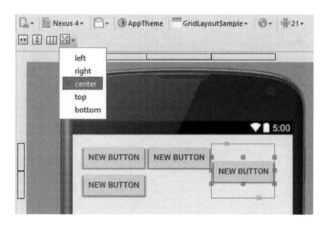

Figure 18-9

Having set this property, the Button view will now be centered vertically between the two cells:

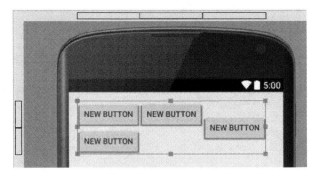

Figure 18-10

An alternative option to centering is for the child view to fill the space available. To achieve this, change the *fill* setting of the *layout:gravity* property to *fill_vertical.* It is important to note that different categories of gravity properties are combined as they are selected. For the selected cell, for example, we have now enabled both *center_vertical* and *fill_vertical* gravity properties. This can be verified by referring to the *layout:gravity* line in the Properties panel as indicated in Figure 18-2:

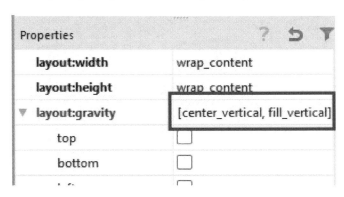

Figure 18-11

Since the *center_vertical* property is no longer required, turn it off by dropping down the center property menu (Figure 18-12) and selecting the *<unset>* option:

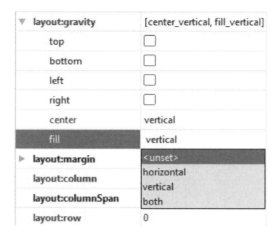

Figure 18-12

Add a gravity property to the second row button, this time enabling the *fill_horizontal* gravity setting. After changing the gravity flags, the two buttons should have expanded to fill the spanned cells:

Figure 18-13

18.9 Summary

The GridLayout class allows views to be arranged in a grid layout where one or more views are contained within grid cells. Each child can be configured to span multiple cells both horizontally and vertically. The position and sizing behavior of a child view within a cell or range of cells is controlled through the configuration of gravity settings.

GridLayouts may be implemented either using the Android Studio Designer in design mode, or through the use of Java code or XML layout resources. This chapter has covered the design mode approach. The next chapter will look at the use of XML layout resources to implement GridLayout configurations.

19. Working with the Android GridLayout using XML Layout Resources

The previous chapter (entitled *Using the Android GridLayout Manager in Android Studio Designer*) introduced the basic concepts of the Android GridLayout manager before explaining how to create a GridLayout based user interface design using the design mode of the Android Studio Designer tool. Visually designing a GridLayout based user interface is not, however, the only available method of working with the GridLayout class. Such layouts may also be implemented by directly writing Java code or manually creating elements in an XML layout file, the latter of which is the topic of this chapter.

19.1 GridLayouts in XML Resource Files

A GridLayout is declared within an XML file using the <GridLayout> element tag. For example:

```
<GridLayout  xmlns:android="http://schemas.android.com/apk/res/android"
    xmlns:tools="http://schemas.android.com/tools"
    android:id="@+id/GridLayout1"
    android:layout_width="wrap_content"
    android:layout_height="wrap_content"
    android:orientation="vertical"
    tools:context=".GridLayoutActivity">

</GridLayout>
```

The above XML syntax applies when the GridLayout is the root element of a user interface design (in other words the top most layout in the view hierarchy). In situations where the GridLayout is nested as a child of another container the syntax changes slightly. The following XML, for example, shows a GridLayout instance embedded in a RelativeLayout manager where the RelativeLayout is the root element of the user interface:

```
<RelativeLayout
xmlns:android="http://schemas.android.com/apk/res/android"
```

```
    xmlns:tools="http://schemas.android.com/tools"
    android:layout_width="match_parent"
    android:layout_height="match_parent"
    tools:context=".GridLayoutActivity">

    <GridLayout
        android:layout_width="wrap_content"
        android:layout_height="wrap_content"
        android:layout_alignParentTop="true"
        android:layout_alignParentLeft="true"
        android:layout_alignParentStart="true"
        android:orientation="vertical">

    </GridLayout>

</RelativeLayout>
```

The number of rows and columns within the grid can be declared using the *android:rowCount* and *android:columnCount* properties. Typically, however, if the number of columns is declared the GridLayout will infer the number of rows based on the number of occupied cells making the use of the rowCount property unnecessary.

Similarly, the orientation of the GridLayout may optionally be defined via the *android:orientation* property. The following example XML declares a 2 x 2 GridLayout configuration in horizontal orientation:

```
<GridLayout xmlns:android="http://schemas.android.com/apk/res/android"
    xmlns:tools="http://schemas.android.com/tools"
    android:id="@+id/GridLayout1"
    android:layout_width="wrap_content"
    android:layout_height="wrap_content"
    android:columnCount="2"
    android:rowCount="2"
    android:orientation="horizontal"
    tools:context=".GridLayoutActivity">

</GridLayout>
```

19.2 Adding Child Views to the GridLayout

Child views can be added to a GridLayout by declaring the elements within the <GridLayout> structure in the XML file. If no row and column values are declared for a child it is positioned automatically by the GridLayout class based on the configuration of the layout and the position of the view in the XML file. The following XML places four buttons within the above GridLayout, with each view placed in the top left hand corner of the encapsulating cell:

```xml
<GridLayout xmlns:android="http://schemas.android.com/apk/res/android"
    xmlns:tools="http://schemas.android.com/tools"
    android:id="@+id/GridLayout1"
    android:layout_width="wrap_content"
    android:layout_height="wrap_content"
    android:columnCount="2"
    android:rowCount="2"
    android:orientation="horizontal"
    tools:context=".GridLayoutActivity">

    <Button
        android:id="@+id/button1"
        android:layout_gravity="left|top"
        android:text="Button" />

    <Button
        android:id="@+id/button2"
        android:layout_gravity="left|top"
        android:text="Button" />

    <Button
        android:id="@+id/button3"
        android:layout_gravity="left|top"
        android:text="Button" />

    <Button
        android:id="@+id/button4"
        android:layout_gravity="left|top"
        android:text="Button" />

</GridLayout>
```

The above layout would be visually represented as illustrated in Figure 19-1:

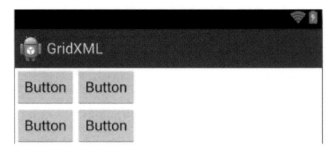

Figure 19-1

A view can be placed within a specific cell by specifying the intersecting row and column number of the destination cell. The following Button view, for example, will be placed in the cell located at row 1, column 2 of the parent GridLayout:

```
<Button
    android:id="@+id/button5"
    android:layout_column="2"
    android:layout_row="1"
    android:layout_gravity="left|top"
    android:text="Button" />
```

19.3 Declaring Cell Spanning, Gravity and Margins

The child of a GridLayout can be configured to span multiple cells using the *android:layout_rowSpan* and *android:layout_columnSpan* properties. The gravity of the child is controlled via the *android:layout_gravity* property.

In the XML fragment below, a Button view is configured to span 3 columns and 2 rows and to fill the space available both horizontally and vertically:

```
<Button
    android:id="@+id/button4"
    android:layout_columnSpan="3"
    android:layout_rowSpan="2"
    android:layout_gravity="fill"
    android:text="Button" />
```

The margins around a view within a cell can be declared for all sides of the view using the *android:layout_margin* margin property. Alternatively, margins for individual sides may be defined using the *topMargin, bottomMargin, leftMargin* and *rightMargin* properties. The following Button view declares a 10dp margin on all four sides:

```
<Button
```

```
android:id="@+id/button3"
android:layout_gravity="left|top"
android:layout_margin="10dp"
android:text="Button" />
```

Bringing this knowledge together, we can now review the XML layout for the GridLayout based user interface created in the previous chapter:

```
<GridLayout
    android:layout_width="wrap_content"
    android:layout_height="wrap_content"
    android:layout_alignParentTop="true"
    android:layout_alignParentLeft="true"
    android:layout_alignParentStart="true"
    android:orientation="vertical">

    <Button
        android:layout_width="wrap_content"
        android:layout_height="wrap_content"
        android:text="New Button"
        android:id="@+id/button4"
        android:layout_row="1"
        android:layout_column="0"
        android:layout_columnSpan="2"
        android:layout_gravity="fill_horizontal" />

    <Button
        android:layout_width="wrap_content"
        android:layout_height="wrap_content"
        android:text="New Button"
        android:id="@+id/button"
        android:layout_row="0"
        android:layout_column="1" />

    <Button
        android:layout_width="wrap_content"
        android:layout_height="wrap_content"
        android:text="New Button"
        android:id="@+id/button3"
        android:layout_row="0"
        android:layout_column="0" />

    <Button
        android:layout_width="wrap_content"
```

```
                android:layout_height="wrap_content"
                android:text="New Button"
                android:id="@+id/button2"
                android:layout_row="0"
                android:layout_column="2"
                android:layout_rowSpan="2"
                android:layout_gravity="fill_vertical" />
    </GridLayout>
```

The above resource file fragment appears exactly as it was created within the Android Studio Designer tool in the preceding chapter. As can be seen, it contains a GridLayout manager and four Button views with cell positions specified by row and column properties. Finally, the row and column span values, along with gravity properties are used to make two of the buttons span multiple cells. When deployed within an application, this XML layout would appear as illustrated in Figure 18-13.

19.4 **Summary**

As an alternative to using the Android Studio Designer tool in design mode to create GridLayout based user interface elements, the same objective may also be achieved by manually creating XML layout resources. Having covered the use of the graphical layout approach in the previous chapter, this chapter has covered the concepts of declaring a GridLayout and positioning and configuring child views within an XML resource file.

20. An Overview and Example of Android Event Handling

Much has been covered in the previous chapters relating to the design of user interfaces for Android applications. An area that has yet to be covered, however, involves the way in which a user's interaction with the user interface triggers the underlying activity to perform a task. In other words, we know from the previous chapters how to create a user interface containing a button view, but not how to make something happen within the application when it is touched by the user.

The primary objective of this chapter, therefore, is to provide an overview of event handling in Android applications together with an Android Studio based example project. Once the basics of event handling have been covered, the next chapter will cover touch event handling in terms of detecting multiple touches and touch motion.

20.1 Understanding Android Events

Events in Android can take a variety of different forms, but are usually generated in response to an external action. The most common form of events, particularly for devices such as tablets and smartphones, involve some form of interaction with the touch screen. Such events fall into the category of *input events*.

The Android framework maintains an *event queue* into which events are placed as they occur. Events are then removed from the queue on a first-in, first-out (FIFO) basis. In the case of an input event such as a touch on the screen, the event is passed to the view positioned at the location on the screen where the touch took place. In addition to the event notification, the view is also passed a range of information (depending on the event type) about the nature of the event such as the coordinates of the point of contact between the user's fingertip and the screen.

In order to be able to handle the event that it has been passed, the view must have in place an *event listener*. The Android View class, from which all user interface components are derived, contains a range of event listener interfaces, each of which contains an abstract declaration for a callback method. In order to be able to respond to an event of a particular type, a view must register the appropriate event listener and implement the corresponding callback. For example, if a button is to respond to a *click* event (the equivalent to the user touching and releasing the button view as though clicking on a physical button) it must both register the *View.onClickListener* event listener (via a call to the target view's *setOnClickListener()* method) and implement the corresponding *onClick()* callback method. In the event that a "click" event is detected on the screen at the location of the button view, the Android framework will call the *onClick()* method of that view when that event is removed from the event queue. It is, of course, within the implementation of the *onClick()* callback method that any tasks should be performed or other methods called in response to the button click.

20.2 Using the *android:onClick* Resource

Before exploring event listeners in more detail it is worth noting that a shortcut is available when all that is required is for a callback method to be called when a user "clicks" on a button view in the user interface. Consider a user interface layout containing a button view named *button1* with the requirement that when the user touches the button, a method called *buttonClick()* declared in the activity class is called. All that is required to implement this behavior is to write the *buttonClick()* method (which takes as an argument a reference to the view that triggered the click event) and add a single line to the declaration of the button view in the XML file. For example:

```
<Button
        android:id="@+id/button1"
        android:layout_width="wrap_content"
        android:layout_height="wrap_content"
        android:onClick="buttonClick"
        android:text="Click me" />
```

This provides a simple way to capture click events. It does not, however, provide the range of options offered by event handlers, which are the topic of the rest of this chapter. When working within Android Studio Designer, the onClick property can be found and configured in the Properties panel when a suitable view type is selected in the device screen layout.

20.3 Event Listeners and Callback Methods

In the example activity outlined later in this chapter the steps involved in registering an event listener and implementing the callback method will be covered in detail. Before doing so, however, it is worth taking some time to outline the event listeners that are available in the Android framework and the callback methods associated with each one.

- **onClickListener** – Used to detect click style events whereby the user touches and then releases an area of the device display occupied by a view. Corresponds to the *onClick()* callback method which is passed a reference to the view that received the event as an argument.
- **onLongClickListener** – Used to detect when the user maintains the touch over a view for an extended period. Corresponds to the *onLongClick()* callback method which is passed as an argument the view that received the event.

- **onTouchListener** – Used to detect any form of contact with the touch screen including individual or multiple touches and gesture motions. Corresponding with the *onTouch()* callback, this topic will be covered in greater detail in the chapter entitled *Android Touch and Multi-touch Event Handling*. The callback method is passed as arguments the view that received the event and a MotionEvent object.

- **onCreateContextMenuListener** – Listens for the creation of a context menu as the result of a long click. Corresponds to the *onCreateContextMenu()* callback method. The callback is passed the menu, the view that received the event and a menu context object.

- **onFocusChangeListener** – Detects when focus moves away from the current view as the result of interaction with a track-ball or navigation key. Corresponds to the *onFocusChange()* callback method which is passed the view that received the event and a Boolean value to indicate whether focus was gained or lost.

- **onKeyListener** – Used to detect when a key on a device is pressed while a view has focus. Corresponds to the *onKey()* callback method. Passed as arguments are the view that received the event, the KeyCode of the physical key that was pressed and a KeyEvent object.

20.4 **An Event Handling Example**

In the remainder of this chapter, we will work through the creation of a simple Android Studio project designed to demonstrate the implementation of an event listener and corresponding callback method to detect when the user has clicked on a button. The code within the callback method will update a text view to indicate that the event has been processed.

Create a new project in Android Studio, entering *EventExample* into the Application name field and *ebookfrenzy.com* as the Company Domain setting before clicking on the *Next* button.

On the form factors screen, enable the *Phone and Tablet* option and set the minimum SDK setting to API 8: Android 2.2 (Froyo). Continue to proceed through the screens, requesting the creation of a blank activity named *EventExampleActivity* with corresponding layout and menu resource files named *activity_event_example* and *menu_event_example* respectively.

20.5 **Designing the User Interface**

The user interface layout for the *EventExampleActivity* class in this example is to consist of a RelativeLayout view, a Button and a TextView as illustrated in Figure 20-1.

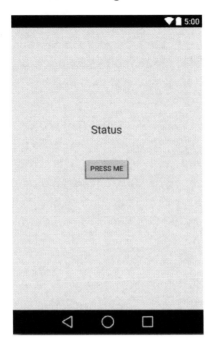

Figure 20-1

Locate and select the *activity_event_example.xml* file created by Android Studio (located in the Project tool window under *app -> res -> layouts*) and double click on it to load it into the Designer tool. Switch from Design mode to Text mode using the tab at the bottom of the Designer panel and delete the current content of the file. With a blank canvas, either use Design mode to visually design the user interface from Figure 20-1 (making sure to change the IDs of the Button and TextView objects to *myButton* and *myTextView* respectively), or directly enter the following XML using Text mode:

```xml
<?xml version="1.0" encoding="utf-8"?>
<RelativeLayout
xmlns:android="http://schemas.android.com/apk/res/android"
    android:id="@+id/myLayout"
    android:layout_width="fill_parent"
    android:layout_height="fill_parent" >

    <Button
        android:id="@+id/myButton"
        android:layout_width="wrap_content"
        android:layout_height="wrap_content"
        android:layout_centerHorizontal="true"
        android:layout_centerVertical="true"
        android:text="Press Me" />
```

```
    <TextView
        android:id="@+id/myTextView"
        android:layout_width="wrap_content"
        android:layout_height="wrap_content"
        android:layout_above="@+id/myButton"
        android:layout_centerHorizontal="true"
        android:layout_marginBottom="41dp"
        android:text="Status"
        android:textAppearance="?android:attr/textAppearanceLarge" />

</RelativeLayout>
```

Switch to Design mode, and select the Status label in the device screen layout. When the light bulb icon appears, click on it and select the I18N hardcoded string warning message to display the *Extract Resource* dialog. Within the dialog, name the resource string *status_string* and click on the *OK* button. Repeat these steps for the button view, this time naming the string resource *button_string*.

With the user interface layout now completed, the next step is to register the event listener and callback method.

20.6 **The Event Listener and Callback Method**

For the purposes of this example, an *onClickListener* needs to be registered for the *myButton* view. This is achieved by making a call to the *setOnClickListener()* method of the button view, passing through a new *onClickListener* object as an argument and implementing the *onClick()* callback method. Since this is a task that only needs to be performed when the activity is created, a good location is the *onCreate()* method of the EventExampleActivity class.

If the *EventExampleActivity.java* file is already open within an editor session, select it by clicking on the tab in the editor panel. Alternatively locate it within the Project tool window by navigating to (*app -> java -> com.ebookfrenzy.eventexample -> EventExampleActivity*) and double click on it to load it into the code editor. Once loaded, locate the template *onCreate()* method and modify it to obtain a reference to the button view, register the event listener and implement the *onClick()* callback method:

```
package com.ebookfrenzy.eventexample;

import android.support.v7.app.ActionBarActivity;
import android.os.Bundle;
import android.view.Menu;
import android.view.MenuItem;
import android.view.View;
import android.widget.Button;
import android.widget.TextView;
```

```java
public class EventExampleActivity extends ActionBarActivity {

    @Override
    protected void onCreate(Bundle savedInstanceState) {
        super.onCreate(savedInstanceState);
        setContentView(R.layout.activity_event_example);
        Button button = (Button)findViewById(R.id.myButton);

        button.setOnClickListener(
                new Button.OnClickListener() {
                    public void onClick(View v) {

                    }
                }
        );
    }
    .
    .
    .
}
```

The above code has now registered the event listener on the button and implemented the *onClick()* method. If the application were to be run at this point, however, there would be no indication that the event listener installed on the button was working since there is, as yet, no code implemented within the body of the *onClick()* callback method. The goal for the example is to have a message appear on the TextView when the button is clicked, so some further code changes need to be made:

```java
@Override
protected void onCreate(Bundle savedInstanceState) {
        super.onCreate(savedInstanceState);
        setContentView(R.layout.activity_event_example);

        Button button = (Button)findViewById(R.id.myButton);

        button.setOnClickListener(
                new Button.OnClickListener() {
                        public void onClick(View v) {
                            TextView myTextView =
                                (TextView)findViewById(R.id.myTextView);
                            myTextView.setText("Button clicked");
                        }
                }
```

```
        );
}
```

Complete this phase of the tutorial by compiling and running the application on either an AVD emulator or physical Android device. On touching and releasing the button view (otherwise known as "clicking") the text view should change to display the "Button clicked" text.

20.7 Consuming Events

The detection of standard clicks (as opposed to long clicks) on views is a very simple case of event handling. The example will now be extended to include the detection of long click events which occur when the user clicks and holds a view on the screen and, in doing so, cover the topic of event consumption.

Consider the code for the *onClick()* method in the above section of this chapter. The callback is declared as *void* and, as such, does not return a value to the Android framework after it has finished executing.

The *onLongClick()* callback method of the *onLongClickListener* interface, on the other hand, is required to return a Boolean value to the Android framework. The purpose of this return value is to indicate to the Android runtime whether or not the callback has *consumed* the event. If the callback returns a *true* value, the event is discarded by the framework. If, on the other hand, the callback returns a *false* value the Android framework will consider the event still to be active and will consequently pass it along to the next matching event listener that is registered on the same view.

As with many programming concepts this is, perhaps, best demonstrated with an example. The first step is to add an event listener and callback method for long clicks to the button view in the example activity:

```
@Override
protected void onCreate(Bundle savedInstanceState) {
        super.onCreate(savedInstanceState);
        setContentView(R.layout.activity_event_example);

        Button button = (Button)findViewById(R.id.myButton);

        button.setOnClickListener(
                new Button.OnClickListener() {
                        public void onClick(View v) {
                           TextView myTextView =
                           (TextView)findViewById(R.id.myTextView);
                          myTextView.setText("Button clicked");
                           }
```

```
                    }
            );

        button.setOnLongClickListener(
                new Button.OnLongClickListener() {
                    public boolean onLongClick(View v) {
                        TextView myTextView =

(TextView)findViewById(R.id.myTextView);
                        myTextView.setText("Long button click");
                        return true;
                    }
                }
            );
        }
```

Clearly, when a long click is detected, the *onLongClick()* callback method will display "Long button click" on the text view. Note, however, that the callback method also returns a value of *true* to indicate that it has consumed the event. Compile and run the application and press and hold a fingertip over the button view until the "Long button click" text appears in the text view. On releasing the button, the text view continues to display the "Long button click" text indicating that the *onClick()* callback method was not called.

Next, modify the code such that the *onLongClick()* method now returns a *false* value:

```
button.setOnLongClickListener(
                new Button.OnLongClickListener() {
                    public boolean onLongClick(View v) {
                        TextView myTextView =
(TextView)findViewById(R.id.myTextView);
                        myTextView.setText("Long button click");
                        return false;
                    }
                }
            );
```

Once again, compile and run the application and perform a long click on the button until the long click message appears. Upon releasing the button this time, however, note that the *onClick()* callback is also triggered and the text changes to "Button click". This is because the *false* value returned by the *onLongClick()* callback method indicated to the Android framework that the event was not consumed by the method and was eligible to be passed on to the next registered listener on the view. In this case, the runtime ascertained that the onClickListener on the button was also interested in events of this type and subsequently called the *onClick()* callback method.

20.8 **Summary**

A user interface is of little practical use if the views it contains do not do anything in response to user interaction. Android bridges the gap between the user interface and the back end code of the application through the concepts of event listeners and callback methods. The Android View class defines a set of event listeners, which can be registered on view objects. Each event listener also has associated with it a callback method.

When an event takes place on a view in a user interface, that event is placed into an event queue and handled on a first in, first out basis by the Android runtime. If the view on which the event took place has registered a listener that matches the type of event, the corresponding callback method is called. The callback method then performs any tasks required by the activity before returning. Some callback methods are required to return a Boolean value to indicate whether the event needs to be passed on to any other event listeners registered on the view or discarded by the system.

Having covered the basics of event handling, the next chapter will explore in some depth the topic of touch events with a particular emphasis on handling multiple touches.

21. Android Touch and Multi-touch Event Handling

Most Android based devices use a touch screen as the primary interface between user and device. The previous chapter introduced the mechanism by which a touch on the screen translates into an action within a running Android application. There is, however, much more to touch event handling than responding to a single finger tap on a view object. Most Android devices can, for example, detect more than one touch at a time. Nor are touches limited to a single point on the device display. Touches can, of course, be dynamic as the user slides one or more points of contact across the surface of the screen.

Touches can also be interpreted by an application as a *gesture*. Consider, for example, that a horizontal swipe is typically used to turn the page of an eBook, or how a pinching motion can be used to zoom in and out of an image displayed on the screen.

The objective of this chapter is to highlight the handling of touches that involve motion and to explore the concept of intercepting multiple concurrent touches. The topic of identifying distinct gestures will be covered in the next chapter.

21.1 Intercepting Touch Events

Touch events can be intercepted by a view object through the registration of an *onTouchListener* event listener and the implementation of the corresponding *onTouch()* callback method. The following code, for example, ensures that any touches on a RelativeLayout view instance named *myLayout* result in a call to the *onTouch()* method:

```
myLayout.setOnTouchListener(
        new RelativeLayout.OnTouchListener() {
                public boolean onTouch(View v, MotionEvent m) {
                        // Perform tasks here

                        return true;
                }
        }
```

```
);
```

As indicated in the code example, the *onTouch()* callback is required to return a Boolean value indicating to the Android runtime system whether or not the event should be passed on to other event listeners registered on the same view or discarded. The method is passed both a reference to the view on which the event was triggered and an object of type *MotionEvent*.

21.2 **The MotionEvent Object**

The MotionEvent object passed through to the *onTouch()* callback method is the key to obtaining information about the event. Information contained within the object includes the location of the touch within the view and the type of action performed. The MotionEvent object is also the key to handling multiple touches.

21.3 **Understanding Touch Actions**

An important aspect of touch event handling involves being able to identify the type of action performed by the user. The type of action associated with an event can be obtained by making a call to the *getActionMasked()* method of the MotionEvent object which was passed through to the *onTouch()* callback method. When the first touch on a view occurs, the MotionEvent object will contain an action type of ACTION_DOWN together with the coordinates of the touch. When that touch is lifted from the screen, an ACTION_UP event is generated. Any motion of the touch between the ACTION_DOWN and ACTION_UP events will be represented by ACTION_MOVE events.

When more than one touch is performed simultaneously on a view, the touches are referred to as *pointers*. In a multi-touch scenario, pointers begin and end with event actions of type ACTION_POINTER_UP and ACTION_POINTER_DOWN respectively. In order to identify the index of the pointer that triggered the event, the *getActionIndex()* callback method of the MotionEvent object must be called.

21.4 **Handling Multiple Touches**

The previous chapter began exploring event handling within the narrow context of a single touch event. In practice, most Android devices possess the ability to respond to multiple consecutive touches (though it is important to note that the number of simultaneous touches that can be detected varies depending on the device).

As previously discussed, each touch in a multi-touch situation is considered by the Android framework to be a *pointer*. Each pointer, in turn, is referenced by an *index* value and assigned an *ID*. The current number of pointers can be obtained via a call to the *getPointerCount()* method of the current MotionEvent object. The ID for a pointer at a particular index in the list of current pointers may be obtained via a call to the MotionEvent *getPointerId()* method. For example, the following code excerpt obtains a count of pointers and the ID of the pointer at index 0:

```
public boolean onTouch(View v, MotionEvent m) {
        int pointerCount = m.getPointerCount();
        int pointerId = m.getPointerId(0);
        return true;
}
```

Note that the pointer count will always be greater than or equal to 1 when an *onTouch()* method is called (since at least one touch must have occurred for the callback to be triggered).

A touch on a view, particularly one involving motion across the screen, will generate a stream of events before the point of contact with the screen is lifted. As such, it is likely that an application will need to track individual touches over multiple touch events. Whilst the ID of a specific touch gesture will not change from one event to the next, it is important to keep in mind that the index value will change as other touch events come and go. When working with a touch gesture over multiple events, therefore, it is essential that the ID value be used as the touch reference in order to make sure the same touch is being tracked. When calling methods that require an index value, this should be obtained by converting the ID for a touch to the corresponding index value via a call to the *findPointerIndex()* method of the *MotionEvent* object.

21.5 **An Example Multi-Touch Application**

The example application created in the remainder of this chapter will track up to two touch gestures as they move across a layout view. As the events for each touch are triggered, the coordinates, index and ID for each touch will be displayed on the screen.

Create a new project in Android Studio, entering *MotionEvent* into the Application name field and *ebookfrenzy.com* as the Company Domain setting before clicking on the *Next* button.

On the form factors screen, enable the *Phone and Tablet* option and set the minimum SDK setting to API 8: Android 2.2 (Froyo). Continue to proceed through the screens, requesting the creation of a blank activity named *MotionEventActivity* with corresponding layout and menu resource files named *activity_motion_event* and *menu_motion_event* respectively.

Click on the *Finish* button to initiate the project creation process.

21.6 **Designing the Activity User Interface**

The user interface for the application's sole activity is to consist of a RelativeLayout view containing two TextView objects. Within the Project tool window, navigate to *app -> res -> layout* and double click on the *activity_motion_event.xml* layout resource file to load it into the Android Studio Designer tool.

One option is to design the layout illustrated in Figure 21-1 using a RelativeLayout as the root view and keeping in mind that the lower TextView component is centered horizontally within the parent view and the upper TextView is positioned a relative distance above the lower TextView. When the layout design is complete, double click on the RelativeLayout (essentially the background of the layout) and set the ID to *RelativeLayout1*. Repeat these steps to assign IDs *textView1* and *textView2* to the TextView components.

Alternatively, switch to the XML editor by selecting the *Text* tab at the bottom of the Designer panel and replace the current XML with the following:

```
<RelativeLayout
xmlns:android="http://schemas.android.com/apk/res/android"
    android:id="@+id/RelativeLayout1"
    android:layout_width="fill_parent"
    android:layout_height="fill_parent" >

    <TextView
        android:id="@+id/textView2"
        android:layout_width="wrap_content"
        android:layout_height="wrap_content"
        android:layout_centerHorizontal="true"
        android:layout_centerVertical="true"
        android:text="Touch Two Status" />

    <TextView
        android:id="@+id/textView1"
        android:layout_width="wrap_content"
        android:layout_height="wrap_content"
        android:layout_above="@+id/textView2"
        android:layout_alignLeft="@+id/textView2"
        android:layout_marginBottom="47dp"
        android:text="Touch One Status" />
</RelativeLayout>
```

Switch to Design mode, and select the upper TextView in the device screen layout. When the light bulb icon appears, click on it and select the I18N hardcoded string warning message to display the *Extract Resource* dialog. Within the dialog, name the resource string *status1_string* and click on the *OK* button. Repeat these steps for the second TextView component, this time naming the string resource *status2_string*.

Figure 21-1

21.7 **Implementing the Touch Event Listener**

In order to receive touch event notifications it will be necessary to register a touch listener on the *RelativeLayout1* view within the *onCreate()* method of the *MotionEventActivity* activity class. Select the *MotionEventActivity.java* tab from the Android Studio editor panel to display the source code. Within the *onCreate()* method, add code to identify the RelativeLayout view object, register the touch listener and implement the *onTouch()* callback method which, in this case, is going to call a second method named *handleTouch()* to which is passed the MotionEvent object:

```
package com.ebookfrenzy.motionevent;

import android.support.v7.app.ActionBarActivity;
import android.os.Bundle;
import android.view.Menu;
import android.view.MenuItem;
import android.view.MotionEvent;
import android.view.View;
import android.widget.RelativeLayout;
import android.widget.TextView;

public class MotionEventActivity extends ActionBarActivity {
```

```
        @Override
        protected void onCreate(Bundle savedInstanceState) {
            super.onCreate(savedInstanceState);
            setContentView(R.layout.activity_motion_event);
            RelativeLayout myLayout =
                    (RelativeLayout)findViewById(R.id.RelativeLayout1);

            myLayout.setOnTouchListener(
                    new RelativeLayout.OnTouchListener() {
                        public boolean onTouch(View v,
                                                MotionEvent m) {
                            handleTouch(m);
                            return true;
                        }
                    }
            );

        }
        .
        .
        .
}
```

The final task before testing the application is to implement the *handleTouch()* method called by the *onTouch()* callback method. The code for this method reads as follows:

```
void handleTouch(MotionEvent m)
{
        TextView textView1 = (TextView)findViewById(R.id.textView1);
        TextView textView2 = (TextView)findViewById(R.id.textView2);

        int pointerCount = m.getPointerCount();

        for (int i = 0; i < pointerCount; i++)
        {
                int x = (int) m.getX(i);
                int y = (int) m.getY(i);
                int id = m.getPointerId(i);
                int action = m.getActionMasked();
                int actionIndex = m.getActionIndex();
                String actionString;


                switch (action)
```

```
                        {
                                case MotionEvent.ACTION_DOWN:
                                        actionString = "DOWN";
                                        break;
                                case MotionEvent.ACTION_UP:
                                        actionString = "UP";
                                        break;
                                case MotionEvent.ACTION_POINTER_DOWN:
                                        actionString = "PNTR DOWN";
                                        break;
                                case MotionEvent.ACTION_POINTER_UP:
                                        actionString = "PNTR UP";
                                        break;
                                case MotionEvent.ACTION_MOVE:
                                        actionString = "MOVE";
                                        break;
                                default:
                                        actionString = "";
                        }


                String touchStatus = "Action: " + actionString + "
Index: " + actionIndex + " ID: " + id + " X: " + x + " Y: " + y;

                if (id == 0)
                        textView1.setText(touchStatus);
                else
                        textView2.setText(touchStatus);
        }
}
```

Before compiling and running the application, it is worth taking the time to walk through this code systematically to highlight the tasks that are being performed.

The code begins by obtaining references to the two TextView objects in the user interface and identifying how many pointers are currently active on the view:

```
TextView textView1 = (TextView)findViewById(R.id.textView1);
TextView textView2 = (TextView)findViewById(R.id.textView2);

int pointerCount = m.getPointerCount();
```

Next, the *pointerCount* variable is used to initiate a *for* loop which performs a set of tasks for each active pointer. The first few lines of the loop obtain the X and Y coordinates of the touch together with the corresponding event ID, action type and action index. Lastly, a string variable is declared:

```
for (int i = 0; i < pointerCount; i++)
{
                int x = (int) m.getX(i);
                int y = (int) m.getY(i);
                int id = m.getPointerId(i);
                int action = m.getActionMasked();
                int actionIndex = m.getActionIndex();
                String actionString;
```

Since action types equate to integer values, a *switch* statement is used to convert the action type to a more meaningful string value, which is stored in the previously declared *actionString* variable:

```
switch (action)
                {
                case MotionEvent.ACTION_DOWN:
                        actionString = "DOWN";
                        break;
                case MotionEvent.ACTION_UP:
                        actionString = "UP";
                        break;
                case MotionEvent.ACTION_POINTER_DOWN:
                        actionString = "PNTR DOWN";
                        break;
                case MotionEvent.ACTION_POINTER_UP:
                        actionString = "PNTR UP";
                        break;
                case MotionEvent.ACTION_MOVE:
                        actionString = "MOVE";
                        break;
                default:
                        actionString = "";
                }
```

Lastly, the string message is constructed using the *actionString* value, the action index, touch ID and X and Y coordinates. The ID value is then used to decide whether the string should be displayed on the first or second TextView object:

```
String touchStatus = "Action: " + actionString + " Index: "
        + actionIndex + " ID: " + id + " X: " + x + " Y: " + y;

            if (id == 0)
                    textView1.setText(touchStatus);
            else
                    textView2.setText(touchStatus);
```

21.8 Running the Example Application

Since the Android emulator environment does not support multi-touch, compile and run the application on a physical Android device. Once launched, experiment with single and multiple touches on the screen and note that the text views update to reflect the events as illustrated in Figure 21-2:

Figure 21-2

21.9 Summary

Activities receive notifications of touch events by registering an onTouchListener event listener and implementing the *onTouch()* callback method which, in turn, is passed a MotionEvent object when called by the Android runtime. This object contains information about the touch such as the type of touch event, the coordinates of the touch and a count of the number of touches currently in contact with the view.

When multiple touches are involved, each point of contact is referred to as a pointer with each assigned an index and an ID. Whilst the index of a touch can change from one event to another, the ID will remain unchanged until the touch ends.

This chapter has worked through the creation of an example Android application designed to display the coordinates and action type of up to two simultaneous touches on a device display.

Having covered touches in general, the next chapter (entitled *Detecting Common Gestures using the Android Gesture Detector Class*) will look further at touch screen event handling through the implementation of gesture recognition.

22. Detecting Common Gestures using the Android Gesture Detector Class

The term "gesture" is used to define a contiguous sequence of interactions between the touch screen and the user. A typical gesture begins at the point that the screen is first touched and ends when the last finger or pointing device leaves the display surface. When correctly harnessed, gestures can be implemented as a form of communication between user and application. Swiping motions to turn the pages of an eBook, or a pinching movement involving two touches to zoom in or out of an image are prime examples of the ways in which gestures can be used to interact with an application.

The Android SDK provides mechanisms for the detection of both common and custom gestures within an application. Common gestures involve interactions such as a tap, double tap, long press or a swiping motion in either a horizontal or a vertical direction (referred to in Android nomenclature as a *fling*).

The goal of this chapter is to explore the use of the Android GestureDetector class to detect common gestures performed on the display of an Android device. The next chapter, entitled *Implementing Custom Gesture and Pinch Recognition on Android*, will cover the detection of more complex, custom gestures such as circular motions and pinches.

22.1 Implementing Common Gesture Detection

When a user interacts with the display of an Android device, the *onTouchEvent()* method of the currently active application is called by the system and passed MotionEvent objects containing data about the user's contact with the screen. This data can be interpreted to identify if the motion on the screen matches a common gesture such as a tap or a swipe. This can be achieved with very little programming effort by making use of the Android GestureDetectorCompat class. This class is designed specifically to receive motion event information from the application and to trigger method calls based on the type of common gesture, if any, detected.

The basic steps in detecting common gestures are as follows:

1. Declaration of a class which implements the GestureDetector.OnGestureListener interface including the required *onFling()*, *onDown()*, *onScroll()*, *onShowPress*, *onSingleTapUp()* and *onLongPress()* callback methods. Note that this can be either an entirely new class, or the

enclosing activity class. In the event that double tap gesture detection is required, the class must also implement the GestureDetector.OnDoubleTapListener interface and include the corresponding *onDoubleTap()* method.

2. Creation of an instance of the Android GestureDetectorCompat class, passing through an instance of the class created in step 1 as an argument.
3. An optional call to the *setOnDoubleTapListener()* method of the GestureDetectorCompat instance to enable double tap detection if required.
4. Implementation of the *onTouchEvent()* callback method on the enclosing activity which, in turn, must call the *onTouchEvent()* method of the GestureDetectorCompat instance, passing through the current motion event object as an argument to the method.

Once implemented, the result is a set of methods within the application code that will be called when a gesture of a particular type is detected. The code within these methods can then be implemented to perform any tasks that need to be performed in response to the corresponding gesture.

In the remainder of this chapter, we will work through the creation of an example project intended to put the above steps into practice.

22.2 Creating an Example Gesture Detection Project

The goal of this project is to detect the full range of common gestures currently supported by the GestureDetectorCompat class and to display status information to the user indicating the type of gesture that has been detected.

Create a new project in Android Studio, entering *CommonGestures* into the Application name field and *ebookfrenzy.com* as the Company Domain setting before clicking on the *Next* button.

On the form factors screen, enable the *Phone and Tablet* option and set the minimum SDK setting to API 8: Android 2.2 (Froyo). Continue to proceed through the screens, requesting the creation of a blank activity named *CommonGesturesActivity* with corresponding layout and menu resource files named *activity_common_gestures* and *menu_common_gestures* respectively.

Click on the *Finish* button to initiate the project creation process.

Once the new project has been created, navigate to the *app -> res -> layout -> activity_common_gestures.xml* file in the Project tool window and double click on it to load it into the Designer tool.

Within the Designer tool, double click on the *Hello, World!* TextView component and, in the property popup window, enter *gestureStatusText* as the ID. Finally, move the TextView so that it is positioned in the center of the display.

22.3 **Implementing the Listener Class**

As previously outlined, it is necessary to create a class that implements the GestureDetector.OnGestureListener interface and, if double tap detection is required, the GestureDetector.OnDoubleTapListener interface. Whilst this can be an entirely new class, it is also perfectly valid to implement this within the current activity class. For the purposes of this example, therefore, we will modify the CommonGesturesActivity class to implement these listener interfaces. Edit the *CommonGesturesActivity.java* file so that it reads as follows to declare the interfaces and to extract and store a reference to the TextView component in the user interface:

```
package com.ebookfrenzy.commongestures;

import android.support.v7.app.ActionBarActivity;
import android.os.Bundle;
import android.view.Menu;
import android.view.MenuItem;
import android.view.GestureDetector;
import android.widget.TextView;


public class CommonGesturesActivity extends ActionBarActivity
        implements GestureDetector.OnGestureListener,
        GestureDetector.OnDoubleTapListener {

    private TextView gestureText;

    @Override
    protected void onCreate(Bundle savedInstanceState) {
        super.onCreate(savedInstanceState);
        setContentView(R.layout.activity_common_gestures);
        gestureText =
                (TextView)findViewById(R.id.gestureStatusText);

    }
    .
    .
    .
}
```

Declaring that the class implements the listener interfaces mandates that the corresponding methods also be implemented in the class:

```
package com.ebookfrenzy.commongestures;
```

```
import android.support.v7.app.ActionBarActivity;
import android.os.Bundle;
import android.view.Menu;
import android.view.MenuItem;
import android.view.GestureDetector;
import android.widget.TextView;
import android.view.MotionEvent;


public class CommonGesturesActivity extends ActionBarActivity
        implements GestureDetector.OnGestureListener,
        GestureDetector.OnDoubleTapListener {

    private TextView gestureText;

    @Override
    protected void onCreate(Bundle savedInstanceState) {
        super.onCreate(savedInstanceState);
        setContentView(R.layout.activity_common_gestures);
        gestureText =
                (TextView)findViewById(R.id.gestureStatusText);
    }

    @Override
    public boolean onDown(MotionEvent event) {
        gestureText.setText ("onDown");
        return true;
    }

    @Override
    public boolean onFling(MotionEvent event1, MotionEvent event2,
                           float velocityX, float velocityY) {
        gestureText.setText("onFling");
        return true;
    }

    @Override
    public void onLongPress(MotionEvent event) {
        gestureText.setText("onLongPress");
    }

    @Override
```

```
        public boolean onScroll(MotionEvent e1, MotionEvent e2,
                            float distanceX, float distanceY) {
            gestureText.setText("onScroll");
            return true;
        }

        @Override
        public void onShowPress(MotionEvent event) {
            gestureText.setText("onShowPress");
        }

        @Override
        public boolean onSingleTapUp(MotionEvent event) {
            gestureText.setText("onSingleTapUp");
            return true;
        }

        @Override
        public boolean onDoubleTap(MotionEvent event) {
            gestureText.setText("onDoubleTap");
            return true;
        }

        @Override
        public boolean onDoubleTapEvent(MotionEvent event) {
            gestureText.setText("onDoubleTapEvent");
            return true;
        }

        @Override
        public boolean onSingleTapConfirmed(MotionEvent event) {
            gestureText.setText("onSingleTapConfirmed");
            return true;
        }
    .
    .
    .
}
```

Note that all of these methods return *true*. This indicates to the Android Framework that the event has been consumed by the method and does not need to be passed to the next event handler in the stack.

22.4 **Creating the GestureDetectorCompat Instance**

With the activity class now updated to implement the listener interfaces, the next step is to create an instance of the GestureDetectorCompat class. Since this only needs to be performed once at the point that the activity is created, the best place for this code is in the *onCreate()* method. Since we also want to detect double taps, the code also needs to call the *setOnDoubleTapListener()* method of the GestureDetectorCompat instance:

```
package com.ebookfrenzy.commongestures;

import android.support.v7.app.ActionBarActivity;
import android.os.Bundle;
import android.view.Menu;
import android.view.MenuItem;
import android.view.GestureDetector;
import android.widget.TextView;
import android.view.MotionEvent;
import android.support.v4.view.GestureDetectorCompat;

public class CommonGesturesActivity extends ActionBarActivity
        implements GestureDetector.OnGestureListener,
        GestureDetector.OnDoubleTapListener {

    private TextView gestureText;
    private GestureDetectorCompat gDetector;

    @Override
    protected void onCreate(Bundle savedInstanceState) {
        super.onCreate(savedInstanceState);
        setContentView(R.layout.activity_common_gestures);
        gestureText =
                (TextView) findViewById(R.id.gestureStatusText);

        this.gDetector = new GestureDetectorCompat(this,this);
        gDetector.setOnDoubleTapListener(this);
    }
    .
    .
}
```

22.5 **Implementing the onTouchEvent() Method**

If the application were to be compiled and run at this point, nothing would happen if gestures were performed on the device display. This is because no code has been added to intercept touch events and to pass them through to the GestureDetectorCompat instance. In order to achieve this, it is necessary to override the *onTouchEvent()* method within the activity class and implement it such that it calls the *onTouchEvent()* method of the GestureDetectorCompat instance. Remaining in the *CommonGesturesActivity.java* file, therefore, implement this method so that it reads as follows:

```
@Override
public boolean onTouchEvent(MotionEvent event) {
        this.gDetector.onTouchEvent(event);
        // Be sure to call the superclass implementation
        return super.onTouchEvent(event);
}
```

22.6 Testing the Application

Compile and run the application on either a physical Android device or an AVD emulator. Once launched, experiment with swipes, presses, scrolling motions and double and single taps. Note that the text view updates to reflect the events as illustrated in Figure 22-1:

Figure 22-1

22.7 Summary

Any physical contact between the user and the touch screen display of a device can be considered a "gesture". Lacking the physical keyboard and mouse pointer of a traditional computer system, gestures are widely used as a method of interaction between user and application. Whilst a gesture can be comprised of just about any sequence of motions, there is a widely used set of gestures with which users of touch screen devices have become familiar. A number of these so-called "common gestures" can be easily detected within an application by making use of the Android Gesture Detector classes. In this chapter, the use of this technique has been outlined both in theory and through the implementation of an example project.

Having covered common gestures in this chapter, the next chapter will look at detecting a wider range of gesture types including the ability to both design and detect your own gestures.

23. Implementing Custom Gesture and Pinch Recognition on Android

The previous chapter looked at the steps involved in detecting what are referred to as "common gestures" from within an Android application. In practice, however, a gesture can conceivably involve just about any sequence of touch motions on the display of an Android device. In recognition of this fact, the Android SDK allows custom gestures of just about any nature to be defined by the application developer and used to trigger events when performed by the user. This is a multistage process, the details of which are the topic of this chapter.

23.1 The Android Gesture Builder Application

The Android SDK allows developers to design custom gestures which are then stored in a gesture file bundled with an Android application package. These custom gesture files are most easily created using the *Gesture Builder* application which is bundled with the samples package supplied as part of the Android SDK. The creation of a gestures file involves launching the Gesture Builder application, either on a physical device or emulator, and "drawing" the gestures that will need to be detected by the application. Once the gestures have been designed, the file containing the gesture data can be pulled off the SD card of the device or emulator and added to the application project. Within the application code, the file is then loaded into an instance of the *GestureLibrary* class where it can be used to search for matches to any gestures performed by the user on the device display.

23.2 The GestureOverlayView Class

In order to facilitate the detection of gestures within an application, the Android SDK provides the GestureOverlayView class. This is a transparent view that can be placed over other views in the user interface for the sole purpose of detecting gestures.

23.3 Detecting Gestures

Gestures are detected by loading the gestures file created using the Gesture Builder app and then registering a *GesturePerformedListener* event listener on an instance of the GestureOverlayView class. The enclosing class is then declared to implement both the *OnGesturePerformedListener* interface and the corresponding *onGesturePerformed* callback method required by that interface. In the event that a gesture is detected by the listener, a call to the *onGesturePerformed* callback method is triggered by the Android runtime system.

23.4 **Identifying Specific Gestures**

When a gesture is detected, the *onGesturePerformed* callback method is called and passed as arguments a reference to the GestureOverlayView object on which the gesture was detected, together with a Gesture object containing information about the gesture.

With access to the Gesture object, the GestureLibrary can then be used to compare the detected gesture to those contained in the gestures file previously loaded into the application. The GestureLibrary reports the probability that the gesture performed by the user matches an entry in the gestures file by calculating a *prediction score* for each gesture. A prediction score of 1.0 or greater is generally accepted to be a good match between a gesture stored in the file and that performed by the user on the device display.

23.5 **Building and Running the Gesture Builder Application**

The Gesture Builder application is bundled by default with the AVD emulator profile for most versions of the SDK. It is not, however, pre-installed on most physical Android devices. If the utility is pre-installed, it will be listed along with the other apps installed in the device or AVD instance. In the event that it is not installed, the source code for the utility is included amongst the standard Android SDK samples and consequently may be imported as an Android Studio project and compiled and run on any Android device or emulator.

To install and build the GestureBuilder utility, begin by installing the SDK samples. To do this, open the Android SDK Manager by selecting the *Tools -> Android -> SDK Manager* menu bar option from the project main window.

Once the manager has loaded, locate the *Samples for SDK* package located beneath the section for the Android version for which you are currently developing (for example Android 5.0.1 (API 21)). If the package is not already installed, set the checkbox next to the package and click on the *Install 1 Package* button to initiate the installation.

Once the installation is complete, the SDK samples will be installed in the following directory (where *<path_to_installation>* represents the location on your system where the SDK was originally installed as shown at the top of the SDK Manager window):

```
<path_to_installation>/sdk/samples/android-21
```

The source code for the Gesture Builder application is located within this directory in a folder named *GestureBuilder* within the *legacy* sub-folder.

From the Android Studio main window for an existing project, select the *File -> Import Project...* menu option and, within the resulting dialog, navigate to and select the GestureBuilder folder within the SDK samples directory and click on *OK*. Confirm the destination directory and click on *Next* followed by *Finish* to accept the default settings on the final screen. At this point, Android Studio will import the project into the designated folder and convert it to match the Android Studio project file and build structure.

Once imported, install and run the GestureBuilder utility on an Android device attached to the development system.

23.6 **Creating a Gestures File**

Once the Gesture Builder application has loaded, it should indicate that no gestures have yet been created. To create a new gesture, click on the *Add gesture* button located at the bottom of the device screen, enter the name *Circle Gesture* into the *Name* text box and then "draw" a gesture using a circular motion on the screen as illustrated in Figure 23-1. Assuming that the gesture appears as required (represented by the yellow line on the device screen), click on the *Done* button to add the gesture to the gestures file:

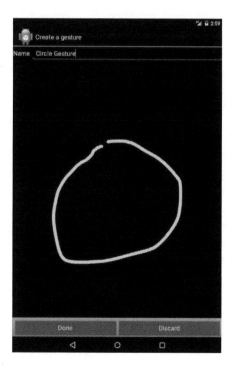

Figure 23-1

After the gesture has been saved, the Gesture Builder app will display a list of currently defined gestures, which, at this point, will consist solely of the new *Circle Gesture*.

Repeat the gesture creation process to add a further gesture to the file. This should involve a two-stroke gesture creating an X on the screen named *X Gesture*. When creating gestures involving multiple strokes, be sure to allow as little time as possible between each stroke so that the builder knows that the strokes are part of the same gesture. Once this gesture has been added, the list within the Gesture Builder application should resemble that outlined in Figure 23-2:

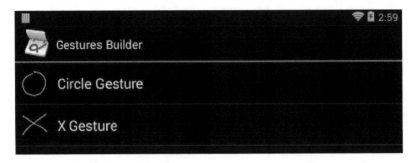

Figure 23-2

23.7 **Extracting the Gestures File from the SD Card**

As each gesture was created within the Gesture Builder application, it was added to a file named *gestures* located on the SD Card of the emulator or device on which the app was running. Before this file can be added to an Android Studio project, however, it must first be pulled off the SD Card and saved to the local file system. This is most easily achieved by using the *adb* command-line tool. Open a Terminal or Command Prompt window, therefore, and execute the following command:

```
adb devices
```

In the event that the adb command is not found, refer to *Setting up an Android Studio Development Environment* for guidance on adding this to the PATH environment variable of your system.

Once executed, the command will list all active physical devices and AVD instances attached to the system. The following output, for example, indicates that both a physical device and one AVD emulator have been detected on the development computer system:

```
List of devices attached
emulator-5554    device
74CE000600000001      device
```

In order to pull the gestures file from the emulator in the above example and place it into the current working directory of the Terminal or Command Prompt window, the following command would need to be executed:

```
adb -s emulator-5554 pull /sdcard/gestures .
```

Alternatively, the gestures file can be pulled from a device connected via adb using the following command (where the –d flag is used to indicate a physical device):

```
adb -d pull /sdcard/gestures .
```

Once the gestures file has been created and pulled off the SD Card, it is ready to be added to an Android Studio project as a resource file. The next step, therefore, is to create a new project.

23.8 **Creating the Example Project**

Create a new project in Android Studio, entering *CustomGestures* into the Application name field and *ebookfrenzy.com* as the Company Domain setting before clicking on the *Next* button.

On the form factors screen, enable the *Phone and Tablet* option and set the minimum SDK setting to API 8: Android 2.2 (Froyo). Continue to proceed through the screens, requesting the creation of a blank activity named *CustomGesturesActivity* with corresponding layout and menu resource files named *activity_custom_gestures* and *menu_custom_gestures.*

Click on the *Finish* button to initiate the project creation process.

23.9 **Adding the Gestures File to the Project**

Within the Android Studio Project tool window, locate and right-click on the *res* folder (located under *app*) and select *New -> Directory* from the resulting menu. In the New Directory dialog, enter *raw* as the folder name and click on the *OK* button. Using the appropriate file explorer utility for your operating system type, locate the *gestures* file previously pulled from the SD Card and copy and paste it into the new *raw* folder in the Project tool window.

23.10 **Designing the User Interface**

This example application calls for a very simple user interface consisting of a LinearLayout view with a GestureOverlayView layered on top of it to intercept any gestures performed by the user. Locate the *app -> res -> layout -> activity_custom_gestures.xml* file and double click on it to load it into the Designer tool.

By default, Android Studio has provided a RelativeLayout component as the root element of the user interface layout so this will need to be deleted and replaced with a LinearLayout.

Switch the Designer tool to Text mode using the *Text* tab along the bottom edge of the panel and modify the XML for the layout so that it matches the following listing:

```
<LinearLayout
    android:orientation="vertical"
    android:layout_width="fill_parent"
```

```
        android:layout_height="fill_parent"
        xmlns:android="http://schemas.android.com/apk/res/android">


</LinearLayout>
```

Return to Design mode, locate the *Expert* section of the Palette and drag and drop a *GestureOverlayView* object onto the layout canvas. Select the *GestureOverlayView* instance in the layout and use the Properties panel or Designer toolbar buttons to change the *layout:width* and *layout:height* properties to *match_parent* so that the view fills the available space.

Double click on the GestureOverlayView instance and use the popup property panel to change the ID to *gOverlay.* When completed, the *activity_custom_gestures.xml* file should read as follows:

```
<LinearLayout
    android:orientation="vertical"
    android:layout_width="fill_parent"
    android:layout_height="fill_parent"
    xmlns:android="http://schemas.android.com/apk/res/android"
    android:weightSum="1">

    <android.gesture.GestureOverlayView
        android:layout_width="match_parent"
        android:layout_height="match_parent"
        android:id="@+id/gOverlay"
        android:layout_gravity="center_horizontal">
        </android.gesture.GestureOverlayView>
</LinearLayout>
```

23.11 Loading the Gestures File

Now that the gestures file has been added to the project, the next step is to write some code so that the file is loaded when the activity starts up. For the purposes of this project, the code to achieve this will be placed in the *onCreate()* method of the *CustomGesturesActivity* class located in the *CustomGesturesActivity.java* source file as follows:

```
package com.ebookfrenzy.customgestures;

import android.support.v7.app.ActionBarActivity;
import android.os.Bundle;
import android.view.Menu;
import android.view.MenuItem;
import android.gesture.GestureLibraries;
import android.gesture.GestureLibrary;
```

```
import android.gesture.GestureOverlayView;
import android.gesture.GestureOverlayView.OnGesturePerformedListener;

public class CustomGesturesActivity extends ActionBarActivity
implements OnGesturePerformedListener {

    private GestureLibrary gLibrary;

    @Override
    protected void onCreate(Bundle savedInstanceState) {
        super.onCreate(savedInstanceState);
        setContentView(R.layout.activity_custom_gestures);

        gLibrary =
                GestureLibraries.fromRawResource(this,
R.raw.gestures);
        if (!gLibrary.load()) {
            finish();
        }
    }
    .
    .
    .
}
```

In addition to some necessary import directives, the above code changes to the *onCreate()* method also create a *GestureLibrary* instance named *gLibrary* and then loads into it the contents of the gestures file located in the *raw* resources folder. The activity class has also been modified to implement the *OnGesturePerformedListener* interface, which requires the implementation of the *onGesturePerformed* callback method (which will be created in a later section of this chapter).

23.12 Registering the Event Listener

In order for the activity to receive notification that the user has performed a gesture on the screen, it is necessary to register the *OnGesturePerformedListener* event listener on the *gLayout* view, a reference to which can be obtained using the *findViewById* method as outlined in the following code fragment:

```
@Override
protected void onCreate(Bundle savedInstanceState) {
    super.onCreate(savedInstanceState);
    setContentView(R.layout.activity_custom_gestures);
```

```
        gLibrary =
            GestureLibraries.fromRawResource(this, R.raw.gestures);
        if (!gLibrary.load()) {
            finish();
        }

        GestureOverlayView gOverlay =
                (GestureOverlayView) findViewById(R.id.gOverlay);
        gOverlay.addOnGesturePerformedListener(this);
}
```

23.13 Implementing the onGesturePerformed Method

All that remains before an initial test run of the application can be performed is to implement the *OnGesturePerformed* callback method. This is the method which will be called when a gesture is performed on the GestureOverlayView instance:

```
package com.ebookfrenzy.customgestures;

import android.support.v7.app.ActionBarActivity;
import android.os.Bundle;
import android.view.Menu;
import android.view.MenuItem;
import android.gesture.GestureLibraries;
import android.gesture.GestureLibrary;
import android.gesture.GestureOverlayView;
import android.gesture.GestureOverlayView.OnGesturePerformedListener;
import android.gesture.Prediction;
import android.widget.Toast;
import android.gesture.Gesture;
import java.util.ArrayList;

public class CustomGesturesActivity extends ActionBarActivity
implements OnGesturePerformedListener {

    private GestureLibrary gLibrary;

    @Override
    protected void onCreate(Bundle savedInstanceState) {
        super.onCreate(savedInstanceState);
        setContentView(R.layout.activity_custom_gestures);

        gLibrary =
```

```
                  GestureLibraries.fromRawResource(this,
R.raw.gestures);
        if (!gLibrary.load()) {
            finish();
        }

        GestureOverlayView gOverlay =
                (GestureOverlayView) findViewById(R.id.gOverlay);
        gOverlay.addOnGesturePerformedListener(this);
    }

    public void onGesturePerformed(GestureOverlayView overlay, Gesture
            gesture) {
        ArrayList<Prediction> predictions =
                gLibrary.recognize(gesture);

        if (predictions.size() > 0 && predictions.get(0).score > 1.0)
{

            String action = predictions.get(0).name;

            Toast.makeText(this, action, Toast.LENGTH_SHORT).show();
        }
    }
    .
    .
    .
}
```

When a gesture on the gesture overlay view object is detected by the Android runtime, the *onGesturePerformed* method is called. Passed through as arguments are a reference to the GestureOverlayView object on which the gesture was detected together with an object of type *Gesture*. The Gesture class is designed to hold the information that defines a specific gesture (essentially a sequence of timed points on the screen depicting the path of the strokes that comprise a gesture).

The Gesture object is passed through to the *recognize()* method of our *gLibrary* instance, the purpose of which is to compare the current gesture with each gesture loaded from the gestures file. Once this task is complete, the *recognize()* method returns an ArrayList object containing a Prediction object for each comparison performed. The list is ranked in order from the best match (at position 0 in the array) to the worst. Contained within each prediction object is the name of the corresponding gesture from the gestures file and a prediction score indicating how closely it matches the current gesture.

The code in the above method, therefore, takes the prediction at position 0 (the closest match) makes sure it has a score of greater than 1.0 and then displays a Toast message (an Android class designed to display notification pop ups to the user) displaying the name of the matching gesture.

23.14 Testing the Application

Build and run the application on either an emulator or a physical Android device and perform the circle and swipe gestures on the display. When performed, the toast notification should appear containing the name of the gesture that was performed. Note, however, that when attempting to perform the X Gesture that the gesture is not recognized. Also, note that when a gesture is recognized, it is outlined on the display with a bright yellow line whilst gestures about which the overlay is uncertain appear as a faded yellow line. Whilst useful during development, this is probably not ideal for a real world application. Clearly, therefore, there is still some more configuration work to do.

23.15 Configuring the GestureOverlayView

By default, the GestureOverlayView is configured to display yellow lines during gestures and to recognize only single stroke gestures. Multi-stroke gestures can be detected by setting the *android:gestureStrokeType* property to *multiple.*

Similarly, the color used to draw recognized and unrecognized gestures can be defined via the *android:gestureColor* and *android:uncertainGestureColor* properties. For example, to hide the gesture lines and recognize multi-stroke gestures, modify the *activity_custom_gestures.xml* file in the example project as follows:

```xml
<LinearLayout
    android:orientation="vertical"
    android:layout_width="fill_parent"
    android:layout_height="fill_parent"
    xmlns:android="http://schemas.android.com/apk/res/android"
    android:weightSum="1">

    <android.gesture.GestureOverlayView
        android:layout_width="match_parent"
        android:layout_height="match_parent"
        android:id="@+id/gOverlay"
        android:layout_gravity="center_horizontal"
        android:gestureColor="#00000000"
        android:uncertainGestureColor="#00000000"
        android:gestureStrokeType="multiple" >
    </android.gesture.GestureOverlayView>
</LinearLayout>
```

On re-running the application, gestures should now be invisible (since they are drawn in white on the white background of the LinearLayout view).

23.16 Intercepting Gestures

The GestureOverlayView is, as previously described, a transparent overlay that may be positioned over the top of other views. This leads to the question as to whether events intercepted by the gesture overlay should then be passed on to the underlying views when a gesture has been recognized. This is controlled via the *android:eventsInterceptionEnabled* property of the GestureOverlayView instance. When set to true, the gesture events are not passed to the underlying views when a gesture is recognized. This can be a particularly useful setting when gestures are being performed over a view that might be configured to scroll in response to certain gestures. Setting this property to *true* will avoid gestures also being interpreted as instructions to the underlying view to scroll in a particular direction.

23.17 Detecting Pinch Gestures

Before moving on from touch handling in general and gesture recognition in particular, the last topic of this chapter is that of handling pinch gestures. Whilst it is possible to create and detect a wide range of gestures using the steps outlined in the previous sections of this chapter it is, in fact, not possible to detect a pinching gesture (where two fingers are used in a stretching and pinching motion, typically to zoom in and out of a view or image) using the techniques discussed so far.

The simplest method for detecting pinch gestures is to use the Android *ScaleGestureDetector* class. In general terms, detecting pinch gestures involves the following three steps:

1. Declaration of a new class which implements the SimpleOnScaleGestureListener interface including the required *onScale()*, *onScaleBegin()* and *onScaleEnd()* callback methods.
2. Creation of an instance of the ScaleGestureDetector class, passing through an instance of the class created in step 1 as an argument.
3. Implementing the *onTouchEvent()* callback method on the enclosing activity which, in turn, calls the *onTouchEvent()* method of the ScaleGestureDetector class.

In the remainder of this chapter, we will create a very simple example designed to demonstrate the implementation of pinch gesture recognition.

23.18 A Pinch Gesture Example Project

Create a new project in Android Studio, entering *PinchExample* into the Application name field and *ebookfrenzy.com* as the Company Domain setting before clicking on the *Next* button.

On the form factors screen, enable the *Phone and Tablet* option and set the minimum SDK setting to API 8: Android 2.2 (Froyo). Continue to proceed through the screens, requesting the creation of a blank

Implementing Custom Gesture and Pinch Recognition on Android

activity named *PinchExampleActivity* with layout and menu resource files named *activity_pinch_example* and *menu_pinch_example* respectively.

Within the *activity_pinch_example.xml* file, locate the TextView object and double click on it to change the ID to *myTextView*.

Locate and load the *PinchExampleActivity.java* file into the Android Studio editor and modify the file as follows:

```java
package com.ebookfrenzy.pinchexample;

import android.support.v7.app.ActionBarActivity;
import android.os.Bundle;
import android.view.Menu;
import android.view.MenuItem;
import android.view.MotionEvent;
import android.view.ScaleGestureDetector;
import android.view.ScaleGestureDetector.SimpleOnScaleGestureListener;
import android.widget.TextView;

public class PinchExampleActivity extends ActionBarActivity {

    TextView scaleText;
    ScaleGestureDetector scaleGestureDetector;

    @Override
    protected void onCreate(Bundle savedInstanceState) {
        super.onCreate(savedInstanceState);
        setContentView(R.layout.activity_pinch_example);

        scaleText = (TextView)findViewById(R.id.myTextView);

        scaleGestureDetector =
                new ScaleGestureDetector(this,
                        new MyOnScaleGestureListener());
    }

    @Override
    public boolean onTouchEvent(MotionEvent event) {
        scaleGestureDetector.onTouchEvent(event);
        return true;
    }
```

```
public class MyOnScaleGestureListener extends
        SimpleOnScaleGestureListener {

    @Override
    public boolean onScale(ScaleGestureDetector detector) {

        float scaleFactor = detector.getScaleFactor();

        if (scaleFactor > 1) {
            scaleText.setText("Zooming Out");
        } else {
            scaleText.setText("Zooming In");
        }
        return true;
    }

    @Override
    public boolean onScaleBegin(ScaleGestureDetector detector) {
        return true;
    }

    @Override
    public void onScaleEnd(ScaleGestureDetector detector) {

    }
}
.
.
.
}
```

The code begins by declaring TextView and ScaleGestureDetector variables. A new class named MyOnScaleGestureListener is declared which extends the Android SimpleOnScaleGestureListener class. This interface requires that three methods (*onScale()*, *onScaleBegin()* and *onScaleEnd()*) be implemented. In this instance the *onScale()* method identifies the scale factor and displays a message on the text view indicating the type of pinch gesture detected.

Within the *onCreate()* method, a reference to the text view object is obtained and assigned to the scaleText variable. Next, a new *ScaleGestureDetector* instance is created, passing through a reference to the enclosing activity and an instance of our new *MyOnScaleGestureListener* class as arguments. Finally, an *onTouchEvent()* callback method is implemented for the activity, which simply calls the corresponding *onTouchEvent()* method of the *ScaleGestureDetector* object, passing through the MotionEvent object as an argument.

Compile and run the application on a physical Android device and perform pinching gestures on the screen, noting that the text view displays either the zoom in or zoom out message depending on the pinching motion.

23.19 **Summary**

A gesture is essentially the motion of points of contact on a touch screen involving one or more strokes and can be used as a method of communication between user and application. Android allows gestures to be designed using the Gesture Builder application. Once created, gestures can be saved to a gestures file and loaded into an activity at application runtime using the GestureLibrary.

Gestures can be detected on areas of the display by overlaying existing views with instances of the transparent *GestureOverlayView* class and implementing an *OnGesturePerformedListener* event listener. Using the GestureLibrary, a ranked list of matches between a gesture performed by the user and the gestures stored in a gestures file may be generated, using a prediction score to decide whether a gesture is a close enough match.

Pinch gestures may be detected through the implementation of the ScaleGestureDetector class, an example of which was also provided in this chapter.

24. An Introduction to Android Fragments

As you progress through the chapters of this book it will become increasingly evident that many of the design concepts behind the Android system were conceived with the goal of promoting reuse of, and interaction between the different elements that make up an application. One such area that will be explored in this chapter involves the use of Fragments.

This chapter will provide an overview of the basics of fragments in terms of what they are and how they can be created and used within applications. The next chapter will work through a tutorial designed to show fragments in action when developing applications in Android Studio, including the implementation of communication between fragments.

24.1 What is a Fragment?

A fragment is a self-contained, modular section of an application's user interface and corresponding behavior that can be embedded within an activity. Fragments can be assembled to create an activity during the application design phase, and added to, or removed from an activity during application runtime to create a dynamically changing user interface.

Fragments may only be used as part of an activity and cannot be instantiated as standalone application elements. That being said, however, a fragment can be thought of as a functional "sub-activity" with its own lifecycle similar to that of a full activity.

Fragments are stored in the form of XML layout files and may be added to an activity either by placing appropriate <fragment> elements in the activity's layout file, or directly through code within the activity's class implementation.

Before starting to use Fragments in an Android application, it is important to be aware that Fragments were not introduced to Android until version 3.0 of the Android SDK. An application that uses Fragments must, therefore, make use of the *android-support-v4* Android Support Library in order to be compatible with older Android versions. The steps to achieve this will be covered in the next chapter, entitled *Using Fragments in Android Studio - A Worked Example*.

24.2 Creating a Fragment

The two components that make up a fragment are an XML layout file and a corresponding Java class. The XML layout file for a fragment takes the same format as a layout for any other activity layout and can contain any combination and complexity of layout managers and views. The following XML layout, for example, is for a fragment consisting simply of a RelativeLayout with a red background containing a single TextView:

```xml
<?xml version="1.0" encoding="utf-8"?>
<RelativeLayout
xmlns:android="http://schemas.android.com/apk/res/android"
    android:layout_width="match_parent"
    android:layout_height="match_parent"
    android:background="@color/red" >

    <TextView
        android:id="@+id/textView1"
        android:layout_width="wrap_content"
        android:layout_height="wrap_content"
        android:layout_centerHorizontal="true"
        android:layout_centerVertical="true"
        android:text="@string/fragone_label_text"
        android:textAppearance="?android:attr/textAppearanceLarge" />
</RelativeLayout>
```

The corresponding class to go with the layout must be a subclass of the Android *Fragment* class. If the application is to be compatible with devices running versions of Android predating version 3.0 then the class file must import *android.support.v4.app.Fragment*. The class should, at a minimum, override the *onCreateView()* method which is responsible for loading the fragment layout. For example:

```java
package com.example.myfragmentdemo;

import android.os.Bundle;
import android.support.v4.app.Fragment;
import android.view.LayoutInflater;
import android.view.View;
import android.view.ViewGroup;

public class FragmentOne extends Fragment {
        @Override
         public View onCreateView(LayoutInflater inflater,
            ViewGroup container,
             Bundle savedInstanceState) {
```

```
                    // Inflate the layout for this fragment
                    return inflater.inflate(R.layout.fragment_one_layout,
                        container, false);
            }
    }
```

In addition to the *onCreateView()* method, the class may also override the standard lifecycle methods.

Note that in order to make the above fragment compatible with Android versions prior to version 3.0, the Fragment class from the v4 support library has been imported.

Once the fragment layout and class have been created, the fragment is ready to be used within application activities.

24.3 Adding a Fragment to an Activity using the Layout XML File

Fragments may be incorporated into an activity either by writing Java code or by embedding the fragment into the activity's XML layout file. Regardless of the approach used, a key point to be aware of is that when the support library is being used for compatibility with older Android releases, any activities using fragments must be implemented as a subclass of *FragmentActivity* instead of the traditional *Activity* class:

```
package com.example.myfragmentdemo;

import android.os.Bundle;
import android.support.v4.app.FragmentActivity;
import android.view.Menu;

public class FragmentDemoActivity extends FragmentActivity {

    @Override
    protected void onCreate(Bundle savedInstanceState) {
            super.onCreate(savedInstanceState);
            setContentView(R.layout.activity_fragment_demo);
    }

    @Override
    public boolean onCreateOptionsMenu(Menu menu) {

    getMenuInflater().inflate(R.menu.activity_fragment_demo,
                        menu);
            return true;
    }
```

```
}
```

Fragments are embedded into activity layout files using the <fragment> element. The following example layout embeds the fragment created in the previous section of this chapter into an activity layout:

```
<RelativeLayout
xmlns:android="http://schemas.android.com/apk/res/android"
    xmlns:tools="http://schemas.android.com/tools"
    android:layout_width="match_parent"
    android:layout_height="match_parent"
    tools:context=".FragmentDemoActivity" >

    <fragment
        android:id="@+id/fragment_one"

android:name="com.example.myfragmentdemo.myfragmentdemo.FragmentOne"
        android:layout_width="match_parent"
        android:layout_height="wrap_content"
        android:layout_alignParentLeft="true"
        android:layout_centerVertical="true"
        tools:layout="@layout/fragment_one_layout" />

</RelativeLayout>
```

The key properties within the <fragment> element are *android:name*, which must reference the class associated with the fragment, and *tools:layout*, which must reference the XML resource file containing the layout of the fragment.

Once added to the layout of an activity, fragments may be viewed and manipulated within the Android Studio Designer tool. Figure 24-1, for example, shows the above layout with the embedded fragment within the Android Studio Designer:

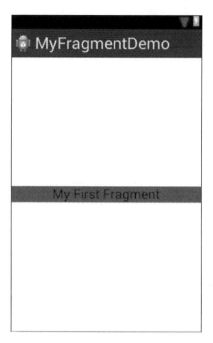

Figure 24-1

24.4 Adding and Managing Fragments in Code

The ease of adding a fragment to an activity via the activity's XML layout file comes at the cost of the activity not being able to remove the fragment at runtime. In order to achieve full dynamic control of fragments during runtime, those activities must be added via code. This has the advantage that the fragments can be added, removed and even made to replace one another dynamically while the application is running.

When using code to manage fragments, the fragment itself will still consist of an XML layout file and a corresponding class. The difference comes when working with the fragment within the hosting activity. There is a standard sequence of steps when adding a fragment to an activity using code. These steps are as follows:

1. Create an instance of the fragment's class.
2. Pass any additional intent arguments through to the class.
3. Obtain a reference to the *fragment manager* instance.
4. Call the *beginTransaction()* method on the fragment manager instance. This returns a *fragment transaction* instance.
5. Call the *add()* method of the fragment transaction instance, passing through as arguments the resource id of the view that is to contain the fragment and the fragment class instance.
6. Call the *commit()* method of the fragment transaction.

The following code, for the sake of an example, adds a fragment defined by the FragmentOne class so that it appears in the container view with an id of LinearLayout1:

```
FragmentOne firstFragment = new FragmentOne();
firstFragment.setArguments(getIntent().getExtras());

FragmentManager fragManager = getSupportFragmentManager();
FragmentTransaction transaction =
fragManager.beginTransaction();

transaction.add(R.id.LinearLayout1, firstFragment);
transaction.commit();
```

The above code breaks down each step into a separate statement for the purposes of clarity. The last four lines can, however, be abbreviated into a single line of code as follows:

```
getSupportFragmentManager().beginTransaction()
        .add(R.id.LinearLayout1, firstFragment).commit();
```

Once added to a container, a fragment may subsequently be removed via a call to the *remove()* method of the fragment transaction instance, passing through a reference to the fragment instance that is to be removed:

```
transaction.remove(firstFragment);
```

Similarly, one fragment may be replaced with another by a call to the *replace()* method of the fragment transaction instance. This takes as arguments the id of the view containing the fragment and an instance of the new fragment. The replaced fragment may also be placed on what is referred to as the *back* stack so that it can be quickly restored in the event that the user navigates back to it. This is achieved by making a call to the *addToBackStack()* method of the fragment transaction object before making the *commit()* method call:

```
FragmentTwo secondFragment = new FragmentTwo();
transaction.replace(R.id.LinearLayout1, secondFragment);
transaction.addToBackStack(null);
transaction.commit();
```

24.5 Handling Fragment Events

As previously discussed, a fragment is very much like a sub-activity with its own layout, class and lifecycle. The view components (such as buttons and text views) within a fragment are able to generate events just like those in a regular activity. This raises the question as to which class receives an event from a view in a fragment; the fragment itself, or the activity in which the fragment is embedded. The answer to this question depends on how the event handler is declared.

In the chapter entitled *An Overview and Example of Android Event Handling*, two approaches to event handling were discussed. The first method involved configuring an event listener and callback method within the code of the activity. For example:

```
Button button = (Button)findViewById(R.id.myButton);

button.setOnClickListener(
        new Button.OnClickListener() {
            public void onClick(View v) {
                // Code to be performed when
                // the button is clicked
            }
        }
    );
```

In the case of intercepting click events, the second approach involved setting the *android:onClick* property within the XML layout file:

```
<Button
    android:id="@+id/button1"
    android:layout_width="wrap_content"
    android:layout_height="wrap_content"
    android:onClick="onClick"
    android:text="Click me" />
```

The general rule for events generated by a view in a fragment is that if the event listener was declared in the fragment class using the event listener and callback method approach, then the event will be handled first by the fragment. If the *android:onClick* resource is used, however, the event will be passed directly to the activity containing the fragment.

24.6 Implementing Fragment Communication

Once one or more fragments are embedded within an activity, the chances are good that some form of communication will need to take place both between the fragments and the activity and between one fragment and another. In fact, fragments should not communicate directly with each other. All communication should take place via the encapsulating activity.

In order for an activity to communicate with a fragment, the activity must identify the fragment object via the ID assigned to it using the *findViewById()* method. Once this reference has been obtained, the activity can simply call the public methods of the fragment object.

Communicating in the other direction (from fragment to activity) is a little more complicated. In the first instance, the fragment must define a listener interface, which is then implemented within the activity class. For example, the following code declares an interface named ToolbarListener on a fragment class named ToolbarFragment. The code also declares a variable in which a reference to the activity will later be stored:

```
public class ToolbarFragment extends Fragment {

        ToolbarListener activityCallback;

        public interface ToolbarListener {
                public void onButtonClick(int position, String text);
        }
 .

 .

}
```

The above code dictates that any class that implements the ToolbarListener interface must also implement a callback method named *onButtonClick* which, in turn, accepts an integer and a String as arguments.

Next, the *onAttach()* method of the fragment class needs to be overridden and implemented. This method is called automatically by the Android system when the fragment has been initialized and associated with an activity. The method is passed a reference to the activity in which the fragment is contained. The method must store a local reference to this activity and verify that it implements the ToolbarListener interface:

```
@Override
public void onAttach(Activity activity) {
    super.onAttach(activity);

    try {
        activityCallback = (ToolbarListener) activity;
    } catch (ClassCastException e) {
        throw new ClassCastException(activity.toString()
                + " must implement ToolbarListener");
    }
}
```

Upon execution of this example, a reference to the activity will be stored in the local *activityCallback* variable, and an exception will be thrown if that activity does not implement the ToolbarListener interface.

The next step is to call the callback method of the activity from within the fragment. When and how this happens is entirely dependent on the circumstances under which the activity needs to be contacted by the fragment. For the sake of an example, the following code calls the callback method on the activity when a button is clicked:

```
public void buttonClicked (View view) {
    activityCallback.onButtonClick(arg1, arg2);
}
```

All that remains is to modify the activity class so that it implements the ToolbarListener interface. For example:

```
public class FragmentExampleActivity extends FragmentActivity
implements
ToolbarFragment.ToolbarListener {
        public void onButtonClick(String arg1, int arg2) {
        // Implement code for callback method
        }
    .
    .
}
```

As we can see from the above code, the activity declares that it implements the ToolbarListener interface of the ToolbarFragment class and then proceeds to implement the *onButtonClick()* method as required by the interface.

24.7 **Summary**

Fragments provide a powerful mechanism for creating re-usable modules of user interface layout and application behavior, which, once created, can be embedded in activities. A fragment consists of a user interface layout file and a class. Fragments may be utilized in an activity either by adding the fragment to the activity's layout file, or by writing code to manage the fragments at runtime. Fragments added to an activity in code can be removed and replaced dynamically at runtime. All communication between fragments should be performed via the activity within which the activities are embedded.

Having covered the basics of fragments in this chapter, the next chapter will work through a tutorial designed to reinforce the techniques outlined in this chapter.

25. Using Fragments in Android Studio - An Example

As outlined in the previous chapter, fragments provide a convenient mechanism for creating reusable modules of application functionality consisting of both sections of a user interface and the corresponding behavior. Once created, fragments can be embedded within activities.

Having explored the overall theory of fragments in the previous chapter, the objective of this chapter is to create an example Android application using Android Studio designed to demonstrate the actual steps involved in both creating and using fragments, and also implementing communication between one fragment and another within an activity.

25.1 About the Example Fragment Application

The application created in this chapter will consist of a single activity and two fragments. The user interface for the first fragment will contain a toolbar of sorts consisting of an EditText view, a SeekBar and a Button, all contained within a RelativeLayout view. The second fragment will consist solely of a TextView object, also contained within a RelativeLayout view.

The two fragments will be embedded within the main activity of the application and communication implemented such that when the button in the first fragment is pressed, the text entered into the EditText view will appear on the TextView of the second fragment using a font size dictated by the position of the SeekBar in the first fragment.

Since this application is intended to work on earlier versions of Android, it will also be necessary to make use of the appropriate Android support library.

25.2 Creating the Example Project

Create a new project in Android Studio, entering *FragmentExample* into the Application name field and *ebookfrenzy.com* as the Company Domain setting before clicking on the *Next* button.

On the form factors screen, enable the *Phone and Tablet* option and set the minimum SDK setting to API 8: Android 2.2 (Froyo). Continue to proceed through the screens, requesting the creation of a blank activity named *FragmentExampleActivity* with corresponding layout and menu resource files named *activity_fragment_example* and *menu_fragment_example* respectively.

Click the *Finish* button to begin the project creation process.

25.3 Creating the First Fragment Layout

The next step is to create the user interface for the first fragment that will be used within our activity.

This user interface will, of course, reside in an XML layout file so begin by navigating to the *layout* folder located under *app -> res* in the Project tool window. Once located, right-click on the *layout* entry and select the *New -> Layout resource file* menu option as illustrated in Figure 25-1:

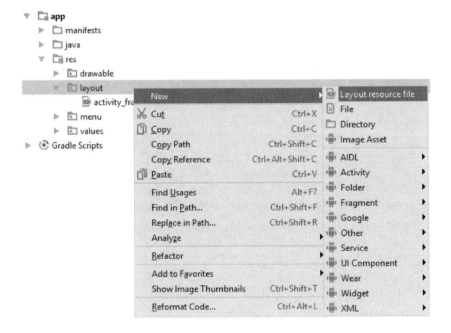

Figure 25-1

In the resulting dialog, name the layout *toolbar_fragment* and change the root element from LinearLayout to RelativeLayout before clicking on OK to create the new resource file.

The new resource file will appear within the Designer tool ready to be designed. Switch the Designer to Text mode and modify the XML so that it reads as outlined in the following listing to add three new view elements to the layout:

```
<?xml version="1.0" encoding="utf-8"?>

<RelativeLayout
    xmlns:android="http://schemas.android.com/apk/res/android"
```

```xml
        android:layout_width="match_parent"
        android:layout_height="match_parent">

    <Button
        android:id="@+id/button1"
        android:layout_width="wrap_content"
        android:layout_height="wrap_content"
        android:layout_below="@+id/seekBar1"
        android:layout_centerHorizontal="true"
        android:layout_marginTop="17dp"
        android:text="Change Text" />

    <EditText
        android:id="@+id/editText1"
        android:layout_width="wrap_content"
        android:layout_height="wrap_content"
        android:layout_alignParentTop="true"
        android:layout_centerHorizontal="true"
        android:layout_marginTop="16dp"
        android:ems="10"
        android:inputType="text" >
        <requestFocus />
    </EditText>

    <SeekBar
        android:id="@+id/seekBar1"
        android:layout_width="match_parent"
        android:layout_height="wrap_content"
        android:layout_alignParentLeft="true"
        android:layout_below="@+id/editText1"
        android:layout_marginTop="14dp" />

</RelativeLayout>
```

Once the changes have been made, switch the Designer tool back to Design mode. Select the button view and click on the light bulb icon followed by the I18N message to display the *Extract Resource* dialog. Name the resource *button_text* and click on *OK* to create a string resource for the button.

Upon completion of these steps, the user interface layout should resemble that of Figure 25-2:

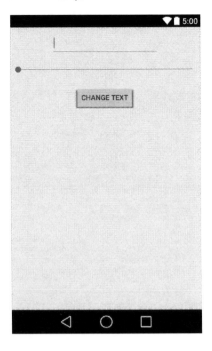

Figure 25-2

With the layout for the first fragment implemented, the next step is to create a class to go with it.

25.4 Creating the First Fragment Class

In addition to a user interface layout, a fragment also needs to have a class associated with it to do the actual work behind the scenes. Add a class for this purpose to the project by unfolding the *app -> java* folder under the FragmentExample project in the Project tool window and right-clicking on the package name given to the project when it was created (in this instance *com.ebookfrenzy.fragmentexample*). From the resulting menu, select the *New -> Java Class* option. In the resulting *Create New Class* dialog, name the class *ToolbarFragment* and click on *OK* to create the new class.

Once the class has been created, it should, by default, appear in the editing panel where it will read as follows:

```
package com.ebookfrenzy.fragmentexample;

/**
 * Created by <name> on <date>.
 */
public class ToolbarFragment {
}
```

For the time being, the only changes to this class are to add some import directives and to override the *onCreateView()* method to make sure the layout file is inflated and displayed when the fragment is used within an activity. The class declaration also needs to indicate that the class extends the Android Fragment class:

```
package com.ebookfrenzy.fragmentexample;

import android.os.Bundle;
import android.support.v4.app.Fragment;
import android.view.LayoutInflater;
import android.view.View;
import android.view.ViewGroup;

public class ToolbarFragment extends Fragment {

    @Override
    public View onCreateView(LayoutInflater inflater,
                             ViewGroup container, Bundle
                             savedInstanceState) {

        // Inflate the layout for this fragment
        View view =  inflater.inflate(R.layout.toolbar_fragment,
                container, false);
        return view;
    }

}
```

Later in this chapter, more functionality will be added to this class. Before that, however, we need to create the second fragment.

25.5 Creating the Second Fragment Layout

Add a second new Android XML layout resource file to the project, once again selecting a RelativeLayout as the root element. Name the layout *text_fragment* and click *OK*. When the layout loads into the Designer tool, change to Text mode and modify the XML to add a TextView to the fragment layout as follows:

```
<?xml version="1.0" encoding="utf-8"?>

<RelativeLayout
xmlns:android="http://schemas.android.com/apk/res/android"
    android:layout_width="match_parent"
```

```
        android:layout_height="match_parent">

    <TextView
        android:id="@+id/textView1"
        android:layout_width="wrap_content"
        android:layout_height="wrap_content"
        android:layout_centerHorizontal="true"
        android:layout_centerVertical="true"
        android:text="Fragment Two"
        android:textAppearance="?android:attr/textAppearanceLarge" />

</RelativeLayout>
```

Once the XML changes have been made, switch back to Design mode, select the TextView component and click on the light bulb icon followed by the I18N message to display the *Extract Resource* dialog. Name the resource *text_label* and click on *OK* to create a string resource for the button. Upon completion of these steps, the user interface layout for this second fragment should resemble that of Figure 25-3:

Figure 25-3

As with the first fragment, this one will also need to have a class associated with it. Right-click on *app -> java -> com.ebookfrenzy.fragmentexample* in the Project tool window. From the resulting menu, select the *New -> Java Class* option. Name the fragment *TextFragment* and click *OK* to create the class.

Edit the new *TextFragment.java* class file and modify it to implement the *onCreateView()* method and designate the class as extending the Android *Fragment* class:

```
package com.ebookfrenzy.fragmentexample;

import android.os.Bundle;
import android.support.v4.app.Fragment;
import android.view.LayoutInflater;
import android.view.View;
import android.view.ViewGroup;

public class TextFragment extends Fragment {

    @Override
    public View onCreateView(LayoutInflater inflater,
                             ViewGroup container,
                             Bundle savedInstanceState) {
        View view = inflater.inflate(R.layout.text_fragment,
                container, false);

        return view;
    }
}
```

Now that the basic structure of the two fragments has been implemented, they are ready to be embedded in the application's main activity.

25.6 Adding the Fragments to the Activity

The main activity for the application has associated with it an XML layout file named *activity_fragment_example.xml*. For the purposes of this example, the fragments will be added to the activity using the <fragment> element within this file. Using the Project tool window, navigate to the *app -> res -> layout* section of the *FragmentExample* project and double click on the *activity_fragment_example.xml* file to load it into the Android Studio Designer tool.

With the Designer tool in Design mode, select and delete the default TextView object from the layout and scroll down the palette until the *Custom* section comes into view. Click on the *<fragment>* entry to display a list of Fragments available within the current project as illustrated in Figure 25-4:

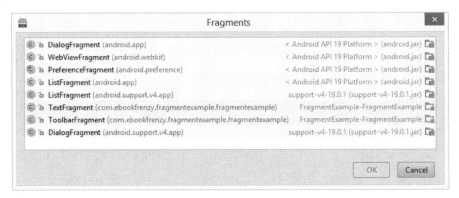

Figure 25-4

Select the ToolbarFragment entry from the list and click on the OK button to dismiss the Fragments dialog. Move the mouse pointer to the top center edge of the parent layout area so that the *centerHorizontal* and *alignParentTop* options are displayed (Figure 25-5).

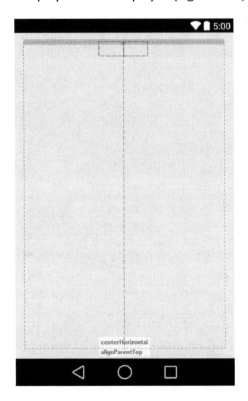

Figure 25-5

Once correctly positioned, release the fragment to add it to the layout. Once added, a message panel will appear (Figure 25-6) indicating that the Designer tool needs to know which fragment to display during the preview session. Display the ToolbarFragment fragment by clicking on the *Use @layout/toolbar_fragment* link within the message:

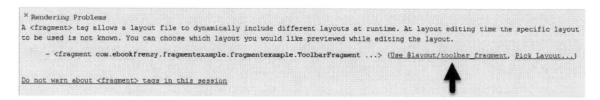

Figure 25-6

Click on the <fragment> entry in the Custom section of the palette once again, this time selecting the *TextFragment* entry from the fragment dialog before clicking on the OK button. Move the mouse pointer to the center of the layout so that the *centerHorizontal* and *centerVertical* properties are activated and release the fragment. When the rendering message appears, click on the *Use @layout/text_fragment* option. Note that the fragments are now visible in the layout as demonstrated in Figure 25-7:

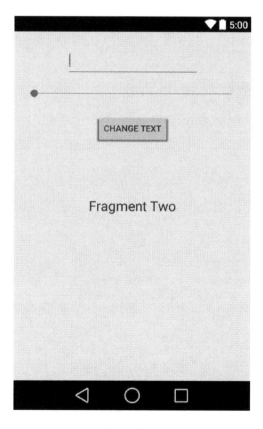

Figure 25-7

Before proceeding to the next step, double click on the TextFragment instance in the layout and, within the resulting panel, change the id of the fragment to *text_fragment*.

25.7 **Making the Toolbar Fragment Talk to the Activity**

When the user touches the button in the toolbar fragment, the fragment class is going to need to get the text from the EditText view and the current value of the SeekBar and send them to the text fragment. As outlined in *An Introduction to Android Fragments*, fragments should not communicate with each other directly, instead using the activity in which they are embedded as an intermediary.

The first step in this process is to make sure that the toolbar fragment responds to the button being clicked. We also need to implement some code to keep track of the value of the SeekBar view. For the purposes of this example, we will implement these listeners within the ToolbarFragment class. Select the *ToolbarFragment.java* file and modify it so that it reads as shown in the following listing:

```
package com.ebookfrenzy.fragmentexample;

import android.os.Bundle;
import android.support.v4.app.Fragment;
import android.view.LayoutInflater;
import android.view.View;
import android.view.ViewGroup;
import android.app.Activity;
import android.widget.Button;
import android.widget.EditText;
import android.widget.SeekBar;
import android.widget.SeekBar.OnSeekBarChangeListener;

public class ToolbarFragment extends Fragment implements
OnSeekBarChangeListener {

    private static int seekvalue = 10;
    private static EditText edittext;

    @Override
    public View onCreateView(LayoutInflater inflater,
                             ViewGroup container, Bundle
                             savedInstanceState) {

        // Inflate the layout for this fragment
        View view =  inflater.inflate(R.layout.toolbar_fragment,
               container, false);
```

```
        edittext = (EditText) view.findViewById(R.id.editText1);
        final SeekBar seekbar =
                (SeekBar) view.findViewById(R.id.seekBar1);

        seekbar.setOnSeekBarChangeListener(this);

        final Button button =
                (Button) view.findViewById(R.id.button1);
        button.setOnClickListener(new View.OnClickListener() {
            public void onClick(View v) {
                buttonClicked(v);
            }
        });

        return view;
    }

    public void buttonClicked (View view) {

    }

    @Override
    public void onProgressChanged(SeekBar seekBar, int progress,
                                    boolean fromUser) {
        seekvalue = progress;
    }

    @Override
    public void onStartTrackingTouch(SeekBar arg0) {

    }

    @Override
    public void onStopTrackingTouch(SeekBar arg0) {

    }
}
```

Before moving on, we need to take some time to explain the above code changes. First, the class is declared as implementing the OnSeekBarChangeListener interface. This is because the user interface contains a SeekBar instance and the fragment needs to receive notifications when the user slides the bar to change the font size. Implementation of the OnSeekBarChangeListener interface requires that the *onProgressChanged()*, *onStartTrackingTouch()* and *onStopTrackingTouch()* methods be implemented. These methods have been implemented but only the *onProgressChanged()* method is actually required to perform a task, in this case storing the new value in a variable named seekvalue which has been declared at the start of the class. Also declared is a variable in which to store a reference to the EditText object.

The *onCreateView()* method has been modified to obtain references to the EditText, SeekBar and Button views in the layout. Once a reference to the button has been obtained it is used to set up an onClickListener on the button which is configured to call a method named *buttonClicked()* when a click event is detected. This method is also then implemented, though at this point it does not do anything.

The next phase of this process is to set up the listener that will allow the fragment to call the activity when the button is clicked. This follows the mechanism outlined in the previous chapter:

```
public class ToolbarFragment extends Fragment implements
OnSeekBarChangeListener {

        private static int seekvalue = 10;
        private static EditText edittext;

        ToolbarListener activityCallback;

        public interface ToolbarListener {
                public void onButtonClick(int position, String text);
        }

        @Override
        public void onAttach(Activity activity) {
                super.onAttach(activity);
                try {
                    activityCallback = (ToolbarListener) activity;
                } catch (ClassCastException e) {
                    throw new ClassCastException(activity.toString()
                        + " must implement ToolbarListener");
                }
        }

        @Override
        public View onCreateView(LayoutInflater inflater,
            ViewGroup container, Bundle savedInstanceState) {
                // Inflate the layout for this fragment

            View view =
inflater.inflate(R.layout.toolbar_fragment,
```

```
                     container, false);

            edittext = (EditText)
view.findViewById(R.id.editText1);
            final SeekBar seekbar =
               (SeekBar) view.findViewById(R.id.seekBar1);

            seekbar.setOnSeekBarChangeListener(this);

            final Button button =
               (Button) view.findViewById(R.id.button1);
            button.setOnClickListener(new View.OnClickListener() {
                public void onClick(View v) {
                    buttonClicked(v);
                }
            });

            return view;
        }

        public void buttonClicked (View view) {
                activityCallback.onButtonClick(seekvalue,
                    edittext.getText().toString());
        }

        .
        .
        .
}
```

The above implementation will result in a method named *onButtonClick()* belonging to the activity class being called when the button is clicked by the user. All that remains, therefore, is to declare that the activity class implements the newly created ToolbarListener interface and to implement the *onButtonClick()* method.

Since the Android Support Library is being used for fragment support in earlier Android versions, the activity also needs to be changed to subclass from *FragmentActivity* instead of *ActionBarActivity*. Bringing these requirements together results in the following modified *FragmentExampleActivity.java* file:

```
package com.ebookfrenzy.fragmentexample;

import android.support.v7.app.ActionBarActivity;
import android.support.v4.app.FragmentActivity;
```

```
import android.os.Bundle;
import android.view.Menu;
import android.view.MenuItem;

public class FragmentExampleActivity extends FragmentActivity
implements ToolbarFragment.ToolbarListener {

    @Override
    protected void onCreate(Bundle savedInstanceState) {
        super.onCreate(savedInstanceState);
        setContentView(R.layout.activity_fragment_example);
    }

    public void onButtonClick(int fontsize, String text) {

    }
.
.
.
}
```

With the code changes as they currently stand, the toolbar fragment will detect when the button is clicked by the user and call a method on the activity passing through the content of the EditText field and the current setting of the SeekBar view. It is now the job of the activity to communicate with the Text Fragment and to pass along these values so that the fragment can update the TextView object accordingly.

25.8 Making the Activity Talk to the Text Fragment

As outlined in *An Introduction to Android Fragments*, an activity can communicate with a fragment by obtaining a reference to the fragment class instance and then calling public methods on the object. As such, within the TextFragment class we will now implement a public method named *changeTextProperties()* which takes as arguments an integer for the font size and a string for the new text to be displayed. The method will then use these values to modify the TextView object. Within the Android Studio editing panel, locate and modify the *TextFragment.java* file to add this new method and to add code to the *onCreateView()* method to obtain the ID of the TextView object:

```
package com.ebookfrenzy.fragmentexample;

import android.os.Bundle;
import android.support.v4.app.Fragment;
import android.view.LayoutInflater;
import android.view.View;
```

```
import android.view.ViewGroup;
import android.widget.TextView;

public class TextFragment extends Fragment {

    private static TextView textview;

    @Override
    public View onCreateView(LayoutInflater inflater,
                             ViewGroup container,
                             Bundle savedInstanceState) {
        View view = inflater.inflate(R.layout.text_fragment,
                container, false);

        textview = (TextView) view.findViewById(R.id.textView1);

        return view;
    }

    public void changeTextProperties(int fontsize, String text)
    {
        textview.setTextSize(fontsize);
        textview.setText(text);
    }

}
```

When the TextFragment fragment was placed in the layout of the activity, it was given an ID of *text_fragment.* Using this ID, it is now possible for the activity to obtain a reference to the fragment instance and call the *changeTextProperties()* method on the object. Edit the *FragmentExampleActivity.java* file and modify the *onButtonClick()* method as follows:

```
public void onButtonClick(int fontsize, String text) {

    TextFragment textFragment =
      (TextFragment)

getSupportFragmentManager().findFragmentById(R.id.text_fragment);

    textFragment.changeTextProperties(fontsize, text);
}
```

25.9 **Testing the Application**

With the coding for this project now complete, the last remaining task is to run the application. When the application is launched, the main activity will start and will, in turn, create and display the two fragments. When the user touches the button in the toolbar fragment, the *onButtonClick()* method of the activity will be called by the toolbar fragment and passed the text from the EditText view and the current value of the SeekBar. The activity will then call the *changeTextProperties()* method of the second fragment, which will modify the TextView to reflect the new text and font size:

Figure 25-8

25.10 **Summary**

The goal of this chapter has been to work through the creation of an example project intended specifically to demonstrate the steps involved in using fragments within an Android application. Topics covered included the use of the Android Support Library for compatibility with Android versions predating the introduction of fragments, the inclusion of fragments within an activity layout and the implementation of inter-fragment communication.

26. An Android Studio Master/Detail Flow Tutorial

A clear understanding of how to use fragments (as outlined in the preceding chapters) is essential in order to be able to make use of the Master/Detail Flow template. This chapter will apply these skills to explain the concept of the Master/Detail user interface design before exploring in detail the elements that make up the Master/Detail Flow template included with Android Studio. Finally, an example application will be created that demonstrates the steps involved in modifying the template to meet the specific needs of the application developer.

26.1 The Master/Detail Flow

A master/detail flow is an interface design concept whereby a list of items (referred to as the *master list*) is displayed to the user. On selecting an item from the list, additional information relating to that item is then presented to the user within a *details* panel. An email application might, for example, consist of a master list of received messages consisting of the address of the sender and the subject of the message. Upon selection of a message from the master list, the body of the email message would appear within the detail panel.

On tablet sized Android device displays, the master list appears in a narrow vertical panel along the left hand edge of the screen. The remainder of the display is devoted to the detail panel in an arrangement referred to as *two-pane mode*. Figure 26-1, for example, shows the master/detail two-pane arrangement with three master items listed and the content of item three listed in the detail panel:

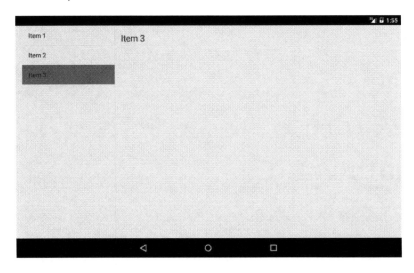

Figure 26-1

On smaller, phone sized Android devices, the master list takes up the entire screen and the detail panel appears on a separate screen which appears when a selection is made from the master list. In this mode, the detail screen includes an action bar entry to return to the master list. Figure 26-2, for example, illustrates both the master and detail screens for the same three item list on a 4" phone screen:

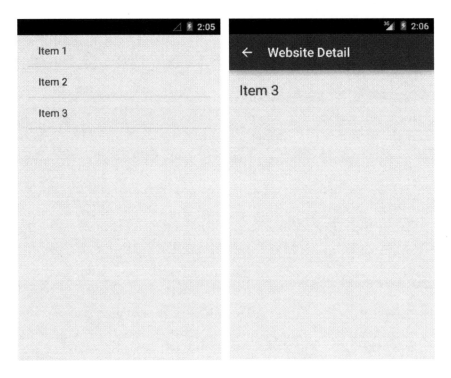

Figure 26-2

26.2 **Creating a Master/Detail Flow Activity**

In the next section of this chapter, the different elements that comprise the Master/Detail Flow template will be covered in some detail. This is best achieved by creating a project using the Master/Detail Flow template to use while working through the information. This project will subsequently be used as the basis for the tutorial at the end of the chapter.

Create a new project in Android Studio, entering *MasterDetailFlow* into the Application name field and *ebookfrenzy.com* as the Company Domain setting before clicking on the *Next* button.

On the form factors screen, enable the *Phone and Tablet* option and set the minimum SDK setting to API 8: Android 2.2 (Froyo).

When the activity configuration screen of the New Project dialog appears, select the *Master/Detail Flow* option as illustrated in Figure 26-3 before clicking on *Next* once again:

Figure 26-3

The next screen (Figure 26-4) provides the opportunity to configure the objects that will be displayed within the master/detail activity. In the tutorial later in this chapter, the master list will contain a number of web site names which, when selected, will load the chosen web site into a web view within the detail panel. With these requirements in mind, set the *Object Kind* field to "Website" and the *Object Kind Plural* and *Title* settings to "Websites".

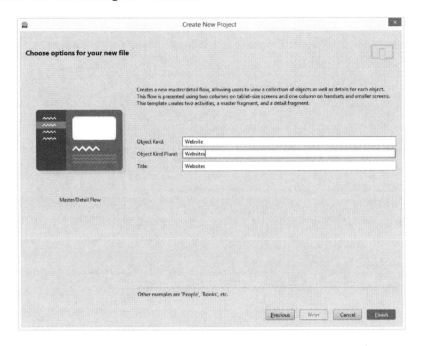

Figure 26-4

Finally, click finish to create the new Master/Detail Flow based application project.

26.3 The Anatomy of the Master/Detail Flow Template

Once a new project has been created using the Master/Detail Flow template, a number of Java and XML layout resource files will have been created automatically. It is important to gain an understanding of these different files in order to be able to adapt the template to specific requirements. A review of the project within the Android Studio Project tool window will reveal the following files, where *<kind_name>* is replaced by the Object Kind name that was specified when the project was created (this being "Website" in the case of the *MasterDetailFlow* example project):

- **<kind_name>ListActivity.java** – This is the main activity of the project, the purpose of which is to display the master list to the user (the layout for which is stored in the *activity_<kind_name>_list.xml* XML fragment resource file). If the class detects that the display is large enough to support two-pane mode, an instance of the *<kind_name>_list* fragment from the *activity_<kind_name>_twopane.xml* file is created and displayed, otherwise, the instance contained in the *activity_<kind_name>_list.xml* file is used. This class also implements and sets up the *onItemSelected()* callback method that will be called when the user makes a selection from the master list. It is the responsibility of this method to create and display an instance of the detail panel. In the case of two-pane mode, the detail panel is handled by creating an instance of the *<kind_name>*DetailFragment class and adding it to the current activity. On smaller device displays, this instead involves launching a second activity in the form of the *<kind_name>*DetailActivity class (which will then, in turn, create an instance of the *<kind_name>*DetailFragment class).

- **activity_*<kind_name>*_twopane.xml** – Contains both the *<kind_name>_list* master list fragment and *<kind_name>_detail_container* FrameLayout declarations for the detail pane to be used when the application is running on a device display large enough to support two-pane mode.

- **activity_*<kind_name>*_list.xml** – The XML layout resource file containing the *<kind_name>_list* fragment for the master list to be used on displays too small to support two-pane mode.

- ***<kind_name>*ListFragment.java** – The Java class that accompanies the *activity_<kind_name>_list.xml* fragment resource file. This class contains a number of methods that serve to identify and highlight the user's current master list selection.

- ***<kind_name>*DetailActivity.java** – The Java class representing the activity for the detail panel for use on devices too small to handle two-pane mode. This class creates an instance of the *<kind_name>*FragmentDetail class and displays the *<kind_name>_detail_container* FrameLayout container declared in the *activity_<kind_name>_detail.xml* file.

- **activity_*<kind_name>*_detail.xml** – The XML resource layout that accompanies the *<kind_name>*ActivityDetail.java* class file used on small screen devices. By default, this contains a FrameLayout instance to which will be added user interface elements declared by the *<kind_name>*FragmentDetail class.

- ***<kind_name>*DetailFragment.java** – The Java class that accompanies the *fragment_<kind_name>_detail.xml* XML resource file. The code in this method loads the data associated with the master list and displays the content of the *fragment_<kind_name>_detail.xml* file to the user.

- **fragment_*<kind_name>*_detail.xml** – The *<kind_name>_detail* user interface for the detail pane that is displayed within the *onCreateView()* method of the *<kind_name>*DetailFragment class. By default, this contains a single TextView object instance and is used in both two-pane and small screen modes.

- **DummyContent.java** – A class file intended to provide sample data for the template. This class can either be modified to meet application needs, or replaced entirely. By default, the content provided by this class simply consists of a number of string items.

Two additional files are also of interest purely for the sake of understanding how the application is able to identify whether to use two-pane mode or not. These files are *res/values-large/refs.xml* and *res/values-sw600dp/refs.xml*.

As will be outlined in greater detail in the chapter entitled *Handling Different Android Devices and Displays*, each application project has multiple sets of resources that target different display sizes. At runtime, the Android system automatically uses the resource set that most closely matches the physical display size of the device. The *values-large* and *values-sw600dp* resources are, of course, used in devices with larger displays. The *ref.xml* files in these folders simply declare an alias that causes the two-pane mode layouts to be used:

```
<item name="activity_item_list"
type="layout">@layout/activity_item_twopane</item>
```

26.4 **Modifying the Master/Detail Flow Template**

Whilst the structure of the Master/Detail Flow template can appear confusing at first, the concepts will become clearer as the default template is modified in the remainder of this chapter. As will become evident, much of the functionality provided by the template can remain unchanged for many master/detail implementation requirements.

In the rest of this chapter, the *MasterDetailFlow* project will be modified such that the master list displays a list of web site names and the detail pane altered to contain a WebView object instead of the current TextView. When a web site is selected by the user, the corresponding web page will subsequently load and display in the detail pane.

26.5 **Changing the Content Model**

The content for the example as it currently stands is defined by the *DummyContent* class file. Begin, therefore, by selecting the *DummyContent.java* file (located in the Project tool window in the *app -> java -> com.ebookfrenzy.masterdetailflow -> dummy* folder) and reviewing the code. At the bottom of the file is a declaration for a class named *DummyItem* which is currently able to store two String objects representing a content string and an ID. The updated project, on the other hand, will need each item object to contain an ID string, a string for the web site name, and a string for the corresponding URL of the web site. To add these features, modify the *DummyItem* class so that it reads as follows:

```
public static class DummyItem {
    public String id;
    public String website_name;
    public String website_url;

    public DummyItem(String id, String website_name,
        String website_url)
    {
        this.id = id;
        this.website_name = website_name;
        this.website_url = website_url;
    }

    @Override
```

```
        public String toString() {
                return website_name;
        }
}
```

Note that the encapsulating DummyContent class currently adds three items in the form of strings that read "Item 1", "Item 2" and "Item 3":

```
public static Map<String, DummyItem> ITEM_MAP = new HashMap<String,
DummyItem>();

static {
    // Add 3 sample items.
    addItem(new DummyItem("1", "Item 1"));
    addItem(new DummyItem("2", "Item 2"));
    addItem(new DummyItem("3", "Item 3"));
}
```

This code needs to be modified to initialize the data model with the required web site data:

```
public static Map<String, DummyItem> ITEM_MAP =
        new HashMap<String, DummyItem>();

static {
        // Add 3 sample items.
        addItem(new DummyItem("1", "eBookFrenzy",
                "http://www.ebookfrenzy.com"));
        addItem(new DummyItem("2", "Amazon",
                "http://www.amazon.com"));
        addItem(new DummyItem("3", "Wikipedia",
                "http://www.wikipedia.org"));
}
```

The code now takes advantage of the modified DummyItem class to store an ID, web site name and URL for each item.

26.6 Changing the Detail Pane

The detail information shown to the user when an item is selected from the master list is currently displayed via the layout contained in the *fragment_website_detail.xml* file. By default this contains a single view in the form of a TextView. Since the TextView class is not capable of displaying a web page, this needs to be changed to a WebView object for the purposes of this tutorial. To achieve this, navigate to the *app -> res -> layout -> fragment_website_detail.xml* file in the Project tool window and double click on it to load it into the Designer tool. Switch to Text mode and delete the current XML content from the file. Replace this content with the following XML:

```xml
<WebView
    android:layout_width="match_parent"
    android:layout_height="match_parent"
    xmlns:android="http://schemas.android.com/apk/res/android"
    android:id="@+id/website_detail"></WebView>
```

Switch to Design mode and verify that the layout now matches that shown in Figure 26-5:

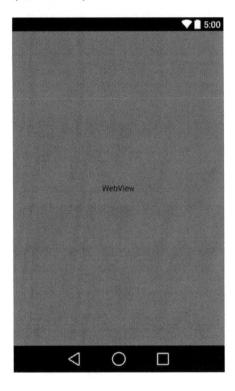

Figure 26-5

26.7 Modifying the WebsiteDetailFragment Class

At this point the user interface detail panel has been modified but the corresponding Java class is still designed for working with a TextView object instead of a WebView. Load the source code for this class by double clicking on the *WebsiteDetailFragment.java* file in the Project tool window. Within the source file locate the *onCreateView()* method which should read as outlined in the following listing:

```java
package com.ebookfrenzy.masterdetailflow;

import android.os.Bundle;
```

```
import android.support.v4.app.Fragment;
import android.view.LayoutInflater;
import android.view.View;
import android.view.ViewGroup;
import android.widget.TextView;

import com.example.masterdetailflow.dummy.DummyContent;

public class WebsiteDetailFragment extends Fragment {
.
.
@Override
public View onCreateView(LayoutInflater inflater, ViewGroup container,
            Bundle savedInstanceState) {

    View rootView =
            inflater.inflate(R.layout.fragment_website_detail,
                    container, false);

    // Show the dummy content as text in a TextView.
    if (mItem != null) {
            ((TextView) rootView.findViewById(R.id.website_detail))
                            .setText(mItem.content);
    }

    return rootView;
}
}
```

In order to load the web page URL corresponding to the currently selected item only one line of code needs to be changed. Once this change has been made, the method should read as follows (note also the addition of the import directive for the android.webkit.WebView library):

```
package com.ebookfrenzy.masterdetailflow;

import android.os.Bundle;
import android.support.v4.app.Fragment;
import android.view.LayoutInflater;
import android.view.View;
import android.view.ViewGroup;
import android.widget.TextView;
import android.webkit.WebView;
```

```
import
com.example.masterdetailflow.masterdetailflow.dummy.DummyContent;


public class WebsiteDetailFragment extends Fragment {
.

.

.

    @Override
    public View onCreateView(LayoutInflater inflater, ViewGroup
       container, Bundle savedInstanceState) {
        View rootView =
              inflater.inflate(R.layout.fragment_website_detail,
                                    container, false);

        // Show the dummy content as text in a TextView.
        if (mItem != null) {
            ((WebView) rootView.findViewById(R.id.website_detail))
                    .loadUrl(mItem.website_url);
        }
        return rootView;
    }
}
```

All that this change does is find the view with the ID of *website_detail* (this was formally the TextView but is now a WebView), extracts the URL of the web site from the selected item and instructs the WebView object to load that page.

26.8 Adding Manifest Permissions

The final step is to add internet permission to the application via the manifest file. This will enable the WebView object to access the internet and download web pages. Navigate to and load the *AndroidManifest.xml* file in the Project tool window (*app -> manifests*) and double click on it to load it into the editor. Once loaded, add the appropriate permission line to the file:

```
<?xml version="1.0" encoding="utf-8"?>
<manifest xmlns:android="http://schemas.android.com/apk/res/android"
    package="com.example.masterdetailflow.masterdetailflow" >

    <uses-permission android:name="android.permission.INTERNET" />

    <application
        android:allowBackup="true"
        android:icon="@mipmap/ic_launcher"
```

```
            android:label="@string/app_name"
            android:theme="@style/AppTheme" >.
    .
    .
</manifest>
```

26.9 **Running the Application**

Compile and run the application on a suitably configured emulator or an attached Android device. Depending on the size of the display, the application will appear either in small screen or two-pane mode. Regardless, the master list should appear primed with the names of the three web sites defined in the content model. Selecting an item should cause the corresponding web site to appear in the detail panel as illustrated in two-pane mode in Figure 26-6:

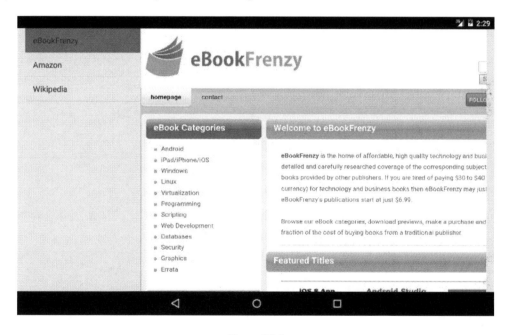

Figure 26-6

26.10 **Summary**

A master/detail user interface consists of a master list of items which, when selected, display additional information about that selection within a detail panel. The Master/Detail Flow is a template provided with Android Studio that allows a master/detail arrangement to be created quickly and with relative ease. As demonstrated in this chapter, with minor modifications to the default template files, a wide range of master/detail based functionality can be implemented with minimal coding and design effort.

27. Creating and Managing Overflow Menus on Android

An area of user interface design that has not yet been covered in this book relates to the concept of menus within an Android application. Menus provide a mechanism for offering additional choices to the user beyond the view components that are present in the user interface layout. Whilst there are a number of different menu systems available to the Android application developer, this chapter will focus on the more commonly used Overflow menu.

27.1 The Overflow Menu

The overflow menu (also referred to as the options menu) is a menu that is accessible to the user from the device display and allows the developer to include other application options beyond those included in the user interface of the application. The location of the overflow menu is dependent upon the version of Android that is running on the device. On a device running Android 2.3.3, for example, the overflow menu is represented by the menu icon located in the center (between the back and search buttons) of the bottom soft key toolbar as illustrated in Figure 27-1:

Figure 27-1

With the Android 4.0 release and later, on the other hand, the overflow menu button is located in the top right hand corner (Figure 27-2) in the action toolbar represented by the stack of three squares:

Figure 27-2

27.2 **Creating an Overflow Menu**

The items in a menu can be declared within an XML file, which is then inflated and displayed to the user on demand. This involves the use of the <menu> element, containing an <item> sub-element for each menu item. The following XML, for example, defines a menu consisting of two menu items relating to color choices:

```
<menu xmlns:android="http://schemas.android.com/apk/res/android"
    xmlns:app="http://schemas.android.com/apk/res-auto"
    xmlns:tools="http://schemas.android.com/tools"
    tools:context=
          ".MenuExampleActivity" >
    <item
        android:id="@+id/menu_red"
        android:orderInCategory="1"
        app:showAsAction="never"
        android:title="@string/red_string"/>
      <item
        android:id="@+id/menu_green"
        android:orderInCategory="2"
        app:showAsAction="never"
        android:title="@string/green_string"/>
</menu>
```

In the above XML, the *android:orderInCategory* property dictates the order in which the menu items will appear within the menu when it is displayed. The *app:showAsAction* property, on the other hand, controls the conditions under which the corresponding item appears as an item within the action bar itself. If set to *ifRoom*, for example, the item will appear in the action bar if there is enough room. Figure 27-3 shows the effect of setting this property to *ifRoom* for both menu items:

Figure 27-3

This property should be used sparingly to avoid over cluttering the action bar.

By default, a menu XML file is created by Android Studio when a new Android application project is created. This file is located in the *app -> res -> menu* project folder and contains a single menu item entitled "Settings":

```
<menu xmlns:android="http://schemas.android.com/apk/res/android"
    xmlns:app="http://schemas.android.com/apk/res-auto"
    xmlns:tools="http://schemas.android.com/tools"
    tools:context=".MainActivity">
        <item android:id="@+id/action_settings"
            android:title="@string/action_settings"
            android:orderInCategory="100"
            app:showAsAction="never" />
</menu>
```

This menu is already configured to be displayed when the user selects the overflow menu on the user interface when the app is running, so simply modify this one to meet your needs.

27.3 Displaying an Overflow Menu

An overflow menu is created by overriding the *onCreateOptionsMenu()* method of the corresponding activity and then inflating the menu's XML file. For example, the following code creates the menu contained within a menu XML file named *menu_menu_example*:

```
@Override
public boolean onCreateOptionsMenu(Menu menu) {
        getMenuInflater().inflate(R.menu.menu_menu_example, menu);
        return true;
}
```

As with the menu XML file, Android Studio will already have overridden this method in the main activity of a newly created Android application project. In the event that an overflow menu is not required in your activity, either remove or comment out this method.

27.4 **Responding to Menu Item Selections**

Once a menu has been implemented, the question arises as to how the application receives notification when the user makes menu item selections. All that an activity needs to do to receive menu selection notifications is to override the *onOptionsItemSelected()* method. Passed as an argument to this method is a reference to the selected menu item. The *getItemId()* method may then be called on the item to obtain the ID which may, in turn, be used to identify which item was selected. For example:

```
@Override
public boolean onOptionsItemSelected(MenuItem item) {
        switch (item.getItemId()) {
          case R.id.menu_red:
              // Red item was selected
              return true;
          case R.id.menu_green:
              // Green item was selected
              return true;
          default:
              return super.onOptionsItemSelected(item);
        }
}
```

27.5 **Creating Checkable Item Groups**

In addition to configuring independent menu items, it is also possible to create groups of menu items. This is of particular use when creating checkable menu items whereby only one out of a number of choices can be selected at any one time. Menu items can be assigned to a group by wrapping them in the *<group>* tag. The group is declared as checkable using the *android:checkableBehavior* property, setting the value to either *single, all or none*. The following XML declares that two menu items make up a group wherein only one item may be selected at any given time:

```
<menu xmlns:android="http://schemas.android.com/apk/res/android" >
<group android:checkableBehavior="single">
    <item
        android:id="@+id/menu_red"
        android:orderInCategory="1"
        app:showAsAction="never"
        android:title="@string/red_string"/>
      <item
        android:id="@+id/menu_green"
        android:orderInCategory="2"
        app:showAsAction="never"
```

```
        android:title="@string/green_string"/>
</group>
</menu>
```

When a menu group is configured to be checkable, a small circle appears next to the item in the menu as illustrated in Figure 27-4. It is important to be aware that the setting and unsetting of this indicator does not take place automatically. It is, therefore, the responsibility of the application to check and uncheck the menu item.

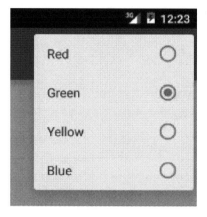

Figure 27-4

Continuing the color example used previously in this chapter, this would be implemented as follows:

```
@Override
public boolean onOptionsItemSelected(MenuItem item) {
        switch (item.getItemId()) {
          case R.id.menu_red:
                if (item.isChecked()) item.setChecked(false);
              else item.setChecked(true);
              mainLayout.setBackgroundColor(android.graphics.Color.RED);
              return true;
          case R.id.menu_green:
                if (item.isChecked()) item.setChecked(false);
              else item.setChecked(true);

mainLayout.setBackgroundColor(android.graphics.Color.GREEN);
              return true;
          default:
              return super.onOptionsItemSelected(item);
        }
}
```

27.6 **Creating the Example Project**

To see the overflow menu in action, create a new project in Android Studio, entering *MenuExample* into the Application name field and *ebookfrenzy.com* as the Company Domain setting before clicking on the *Next* button.

On the form factors screen, enable the *Phone and Tablet* option and set the minimum SDK setting to API 8: Android 2.2 (Froyo). Continue to proceed through the screens, requesting the creation of a blank activity named *MenuExampleActivity* with corresponding layout and menu resource files named *activity_menu_example* and *menu_menu_example*.

When the project has been created, navigate to the *app -> res -> layout* folder in the Project tool window and double click on the *activity_menu_example.xml* file to load it into the Android Studio Designer tool. Switch the tool to Design mode, double click on the background of the layout (the area representing the RelativeLayout view) and enter *layoutView* into the id field of the popup panel.

27.7 **Modifying the Menu Description**

Within the Project tool window, locate the project's *app -> res -> menu -> menu_menu_example.xml* file and double click on it to load it into the editing panel. Delete the default Settings menu item added by Android Studio and then add new items as a checkable group so that the XML file is structured as follows:

```xml
<menu xmlns:android="http://schemas.android.com/apk/res/android"
    xmlns:app="http://schemas.android.com/apk/res-auto"
    xmlns:tools="http://schemas.android.com/tools"
    tools:context=".MenuExampleActivity" >

    <group android:checkableBehavior="single">
        <item
            android:id="@+id/menu_red"
            android:orderInCategory="1"
            app:showAsAction="never"
            android:title="@string/red_string"/>

        <item
            android:id="@+id/menu_green"
            android:orderInCategory="2"
            app:showAsAction="never"
            android:title="@string/green_string"/>

        <item
            android:id="@+id/menu_yellow"
```

```
                android:orderInCategory="3"
                app:showAsAction="never"
                android:title="@string/yellow_string"/>

        <item
                android:id="@+id/menu_blue"
                android:orderInCategory="4"
                app:showAsAction="never"
                android:title="@string/blue_string"/>
    </group>
```

```
</menu>
```

Locate and double click on the *app -> res -> values -> strings.xml* file. Within the file, add new string resources for the color names as referenced by the menu items:

```xml
<?xml version="1.0" encoding="utf-8"?>
<resources>
    <string name="app_name">MenuExample</string>
    <string name="hello_world">Hello world!</string>
    <string name="menu_settings">Settings</string>
    <string name="red_string">Red</string>
    <string name="green_string">Green</string>
    <string name="yellow_string">Yellow</string>
    <string name="blue_string">Blue</string>
</resources>
```

27.8 Modifying the *onOptionsItemSelected()* Method

When items are selected from the menu, the overridden *onOptionsItemsSelected()* method of the application's activity will be called. The role of this method will be to identify which item was selected and change the background color of the layout view to the corresponding color. Locate and double click on the *app -> java -> com.ebookfrenzy.menuexample -> MenuExampleActivity* file and modify the method as follows:

```java
package com.ebookfrenzy.menuexample;

import android.support.v7.app.ActionBarActivity;
import android.os.Bundle;
import android.view.Menu;
import android.view.MenuItem;
import android.widget.RelativeLayout;
```

```
public class MenuExampleActivity extends ActionBarActivity {
    .
    .
    .

    @Override
    public boolean onOptionsItemSelected(MenuItem item) {

        RelativeLayout mainLayout =
                (RelativeLayout) findViewById(R.id.layoutView);

        switch (item.getItemId()) {
            case R.id.menu_red:
                if (item.isChecked()) item.setChecked(false);
                else item.setChecked(true);

mainLayout.setBackgroundColor(android.graphics.Color.RED);
                return true;
            case R.id.menu_green:
                if (item.isChecked()) item.setChecked(false);
                else item.setChecked(true);

mainLayout.setBackgroundColor(android.graphics.Color.GREEN);
                return true;
            case R.id.menu_yellow:
                if (item.isChecked()) item.setChecked(false);
                else item.setChecked(true);

mainLayout.setBackgroundColor(android.graphics.Color.YELLOW);
                return true;
            case R.id.menu_blue:
                if (item.isChecked()) item.setChecked(false);
                else item.setChecked(true);

mainLayout.setBackgroundColor(android.graphics.Color.BLUE);
                return true;
            default:
                return super.onOptionsItemSelected(item);
        }

    }
    .
    .
    .
}
```

27.9 **Testing the Application**

Build and run the application on either an emulator or physical Android device. Using the overflow menu, select menu items and verify that the layout background color changes appropriately. Note that the currently selected color is displayed as the checked item in the menu.

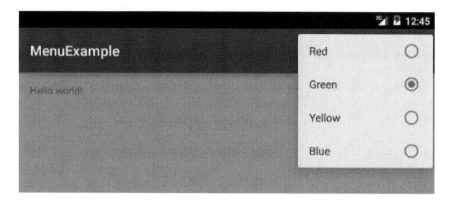

Figure 27-5

27.10 **Summary**

On earlier versions of Android, the overflow menu is accessible from the soft key toolbar at the bottom of the screen. On Android 4.0 and later, the menu is accessed from the far right of the actions toolbar at the top of the display. This menu provides a location for applications to provide additional options to the user.

The structure of the menu is most easily defined within an XML file and the application activity receives notifications of menu item selections by overriding and implementing the *onOptionsItemSelected()* method.

28. Animating User Interfaces with the Android Transitions Framework

The Android Transitions framework was introduced as part of the Android 4.4 KitKat release and is designed to make it easy for you, as an Android developer, to add animation effects to the views that make up the screens of your applications. As will be outlined in both this and subsequent chapters, animated effects such as making the views in a user interface gently fade in and out of sight and glide smoothly to new positions on the screen can be implemented with just a few simple lines of code when using the Transitions framework in Android Studio.

28.1 Introducing Android Transitions and Scenes

Transitions allow the changes made to the layout and appearance of the views in a user interface to be animated during application runtime. Whilst there are a number of different ways to implement Transitions from within application code, perhaps the most powerful mechanism involves the use of *Scenes*. A scene represents either the entire layout of a user interface screen, or a subset of the layout (represented by a ViewGroup).

To implement transitions using this approach, scenes are defined that reflect the two different user interface states (these can be thought of as the "before" and "after" scenes). One scene, for example, might consist of a TextEdit, Button and TextView positioned near the top of the screen. The second scene might remove the Button view and move the remaining TextEdit and TextView objects to the bottom of the screen to make room for the introduction of a MapView instance. Using the transition framework, the changes between these two scenes can be animated so that the Button fades from view, the TextEdit and TextView slide to the new locations and the map gently fades into view.

Scenes can be created in code from ViewGroups, or implemented in layout resource files that are loaded into Scene instances at application runtime.

Transitions can also be implemented dynamically from within application code. Using this approach, scenes are created by referencing collections of user interface views in the form of ViewGroups with transitions then being performed on those elements using the TransitionManager class, which provides a range of methods for triggering and managing the transitions between scenes.

Perhaps the simplest form of transition involves the use of the *beginDelayedTransition()* method of the TransitionManager class. When called and passed the ViewGroup representing a scene, any subsequent changes to any views within that scene (such as moving, resizing, adding or deleting views) will be animated by the Transition framework.

The actual animation is handled by the Transition framework via instances of the *Transition* class. Transition instances are responsible for detecting changes to the size, position and visibility of the views within a scene and animating those changes accordingly.

By default, transitions will be animated using a set of criteria defined by the AutoTransition class. Custom transitions can be created either via settings in XML transition files or directly within code. Multiple transitions can be combined together in a TransitionSet and configured to be performed either in parallel or sequentially.

28.2 Using Interpolators with Transitions

The Transitions framework makes extensive use of the Android Animation framework to implement animation effects. This fact is largely incidental when using transitions since most of this work happens behind the scenes, thereby shielding the developer from some of the complexities of the Animation framework. One area where some knowledge of the Animation framework is beneficial when using Transitions, however, involves the concept of interpolators.

Interpolators are a feature of the Android Animation framework that allow animations to be modified in a number of pre-defined ways. At present the Animation framework provides the following interpolators, all of which are available for use in customizing transitions:

- **AccelerateDecelerateInterpolator** – By default, animation is performed at a constant rate. The AccelerateDecelerateInterpolator can be used to cause the animation to begin slowly and then speed up in the middle before slowing down towards the end of the sequence.
- **AccelerateInterpolator** – As the name suggests, the AccelerateInterpolator begins the animation slowly and accelerates at a specified rate with no deceleration at the end.
- **AnticipateInterpolator** – The AnticipateInterpolator provides an effect similar to that of a sling shot. The animated view moves in the opposite direction to the configured animation for a short distance before being flung forward in the correct direction. The amount of backward force can be controlled through the specification of a tension value.
- **AnticipateOvershootInterpolator** – Combines the effect provided by the AnticipateInterpolator with the animated object overshooting and then returning to the destination position on the screen.
- **BounceInterpolator** – Causes the animated view to bounce on arrival at its destination position.
- **CycleInterpolator** – Configures the animation to be repeated a specified number of times.

- **DecelerateInterpolator** – The DecelerateInterpolator causes the animation to begin quickly and then decelerate by a specified factor as it nears the end.
- **LinearInterpolator** – Used to specify that the animation is to be performed at a constant rate.
- **OvershootInterpolator** – Causes the animated view to overshoot the specified destination position before returning. The overshoot can be configured by specifying a tension value.

As will be demonstrated in this and later chapters, interpolators can be specified both in code and XML files.

28.3 Working with Scene Transitions

Scenes can be represented by the content of an Android Studio XML layout file. The following XML, for example, could be used to represent a scene consisting of three button views within a RelativeLayout parent:

```xml
<?xml version="1.0" encoding="utf-8"?>
<RelativeLayout
xmlns:android="http://schemas.android.com/apk/res/android"
    android:id="@+id/RelativeLayout1"
    android:layout_width="match_parent"
    android:layout_height="match_parent"
    android:orientation="vertical" >

    <Button
        android:id="@+id/button1"
        android:layout_width="wrap_content"
        android:layout_height="wrap_content"
        android:layout_alignParentLeft="true"
        android:layout_alignParentTop="true"
        android:onClick="goToScene2"
        android:text="@string/one_string" />

    <Button
        android:id="@+id/button2"
        android:layout_width="wrap_content"
        android:layout_height="wrap_content"
        android:layout_alignParentRight="true"
        android:layout_alignParentTop="true"
        android:onClick="goToScene1"
        android:text="@string/two_string" />

    <Button
        android:id="@+id/button3"
```

```
            android:layout_width="wrap_content"
            android:layout_height="wrap_content"
            android:layout_centerHorizontal="true"
            android:layout_centerVertical="true"
            android:text="@string/three_string" />


</RelativeLayout>
```

Assuming that the above layout resides in a file named *scene1_layout.xml* located in the *res/layout* folder of the project, the layout can be loaded into a scene using the *getSceneForLayout()* method of the Scene class. For example:

```
Scene scene1 = Scene.getSceneForLayout(rootContainer,
                  R.layout.scene1_layout, this);
```

Note that the method call requires a reference to the root container. This is the view at the top of the view hierarchy in which the scene is to be displayed.

To display a scene to the user without any transition animation, the *enter()* method is called on the scene instance:

```
scene1.enter();
```

Transitions between two scenes using the default AutoTransition class can be triggered using the *go()* method of the TransitionManager class:

```
TransitionManager.go(scene2);
```

Scene instances can be created easily in code by bundling the view elements into one or more ViewGroups and then creating a scene from those groups. For example:

```
Scene scene1 = Scene(viewGroup1);
Scene scene2 = Scene(viewGroup2, viewGroup3);
```

28.4 Custom Transitions and TransitionSets in Code

The examples outlined so far in this chapter have used the default transition settings in which resizing, fading and motion are animated using pre-configured behavior. These can be modified by creating custom transitions which are then referenced during the transition process. Animations are categorized as either *change bounds* (relating to changes in the position and size of a view) and *fade* (relating to the visibility or otherwise of a view).

A single Transition can be created as follows:

```
Transition myChangeBounds = new ChangeBounds();
```

This new transition can then be used when performing a transition:

```
TransitionManager.go(scene2, myChangeBounds);
```

Multiple transitions may be bundled together into a TransitionSet instance. The following code, for example, creates a new TransitionSet object consisting of both change bounds and fade transition effects:

```
TransitionSet myTransition = new TransitionSet();
myTransition.addTransition(new ChangeBounds());
myTransition.addTransition(new Fade());
```

Transitions can be configured to target specific views (referenced by view ID). For example, the following code will configure the previous fade transition to target only the view with an ID that matches *myButton1*:

```
TransitionSet myTransition = new TransitionSet();
myTransition.addTransition(new ChangeBounds());
Transition fade = new Fade();
fade.addTarget(R.id.myButton1);
myTransition.addTransition(fade);
```

Additional aspects of the transition may also be customized, such as the duration of the animation. The following code specifies the duration over which the animation is to be performed:

```
Transition changeBounds = new ChangeBounds();
changeBounds.setDuration(2000);
```

As with Transition instances, once a TransitionSet instance has been created, it can be used in a transition via the TransitionManager class. For example:

```
TransitionManager.go(scene1, myTransition);
```

28.5 Custom Transitions and TransitionSets in XML

Whilst custom transitions can be implemented in code, it is often easier to do so via XML transition files using the <fade> and <changeBounds> tags together with some additional options. The following XML includes a single changeBounds transition:

```
<?xml version="1.0" encoding="utf-8"?>
<changeBounds/>
```

Animating User Interfaces with the Android Transitions Framework

As with the code based approach to working with transitions, each transition entry in a resource file may be customized. The XML below, for example, configures a duration for a change bounds transition:

```
<changeBounds android:duration="5000" >
```

Multiple transitions may be bundled together using the <transitionSet> element:

```
<?xml version="1.0" encoding="utf-8"?>
<transitionSet
  xmlns:android="http://schemas.android.com/apk/res/android" >

  <fade
    android:duration="2000"
    android:fadingMode="fade_out" />

  <changeBounds
    android:duration="5000" >

    <targets>
      <target android:targetId="@id/button2" />
    </targets>

  </changeBounds>

  <fade
    android:duration="2000"
    android:fadingMode="fade_in" />
</transitionSet>
```

Transitions contained within an XML resource file should be stored in the *res/transition* folder of the project in which they are being used and must be inflated before being referenced in the code of an application. The following code, for example, inflates the transition resources contained within a file named *transition.xml* and assigns the results to a reference named *myTransition*:

```
Transition myTransition = TransitionInflater.from(this)
    .inflateTransition(R.transition.transition);
```

Once inflated, the new transition can be referenced in the usual way:

```
TransitionManager.go(scene1, myTransition);
```

By default, transition effects within a TransitionSet are performed in parallel. To instruct the Transition framework to perform the animations sequentially, add the appropriate *android:transitionOrdering* property to the transitionSet element of the resource file:

```xml
<?xml version="1.0" encoding="utf-8"?>

<transitionSet
  xmlns:android="http://schemas.android.com/apk/res/android"
  android:transitionOrdering="sequential">

    <fade
       android:duration="2000"
       android:fadingMode="fade_out" />

    <changeBounds
       android:duration="5000" >
  </changeBounds>
</transitionSet>
```

Change the value from "sequential" to "together" to indicate that the animation sequences are to be performed in parallel.

28.6 Working with Interpolators

As previously discussed, interpolators can be used to modify the behavior of a transition in a variety of ways and may be specified either in code or via the settings within a transition XML resource file.

When working in code, new interpolator instances can be created by calling the constructor method of the required interpolator class and, where appropriate, passing through values to further modify the interpolator behavior:

* AccelerateDecelerateInterpolator()
* AccelerateInterpolator(float factor)
* AnticipateInterpolator(float tension)
* AnticipateOvershootInterpolator(float tension)
* BounceInterpolator()
* CycleInterpolator(float cycles)
* DecelerateInterpolator(float factor)
* LinearInterpolator()
* OvershootInterpolator(float tension)

Once created, an interpolator instance can be attached to a transition using the *setInterpolator()* method of the Transition class. The following code, for example, adds a bounce interpolator to a change bounds transition:

```
Transition changeBounds = new ChangeBounds();
changeBounds.setInterpolator(new BounceInterpolator());
```

Similarly, the following code adds an accelerate interpolator to the same transition, specifying an acceleration factor of 1.2:

```
changeBounds.setInterpolator(new AccelerateInterpolator(1.2f));
```

In the case of XML based transition resources, a default interpolator is declared using the following syntax:

```
android:interpolator="@android:anim/<interpolator_element>"
```

In the above syntax, *<interpolator_element>* must be replaced by the resource ID of the corresponding interpolator selected from the following list:

- accelerate_decelerate_interpolator
- accelerate_interpolator
- anticipate_interpolator
- anticipate_overshoot_interpolator
- bounce_interpolator
- cycle_interpolator
- decelerate_interpolator
- linear_interpolator
- overshoot_interpolator

The following XML fragment, for example, adds a bounce interpolator to a change bounds transition contained within a transition set:

```
<?xml version="1.0" encoding="utf-8"?>
<transitionSet
  xmlns:android="http://schemas.android.com/apk/res/android"
  android:transitionOrdering="sequential">

  <changeBounds
    android:interpolator="@android:anim/bounce_interpolator"
    android:duration="2000" />

  <fade
```

```
    android:duration="1000"
    android:fadingMode="fade_in" />
</transitionSet>
```

This approach to adding interpolators to transitions within XML resources works well when the default behavior of the interpolator is required. The task becomes a little more complex when the default behavior of an interpolator needs to be changed. Take, for the sake of an example, the cycle interpolator. The purpose of this interpolator is to make an animation or transition repeat a specified number of times. In the absence of a *cycles* attribute setting, the cycle interpolator will perform only one cycle. Unfortunately there is no way to directly specify the number of cycles (or any other interpolator attribute for that matter) when adding an interpolator using the above technique. Instead, a custom interpolator must be created and then referenced within the transition file.

28.7 Creating a Custom Interpolator

A custom interpolator must be declared in a separate XML file and stored within the *res/anim* folder of the project. The name of the XML file will be used by the Android system as the resource ID for the custom interpolator.

Within the custom interpolator XML resource file, the syntax should read as follows:

```
<?xml version="1.0" encoding="utf-8"?>
<interpolatorElement
xmlns:android="http://schemas.android.com/apk/res/android"
android:attribute="value" />
```

In the above syntax, *interpolatorElement* must be replaced with the element name of the required interpolator selected from the following list:

- accelerateDecelerateInterpolator
- accelerateInterpolator
- anticipateInterpolator
- anticipateOvershootInterpolator
- bounceInterpolator
- cycleInterpolator
- decelerateInterpolator
- linearInterpolator
- overshootInterpolator

The *attribute* keyword is replaced by the name attribute of the interpolator for which the value is to be changed (for example *tension* to change the tension attribute of an overshoot interpolator). Finally, *value* represents the value to be assigned to the specified attribute. The following XML, for example, contains a custom cycle interpolator configured to cycle 7 times:

```
<?xml version="1.0" encoding="utf-8"?>
<cycleInterpolator
xmlns:android="http://schemas.android.com/apk/res/android"
android:cycles="7" />
```

Assuming that the above XML was stored in a resource file named *my_cycle.xml* stored in the *res/anim* project folder, the custom interpolator could be added to a transition resource file using the following XML syntax:

```
<changeBounds
    xmlns:android="http://schemas.android.com/apk/res/android"
    android:duration="5000"
    android:interpolator="@anim/my_cycle" >
```

28.8 Using the beginDelayedTransition Method

Perhaps the simplest form of Transition based user interface animation involves the use of the *beginDelayedTransition()* method of the TransitionManager class. This method is passed a reference to the root view of the viewgroup representing the scene for which animation is required. Subsequent changes to the views within that sub view will then be animated using the default transition settings:

```
myLayout = (ViewGroup) findViewById(R.id.myLayout);
TransitionManager.beginDelayedTransition(myLayout);
// Make changes to the scene
```

If behavior other than the default animation behavior is required, simply pass a suitably configured Transition or TransitionSet instance through to the method call:

```
TransitionManager.beginDelayedTransition(myLayout, myTransition);
```

28.9 Summary

The Android 4.4 KitKat SDK release introduced the Transition Framework, the purpose of which is to simplify the task of adding animation to the views that make up the user interface of an Android application. With some simple configuration and a few lines of code, animation effects such as movement, visibility and resizing of views can be animated by making use of the Transition framework. A number of different approaches to implementing transitions are available involving a combination of Java code and XML resource files. The animation effects of transitions may also be enhanced through the use of a range of interpolators.

Having covered some of the theory of Transitions in Android, the next two chapters will put this theory into practice by working through some example Android Studio based transition implementations.

29. An Android Transition Tutorial using beginDelayedTransition

The previous chapter, entitled *Animating User Interfaces with the Android Transitions Framework*, provided an introduction to the animation of user interfaces using the Android Transitions framework. This chapter uses a tutorial based approach to demonstrate Android transitions in action using the *beginDelayedTransition()* method of the TransitionManager class.

The next chapter will create a more complex example that uses layout files and transition resource files to animate the transition from one scene to another within an application.

29.1 Creating the Android Studio TransitionDemo Project

Create a new project in Android Studio, entering *TransitionDemo* into the Application name field and *ebookfrenzy.com* as the Company Domain setting before clicking on the *Next* button.

On the form factors screen, enable the *Phone and Tablet* option and set the minimum SDK setting to API 19: Android 4.4 (KitKat). Continue to proceed through the screens, requesting the creation of a blank activity named *TransitionDemoActivity* with layout and menu resource files named *activity_transition_demo* and *menu_transition_demo* respectively.

29.2 Preparing the Project Files

The first example transition animation will be implemented through the use of the *beginDelayedTransition()* method of the TransitionManager class. The first step, however, is to assign an ID to the parent layout view element in the user interface layout created for us by Android Studio. If Android Studio does not automatically load the file, locate and double click on the *app -> res -> layout -> activity_transition_demo.xml* file in the Project tool window panel to load it into the Designer tool. Once loaded, switch to Design mode and double click on the background of the view canvas that represents the parent RelativeLayout container and, in the resulting panel, name the layout view *myLayout* and press Enter to commit the change.

Select the TextView object that currently displays the *Hello world!* text and press the keyboard delete key to remove it from the layout. Drag a Button from the Widget section of the Designer palette and position it in the top left hand corner of the device screen layout. Once positioned, double click on it and specify an ID of *myButton1*.

29.3 Implementing beginDelayedTransition Animation

The objective for the initial phase of this tutorial is to implement a touch handler so that when the user taps on the layout view the button view moves to the lower right hand corner of the screen and increases in size.

Locate the *TransitionDemoActivity.java* file (located in the Project tool window under *app -> java -> com.ebookfrenzy.transitiondemo*) and modify the *onCreate()* method to implement the onTouch handler:

```
package com.ebookfrenzy.transitiondemo;

import android.support.v7.app.ActionBarActivity;
import android.os.Bundle;
import android.view.Menu;
import android.view.MenuItem;
import android.view.MotionEvent;
import android.view.View;
import android.view.ViewGroup;
import android.widget.RelativeLayout;

public class TransitionDemoActivity extends ActionBarActivity {

    ViewGroup myLayout;

    @Override
    protected void onCreate(Bundle savedInstanceState) {
        super.onCreate(savedInstanceState);
        setContentView(R.layout.activity_transition_demo);

        myLayout = (ViewGroup) findViewById(R.id.myLayout);

        myLayout.setOnTouchListener(
                new RelativeLayout.OnTouchListener() {
                    public boolean onTouch(View v,
                                             MotionEvent m) {
                        handleTouch();
                        return true;
                    }
                }
```

```
        );


    }
    .
    .
    .
}
```

The above code simply sets up a touch listener on the RelativeLayout container and configures it to call a method named *handleTouch()* when a touch is detected. The next task, therefore, is to implement the *handleTouch()* method as follows:

```
public void handleTouch() {
        View view = findViewById(R.id.myButton1);

        RelativeLayout.LayoutParams params = new
RelativeLayout.LayoutParams(RelativeLayout.LayoutParams.WRAP_CONTENT,
                RelativeLayout.LayoutParams.WRAP_CONTENT);

        params.addRule(RelativeLayout.ALIGN_PARENT_RIGHT,
                RelativeLayout.TRUE);
        params.addRule(RelativeLayout.ALIGN_PARENT_BOTTOM,
                RelativeLayout.TRUE);
        view.setLayoutParams(params);

        ViewGroup.LayoutParams lparams = view.getLayoutParams();

        lparams.width = 500;
        lparams.height = 350;
        view.setLayoutParams(lparams);
}
```

This method obtains a reference to the button view in the user interface layout and creates a new set of layout parameter rules designed to move the button to the bottom right hand corner of the parent layout and to increase the button's dimensions. Once created, these new parameters are applied to the button.

Test the code so far by compiling and running the application. Once launched, touch the background (not the button) and note that the button moves and resizes as illustrated in Figure 29-1:

An Android Transition Tutorial using beginDelayedTransition

Figure 29-1

Although the layout changes took effect, they did so instantly and without any form of animation. This is where the call to the *beginDelayedTransition()* method of the TransitionManager class comes in. All that is needed to add animation to this layout change is the addition of a single line of code before the layout changes are implemented. Remaining within the *TransitionDemoActivity.java* file, modify the code as follows:

```
package com.ebookfrenzy.transitiondemo;

import android.support.v7.app.ActionBarActivity;
import android.os.Bundle;
import android.view.Menu;
import android.view.MenuItem;
import android.view.MotionEvent;
import android.view.View;
import android.view.ViewGroup;
import android.widget.RelativeLayout;
import android.transition.TransitionManager;

public class TransitionDemoActivity extends ActionBarActivity {

.
.
.
        public void handleTouch() {
                View view = findViewById(R.id.myButton1);

                TransitionManager.beginDelayedTransition(myLayout);
```

```
            RelativeLayout.LayoutParams params = new
RelativeLayout.LayoutParams(RelativeLayout.LayoutParams.WRAP_CONTENT,
                RelativeLayout.LayoutParams.WRAP_CONTENT);

            params.addRule(RelativeLayout.ALIGN_PARENT_RIGHT,
                RelativeLayout.TRUE);

            params.addRule(RelativeLayout.ALIGN_PARENT_BOTTOM,
                RelativeLayout.TRUE);

            params.width = 500;
            params.height = 350;
            view.setLayoutParams(params);
        }
    .
    .
    .
}
```

Compile and run the application once again and note that the transition is now animated.

29.4 Customizing the Transition

The final task in this example is to modify the changeBounds transition so that it is performed over a longer duration and incorporates a bounce effect when the view reaches its new screen location. This involves the creation of a Transition instance with appropriate duration interpolator settings which is, in turn, passed through as an argument to the *beginDelayedTransition()* method:

```
package com.ebookfrenzy.transitiondemo;

import android.support.v7.app.ActionBarActivity;
import android.os.Bundle;
import android.view.Menu;
import android.view.MenuItem;
import android.view.MotionEvent;
import android.view.View;
import android.view.ViewGroup;
import android.widget.RelativeLayout;
import android.transition.TransitionManager;
import android.transition.ChangeBounds;
import android.transition.Transition;
import android.view.animation.BounceInterpolator;

public class TransitionDemoActivity extends ActionBarActivity {
```

```
       .
       .
       .
    public void handleTouch() {
            View view = findViewById(R.id.myButton1);

            Transition changeBounds = new ChangeBounds();
            changeBounds.setDuration(3000);
            changeBounds.setInterpolator(new BounceInterpolator());

            TransitionManager.beginDelayedTransition(myLayout,
                                    changeBounds);

            RelativeLayout.LayoutParams params = new
RelativeLayout.LayoutParams(RelativeLayout.LayoutParams.WRAP_CONTENT,
                    RelativeLayout.LayoutParams.WRAP_CONTENT);

            params.addRule(RelativeLayout.ALIGN_PARENT_RIGHT,
                    RelativeLayout.TRUE);

            params.addRule(RelativeLayout.ALIGN_PARENT_BOTTOM,
                    RelativeLayout.TRUE);

            params.width = 500;
            params.height = 350;
            view.setLayoutParams(params);
    }
```

When the application is now executed, the animation will slow to match the new duration setting and the button will bounce on arrival at the bottom right hand corner of the display.

29.5 **Summary**

The most basic form of transition animation involves the use of the *beginDelayedTransition()* method of the TransitionManager class. Once called, any changes in size and position of the views in the next user interface rendering frame, and within a defined view group, will be animated using the specified transitions. This chapter has worked through a simple Android Studio example that demonstrates the use of this approach to implementing transitions.

30. Implementing Android Scene Transitions – A Tutorial

This chapter will build on the theory outlined in the chapter entitled *Animating User Interfaces with the Android Transitions Framework* by working through the creation of a project designed to demonstrate transitioning from one scene to another using the Android Transition framework.

30.1 An Overview of the Scene Transition Project

The application created in this chapter will consist of two scenes, each represented by an XML layout resource file. A transition will then be used to animate the changes from one scene to another. The first scene will consist of three button views. The second scene will contain two of the buttons from the first scene positioned at different locations on the screen. The third button will be absent from the second scene. Once the transition has been implemented, movement of the first two buttons will be animated with a bounce effect. The third button will gently fade into view as the application transitions back to the first scene from the second.

30.2 Creating the Android Studio SceneTransitions Project

Create a new project in Android Studio, entering *SceneTransitions* into the Application name field and *ebookfrenzy.com* as the Company Domain setting before clicking on the *Next* button.

On the form factors screen, enable the *Phone and Tablet* option and set the minimum SDK setting to API 19: Android 4.4 (KitKat). Continue to proceed through the screens, requesting the creation of a blank activity named *SceneTransitionsActivity* with corresponding layout and menu files named *activity_scene_transitions* and *menu_scene_transitions.*

30.3 Identifying and Preparing the Root Container

When working with transitions it is important to identify the root container for the scenes. This is essentially the parent layout container into which the scenes are going to be displayed. When the project was created, Android Studio created a layout resource file in the *app -> res -> layout* folder named *activity_scene_transitions.xml* and containing a single RelativeLayout container and TextView. When the application is launched, this is the first layout that will be displayed to the user on the device screen and for the purposes of this example, the RelativeLayout container within this layout will act as the root container for the two scenes.

Begin by locating the *activity_scene_transitions.xml* layout resource file and loading it into the Android Studio Designer tool. Switch to Design mode if necessary, select the "Hello World!" TextView object and delete it from the layout using the keyboard delete key. Double click on the layout background and in the resulting panel change the view's ID property to *rootContainer*.

30.4 Designing the First Scene

The first scene is going to consist of a relative layout containing three button views. Create this layout resource file by right-clicking on the *app -> res -> layout* entry in the Project tool window and selecting the *New -> Layout resource file...* menu option. In the resulting dialog, name the file *scene1_layout* and select *RelativeLayout* as the root element before clicking on *OK*.

When the newly created layout file has loaded into the Designer tool drag a Button view from the Widgets section of the palette onto the layout canvas and position it in the top left hand corner of the layout view so that the *alignParentLeft* and *alignParentTop* properties are displayed as illustrated in Figure 30-1. Drop the Button view at this position, double click on it and change the text property to "One". Select the light bulb icon, click on the I18N message and extract the string to a resource named *one_string*.

Figure 30-1

Drag a second Button view from the palette and position it in the top right hand corner of the layout view so that the *alignParentRight* and *alignParentTop* properties are displayed before dropping the view into place. Repeating the steps for the first button, assign text that reads "Two" to the button and extract it into a string resource named and *two_string*.

Drag a third Button view and position it so that it is centered both horizontally and vertically within the layout, this time configuring a string resource named *three_string* that reads "Three".

On completion of the above steps, the layout for the first scene should resemble that shown in Figure 30-2:

Figure 30-2

Switch the Designer tool to Text mode to directly edit the XML resources for the layout. Verify that the XML matches that listed below before adding the onClick properties to the first and second buttons. These methods will be implemented later to trigger the transitions from one scene to another:

```xml
<?xml version="1.0" encoding="utf-8"?>

<RelativeLayout
xmlns:android="http://schemas.android.com/apk/res/android"
    android:layout_width="match_parent"
android:layout_height="match_parent">

    <Button
        android:layout_width="wrap_content"
        android:layout_height="wrap_content"
```

```
        android:text="@string/one_string"
        android:id="@+id/button"
        android:layout_alignParentTop="true"
        android:layout_alignParentLeft="true"
        android:layout_alignParentStart="true"
        android:onClick="goToScene2" />

    <Button
        android:layout_width="wrap_content"
        android:layout_height="wrap_content"
        android:text="@string/two_string"
        android:id="@+id/button2"
        android:layout_alignParentTop="true"
        android:layout_alignParentRight="true"
        android:layout_alignParentEnd="true"
        android:onClick="goToScene1" />

    <Button
        android:layout_width="wrap_content"
        android:layout_height="wrap_content"
        android:text="@string/three_string"
        android:id="@+id/button3"
        android:layout_centerVertical="true"
        android:layout_centerHorizontal="true" />

</RelativeLayout>
```

30.5 Designing the Second Scene

The second scene is simply a modified version of the first scene. The first and second buttons will still be present but will be located in the bottom right and left hand corners of the layout respectively. The third button, on the other hand, will no longer be present in the second scene.

For the purposes of avoiding duplicated effort, the layout file for the second scene will be created by copying and modifying the *scene1_layout.xml* file. Within the Project tool window, locate the *app -> res -> layout -> scene1_layout.xml* file, right-click on it and select the *Copy* menu option. Right-click on the *layout* folder, this time selecting the *Paste* menu option and change the name of the file to *scene2_layout.xml* when prompted to do so.

Double click on the new *scene2_layout.xml* file to load it into the Designer tool and switch to Design mode if necessary. Select and delete the "Three" button and move the first and second buttons to the bottom right and bottom left locations as illustrated in Figure 30-3:

Figure 30-3

Switch Designer to Text mode and verify that the XML matches that listed below:

```xml
<?xml version="1.0" encoding="utf-8"?>

<RelativeLayout
xmlns:android="http://schemas.android.com/apk/res/android"
    android:layout_width="match_parent"
android:layout_height="match_parent">

    <Button
        android:layout_width="wrap_content"
        android:layout_height="wrap_content"
        android:text="@string/one_string"
        android:id="@+id/button"
        android:onClick="goToScene2"
        android:layout_alignParentBottom="true"
        android:layout_alignParentRight="true"
        android:layout_alignParentEnd="true" />

    <Button
        android:layout_width="wrap_content"
        android:layout_height="wrap_content"
        android:text="@string/two_string"
```

```
        android:id="@+id/button2"
        android:onClick="goToScene1"
        android:layout_alignParentBottom="true"
        android:layout_alignParentLeft="true"
        android:layout_alignParentStart="true" />
</RelativeLayout>
```

30.6 **Entering the First Scene**

If the application were to be run now, only the blank layout represented by the *activity_scene_transitions.xml* file would be displayed. Some code must, therefore, be added to the *onCreate()* method located in the *SceneTransitionsActivity.java* file so that the first scene is presented when the activity is created. This can be achieved as follows:

```
package com.ebookfrenzy.scenetransitions;

import android.support.v7.app.ActionBarActivity;
import android.os.Bundle;
import android.view.Menu;
import android.view.MenuItem;
import android.transition.Scene;
import android.transition.Transition;
import android.transition.TransitionManager;
import android.view.ViewGroup;
import android.view.View;

public class SceneTransitionsActivity extends ActionBarActivity {

    ViewGroup rootContainer;
    Scene scene1;

    @Override
    protected void onCreate(Bundle savedInstanceState) {
        super.onCreate(savedInstanceState);
        setContentView(R.layout.activity_scene_transitions);

        rootContainer =
                (ViewGroup) findViewById(R.id.rootContainer);

        scene1 = Scene.getSceneForLayout(rootContainer,
                R.layout.scene1_layout, this);

        scene1.enter();
```

```
        }
    .
    .
    .
}
```

The code added to the activity class declares some variables in which to store references to the root container and first scene and obtains a reference to the root container view. The *getSceneForLayout()* method of the Scene class is then used to create a scene from the layout contained in the *scene1_layout.xml* file to convert that layout into a scene. The scene is then entered via the *enter()* method call so that it is displayed to the user.

Compile and run the application at this point and verify that scene 1 is displayed after the application has launched.

30.7 Loading Scene 2

Before implementing the transition between the first and second scene it is first necessary to add some code to load the layout from the *scene2_layout.xml* file into a Scene instance. Remaining in the *SceneTransitionsActivity.java* file, therefore, add this code as follows:

```
public class SceneTransitionsActivity extends ActionBarActivity {

    ViewGroup rootContainer;
    Scene scene1;
    Scene scene2;

    @Override
    protected void onCreate(Bundle savedInstanceState) {
        super.onCreate(savedInstanceState);
        setContentView(R.layout.activity_scene_transitions);

        rootContainer =
                (ViewGroup) findViewById(R.id.rootContainer);

        scene1 = Scene.getSceneForLayout(rootContainer,
                R.layout.scene1_layout, this);

        scene2 = Scene.getSceneForLayout(rootContainer,
                R.layout.scene2_layout, this);

        scene1.enter();
    }
```

```
    .
}
```

30.8 Implementing the Transitions

The first and second buttons have been configured to call methods named *goToScene2* and *goToScene1* respectively when selected. As the method names suggest, it is the responsibility of these methods to trigger the transitions between the two scenes. Add these two methods within the *SceneTransitionsActivity.java* file so that they read as follows:

```
public void goToScene2 (View view)
{
        TransitionManager.go(scene2);
}

public void goToScene1 (View view)
{
        TransitionManager.go(scene1);
}
```

Run the application and note that selecting the first two buttons causes the layout to switch between the two scenes. Since we have yet to configure any transitions, these layout changes are not yet animated.

30.9 Adding the Transition File

All of the transition effects for this project will be implemented within a single transition XML resource file. As outlined in the chapter entitled *Animating User Interfaces with the Android Transitions Framework*, transition resource files must be placed in the *app -> res -> transition* folder of the project. Begin, therefore, by right-clicking on the *res* folder in the Project tool window and selecting the *New -> Directory* menu option. In the resulting dialog, name the new folder *transition* and click on the *OK* button. Right-click on the new transition folder, this time selecting the *New -> File* option and name the new file *transition.xml*.

With the newly created *transition.xml* file selected and loaded into the editing panel, add the following XML content to add a transition set that enables the change bounds transition animation with a duration attribute setting:

```
<?xml version="1.0" encoding="utf-8"?>

<transitionSet
  xmlns:android="http://schemas.android.com/apk/res/android">
```

```
    <changeBounds
        android:duration="2000">
    </changeBounds>

</transitionSet>
```

30.10 Loading and Using the Transition Set

Although a transition resource file has been created and populated with a change bounds transition, this will have no effect until some code is added to load the transitions into a TransitionManager instance and reference it in the scene changes. The changes to achieve this are as follows:

```
package com.ebookfrenzy.scenetransitions;

import android.support.v7.app.ActionBarActivity;
import android.os.Bundle;
import android.view.Menu;
import android.view.MenuItem;
import android.transition.Scene;
import android.transition.Transition;
import android.transition.TransitionInflater;
import android.transition.TransitionManager;
import android.view.ViewGroup;
import android.view.View;

public class SceneTransitionsActivity extends ActionBarActivity {

        ViewGroup rootContainer;
        Scene scene1;
        Scene scene2;
        Transition transitionMgr;

        @Override
        protected void onCreate(Bundle savedInstanceState) {
                super.onCreate(savedInstanceState);
                setContentView(R.layout.activity_scene_transitions);

                rootContainer =
                        (ViewGroup) findViewById(R.id.rootContainer);

                transitionMgr = TransitionInflater.from(this)
                        .inflateTransition(R.transition.transition);

                scene1 = Scene.getSceneForLayout(rootContainer,
```

```
                        R.layout.scene1_layout, this);

                scene2 = Scene.getSceneForLayout(rootContainer,
                        R.layout.scene2_layout, this);

                scene1.enter();
        }

        public void goToScene2 (View view)
        {
                TransitionManager.go(scene2, transitionMgr);
        }

        public void goToScene1 (View view)
        {
                TransitionManager.go(scene1, transitionMgr);
        }

.
.
.
}
```

When the application is now run the two buttons will gently glide to their new positions during the transition.

30.11 Configuring Additional Transitions

With the transition file integrated into the project, any number of additional transitions may be added to the file without the need to make any further changes to the Java source code of the activity. Take, for example, the following changes to the *transition.xml* file to add a bounce interpolator to the change bounds transition, introduce a fade-in transition targeted at the third button and to change the transitions such that they are performed sequentially:

```
<?xml version="1.0" encoding="utf-8"?>

<transitionSet
  xmlns:android="http://schemas.android.com/apk/res/android"
  android:transitionOrdering="sequential" >


        <fade
          android:duration="2000"
          android:fadingMode="fade_in">
```

```
        <targets>
            <target android:targetId="@id/button3" />
        </targets>
    </fade>


    <changeBounds
        android:duration="2000"
        android:interpolator="@android:anim/bounce_interpolator">
    </changeBounds>
</transitionSet>
```

Buttons one and two will now bounce on arriving at the end destinations and button three will gently fade back into view when transitioning to scene 1 from scene 2.

Take some time to experiment with different transitions and interpolators by making changes to the *transition.xml* file and re-running the application.

30.12 Summary

Scene based transitions provide a flexible approach to animating user interface layout changes within an Android application. This chapter has demonstrated the steps involved in animating the transition between the scenes represented by two layout resource files. In addition, the example also used a transition XML resource file to configure the transition animation effects between the two scenes.

31. An Overview of Android Intents

By this stage of the book, it should be clear that Android applications are comprised, among other things, of one or more activities. An area that has yet to be covered in extensive detail, however, is the mechanism by which one activity can trigger the launch of another activity. As outlined briefly in the chapter entitled *The Anatomy of an Android Application*, this is achieved primarily using *Intents*.

Prior to working through some Android Studio based example implementations of intents in the following chapters, the goal of this chapter is to provide an overview of intents in the form of *explicit intents* and *implicit intents* together with an introduction to *intent filters*.

31.1 **An Overview of Intents**

Intents (*android.content.Intent*) are the messaging system by which one activity is able to launch another activity. An activity can, for example, issue an intent to request the launch of another activity contained within the same application. Intents also, however, go beyond this concept by allowing an activity to request the services of any other appropriately registered activity on the device for which permissions are configured. Consider, for example, an activity contained within an application that requires a web page to be loaded and displayed to the user. Rather than the application having to contain a second activity to perform this task, the code can simply send an intent to the Android runtime requesting the services of any activity that has registered the ability to display a web page. The runtime system will match the request to available activities on the device and either launch the activity that matches or, in the event of multiple matches, allow the user to decide which activity to use.

Intents also allow for the transfer of data from the sending activity to the receiving activity. In the previously outlined scenario, for example, the sending activity would need to send the URL of the web page to be displayed to the second activity. Similarly, the receiving activity may also be configured to return results data to the sending activity when the required tasks are completed.

Though not covered until later chapters, it is also worth highlighting the fact that, in addition to launching activities, intents are also used to launch and communicate with services and broadcast receivers.

Intents are categorized as either *explicit* or *implicit.*

31.2 **Explicit Intents**

An *explicit intent* requests the launch of a specific activity by referencing the *component name* (which is actually the Java class name) of the target activity. This approach is most common when launching an activity residing in the same application as the sending activity (since the Java class name is known to the application developer).

An explicit intent is issued by creating a new instance of the Intent class, passing through the activity context and the component name of the activity to be launched. A call is then made to the *startActivity()* method, passing through the intent object as an argument. For example, the following code fragment issues an intent for the activity with the class name ActivityB to be launched:

```
Intent i = new Intent(this, ActivityB.class);
startActivity(i);
```

Data may be transmitted to the receiving activity by adding it to the intent object before it is started via calls to the *putExtra()* method of the intent object. Data must be added in the form of key-value pairs. The following code extends the previous example to add String and integer values with the keys "myString" and "myInt" respectively to the intent:

```
Intent i = new Intent(this, ActivityB.class);
i.putExtra("myString", "This is a message for ActivityB");
i.putExtra("myInt", 100);

startActivity(i);
```

The data is received at the target activity as part of a Bundle object which can be obtained via a call to *getIntent().getExtras()*. The *getIntent()* method of the Activity class returns the intent that started the activity, whilst the *getExtras()* method (of the Intent class) returns a Bundle object for that intent containing the data. For example, to extract the data values passed to ActivityB:

```
Bundle extras = getIntent().getExtras();

If (extras != null) {
    String myString = extras.getString("myString");
    int myInt = extras.getInt("myInt");
}
```

When using intents to launch other activities within the same application, it is essential that those activities be listed in the application manifest file. The following *AndroidManifest.xml* contents are correctly configured for an application containing activities named ActivityA and ActivityB:

```
<?xml version="1.0" encoding="utf-8"?>
```

```
<manifest xmlns:android="http://schemas.android.com/apk/res/android"
    package="com.ebookfrenzy.intent1.intent1" >

    <application
        android:icon="@mipmap/ic_launcher"
        android:label="@string/app_name" >
        <activity
            android:label="@string/app_name"
            android:name="com.ebookfrenzy.intent1.intent1.ActivityA" >
            <intent-filter >
                <action android:name="android.intent.action.MAIN" />
                <category
android:name="android.intent.category.LAUNCHER" />
            </intent-filter>
        </activity>
        <activity
            android:name="ActivityB"
            android:label="ActivityB" >
        </activity>
    </application>
</manifest>
```

31.3 Returning Data from an Activity

As the example in the previous section stands, whilst data is transferred to ActivityB, there is no way for data to be returned to the first activity (which we will call ActivityA). This can, however, be achieved by launching ActivityB as a *sub-activity* of ActivityA. An activity is started as a sub-activity by starting the intent with a call to the *startActivityForResult()* method instead of using *startActivity()*. In addition to the intent object, this method is also passed a *request code* value which can be used to identify the return data when the sub-activity returns. For example:

```
startActivityForResult(i, REQUEST_CODE);
```

In order to return data to the parent activity, the sub-activity must implement the *finish()* method, the purpose of which is to create a new intent object containing the data to be returned, and then calling the *setResult()* method of the enclosing activity, passing through a *result code* and the intent containing the return data. The result code is typically *RESULT_OK,* or *RESULT_CANCELED*, but may also be a custom value subject to the requirements of the developer. In the event that a sub-activity crashes, the parent activity will receive a *RESULT_CANCELED* result code.

The following code, for example, illustrates the code for a typical sub-activity *finish()* method:

```
public void finish() {
```

```
        Intent data = new Intent();

        data.putExtra("returnString1", "Message to parent activity");
        setResult(RESULT_OK, data);
        super.finish();
}
```

In order to obtain and extract the returned data, the parent activity must implement the *onActivityResult()* method, for example:

```
protected void onActivityResult(int requestCode, int resultCode,
Intent data)
{
    String returnString;
    if (resultCode == RESULT_OK && requestCode == REQUEST_CODE) {
        if (data.hasExtra("returnString1")) {
            returnString =
data.getExtras().getString("returnString1");
        }
    }
}
```

Note that the above method checks the returned request code value to make sure that it matches that passed through to the *startActivityForResult()* method. When starting multiple sub-activities it is especially important to use the request code to track which activity is currently returning results, since all will call the same *onActivityResult()* method on exit.

31.4 Implicit Intents

Unlike explicit intents, which reference the Java class name of the activity to be launched, implicit intents identify the activity to be launched by specifying the action to be performed and the type of data to be handled by the receiving activity. For example, an action type of ACTION_VIEW accompanied by the URL of a web page in the form of a URI object will instruct the Android system to search for, and subsequently launch, a web browser capable activity. The following implicit intent will, when executed on an Android device, result in the designated web page appearing in a Chrome web browser activity:

```
Intent i = new Intent(Intent.ACTION_VIEW,
                Uri.parse("http://www.ebookfrenzy.com"));
```

When the above implicit intent is issued by an activity, the Android system will search for activities on the device that have registered the ability to handle ACTION_VIEW requests on *http* scheme data using a process referred to as *intent resolution*. In the event that a single match is found, that activity will be launched. If more than one match is found, the user will be prompted to choose from the available activity options.

31.5 **Using Intent Filters**

Intent filters are the mechanism by which activities "advertise" supported actions and data handling capabilities to the Android intent resolution process. Continuing the example in the previous section, an activity capable of displaying web pages would include an intent filter section in its manifest file indicating support for ACTION_VIEW type intent requests on http scheme data.

It is important to note that both the sending and receiving activities must have requested permission for the type of action to be performed. This is achieved by adding *<uses-permission>* tags to the manifest files for both activities. For example, the following manifest lines request permission to access the internet and contacts database:

```
<uses-permission android:name="android.permission.READ_CONTACTS" />
<uses-permission android:name="android.permission.INTERNET"/>
```

The following *AndroidManifest.xml* file illustrates a configuration for an activity named *WebViewActivity* with intent filters and permissions enabled for internet access:

```
<?xml version="1.0" encoding="utf-8"?>
<manifest xmlns:android="http://schemas.android.com/apk/res/android"
    package="com.ebookfreny.WebView"
    android:versionCode="1"
    android:versionName="1.0" >

    <uses-sdk android:minSdkVersion="10" />

    <uses-permission android:name="android.permission.INTERNET" />

    <application
        android:icon="@mipmap/ic_launcher"
        android:label="@string/app_name" >
        <activity
            android:label="@string/app_name"
            android:name=".WebViewActivity" >
        <intent-filter >
            <action android:name="android.intent.action.VIEW" />
            <category
android:name="android.intent.category.DEFAULT" />
            <data android:scheme="http" />
        </intent-filter>
```

```
        </activity>
    </application>

</manifest>
```

31.6 Checking Intent Availability

It is generally unwise to assume that an activity will be available for a particular intent, especially since the absence of a matching action will typically result in the application crashing. Fortunately, it is possible to identify the availability of an activity for a specific intent before it is sent to the runtime system. The following method can be used to identify the availability of an activity for a specified intent action type:

```
public static boolean isIntentAvailable(Context context, String
action) {
    final PackageManager packageManager = context.getPackageManager();
    final Intent intent = new Intent(action);
    List<ResolveInfo> list =
            packageManager.queryIntentActivities(intent,
                PackageManager.MATCH_DEFAULT_ONLY);
    return list.size() > 0;
}
```

31.7 Summary

Intents are the messaging mechanism by which one Android activity can launch another. An explicit intent references a specific activity to be launched by referencing the receiving activity by class name. Explicit intents are typically, though not exclusively, used when launching activities contained within the same application. An implicit intent specifies the action to be performed and the type of data to be handled and lets the Android runtime find a matching intent to launch. Implicit intents are generally used when launching activities that reside in different applications.

An activity can send data to the receiving activity by bundling data into the intent object in the form of key-value pairs. Data may only be returned from an activity if it is started as a *sub-activity* of the sending activity.

Activities advertise capabilities to the Android intent resolution process through the specification of intent-filters in the application manifest file. Both sending and receiving activities must also request appropriate permissions to perform tasks such as accessing the device contact database or the internet.

Having covered the theory of intents, the next few chapters will work through the creation of some examples in Android Studio that put both explicit and implicit intents into action.

32. Android Explicit Intents – A Worked Example

The chapter entitled *An Overview of Android Intents* covered the theory of using intents to launch activities. This chapter will put this theory into practice through the creation of an example application.

The example Android Studio application project created in this chapter will demonstrate the use of an explicit intent to launch an activity, including the transfer of data between sending and receiving activities. The next chapter (*Android Implicit Intents – A Worked Example*) will demonstrate the use of implicit intents.

32.1 Creating the Explicit Intent Example Application

Launch Android Studio and create a new project, entering *ExplicitIntent* into the Application name field and *ebookfrenzy.com* as the Company Domain setting before clicking on the *Next* button.

On the form factors screen, enable the *Phone and Tablet* option and set the minimum SDK setting to API 8: Android 2.2 (Froyo). Continue to proceed through the screens, requesting the creation of a blank activity named *ActivityA* with a corresponding layout named *activity_a* and a menu resource file named *menu_activity_a.*

Click *Finish* to create the new project.

32.2 Designing the User Interface Layout for ActivityA

The user interface for ActivityA will consist of a RelativeLayout view containing EditText (Plain Text), TextView and Button views named *editText1*, *textView1* and *button1* respectively. Using the Project tool window, locate the *activity_a.xml* resource file for ActivityA (located under *app -> res -> layout*) and double click on it to load it into the Android Studio Designer tool. Either design the layout in Design mode, or switch to Text mode and enter the following XML. Note that the "Ask Question" text displayed on the button view has been extracted to a string resource named *ask_text.*

Android Explicit Intents – A Worked Example

If designing the user interface using the Designer tool in Design mode, be sure to edit the XML afterwards to add the *onClick* handler property for the button1 view, and note the layout width property of the EditView component has been set to 200dp:

```xml
<RelativeLayout
xmlns:android="http://schemas.android.com/apk/res/android"
    xmlns:tools="http://schemas.android.com/tools"
    android:layout_width="match_parent"
    android:layout_height="match_parent"
    android:paddingLeft="@dimen/activity_horizontal_margin"
    android:paddingRight="@dimen/activity_horizontal_margin"
    android:paddingTop="@dimen/activity_vertical_margin"
    android:paddingBottom="@dimen/activity_vertical_margin"
    tools:context=".ActivityA">

    <TextView
        android:layout_width="wrap_content"
        android:layout_height="wrap_content"
        android:textAppearance="?android:attr/textAppearanceLarge"
        android:text="Large Text"
        android:id="@+id/textView1"
        android:layout_centerVertical="true"
        android:layout_centerHorizontal="true" />

    <EditText
        android:layout_width="200dp"
        android:layout_height="wrap_content"
        android:id="@+id/editText1"
        android:layout_above="@+id/textView1"
        android:layout_centerHorizontal="true"
        android:layout_marginBottom="77dp" />

    <Button
        android:layout_width="wrap_content"
        android:layout_height="wrap_content"
        android:text="Ask Question"
        android:id="@+id/button1"
        android:layout_below="@+id/textView1"
        android:layout_centerHorizontal="true"
        android:onClick="onClick"
        android:layout_marginTop="56dp" />
</RelativeLayout>
```

As covered in *An Overview and Example of Android Event Handling*, the *android:onClick="onClick"* resource line in the above XML listing uses an alternative way to handle simple click events without having to implement an event listener in the Java code of the activity. By specifying the *onClick* event type and the method to be called when such an event is detected, it is quick and easy to wire up basic click event handling on a view. Once the *onClick()* method has been implemented in the *ActivityA.java* file, it will be called whenever the button is touched by the user.

Once the layout is complete, the user interface should resemble that illustrated in Figure 32-1:

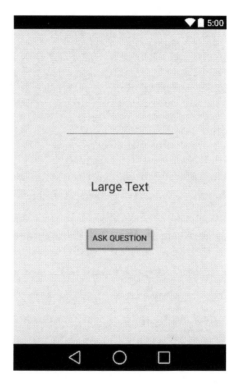

Figure 32-1

32.3 Creating the Second Activity Class

When the "Ask Question" button is touched by the user, an intent will be issued requesting that a second activity be launched into which an answer can be entered by the user. The next step, therefore, is to create the second activity. Within the Project tool window, right-click on the *com.ebookfrenzy.explicitintent* package name located in *app -> java* and select the *New -> Activity -> Blank Activity* menu option to display the *New Blank Activity* dialog as shown in Figure 32-2:

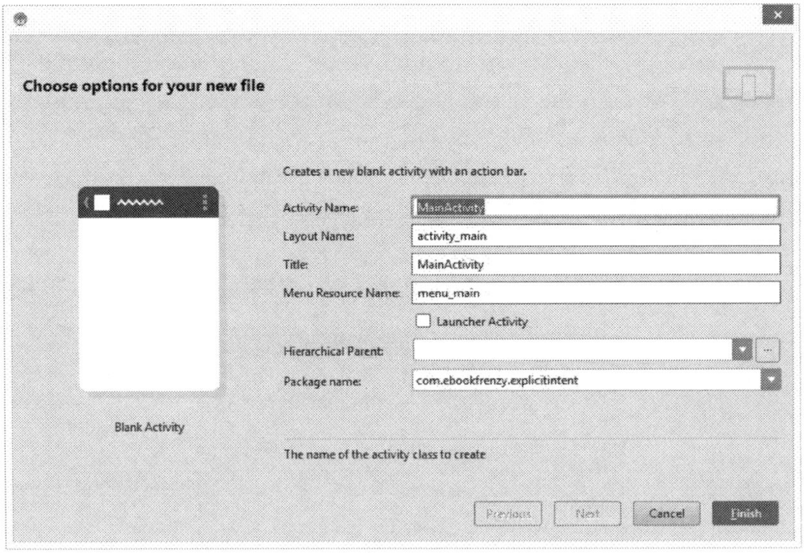

Figure 32-2

Enter *ActivityB* into the Activity Name and Title fields and name the layout and menu files *activity_b* and *menu_activity_b.* Since this activity will not be started when the application is launched (it will instead be launched via an intent by ActivityA when the button is pressed), it is important to make sure that the *Launcher Activity* option is disabled before clicking on the Finish button.

32.4 Designing the User Interface Layout for ActivityB

The only elements that are required for the user interface of the second activity are a Plain Text EditText, TextView and Button view. With these requirements in mind, modify the *activity_b.xml* layout in the Designer tool, either visually using Design mode or by directly inputting the following XML in Text mode. Note that the text on the button (which reads "Answer Question") has been extracted to a string resource named *answer_text*:

```
<RelativeLayout
xmlns:android="http://schemas.android.com/apk/res/android"
    xmlns:tools="http://schemas.android.com/tools"
    android:layout_width="match_parent"
    android:layout_height="match_parent"
tools:context=".ActivityB">

    <Button
        android:id="@+id/button1"
        android:layout_width="wrap_content"
        android:layout_height="wrap_content"
        android:layout_below="@+id/editText1"
```

```
                android:layout_centerHorizontal="true"
                android:layout_marginTop="86dp"
                android:onClick="onClick"
                android:text="@string/answer_text" />

        <TextView
                android:id="@+id/textView1"
                android:layout_width="wrap_content"
                android:layout_height="wrap_content"
                android:layout_alignParentTop="true"
                android:layout_centerHorizontal="true"
                android:layout_marginTop="35dp"
                android:text="Large Text"
                android:textAppearance="?android:attr/textAppearanceLarge" />

        <EditText
                android:id="@+id/editText1"
                android:layout_width="300dp"
                android:layout_height="wrap_content"
                android:layout_below="@+id/textView1"
                android:layout_centerHorizontal="true"
                android:layout_marginTop="66dp"
                android:ems="10"
                android:inputType="text" />

</RelativeLayout>
```

If designing the layout using the Designer tool in Design mode, note that the *onClick* property on the button view has been configured to call a method named *onClick()*, the width of the EditText view has been set to 300dp and the views have been assigned IDs *button1*, *TextView1* and *editText1*. The completed layout should resemble that illustrated in Figure 32-3:

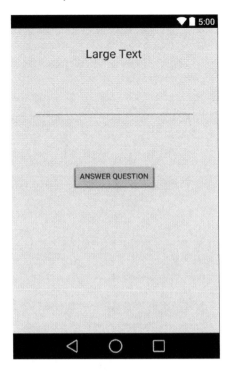

Figure 32-3

32.5 **Reviewing the Application Manifest File**

In order for ActivityA to be able to launch ActivityB using an intent, it is necessary that an entry for ActivityB be present in the *AndroidManifest.xml* file. Locate this file within the Project tool window (*app -> manifests*), double click on it to load it into the editor and verify that Android Studio has automatically added an entry for the activity:

```xml
<?xml version="1.0" encoding="utf-8"?>
<manifest xmlns:android="http://schemas.android.com/apk/res/android"
    package="com.ebookfrenzy.explicitintent" >

    <application
        android:allowBackup="true"
        android:icon="@mipmap/ic_launcher"
        android:label="@string/app_name"
        android:theme="@style/AppTheme" >
        <activity
android:name=".ActivityA"
            android:label="@string/app_name" >
            <intent-filter>
                <action android:name="android.intent.action.MAIN" />
```

```
                    <category
android:name="android.intent.category.LAUNCHER" />
            </intent-filter>
        </activity>
        <activity
            android:name=".ActivityB"
            android:label="@string/title_activity_activity_b" >
        </activity>
    </application>

</manifest>
```

With the second activity created and listed in the manifest file, it is now time to write some code in the ActivityA class to issue the intent.

32.6 Creating the Intent

The objective for ActivityA is to create and start an intent when the user touches the "Ask Question" button. As part of the intent creation process, the question string entered by the user into the EditText view will be added to the intent object as a key-value pair. When the user interface layout was created for ActivityA, the button object was configured to call a method named *onClick()* when "clicked" by the user. This method now needs to be added to the ActivityA class *ActivityA.java* source file as follows:

```
package com.ebookfrenzy.explicitintent;

import android.support.v7.app.ActionBarActivity;
import android.os.Bundle;
import android.view.Menu;
import android.view.MenuItem;
import android.content.Intent;
import android.view.View;
import android.widget.EditText;
import android.widget.TextView;

public class ActivityA extends ActionBarActivity {

    @Override
    protected void onCreate(Bundle savedInstanceState) {
        super.onCreate(savedInstanceState);
        setContentView(R.layout.activity_a);
    }
```

```
    public void onClick(View view) {

        Intent i = new Intent(this, ActivityB.class);

        final EditText editText1 = (EditText)
                findViewById(R.id.editText1);
        String myString = editText1.getText().toString();
        i.putExtra("qString", myString);
        startActivity(i);
    }
    .
    .
    .
}
```

The code for the *onClick()* method follows the techniques outlined in *An Overview of Android Intents*. First, a new Intent instance is created, passing through the current activity and the class name of ActivityB as arguments. Next, the text entered into the EditText object is added to the intent object as a key-value pair and the intent started via a call to *startActivity()*, passing through the intent object as an argument.

Compile and run the application and touch the "Ask Question" button to launch ActivityB and the back button to return to ActivityA.

32.7 **Extracting Intent Data**

Now that ActivityB is being launched from ActivityA, the next step is to extract the String data value included in the intent and assign it to the TextView object in the ActivityB user interface. This involves adding some code to the *onCreate()* method of ActivityB in the *ActivityB.java* source file:

```
package com.ebookfrenzy.explicitintent;

import android.app.Activity;
import android.os.Bundle;
import android.view.Menu;
import android.view.MenuItem;
import android.content.Intent;
import android.view.View;
import android.widget.TextView;
import android.widget.EditText;

public class ActivityB extends Activity {
```

```
        public void onCreate(Bundle savedInstanceState) {
          super.onCreate(savedInstanceState);
          setContentView(R.layout.activityb);

          Bundle extras = getIntent().getExtras();
                if (extras == null) {
                        return;
                }

                String qString = extras.getString("qString");

                final TextView textView = (TextView)
                  findViewById(R.id.textView1);
                textView.setText(qString);
        }
}
```

Compile and run the application either within an emulator or on a physical Android device. Enter a question into the text box in ActivityA before touching the "Ask Question" button. The question should now appear on the TextView component in the ActivityB user interface.

32.8 Launching ActivityB as a Sub-Activity

In order for ActivityB to be able to return data to ActivityA, ActivityB must be started as a *sub-activity* of ActivityA. This means that the call to *startActivity()* in the ActivityA *onClick()* method needs to be replaced with a call to *startActivityForResult()*. Unlike the *startActivity()* method, which takes only the intent object as an argument, *startActivityForResult()* requires that a request code also be passed through. The request code can be any number value and is used to identify which sub-activity is associated with which set of return data. For the purposes of this example, a request code of 5 will be used, giving us a modified ActivityA class that reads as follows:

```
public class ActivityA extends ActionBarActivity {

    private static final int request_code = 5;

    @Override
    public void onCreate(Bundle savedInstanceState) {
        super.onCreate(savedInstanceState);
        setContentView(R.layout.main);
    }

    public void onClick(View view) {
```

```
            Intent i = new Intent(this, ActivityB.class);

            final EditText editText1 = (EditText)
                    findViewById(R.id.editText1);
            String myString = editText1.getText().toString();
            i.putExtra("qString", myString);
            startActivityForResult(i, request_code);

      }
}
```

When the sub-activity exits, the *onActivityResult()* method of the parent activity is called and passed as arguments the request code associated with the intent, a result code indicating the success or otherwise of the sub-activity and an intent object containing any data returned by the sub-activity. Remaining within the ActivityA class source file, this method needs to be implemented as follows:

```
protected void onActivityResult(int requestCode, int resultCode,
Intent data) {
      if ((requestCode == request_code) &&
                  (resultCode == RESULT_OK)) {

            TextView textView1 =
                    (TextView) findViewById(R.id.textView1);

            String returnString =
                    data.getExtras().getString("returnData");

            textView1.setText(returnString);

      }
}
```

The code in the above method begins by checking that the request code matches the one used when the intent was issued and ensuring that the activity was successful. The return data is then extracted from the intent and displayed on the TextView object.

32.9 Returning Data from a Sub-Activity

ActivityB is now launched as a sub-activity of ActivityA, which has, in turn, been modified to handle data returned from ActivityB. All that remains is to modify *ActivityB.java* to implement the *finish()* method and to add code for the *onClick()* method, which is called when the "Answer Question" button is touched. The *finish()* method is triggered when an activity exits (for example when the user selects the back button on the device):

```
public void onClick(View view) {
```

```
            finish();
}

@Override
public void finish() {
      Intent data = new Intent();

      EditText editText1 = (EditText) findViewById(R.id.editText1);

      String returnString = editText1.getText().toString();
      data.putExtra("returnData", returnString);

      setResult(RESULT_OK, data);
      super.finish();
}
```

All that the *finish()* method needs to do is create a new intent, add the return data as a key-value pair and then call the *setResult()* method, passing through a result code and the intent object. The *onClick()* method simply calls the *finish()* method.

32.10 **Testing the Application**

Compile and run the application, enter a question into the text field on ActivityA and touch the "Ask Question" button. When ActivityB appears, enter the answer to the question and use either the back button or the "Submit Answer" button to return to ActivityA where the answer should appear in the text view object.

32.11 **Summary**

Having covered the basics of intents in the previous chapter, the goal of this chapter has been to work through the creation of an application project in Android Studio designed to demonstrate the use of explicit intents together with the concepts of data transfer between a parent activity and sub-activity.

The next chapter will work through an example designed to demonstrate implicit intents in action.

33. Android Implicit Intents – A Worked Example

In this chapter, an example application will be created in Android Studio designed to demonstrate a practical implementation of implicit intents. The goal will be to create and send an intent requesting that the content of a particular web page be loaded and displayed to the user. Since the example application itself will not contain an activity capable of performing this task, an implicit intent will be issued so that the Android intent resolution algorithm can be engaged to identify and launch a suitable activity from another application. This is most likely to be an activity from the Chrome web browser bundled with the Android operating system.

Having successfully launched the built-in browser, a new project will be created that also contains an activity capable of displaying web pages. This will be installed onto the device or emulator and used to demonstrate what happens when two activities match the criteria for an implicit intent.

33.1 Creating the Android Studio Implicit Intent Example Project

Launch Android Studio and create a new project, entering *ImplicitIntent* into the Application name field and *ebookfrenzy.com* as the Company Domain setting before clicking on the *Next* button.

On the form factors screen, enable the *Phone and Tablet* option and set the minimum SDK setting to API 8: Android 2.2 (Froyo). Continue to proceed through the screens, requesting the creation of a blank activity named *ImplicitIntentActivity* with corresponding layout and menu resource files named *activity_implicit_intent* and *menu_implicit_intent* respectively.

Click *Finish* to create the new project.

33.2 Designing the User Interface

The user interface for the *ImplicitIntentActivity* class is very simple, consisting solely of a RelativeLayout view and a button. Within the Project tool window, locate the *app -> res -> layout -> activity_implicit_intent.xml* file and double click on it to load it into the Designer tool. Visually construct the user interface in Design mode so that it resembles Figure 33-1, or enter the following XML in Text mode. Note that in both cases, the text on the button ("Show Web Page") has been extracted to a string resource named *button_text*:

```
<RelativeLayout
xmlns:android="http://schemas.android.com/apk/res/android"
    xmlns:tools="http://schemas.android.com/tools"
    android:layout_width="match_parent"
    android:layout_height="match_parent"

tools:context="com.ebookfrenzy.implicitintent.ImplicitIntentActivity">

    <Button
        android:id="@+id/button1"
        android:layout_width="wrap_content"
        android:layout_height="wrap_content"
        android:layout_centerHorizontal="true"
        android:layout_centerVertical="true"
        android:text="@string/button_text"
        android:onClick="showWebPage" />

</RelativeLayout>
```

Figure 33-1

Note the inclusion of the *onClick* property which will ensure that a method named *showWebPage()* (which has not yet been implemented) will be called when the button is "clicked" by the user.

33.3 **Creating the Implicit Intent**

As outlined above, the implicit intent will be created and issued from within a method named *showWebPage()* which, in turn, needs to be implemented in the *ImplicitIntentActivity* class, the code for which resides in the *ImplicitIntentActivity.java* source file. Locate this file in the Project tool window and double click on it to load it into an editing pane. Once loaded, modify the code to add the *showWebPage()* method together with a few requisite imports:

```
package com.ebookfrenzy.implicitintent;

import android.support.v7.app.ActionBarActivity;
import android.os.Bundle;
import android.view.Menu;
import android.view.MenuItem;
import android.net.Uri;
import android.content.Intent;
import android.view.View;

public class ImplicitIntentActivity extends ActionBarActivity {

    @Override
    protected void onCreate(Bundle savedInstanceState) {
        super.onCreate(savedInstanceState);
        setContentView(R.layout.activity_implicit_intent);
    }

    public void showWebPage(View view) {
        Intent intent = new Intent(Intent.ACTION_VIEW,
                Uri.parse("http://www.ebookfrenzy.com"));

        startActivity(intent);
    }
    .
    .
    .
}
```

The tasks performed by this method are actually very simple. First, a new intent object is created. Instead of specifying the class name of the intent, however, the code simply indicates the nature of the intent (to display something to the user) using the ACTION_VIEW option. The intent object also includes a URI containing the URL to be displayed. This indicates to the Android intent resolution system that the activity is requesting that a web page be displayed. The intent is then issued via a call to the *startActivity()* method.

Compile and run the application on either an emulator or a physical Android device and, once running, touch the *Show Web Page* button. When touched, a web browser view should appear and load the web page designated by the URL. A successful implicit intent has now been executed.

33.4 **Adding a Second Matching Activity**

The remainder of this chapter will be used to demonstrate the effect of the presence of more than one activity installed on the device matching the requirements for an implicit intent. To achieve this, a second application will be created and installed on the device or emulator. Begin, therefore, by creating a new project within Android Studio with the application name set to *MyWebView*, using the same SDK configuration options used when creating the ImplicitIntent project earlier in this chapter. Select a blank activity and, when prompted, name the activity *MyWebViewActivity* and the layout and menu resource files *activity_my_web_view* and *menu_my_web_view*.

33.5 **Adding the Web View to the UI**

The user interface for the sole activity contained within the new *MyWebView* project is going to consist of an instance of the Android WebView widget. Within the Project tool window, locate the *activity_my_web_view.xml* file containing the user interface description for the activity and double click on it to load it into the Designer tool. With the Designer tool in Design mode, select the default TextView widget and remove it from the layout using the keyboard delete key. Switch Designer to Text mode and edit the XML to remove the padding properties and TextView element so that the file reads as follows:

```
<RelativeLayout
xmlns:android="http://schemas.android.com/apk/res/android"
    xmlns:tools="http://schemas.android.com/tools"
    android:layout_width="match_parent"
    android:layout_height="match_parent"
    android:paddingLeft="@dimen/activity_horizontal_margin"
    android:paddingRight="@dimen/activity_horizontal_margin"
    android:paddingTop="@dimen/activity_vertical_margin"
    android:paddingBottom="@dimen/activity_vertical_margin"
    tools:context=".MyWebViewActivity">

    <TextView
        android:text="@string/hello_world"
        android:layout_width="wrap_content"
```

```
        android:layout_height="wrap_content" />

</RelativeLayout>
```

Return the Designer tool to Design mode and drag and drop a WebView object from the *Widgets* section of the palette onto the existing RelativeLayout view. Set the layout height and width properties to *match_parent* using either the Designer toolbar buttons or the Properties panel so that the WebView fills the entire display area as illustrated in Figure 33-2:

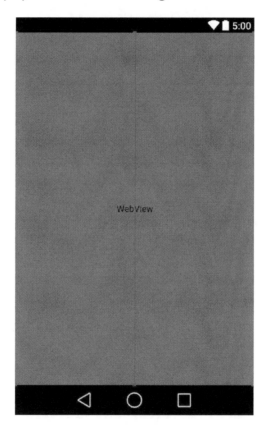

Figure 33-2

Double-click on the WebView instance and change the ID to *webView1*.

33.6 Obtaining the Intent URL

When the implicit intent object is created to display a web browser window, the URL of the web page to be displayed will be bundled into the intent object within a Uri object. The task of the *onCreate()* method within the *MyWebViewActivity* class is to extract this Uri from the intent object, convert it into a URL string and assign it to the WebView object. To implement this functionality, modify the *onCreate()* method in *MyWebViewActivity.java* so that it reads as follows:

```
package com.ebookfrenzy.mywebview;

import android.support.v7.app.ActionBarActivity;
import android.os.Bundle;
import android.view.Menu;
import android.view.MenuItem;
import java.net.URL;
import android.net.Uri;
import android.content.Intent;
import android.webkit.WebView;

public class MyWebViewActivity extends ActionBarActivity {

    @Override
    protected void onCreate(Bundle savedInstanceState) {
        super.onCreate(savedInstanceState);
        setContentView(R.layout.activity_my_web_view);

        Intent intent = getIntent();

        Uri data = intent.getData();
        URL url = null;

        try {
            url = new URL(data.getScheme(),
                    data.getHost(),
                    data.getPath());
        } catch (Exception e) {
            e.printStackTrace();
        }

        WebView webView = (WebView) findViewById(R.id.webView1);
        webView.loadUrl(url.toString());
    }
    .
    .
    .
}
```

The new code added to the *onCreate()* method performs the following tasks:

- Obtains a reference to the intent which caused this activity to be launched
- Extracts the Uri data from the intent object

- Converts the Uri data to a URL object
- Obtains a reference to the WebView object in the user interface
- Loads the URL into the web view, converting the URL to a String in the process

The coding part of the MyWebView project is now complete. All that remains is to modify the manifest file.

33.7 **Modifying the MyWebView Project Manifest File**

There are a number of changes that must be made to the MyWebView manifest file before it can be tested. In the first instance, the activity will need to seek permission to access the internet (since it will be required to load a web page). This is achieved by adding the appropriate permission line to the manifest file:

```
<uses-permission android:name="android.permission.INTERNET" />
```

Further, a review of the contents of the intent filter section of the *AndroidManifest.xml* file for the MyWebView project will reveal the following settings:

```
<intent-filter >
        <action android:name="android.intent.action.MAIN" />
        <category android:name="android.intent.category.LAUNCHER" />
</intent-filter>
```

In the above XML, the *android.intent.action.MAIN* entry indicates that this activity is the point of entry for the application when it is launched without any data input. The *android.intent.category.LAUNCHER* directive, on the other hand, indicates that the activity should be listed within the application launcher screen of the device.

Since the activity is not required to be launched as the entry point to an application, cannot be run without data input (in this case a URL) and is not required to appear in the launcher, neither the MAIN nor LAUNCHER directives are required in the manifest file for this activity.

The intent filter for the *MyWebViewActivity* activity does, however, need to be modified to indicate that it is capable of handling ACTION_VIEW intent actions for http data schemes.

Android also requires that any activities capable of handling implicit intents that do not include MAIN and LAUNCHER entries also include the so-called *default category* in the intent filter. The modified intent filter section should, therefore, read as follows:

```
<intent-filter >
        <action android:name="android.intent.action.VIEW" />
        <category android:name="android.intent.category.DEFAULT" />
```

```
            <data android:scheme="http" />
</intent-filter>
```

Bringing these requirements together results in the following complete *AndroidManifest.xml* file:

```
<?xml version="1.0" encoding="utf-8"?>
<manifest xmlns:android="http://schemas.android.com/apk/res/android"
    package="com.ebookfrenzy.mywebview" >

    <uses-permission android:name="android.permission.INTERNET" />

    <application
        android:allowBackup="true"
        android:icon="@mipmap/ic_launcher"
        android:label="@string/app_name"
        android:theme="@style/AppTheme" >
        <activity
            android:name=".MyWebViewActivity"
            android:label="@string/app_name" >
            <intent-filter >
                <action android:name="android.intent.action.VIEW" />
                <category
                    android:name="android.intent.category.DEFAULT"
/>
                <data android:scheme="http" />
            </intent-filter>

        </activity>
    </application>

</manifest>
```

Load the *AndroidManifest.xml* file into the manifest editor by double clicking on the file name in the Project tool window. Once loaded, modify the XML to match the above changes.

Having made the appropriate modifications to the manifest file, the new activity is ready to be installed on the device.

33.8 Installing the MyWebView Package on a Device

Before the MyWebViewActivity can be used as the recipient of an implicit intent, it must first be installed onto the device. This is achieved by running the application in the normal manner. Because the manifest file contains neither the *android.intent.action.MAIN* nor the *android.intent.category.LAUNCHER* directives, however, Android Studio does not know whether or not to launch the activity once the application has been installed on the device. Consequently, Android Studio will display the *Edit configuration* dialog illustrated in Figure 33-3 when the application is run, requesting instructions on how to proceed once the application package has been installed.

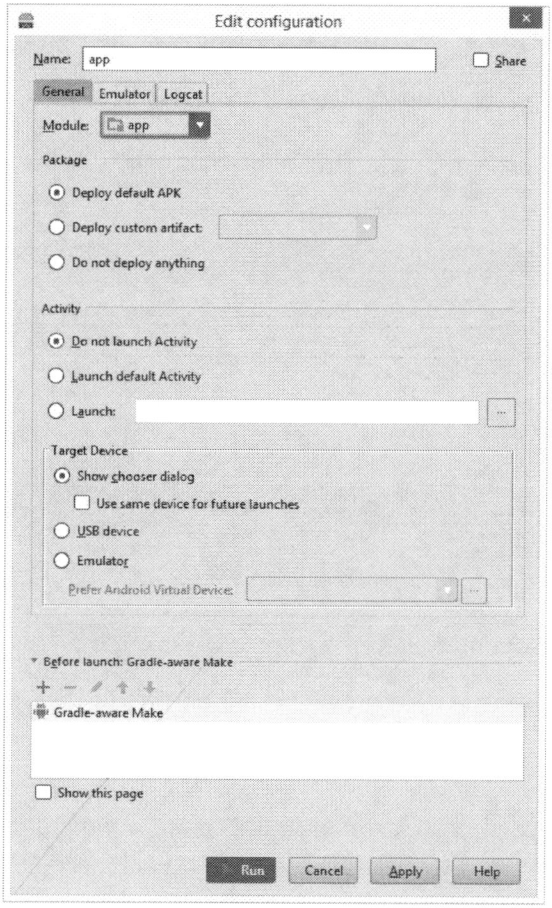

Figure 33-3

Within the Activity section of the configuration dialog, select the *Do not launch Activity* option so that the activity is installed but not launched and click on the *Run* button. The successful installation of the package will be reported in the Android Studio *Run* tool window:

```
Installing com.ebookfrenzy.mywebview
DEVICE SHELL COMMAND: pm install -r
"/data/local/tmp/com.ebookfrenzy.mywebview"
pkg: /data/local/tmp/com.ebookfrenzy.mywebview
Success
```

Once the installation is completed, the activity is ready to be included in the Android framework's intent resolution process.

33.9 **Testing the Application**

In order to test MyWebView, simply re-launch the *ImplicitIntent* application created earlier in this chapter and touch the *Show Web Page* button. This time, however, the intent resolution process will find two activities with intent filters matching the implicit intent. As such, the system will display a dialog (Figure 33-4) providing the user with the choice of activity to launch.

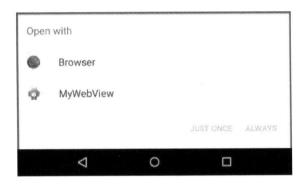

Figure 33-4

Selecting the *MyWebView* option followed by the *Just once* button should cause the intent to be handled by our new *MyWebViewActivity*, which will subsequently appear and display the designated web page.

If the web page loads into the Chrome browser without the above selection dialog appearing, it may be that Chrome has been configured as the default browser on the device. This can be changed by going to *Settings -> Apps* on the device and choosing the *ALL* category. Scroll down the list of apps and select *Chrome*. On the Chrome app info screen, touch the *Clear Defaults* button.

33.10 **Summary**

Implicit intents provide a mechanism by which one activity can request the service of another simply by specifying an action type and, optionally, the data on which that action is to be performed. In order to be eligible as a target candidate for an implicit intent, however, an activity must be configured to extract the appropriate data from the inbound intent object and be included in a correctly configured manifest file, including appropriate permissions and intent filters. When more than one matching activity for an implicit intent is found during an intent resolution search, the user is prompted to make a choice as to which to use.

Within this chapter an example has been created to demonstrate both the issuing of an implicit intent, and the creation of an example activity capable of handling such an intent.

Chapter 34

34. Android Broadcast Intents and Broadcast Receivers

In addition to providing a mechanism for launching application activities, intents are also used as a way to broadcast system wide messages to other components on the system. This involves the implementation of Broadcast Intents and Broadcast Receivers, both of which are the topic of this chapter.

34.1 An Overview of Broadcast Intents

Broadcast intents are Intent objects that are broadcast via a call to the *sendBroadcast()*, *sendStickyBroadcast()* or *sendOrderedBroadcast()* methods of the Activity class (the latter being used when results are required from the broadcast). In addition to providing a messaging and event system between application components, broadcast intents are also used by the Android system to notify interested applications about key system events (such as the external power supply or headphones being connected or disconnected).

When a broadcast intent is created, it must include an *action string* in addition to optional data and a category string. As with standard intents, data is added to a broadcast intent using key-value pairs in conjunction with the *putExtra()* method of the intent object. The optional category string may be assigned to a broadcast intent via a call to the *addCategory()* method.

The action string, which identifies the broadcast event, must be unique and typically uses the application's Java package name syntax. For example, the following code fragment creates and sends a broadcast intent including a unique action string and data:

```
Intent intent = new Intent();
intent.setAction("com.example.Broadcast");
intent.putExtra("MyData", 1000);
sendBroadcast(intent);
```

The above code would successfully launch the corresponding broadcast receiver on a device running an Android version earlier than 3.0. On more recent versions of Android, however, the intent would not be received by the broadcast receiver. This is because Android 3.0 introduced a launch control security measure that prevents components of *stopped* applications from being launched via an intent. An application is considered to be in a stopped state if the application has either just been installed and not previously launched, or been manually stopped by the user using the application manager on the device. To get around this, however, a flag can be added to the intent before it is sent to indicate that the intent is to be allowed to start a component of a stopped application. This flag is FLAG_INCLUDE_STOPPED_PACKAGES and would be used as outlined in the following adaptation of the previous code fragment:

```
Intent intent = new Intent();
intent.addFlags(Intent.FLAG_INCLUDE_STOPPED_PACKAGES);
intent.setAction("com.example.Broadcast");
intent.putExtra("MyData", 1000);
sendBroadcast(intent);
```

34.2 **An Overview of Broadcast Receivers**

An application listens for specific broadcast intents by registering a *broadcast receiver*. Broadcast receivers are implemented by extending the Android BroadcastReceiver class and overriding the *onReceive()* method. The broadcast receiver may then be registered, either within code (for example within an activity), or within a manifest file. Part of the registration implementation involves the creation of intent filters to indicate the specific broadcast intents the receiver is required to listen for. This is achieved by referencing the *action string* of the broadcast intent. When a matching broadcast is detected, the *onReceive()* method of the broadcast receiver is called, at which point the method has 5 seconds within which to perform any necessary tasks before returning. It is important to note that a broadcast receiver does not need to be running all the time. In the event that a matching intent is detected, the Android runtime system will automatically start up the broadcast receiver before calling the *onReceive()* method.

The following code outlines a template Broadcast Receiver subclass:

```
package com.example.broadcastdetector;

import android.content.BroadcastReceiver;
import android.content.Context;
import android.content.Intent;

public class MyReceiver extends BroadcastReceiver {

        public MyReceiver() {
        }

        @Override
```

```
        public void onReceive(Context context, Intent intent) {
            // Implement code here to be performed when
            // broadcast is detected
        }
}
```

When registering a broadcast receiver within a manifest file, a *<receiver>* entry must be added containing one or more intent filters, each containing the action string of the broadcast intent for which the receiver is required to listen.

The following example manifest file registers the above example broadcast receiver to listen for broadcast intents containing an action string of *com.example.Broadcast*:

```
<?xml version="1.0" encoding="utf-8"?>
<manifest xmlns:android="http://schemas.android.com/apk/res/android"
    package=" com.example.broadcastdetector.broadcastdetector "
    android:versionCode="1"
    android:versionName="1.0" >

    <uses-sdk android:minSdkVersion="17" />

    <application
        android:icon="@mipmap/ic_launcher"
        android:label="@string/app_name" >
        <receiver android:name="MyReceiver" >
            <intent-filter>
                <action android:name="com.example.Broadcast" >
                    </action>
            </intent-filter>
        </receiver>
    </application>
</manifest>
```

The same effect can be achieved by registering the broadcast receiver in code using the *registerReceiver()* method of the Activity class together with an appropriately configured IntentFilter object:

```
IntentFilter filter = new IntentFilter("com.example.Broadcast");

MyReceiver receiver = new MyReceiver();
registerReceiver(receiver, filter);
```

When a broadcast receiver registered in code is no longer required, it may be unregistered via a call to the *unregisterReceiver()* method of the activity class, passing through a reference to the receiver object as an argument. For example, the following code will unregister the above broadcast receiver:

```
unregisterReceiver(receiver);
```

It is important to keep in mind that some system broadcast intents can only be detected by a broadcast receiver if it is registered in code rather than in the manifest file. Check the Android Intent class documentation for a detailed overview of the system broadcast intents and corresponding requirements online at:

http://developer.android.com/reference/android/content/Intent.html

34.3 **Obtaining Results from a Broadcast**

When a broadcast intent is sent using the *sendBroadcast()* method, there is no way for the initiating activity to receive results from any broadcast receivers that pick up the broadcast. In the event that return results are required, it is necessary to use the *sendOrderedBroadcast()* method instead. When a broadcast intent is sent using this method, it is delivered in sequential order to each broadcast receiver with a registered interest.

The *sendOrderedBroadcast()* method is called with a number of arguments including a reference to another broadcast receiver (known as the *result receiver*) which is to be notified when all other broadcast receivers have handled the intent, together with a set of data references into which those receivers can place result data. When all broadcast receivers have been given the opportunity to handle the broadcast, the *onReceive()* method of the *result receiver* is called and passed the result data.

34.4 **Sticky Broadcast Intents**

By default, broadcast intents disappear once they have been sent and handled by any interested broadcast receivers. A broadcast intent can, however, be defined as being "sticky". A sticky intent, and the data contained therein, remains present in the system after it has completed. The data stored within a sticky broadcast intent can be obtained via the return value of a call to the *registerReceiver()* method, using the usual arguments (references to the broadcast receiver and intent filter object). Many of the Android system broadcasts are sticky, a prime example being those broadcasts relating to battery level status.

A sticky broadcast may be removed at any time via a call to the *removeStickyBroadcast()* method, passing through as an argument a reference to the broadcast intent to be removed.

34.5 **The Broadcast Intent Example**

The remainder of this chapter will work through the creation of an Android Studio based example of broadcast intents in action. In the first instance, a simple application will be created for the purpose of issuing a custom broadcast intent. A corresponding broadcast receiver will then be created that will display a message on the display of the Android device when the broadcast is detected. Finally, the broadcast receiver will be modified to detect notification by the system that external power has been disconnected from the device.

34.6 **Creating the Example Application**

Launch Android Studio and create a new project, entering *SendBroadcast* into the Application name field and *ebookfrenzy.com* as the Company Domain setting before clicking on the *Next* button.

On the form factors screen, enable the *Phone and Tablet* option and set the minimum SDK setting to API 8: Android 2.2 (Froyo). Continue to proceed through the screens, requesting the creation of a blank activity named *SendBroadcastActivity* with corresponding layout and menu resource files named *activity_send_broadcast* and *menu_send_broadcast* respectively.

Once the new project has been created, locate and load the *activity_send_broadcast.xml* layout file located in the Project tool window under *app -> res -> layout* and, with the Designer tool in Design mode, replace the TextView object with a Button view. Move the button to the center of the display, double click on it and set the text property so that it reads "Send Broadcast". Once the text value has been set, use the light bulb menu icon to extract the string to a resource named *button_text*.

With the button still selected in the layout, locate the *onClick* property in the Properties panel and configure it to call a method named *broadcastIntent.* A useful shortcut for finding properties is to click on the toolbar of the Properties panel and start typing the first few characters of the property name. This will trigger the search system and begin selecting the best matches for the property name.

34.7 **Creating and Sending the Broadcast Intent**

Having created the framework for the *SendBroadcast* application, it is now time to implement the code to send the broadcast intent. This involves implementing the *broadcastIntent()* method specified previously as the *onClick* target of the Button view in the user interface. Locate and double click on the *SendBroadcastActivity.java* file and modify it to add the code to create and send the broadcast intent. Once modified, the source code for this class should read as follows:

```
package com.ebookfrenzy.sendbroadcast;

import android.support.v7.app.ActionBarActivity;
import android.os.Bundle;
```

```
import android.view.Menu;
import android.view.MenuItem;
import android.content.Intent;
import android.view.View;

public class SendBroadcastActivity extends ActionBarActivity {

    @Override
    protected void onCreate(Bundle savedInstanceState) {
        super.onCreate(savedInstanceState);
        setContentView(R.layout.activity_send_broadcast);
    }

    public void broadcastIntent(View view)
    {
        Intent intent = new Intent();
        intent.setAction("com.ebookfrenzy.sendbroadcast");
        intent.addFlags(Intent.FLAG_INCLUDE_STOPPED_PACKAGES);
        sendBroadcast(intent);
    }
    .
    .
    .
}
```

Note that, in this instance, the action string for the intent is *com.ebookfrenzy.sendbroadcast*. When the broadcast receiver class is created in later sections of this chapter, it is essential that the intent filter declaration match this action string.

This concludes the creation of the application to send the broadcast intent. All that remains is to build a matching broadcast receiver.

34.8 Creating the Broadcast Receiver

In order to create the broadcast receiver, a new class needs to be created which subclasses the BroadcastReceiver superclass. Create a new project with the application name set to *BroadcastReceiver* and the company domain name set to *com.ebookfrenzy*, this time selecting the *Add No Activity* option before clicking on *Finish*.

Within the Project tool window, navigate to *app -> java* and right-click on the package name. From the resulting menu, select the *New -> Other -> Broadcast Receiver* menu option, name the class *MyReceiver* and make sure the *Exported* and *Enabled* options are selected. These settings allow the

Android system to launch the receiver when needed and ensure that the class can receive messages sent by other applications on the device. With the class configured, click on *Finish*.

Once created, Android Studio will automatically load the new *MyReceiver.java* class file into the editor where it should read as follows:

```
package com.ebookfrenzy.broadcastreceiver;

import android.content.BroadcastReceiver;
import android.content.Context;
import android.content.Intent;

public class MyReceiver extends BroadcastReceiver {

    public MyReceiver() {
    }

    @Override
    public void onReceive(Context context, Intent intent) {
        // TODO: This method is called when the BroadcastReceiver is
receiving
        // an Intent broadcast.
        throw new UnsupportedOperationException("Not yet
implemented");
    }
}
```

As can be seen in the code, Android Studio has generated a template for the new class and generated a stub for the *onReceive()* method. A number of changes now need to be made to the class to implement the required behavior. Remaining in the *MyReceiver.java* file, therefore, modify the code so that it reads as follows:

```
package com.ebookfrenzy.broadcastreceiver;

import android.content.BroadcastReceiver;
import android.content.Context;
import android.content.Intent;
import android.widget.Toast;

public class MyReceiver extends BroadcastReceiver {

    public MyReceiver() {
    }
```

```
@Override
public void onReceive(Context context, Intent intent) {

    Toast.makeText(context, "Broadcast Intent Detected.",
            Toast.LENGTH_LONG).show();
}
}
```

The code for the broadcast receiver is now complete.

34.9 Configuring a Broadcast Receiver in the Manifest File

In common with other Android projects, BroadcastReceiver has associated with it a manifest file named *AndroidManifest.xml.*

This file needs to publicize the presence of the broadcast receiver and must include an intent filter to specify the broadcast intents in which the receiver is interested. When the BroadcastReceiver class was created in the previous section, Android Studio automatically added a <receiver> element to the manifest file. All that remains, therefore, is to add an *<intent-filter>* element within the <receiver> declaration appropriately configured for the custom action string:

```
<?xml version="1.0" encoding="utf-8"?>
<manifest xmlns:android="http://schemas.android.com/apk/res/android"
    package="com.ebookfrenzy.broadcastreceiver.broadcastreceiver" >

    <application
        android:allowBackup="true"
        android:icon="@mipmap/ic_launcher"
        android:label="@string/app_name"
        android:theme="@style/AppTheme" >
        <receiver
android:name=".MyReceiver"
            android:enabled="true"
            android:exported="true" >
            <intent-filter>
                <action
                    android:name="com.ebookfrenzy.sendbroadcast" >
                </action>
            </intent-filter>
        </receiver>
    </application>
```

```
</manifest>
```

With the manifest file completed, the broadcast example is ready to be tested.

34.10 Testing the Broadcast Example

In order to test the broadcast sender and receiver, begin by running the BroadcastReceiver application on a physical Android device or AVD. When the *Edit configuration* dialog appears, select the *Do not launch Activity* option so that the activity is installed but not launched and click on the *Run* button. The successful installation of the package will be reported in the Android Studio *Run* tool window:

```
Uploading file
       local path:
C:\Users\Neil\AndroidStudioProjects\BroadcastReceiver\app\build\output
s\apk\app-debug.apk
       remote path: /data/local/tmp/com.ebookfrenzy.broadcastreceiver
Installing com.ebookfrenzy.broadcastreceiver
DEVICE SHELL COMMAND: pm install -r
"/data/local/tmp/com.ebookfrenzy.broadcastreceiver"
pkg: /data/local/tmp/com.ebookfrenzy.broadcastreceiver
Success
```

Once the receiver is installed, run the SendBroadcast application on the same device or AVD and wait for it to appear on the display. Once running, touch the button, at which point the toast message reading "Broadcast Intent Detected." should pop up for a few seconds before fading away.

In the event that the toast message does not appear, double check that the BroadcastReceiver application installed correctly and that the intent filter in the manifest file matches the action string used when the intent was broadcast.

34.11 Listening for System Broadcasts

The final stage of this example is to modify the intent filter for the *BroadcastReceiver* to listen also for the system intent that is broadcast when external power is disconnected from the device. The action that the receiver needs to be listening for in this context is *android.intent.action.ACTION_POWER_DISCONNECTED*. The modified manifest file for the BroadcastReceiver project should, therefore, now read as follows:

```
<manifest xmlns:android="http://schemas.android.com/apk/res/android"
    package="com.ebookfrenzy.broadcastreceiver.broadcastreceiver">

    <application android:allowBackup="true"
        android:label="@string/app_name"
        android:icon="@mipmap/ic_launcher"
```

```
        android:theme="@style/AppTheme">

        <receiver android:name=".MyReceiver"
            android:enabled="true"
            android:exported="true" >
            <intent-filter>
                <action
        android:name="com.ebookfrenzy.sendbroadcast" >
                </action>
                <action
        android:name="android.intent.action.ACTION_POWER_DISCONNECTED" >
                </action>

            </intent-filter>
        </receiver>

    </application>

</manifest>
```

Since the *onReceive()* method is now going to be listening for two types of broadcast intent, it is worthwhile modifying the code so that the action string of the current intent is also displayed in the toast message. This string can be obtained via a call to the *getAction()* method of the intent object passed as an argument to the *onReceive()* method:

```
public void onReceive(Context context, Intent intent) {
            String message = "Broadcast intent detected "
                    + intent.getAction();

            Toast.makeText(context, message,
                        Toast.LENGTH_LONG).show();
}
```

Test the receiver by re-installing the modified *BroadcastReceiver* package. Touching the button in the *SendBroadcast* application should now result in a new message containing the custom action string:

```
Broadcast intent detected com.ebookfrenzy.sendbroadcast
```

Next, remove the USB connector that is currently supplying power to the Android device, at which point the receiver should report the following in the toast message:

```
Broadcast intent detected
android.intent.action.ACTION_POWER_DISCONNECTED
```

34.12 **Summary**

Broadcast intents are a mechanism by which an intent can be issued for consumption by multiple components on an Android system. Broadcasts are detected by registering a Broadcast Receiver, which, in turn, is configured to listen for intents that match particular action strings. In general, broadcast receivers remain dormant until woken up by the system when a matching intent is detected. Broadcast intents are also used by the Android system to issue notifications of events such as a low battery warning or the connection or disconnection of external power to the device.

In addition to providing an overview of Broadcast intents and receivers, this chapter has also worked through an example of sending broadcast intents and the implementation of a broadcast receiver to listen for both custom and system broadcast intents.

35. A Basic Overview of Android Threads and Thread Handlers

The next chapter will be the first in a series of chapters intended to introduce the use of Android Services to perform application tasks in the background. It is impossible, however, to understand fully the steps involved in implementing services without first gaining a basic understanding of the concept of threading in Android applications. Threads and thread handlers are, therefore, the topic of this chapter.

35.1 An Overview of Threads

Threads are the cornerstone of any multitasking operating system and can be thought of as mini-processes running within a main process, the purpose of which is to enable at least the appearance of parallel execution paths within applications.

35.2 The Application Main Thread

When an Android application is first started, the runtime system creates a single thread in which all application components will run by default. This thread is generally referred to as the *main thread*. The primary role of the main thread is to handle the user interface in terms of event handling and interaction with views in the user interface. Any additional components that are started within the application will, by default, also run on the main thread.

Any component within an application that performs a time consuming task using the main thread will cause the entire application to appear to lock up until the task is completed. This will typically result in the operating system displaying an "Application is not responding" warning to the user. Clearly, this is far from the desired behavior for any application. In such a situation, this can be avoided simply by launching the task to be performed in a separate thread, allowing the main thread to continue unhindered with other tasks.

35.3 Thread Handlers

Clearly one of the key rules of Android development is never to perform time-consuming operations on the main thread of an application. The second, equally important rule is that the code within a separate thread must never, under any circumstances, directly update any aspect of the user interface.

Any changes to the user interface must always be performed from within the main thread. The reason for this is that the Android UI toolkit is not *thread-safe*. Attempts to work with non thread-safe code from within multiple threads will typically result in intermittent problems and unpredictable application behavior.

In the event that the code executing in a thread needs to interact with the user interface, it must do so by *synchronizing* with the main UI thread. This is achieved by creating a *handler* within the main thread, which, in turn, receives messages from another thread and updates the user interface accordingly.

35.4 **A Basic Threading Example**

The remainder of this chapter will work through some simple examples intended to provide a basic introduction to threads. The first step will be to highlight the importance of performing time-consuming tasks in a separate thread from the main thread. Begin, therefore, by creating a new project in Android Studio, entering *ThreadExample* into the Application name field and *ebookfrenzy.com* as the Company Domain setting before clicking on the *Next* button.

On the form factors screen, enable the *Phone and Tablet* option and set the minimum SDK setting to API 8: Android 2.2 (Froyo). Continue to proceed through the screens, requesting the creation of a blank activity named *ThreadExampleActivity*, using the defaults for the layout and menu resource files.

Click *Finish* to create the new project.

Load the *activity_thread_example.xml* file for the project into the Designer tool. Double click on the TextView component and change the ID for the view to *myTextView*. Next, click and drag the TextView so that it is positioned in the center of the display canvas.

Add a Button view to the user interface, positioned directly beneath the existing TextView object as illustrated in Figure 35-1:

Figure 35-1

Double click on the button view and change the text to "Press Me". Extract the string to a resource named *button_text*. With the button view still selected in the layout, locate the *onClick* property in the Properties panel and enter *buttonClick* as the method name.

Once completed, the XML file content should be similar to the following listing:

```
<RelativeLayout
xmlns:android="http://schemas.android.com/apk/res/android"
    xmlns:tools="http://schemas.android.com/tools"
    android:layout_width="match_parent"
    android:layout_height="match_parent"
    android:paddingLeft="@dimen/activity_horizontal_margin"
    android:paddingRight="@dimen/activity_horizontal_margin"
    android:paddingTop="@dimen/activity_vertical_margin"
    android:paddingBottom="@dimen/activity_vertical_margin"
tools:context=".ThreadExampleActivity">

    <TextView
        android:text="@string/hello_world"
        android:layout_width="wrap_content"
        android:layout_height="wrap_content"
        android:layout_centerVertical="true"
        android:layout_centerHorizontal="true"
```

```
        android:id="@+id/myTextView" />

    <Button
        android:layout_width="wrap_content"
        android:layout_height="wrap_content"
        android:text="@string/button_string"
        android:id="@+id/button"
        android:layout_below="@+id/myTextView"
        android:layout_centerHorizontal="true"
        android:layout_marginTop="45dp"
        android:onClick="buttonClick" />

</RelativeLayout>
```

Next, load the *ThreadExampleActivity.java* file into an editing panel and add code to implement the *buttonClick()* method which will be called when the Button view is touched by the user. Since the goal here is to demonstrate the problem of performing lengthy tasks on the main thread, the code will simply pause for 20 seconds before displaying different text on the TextView object:

```
package com.ebookfrenzy.threadexample;

import android.support.v7.app.ActionBarActivity;
import android.os.Bundle;
import android.view.Menu;
import android.view.MenuItem;
import android.view.View;
import android.widget.TextView;

public class ThreadExampleActivity extends ActionBarActivity {

    @Override
    protected void onCreate(Bundle savedInstanceState) {
        super.onCreate(savedInstanceState);
        setContentView(R.layout.activity_thread_example);
    }

    public void buttonClick(View view)
    {
        long endTime = System.currentTimeMillis() + 20*1000;

        while (System.currentTimeMillis() < endTime) {
            synchronized (this) {
                try {
```

```
                        wait(endTime - System.currentTimeMillis());
                } catch (Exception e) {
                }
            }
        }
        TextView myTextView =
                (TextView)findViewById(R.id.myTextView);
        myTextView.setText("Button Pressed");
    }
    .
    .
    .
}
```

With the code changes complete, run the application on either a physical device or an emulator. Once the application is running, touch the Button, at which point the application will appear to freeze. It will, for example, not be possible to touch the button a second time and in some situations the operating system will, as demonstrated in Figure 35-2, report the application as being unresponsive:

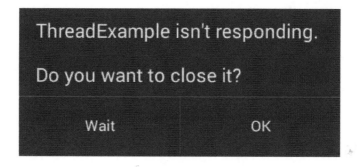

Figure 35-2

Clearly, anything that is going to take time to complete within the *buttonClick()* method needs to be performed within a separate thread.

35.5 Creating a New Thread

In order to create a new thread, the code to be executed in that thread needs to be placed within the *Run()* method of a *Runnable* instance. A new Thread object then needs to be created, passing through a reference to the Runnable instance to the constructor. Finally, the *start()* method of the thread object needs to be called to start the thread running. To perform the task within the *buttonClick()* method, therefore, the following changes need to be made:

```
public void buttonClick(View view)
{
```

```
    Runnable runnable = new Runnable() {
        public void run() {

            long endTime = System.currentTimeMillis()
                                + 20*1000;

            while (System.currentTimeMillis() < endTime) {
                synchronized (this) {
                    try {
                        wait(endTime -
                            System.currentTimeMillis());
                    } catch (Exception e) {}
                }
            }
        }
    };
    Thread mythread = new Thread(runnable);
    mythread.start();
}
```

When the application is now run, touching the button causes the delay to be performed in a new thread leaving the main thread to continue handling the user interface, including responding to additional button presses. In fact, each time the button is touched, a new thread will be created, allowing the task to be performed multiple times concurrently.

A close inspection of the updated code for the *buttonClick()* method will reveal that the code to update the TextView has been removed. As previously stated, updating a user interface element from within a thread other than the main thread violates a key rule of Android development. In order to update the user interface, therefore, it will be necessary to implement a Handler for the thread.

35.6 Implementing a Thread Handler

Thread handlers are implemented in the main thread of an application and are primarily used to make updates to the user interface in response to messages sent by other threads running within the application's process.

Handlers are subclassed from the Android *Handler* class and can be used either by specifying a Runnable to be executed when required by the thread, or by overriding the *handleMessage()* callback method within the Handler subclass which will be called when messages are sent to the handler by a thread.

For the purposes of this example, a handler will be implemented to update the user interface from within the previously created thread. From within Android Studio, load the *ThreadExampleActivity.java* file into the Android Studio editor and modify the code to add a Handler instance to the activity:

```
package com.ebookfrenzy.threadexample;

import android.support.v7.app.ActionBarActivity;
import android.os.Bundle;
import android.view.Menu;
import android.view.MenuItem;
import android.view.View;
import android.widget.TextView;
import android.os.Handler;
import android.os.Message;

public class ThreadExampleActivity extends ActionBarActivity {

    Handler handler = new Handler() {
        @Override
        public void handleMessage(Message msg) {
            TextView myTextView =
                    (TextView)findViewById(R.id.myTextView);
            myTextView.setText("Button Pressed");
        }
    };

    @Override
    protected void onCreate(Bundle savedInstanceState) {
        super.onCreate(savedInstanceState);
        setContentView(R.layout.activity_thread_example);
    }
    .
    .
    .
}
```

The above code changes have declared a handler and implemented within that handler the *handleMessage()* callback which will be called when the thread sends the handler a message. In this instance, the code simply displays a string on the TextView object in the user interface.

All that now remains is to modify the thread created in the *buttonClick()* method to send a message to the handler when the delay has completed:

```
public void buttonClick(View view)
{

        Runnable runnable = new Runnable() {
                public void run() {

                        long endTime = System.currentTimeMillis() +
                                                         20*1000;

                        while (System.currentTimeMillis() < endTime) {
                                synchronized (this) {
                                    try {
                                            wait(endTime -
System.currentTimeMillis());
                                    } catch (Exception e) {}
                                }

                        }
                handler.sendEmptyMessage(0);
                }
        };

        Thread mythread = new Thread(runnable);
        mythread.start();

}
```

Note that the only change that has been made is to make a call to the *sendEmptyMessage()* method of the handler. Since the handler does not currently do anything with the content of any messages it receives it is not necessary to create and send a message object to the handler.

Compile and run the application and, once executing, touch the button. After a 20 second delay, the new text will appear in the TextView object in the user interface.

35.7 Passing a Message to the Handler

Whilst the previous example triggered a call to the *handleMessage()* handler callback, it did not take advantage of the message object to send data to the handler. In this phase of the tutorial, the example will be further modified to pass data between the thread and the handler. First, the updated thread in the *buttonClick()* method will obtain the date and time from the system in string format and store that information in a Bundle object. A call will then be made to the *obtainMessage()* method of the handler object to get a message object from the message pool. Finally, the bundle will be added to the message object before being sent via a call to the *sendMessage()* method of the handler object:

```java
package com.ebookfrenzy.threadexample;

import android.support.v7.app.ActionBarActivity;
import android.os.Bundle;
import android.view.Menu;
import android.view.MenuItem;
import android.view.View;
import android.widget.TextView;
import android.os.Handler;
import android.os.Message;
import java.text.SimpleDateFormat;
import java.util.Date;
import java.util.Locale;

public class ThreadExampleActivity extends ActionBarActivity {
.
.
.
    public void buttonClick(View view)
    {
        Runnable runnable = new Runnable() {
            public void run() {
                Message msg = handler.obtainMessage();
                Bundle bundle = new Bundle();
                SimpleDateFormat dateformat =
                        new SimpleDateFormat("HH:mm:ss MM/dd/yyyy",
                                Locale.US);
                String dateString =
                        dateformat.format(new Date());
                bundle.putString("myKey", dateString);
                msg.setData(bundle);
                handler.sendMessage(msg);
            }
        };
        Thread mythread = new Thread(runnable);
        mythread.start();

    }
.
.
```

```
        .
}
```

Next, update the *handleMessage()* method of the handler to extract the date and time string from the bundle object in the message and display it on the TextView object:

```
Handler handler = new Handler() {
        @Override
        public void handleMessage(Message msg) {
                Bundle bundle = msg.getData();
                String string = bundle.getString("myKey");
                TextView myTextView =
                        (TextView)findViewById(R.id.myTextView);
                myTextView.setText(string);
        }
};
```

Finally, compile and run the application and test that touching the button now causes the current date and time to appear on the TextView object.

35.8 Summary

The goal of this chapter has been to provide an overview of threading within Android applications. When an application is first launched in a process, the runtime system creates a *main thread* in which all subsequently launched application components run by default. The primary role of the main thread is to handle the user interface, so any time consuming tasks performed in that thread will give the appearance that the application has locked up. It is essential, therefore, that tasks likely to take time to complete be started in a separate thread.

Because the Android user interface toolkit is not thread-safe, changes to the user interface should not be made in any thread other than the main thread. User interface changes can be implemented by creating a handler in the main thread to which messages may be sent from within other, non-main threads.

36. An Overview of Android Started and Bound Services

The Android Service class is designed specifically to allow applications to initiate and perform background tasks. Unlike broadcast receivers, which are intended to perform a task quickly and then exit, services are designed to perform tasks that take a long time to complete (such as downloading a file over an internet connection or streaming music to the user) but do not require a user interface.

In this chapter, an overview of the different types of services available will be covered, including *started services*, *bound services* and *intent services*. Once these basics have been covered, subsequent chapters will work through a number of examples of services in action.

36.1 Started Services

Started services are launched by other application components (such as an activity or even a broadcast receiver) and potentially run indefinitely in the background until the service is stopped, or is destroyed by the Android runtime system in order to free up resources. A service will continue to run if the application that started it is no longer in the foreground, and even in the event that the component that originally started the service is destroyed.

By default, a service will run within the same main thread as the application process from which it was launched (referred to as a *local service*). It is important, therefore, that any CPU intensive tasks be performed in a new thread within the service. Instructing a service to run within a separate process (and therefore known as a *remote service*) requires a configuration change within the manifest file.

Unless a service is specifically configured to be private (once again via a setting in the manifest file), that service can be started by other components on the same Android device. This is achieved using the Intent mechanism in the same way that one activity can launch another as outlined in preceding chapters.

Started services are launched via a call to the *startService()* method, passing through as an argument an Intent object identifying the service to be started. When a started service has completed its tasks, it should stop itself via a call to *stopSelf()*. Alternatively, a running service may be stopped by another component via a call to the *stopService()* method, passing through as an argument the matching Intent for the service to be stopped.

Services are given a high priority by the Android system and are typically among the last to be terminated in order to free up resources.

36.2 **Intent Service**

As previously outlined, services run by default within the same main thread as the component from which they are launched. As such, any CPU intensive tasks that need to be performed by the service should take place within a new thread, thereby avoiding impacting the performance of the calling application.

The *IntentService* class is a convenience class (subclassed from the Service class) that sets up a worker thread for handling background tasks and handles each request in an asynchronous manner. Once the service has handled all queued requests, it simply exits. All that is required when using the IntentService class is that the *onHandleIntent()* method be implemented containing the code to be executed for each request.

For services that do not require synchronous processing of requests, IntentService is the recommended option. Services requiring synchronous handling of requests will, however, need to subclass from the Service class and manually implement and manage threading to handle any CPU intensive tasks efficiently.

36.3 **Bound Service**

A *bound service* is similar to a started service with the exception that a started service does not generally return results or permit interaction with the component that launched it. A bound service, on the other hand, allows the launching component to interact with, and receive results from, the service. Through the implementation of interprocess communication (IPC), this interaction can also take place across process boundaries. An activity might, for example, start a service to handle audio playback. The activity will, in all probability, include a user interface providing controls to the user for the purpose of pausing playback or skipping to the next track. Similarly, the service will quite likely need to communicate information to the calling activity to indicate that the current audio track has completed and to provide details of the next track that is about to start playing.

A component (also referred to in this context as a *client*) starts and *binds* to a bound service via a call to the *bindService()* method and multiple components may bind to a service simultaneously. When the service binding is no longer required by a client, a call should be made to the *unbindService()* method. When the last bound client unbinds from a service, the service will be terminated by the Android runtime system. It is important to keep in mind that a bound service may also be started via call to *startService()*. Once started, components may then bind to it via *bindService()* calls. When a bound service is launched via a call to *startService()* it will continue to run even after the last client unbinds from it.

A bound service must include an implementation of the *onBind()* method which is called both when the service is initially created and when other clients subsequently bind to the running service. The purpose of this method is to return to binding clients an object of type *IBinder* containing the information needed by the client to communicate with the service.

In terms of implementing the communication between a client and a bound service, the recommended technique depends on whether the client and service reside in the same or different processes and whether or not the service is private to the client. Local communication can be achieved by extending the Binder class and returning an instance from the *onBind()* method. Interprocess communication, on the other hand, requires Messenger and Handler implementation. Details of both of these approaches will be covered in later chapters.

36.4 **The Anatomy of a Service**

A service must, as has already been mentioned, be created as a subclass of the Android Service class (more specifically *android.app.Service*) or a sub-class thereof (such as *android.app.IntentService*). As part of the subclassing procedure, one or more of the following superclass callback methods must be overridden, depending on the exact nature of the service being created:

- **onStartCommand()** – This is the method that is called when the service is started by another component via a call to the *startService()* method. This method does not need to be implemented for bound services.
- **onBind()** – Called when a component binds to the service via a call to the *bindService()* method. When implementing a bound service, this method must return an *IBinder* object facilitating communication with the client. In the case of *started services*, this method must be implemented to return a NULL value.
- **onCreate()** – Intended as a location to perform initialization tasks, this method is called immediately before the call to either *onStartCommand()* or the *first* call to the *onBind()* method.
- **onDestroy()** – Called when the service is being destroyed.
- **onHandleIntent()** – Applies only to IntentService subclasses. This method is called to handle the processing for the service. It is executed in a separate thread from the main application.

Note that the IntentService class includes its own implementations of the *onStartCommand()* and *onBind()* callback methods so these do not need to be implemented in subclasses.

36.5 **Controlling Destroyed Service Restart Options**

The *onStartCommand()* callback method is required to return an integer value to define what should happen with regard to the service in the event that it is destroyed by the Android runtime system. Possible return values for these methods are as follows:

- **START_NOT_STICKY** – Indicates to the system that the service should not be restarted in the event that it is destroyed unless there are pending intents awaiting delivery.
- **START_STICKY** – Indicates that the service should be restarted as soon as possible after it has been destroyed if the destruction occurred after the *onStartCommand()* method returned. In the event that no pending intents are waiting to be delivered, the *onStartCommand()* callback method is called with a NULL intent value. The intent being processed at the time that the service was destroyed is discarded.
- **START_REDELIVER_INTENT** – Indicates that, if the service was destroyed after returning from the *onStartCommand()* callback method, the service should be restarted with the current intent redelivered to the *onStartCommand()* method followed by any pending intents.

36.6 **Declaring a Service in the Manifest File**

In order for a service to be useable, it must first be declared within a manifest file. This involves embedding an appropriately configured *<service>* element into an existing *<application>* entry. At a minimum, the <service> element must contain a property declaring the class name of the service as illustrated in the following XML fragment:

```xml
<application
    android:icon="@mipmap/ic_launcher"
    android:label="@string/app_name" >
    <activity
        android:label="@string/app_name"
        android:name=".TestActivity" >
        <intent-filter >
            <action android:name="android.intent.action.MAIN" />
            <category
android:name="android.intent.category.LAUNCHER" />
        </intent-filter>
    </activity>
    <service android:name="MyService>
    </service>
</application>
</manifest>
```

By default, services are declared as public, in that they can be accessed by components outside of the application package in which they reside. In order to make a service private, the *android:exported* property must be declared as *false* within the <service> element of the manifest file. For example:

```
<service android:name="MyService"
android:exported="false">
</service>
```

As previously discussed, services run within the same process as the calling component by default. In order to force a service to run within its own process, add an *android:process* property to the <service> element, declaring a name for the process prefixed with a colon (:):

```
<service android:name="MyService"
android:exported="false"
android:process=":myprocess">
</service>
```

The colon prefix indicates that the new process is private to the local application. If the process name begins with a lower case letter instead of a colon, however, the process will be global and available for use by other components.

Finally, using the same intent filter mechanisms outlined for activities, a service may also advertise capabilities to other applications running on the device. For more details on Intent Filters, refer to the chapter entitled *An Overview of Android Intents*.

36.7 **Starting a Service Running on System Startup**

Given the background nature of services, it is not uncommon for a service to need to be started when an Android based system first boots up. This can be achieved by creating a broadcast receiver with an intent filter configured to listen for the system *android.intent.action.BOOT_COMPLETED* intent. When such an intent is detected, the broadcast receiver would simply invoke the necessary service and then return. Note that such a broadcast receiver will need to request the *android.permission.RECEIVE_BOOT_COMPLETED* permission in order to function.

36.8 **Summary**

Android services are a powerful mechanism that allows applications to perform tasks in the background. A service, once launched, will continue to run regardless of whether the calling application is no longer the foreground task and even in the event that the component that initiated the service is destroyed.

Services are subclassed from the Android Service class and fall into the category of either *started services* or *bound services*. Started services run until they are stopped or destroyed and do not inherently provide a mechanism for interaction or data exchange with other components. Bound services, on the other hand, provide a communication interface to other client components and, generally, run until the last client unbinds from the service.

By default, services run locally within the same process and main thread as the calling application. A new thread should, therefore, be created within the service for the purpose of handling CPU intensive tasks. Remote services may be started within a separate process by making a minor configuration change to the corresponding <service> entry in the application manifest file.

The IntentService class (itself a subclass of the Android Service class) provides a convenient mechanism for handling asynchronous service requests within a separate worker thread.

37. Implementing an Android Started Service – A Worked Example

The previous chapter covered a considerable amount of information relating to Android services and, at this point, the concept of services may seem somewhat overwhelming. In order to reinforce the information in the previous chapter, this chapter will work through an Android Studio tutorial intended to gradually introduce the concepts of started service implementation.

Within this chapter, a sample application will be created and used as the basis for implementing an Android service. In the first instance, the service will be created using the *IntentService* class. This example will subsequently be extended to demonstrate the use of the *Service* class. Finally, the steps involved in performing tasks within a separate thread when using the Service class will be implemented. Having covered started services in this chapter, the next chapter, entitled *Android Local Bound Services – A Worked Example*, will focus on the implementation of bound services and client-service communication.

37.1 Creating the Example Project

Launch Android Studio and follow the usual steps to create a new project, entering *ServiceExample* into the Application name field and *ebookfrenzy.com* as the Company Domain setting before clicking on the *Next* button.

On the form factors screen, enable the *Phone and Tablet* option and set the minimum SDK setting to API 8: Android 2.2 (Froyo). Continue to proceed through the screens, requesting the creation of a blank activity named *ServiceExampleActivity* using the default values for the remaining options.

37.2 Creating the Service Class

Before writing any code, the first step is to add a new class to the project to contain the service. The first type of service to be demonstrated in this tutorial is to be based on the IntentService class. As outlined in the preceding chapter (*An Overview of Android Started and Bound Services*), the purpose of the IntentService class is to provide the developer with a convenient mechanism for creating services that perform tasks asynchronously within a separate thread from the calling application.

Implementing an Android Started Service – A Worked Example

Add a new class to the project by right-clicking on the *com.ebookfrenzy.serviceexample* package name located under *app -> java* in the Project tool window and selecting the *New -> Java Class* menu option. Within the resulting *Create New Class* dialog, name the new class *MyIntentService*. Finally, click on the *OK* button to create the new class.

Review the new *MyIntentService.java* file in the Android Studio editor where it should read as follows:

```
package com.ebookfrenzy.serviceexample;

/**
 * Created by <name> on <date>.
 */
public class MyIntentService {
}
```

The class needs to be modified so that it subclasses the IntentService class. When subclassing the IntentService class, there are two rules that must be followed. First, a constructor for the class must be implemented which calls the superclass constructor, passing through the class name of the service. Second, the class must override the *onHandleIntent()* method. Modify the code in the *MyIntentService.java* file, therefore, so that it reads as follows:

```
package com.ebookfrenzy.serviceexample;

import android.app.IntentService;
import android.content.Intent;

public class MyIntentService extends IntentService {

    @Override
    protected void onHandleIntent(Intent arg0) {

    }

    public MyIntentService() {
        super("MyIntentService");
    }
}
```

All that remains at this point is to implement some code within the *onHandleIntent()* method so that the service actually does something when invoked. Ordinarily this would involve performing a task that takes some time to complete such as downloading a large file or playing audio. For the purposes of this example, however, the handler will simply output a message to the Android Studio LogCat panel:

```
package com.ebookfrenzy.serviceexample;

import android.app.IntentService;
import android.content.Intent;
import android.util.Log;

public class MyIntentService extends IntentService {

    private static final String TAG =
            "ServiceExample";

    @Override
    protected void onHandleIntent(Intent arg0) {
        Log.i(TAG, "Intent Service started");
    }

    public MyIntentService() {
        super("MyIntentService");
    }
}
```

37.3 Adding the Service to the Manifest File

Before a service can be invoked, it must first be added to the manifest file of the application to which it belongs. At a minimum, this involves adding a <service> element together with the class name of the service.

Double click on the *AndroidManifest.xml* file (*app -> manifests*) for the current project to load it into the editor and modify the XML to add the service element as shown in the following listing:

```
<?xml version="1.0" encoding="utf-8"?>
<manifest xmlns:android="http://schemas.android.com/apk/res/android"
    package="com.ebookfrenzy.serviceexample" >

    <application
        android:allowBackup="true"
        android:icon="@mipmap/ic_launcher"
        android:label="@string/app_name"
        android:theme="@style/AppTheme" >
        <activity
            android:name=".ServiceExampleActivity"
            android:label="@string/app_name" >
            <intent-filter>
                <action android:name="android.intent.action.MAIN" />
```

```
            <category
android:name="android.intent.category.LAUNCHER" />
            </intent-filter>
        </activity>
        <service android:name=".MyIntentService" />
    </application>

</manifest>
```

37.4 Starting the Service

Now that the service has been implemented and declared in the manifest file, the next step is to add code to start the service when the application launches. As is typically the case, the ideal location for such code is the *onCreate()* callback method of the activity class (which, in this case, can be found in the *ServiceExampleActivity.java* file). Locate and load this file into the editor and modify the *onCreate()* method to add the code to start the service:

```java
package com.ebookfrenzy.serviceexample;

import android.support.v7.app.ActionBarActivity;
import android.os.Bundle;
import android.view.Menu;
import android.view.MenuItem;
import android.content.Intent;

public class ServiceExampleActivity extends ActionBarActivity {

    @Override
    protected void onCreate(Bundle savedInstanceState) {
        super.onCreate(savedInstanceState);
        setContentView(R.layout.activity_service_example);
        Intent intent = new Intent(this, MyIntentService.class);
        startService(intent);
    }
.
.
.
}
```

All that the added code needs to do is to create a new Intent object primed with the class name of the service to start and then use it as an argument to the *startService()* method.

37.5 **Testing the IntentService Example**

The example IntentService based service is now complete and ready to be tested. Since the message displayed by the service will appear in the LogCat panel, it is important that this is configured in the Android Studio environment.

Begin by displaying the Android tool window using either the tools menu button located in the far left corner of the status bar or the *Alt-6* keyboard shortcut. Within the tool window, make sure that the *Devices/logcat* tab is selected before accessing the menu in the upper right hand corner of the panel (which will probably currently read *No Filters*). From this menu, select the *Edit Filter Configuration* menu option.

In the *Create New Logcat Filter* dialog name the filter *ServiceExample* and, in the *by Log Tag (regex)* field, enter the TAG value declared in *ServiceExampleActivity.java* (in the above code example this was *ServiceExample*).

When the changes are complete, click on the *OK* button to create the filter and dismiss the dialog. Instead of listing *No Filters,* the newly created filter should now be selected in the Android tool window.

With the filter configured, run the application on a physical device or AVD emulator session and note that the "Intent Service Started" message appears in the LogCat panel (note that it may be necessary to change the filter menu setting back to ServiceExample after the application has launched):

```
05-20 09:38:50.953   10961-10996/com.ebookfrenzy.serviceexample
I/ServiceExample :  Intent Service started
```

Had the service been tasked with a long-term activity, the service would have continued to run in the background in a separate thread until the task was completed, allowing the application to continue functioning and responding to the user. Since all our service did was log a message, it will have simply stopped upon completion.

37.6 **Using the Service Class**

Whilst the IntentService class allows a service to be implemented with minimal coding, there are situations where the flexibility and synchronous nature of the Service class will be required. As will become evident in this section, this involves some additional programming work to implement.

In order to avoid introducing too many concepts at once, and as a demonstration of the risks inherent in performing time-consuming service tasks in the same thread as the calling application, the example service created here will not run the service task within a new thread, instead relying on the main thread of the application. Creation and management of a new thread within a service will be covered in the next phase of the tutorial.

37.7 Creating the New Service

For the purposes of this example, a new class will be added to the project that will subclass from the Service class. Right-click, therefore, on the package name listed under *app -> java* in the Project tool window and select the *New -> Service -> Service* menu option. Create a new class named *MyService* with both the *Exported* and *Enabled* options selected.

The minimal requirement in order to create an operational service is to implement the *onStartCommand()* callback method which will be called when the service is starting up. In addition, the *onBind()* method must return a null value to indicate to the Android system that this is not a bound service. For the purposes of this example, the *onStartCommand()* method will loop three times performing a 10-second wait on each loop. For the sake of completeness, stub versions of the *onCreate()* and *onDestroy()* methods will also be implemented in the new *MyService.java* file as follows:

```java
package com.ebookfrenzy.serviceexample;

import android.app.Service;
import android.content.Intent;
import android.os.IBinder;
import android.util.Log;

public class MyService extends Service {

    public MyService() {
    }

    private static final String TAG =
            "ServiceExample";

    @Override
    public void onCreate() {
        Log.i(TAG, "Service onCreate");
    }

    @Override
    public int onStartCommand(Intent intent, int flags, int startId) {

        Log.i(TAG, "Service onStartCommand");
```

```
        for (int i = 0; i < 3; i++) {
            long endTime = System.currentTimeMillis() +
                    10 * 1000;
            while (System.currentTimeMillis() < endTime) {
                synchronized (this) {
                    try {
                        wait(endTime - System.currentTimeMillis());
                    } catch (Exception e) {
                    }
                }
            }
            Log.i(TAG, "Service running");
        }
        return Service.START_STICKY;
    }

    @Override
    public IBinder onBind(Intent arg0) {
        Log.i(TAG, "Service onBind");
        return null;
    }

    @Override
    public void onDestroy() {
        Log.i(TAG, "Service onDestroy");
    }
}
```

With the service implemented, load the *AndroidManifest.xml* file into the editor and verify that Android Studio has added an appropriate entry for the new service which should read as follows:

```
<service
  android:name=".MyService"
          android:enabled="true"
          android:exported="true" >
</service>
```

37.8 Modifying the User Interface

As will become evident when the application runs, failing to create a new thread for the service to perform tasks creates a serious usability problem. In order to be able to appreciate fully the magnitude of this issue, it is going to be necessary to add a Button view to the user interface of the *ServiceExampleActivity* activity and configure it to call a method when "clicked" by the user.

Implementing an Android Started Service – A Worked Example

Locate and load the *activity_service_example.xml* file in the Project tool window (*app -> res -> layout -> activity_service_example.xml*). Delete the TextView and add a Button view to the layout. Double click on the new button and change the text to read "Start Service". Use the light bulb icon menu to extract the string to a resource named *button_text*.

With the new Button still selected, locate the *onClick* property in the Properties panel and assign to it a method named *buttonClick*.

On completion, the XML for the user interface layout should resemble the following listing:

```xml
<RelativeLayout
xmlns:android="http://schemas.android.com/apk/res/android"
    xmlns:tools="http://schemas.android.com/tools"
    android:layout_width="match_parent"
    android:layout_height="match_parent"
    android:paddingLeft="@dimen/activity_horizontal_margin"
    android:paddingRight="@dimen/activity_horizontal_margin"
    android:paddingTop="@dimen/activity_vertical_margin"
    android:paddingBottom="@dimen/activity_vertical_margin"
tools:context="com.ebookfrenzy.serviceexample.serviceexample.ServiceEx
ampleActivity">

    <Button
        android:layout_width="wrap_content"
        android:layout_height="wrap_content"
        android:text="@string/button_string"
        android:id="@+id/button"
        android:layout_alignParentTop="true"
        android:layout_alignParentLeft="true"
        android:layout_alignParentStart="true"
        android:onClick="buttonClick" />
</RelativeLayout>
```

Next, edit the *ServiceExampleActivity.java* file to add the *buttonClick()* method and remove the code from the *onCreate()* method that was previously added to launch the MyIntentService service:

```java
package com.ebookfrenzy.serviceexample;

import android.support.v7.app.ActionBarActivity;
import android.os.Bundle;
import android.view.Menu;
import android.view.MenuItem;
import android.content.Intent;
```

```
import android.view.View;

public class ServiceExampleActivity extends ActionBarActivity {

    @Override
    protected void onCreate(Bundle savedInstanceState) {
        super.onCreate(savedInstanceState);
        setContentView(R.layout.activity_service_example);

        Intent intent = new Intent(this, MyIntentService.class);
        startService(intent);
    }

    public void buttonClick(View view)
    {
        Intent intent = new Intent(this, MyService.class);
        startService(intent);
    }
}
```

All that the *buttonClick()* method does is create an intent object for the new service and then start it running.

37.9 **Running the Application**

Run the application and, once loaded, touch the *Start Service* button. Within the LogCat window (using the *ServiceExample* filter created previously) the log messages will appear indicating that the *onCreate()* method was called and that the loop in the *onStartCommand()* method is executing.

Before the final loop message appears, attempt to touch the *Start Service* button a second time. Note that the button is unresponsive. After approximately 20 seconds, the system may display a warning dialog containing the message "ServiceExample isn't responding". The reason for this is that the main thread of the application is currently being held up by the service while it performs the looping task. Not only does this prevent the application from responding to the user, but also to the system, which eventually assumes that the application has locked up in some way.

Clearly, the code for the service needs to be modified to perform tasks in a separate thread from the main thread.

37.10 **Creating a New Thread for Service Tasks**

As outlined in *A Basic Overview of Android Threads and Thread Handlers*, when an Android application is first started, the runtime system creates a single thread in which all application components will run by default. This thread is generally referred to as the *main thread*. The primary role of the main thread is to handle the user interface in terms of event handling and interaction with views in the user interface. Any additional components that are started within the application will, by default, also run on the main thread.

As demonstrated in the previous section, any component that undertakes a time consuming operation on the main thread will cause the application to become unresponsive until that task is complete. It is not surprising, therefore, that Android provides an API that allows applications to create and use additional threads. Any tasks performed in a separate thread from the main thread are essentially performed in the background. Such threads are typically referred to as *background* or *worker* threads.

A very simple solution to this problem involves performing the service task within a new thread. The following *onStartCommand()* method from the *MyService.java* file, for example, has been modified to launch the task within a new thread using the most basic of thread handling examples:

```java
@Override
public int onStartCommand(Intent intent, int flags, int startId) {

    Log.i(TAG, "Service onStartCommand " + startId);

    final int currentId = startId;

    Runnable r = new Runnable() {
        public void run() {

            for (int i = 0; i < 3; i++)
            {
                long endTime = System.currentTimeMillis() +
                                                    10*1000;

                while (System.currentTimeMillis() < endTime) {
                    synchronized (this) {
                        try {
                            wait(endTime -
                            System.currentTimeMillis());
                        } catch (Exception e) {
                        }
                    }
                }
                Log.i(TAG, "Service running " + currentId);
            }
            stopSelf();
        }
```

```
        };

        Thread t = new Thread(r);
        t.start();
        return Service.START_STICKY;
    }
}
```

When the application is now run, it should be possible to touch the *Start Service* button multiple times. Each time a new thread will be created by the service to process the task. The LogCat output will now also include a number referencing the startId of each service request.

With the service now handling requests outside of the main thread, the application remains responsive to both the user and the Android system.

37.11 **Summary**

This chapter has worked through an example implementation of an Android started service using the *IntentService* and *Service* classes. The example also demonstrated the use of threads within a service to avoid making the main thread of the application unresponsive.

38. Android Local Bound Services – A Worked Example

As outlined in some detail in the previous chapters, bound services, unlike started services, provide a mechanism for implementing communication between an Android service and one or more client components. The objective of this chapter is to build on the overview of bound services provided in *An Overview of Android Started and Bound Services* before embarking on an example implementation of a *local* bound service in action.

38.1 Understanding Bound Services

In common with started services, bound services are provided to allow applications to perform tasks in the background. Unlike started services, however, multiple client components may *bind* to a bound service and, once bound, interact with that service using a variety of different mechanisms.

Bound services are created as sub-classes of the Android Service class and must, at a minimum, implement the *onBind()* method. Client components bind to a service via a call to the *bindService()* method. The first bind request to a bound service will result in a call to that service's *onBind()* method (subsequent bind request do not trigger an *onBind()* call). Clients wishing to bind to a service must also implement a ServiceConnection subclass containing *onServiceConnected()* and *onServiceDisconnected()* methods which will be called once the client-server connection has been established or disconnected respectively. In the case of the *onServiceConnected()* method, this will be passed an IBinder object containing the information needed by the client to interact with the service.

38.2 Bound Service Interaction Options

There are two recommended mechanisms for implementing interaction between client components and a bound service. In the event that the bound service is local and private to the same application as the client component (in other words it runs within the same process and is not available to components in other applications), the recommended mechanism is to create a subclass of the Binder class and extend it to provide an interface to the service. An instance of this Binder object is then returned by the *onBind()* method and subsequently used by the client component to directly access methods and data held within the service.

In situations where the bound service is not local to the application (in other words, it is running in a different process from the client component), interaction is best achieved using a Messenger/Handler implementation.

In the remainder of this chapter, an example will be created with the aim of demonstrating the steps involved in creating, starting and interacting with a local, private bound service.

38.3 An Android Studio Local Bound Service Example

The example application created in the remainder of this chapter will consist of a single activity and a bound service. The purpose of the bound service is to obtain the current time from the system and return that information to the activity where it will be displayed to the user. The bound service will be local and private to the same application as the activity.

Launch Android Studio and follow the usual steps to create a new project, entering *LocalBound* into the Application name field and *ebookfrenzy.com* as the Company Domain setting before clicking on the *Next* button.

On the form factors screen, enable the *Phone and Tablet* option and set the minimum SDK setting to API 8: Android 2.2 (Froyo). Continue to proceed through the screens, requesting the creation of a blank activity named *LocalBoundActivity* with the remaining fields set to the default values.

Once the project has been created, the next step is to add a new class to act as the bound service.

38.4 Adding a Bound Service to the Project

To add a new class to the project, right-click on the package name (located under *app -> java -> com.ebookfrenzy.localbound*) within the Project tool window and select the *New -> Service -> Service* menu option. Specify *BoundService* as the class name and make sure that both the *Exported* and *Enabled* options are selected before clicking on *Finish* to create the class. By default Android Studio will load the *BoundService.java* file into the editor where it will read as follows:

```
package com.ebookfrenzy.localbound;

import android.app.Service;
import android.content.Intent;
import android.os.IBinder;

public class BoundService extends Service {
    public BoundService() {
    }

    @Override
```

```
    public IBinder onBind(Intent intent) {
        // TODO: Return the communication channel to the service.
        throw new UnsupportedOperationException("Not yet
implemented");
    }
}
```

38.5 Implementing the Binder

As previously outlined, local bound services can communicate with bound clients by passing an appropriately configured Binder object to the client. This is achieved by creating a Binder subclass within the bound service class and extending it by adding one or more new methods that can be called by the client. In most cases, this simply involves implementing a method that returns a reference to the bound service instance. With a reference to this instance, the client can then access data and call methods within the bound service directly.

For the purposes of this example, therefore, some changes are needed to the template *BoundService* class created in the preceding section. In the first instance, a Binder subclass needs to be declared. This class will contain a single method named *getService()* which will simply return a reference to the current service object instance (represented by the *this* keyword). With these requirements in mind, edit the *BoundService.java* file and modify it as follows:

```
package com.ebookfrenzy.localbound;

import android.app.Service;
import android.content.Intent;
import android.os.IBinder;
import android.os.Binder;

public class BoundService extends Service {

    private final IBinder myBinder = new MyLocalBinder();

    public BoundService() {
    }

    @Override
    public IBinder onBind(Intent intent) {
        // TODO: Return the communication channel to the service.
        throw new UnsupportedOperationException("Not yet
implemented");
    }
```

```
        public class MyLocalBinder extends Binder {
            BoundService getService() {
                return BoundService.this;
            }
        }
    }
}
```

Having made the changes to the class, it is worth taking a moment to recap the steps performed here. Firstly, a new subclass of Binder (named *MyLocalBinder*) is declared. This class contains a single method for the sole purpose of returning a reference to the current instance of the *BoundService* class. A new instance of the *MyLocalBinder* class is created and assigned to the *myBinder* IBinder reference (since Binder is a subclass of IBinder there is no type mismatch in this assignment).

Next, the *onBind()* method needs to be modified to return a reference to the *myBinder* object and a new public method implemented to return the current time when called by any clients that bind to the service:

```java
package com.ebookfrenzy.localbound;

import java.text.SimpleDateFormat;
import java.util.Date;
import java.util.Locale;

import android.app.Service;
import android.content.Intent;
import android.os.IBinder;
import android.os.Binder;

public class BoundService extends Service {

    private final IBinder myBinder = new MyLocalBinder();

    public BoundService() {
    }

    @Override
    public IBinder onBind(Intent intent) {
        return myBinder;
    }

    public String getCurrentTime() {
        SimpleDateFormat dateformat =
                new SimpleDateFormat("HH:mm:ss MM/dd/yyyy",
```

```
                        Locale.US);
        return (dateformat.format(new Date()));
    }


    public class MyLocalBinder extends Binder {
        BoundService getService() {
            return BoundService.this;
        }
    }
}
```

At this point, the bound service is complete and is ready to be added to the project manifest file. Locate and double click on the *AndroidManifest.xml* file for the *LocalBound* project in the Project tool window and, once loaded into the Manifest Editor, verify that Android Studio has already added a <service> entry for the service as follows:

```
<?xml version="1.0" encoding="utf-8"?>
<manifest xmlns:android="http://schemas.android.com/apk/res/android"
    package="com.ebookfrenzy.localbound.localbound" >

    <application
        android:allowBackup="true"
        android:icon="@mipmap/ic_launcher"
        android:label="@string/app_name"
        android:theme="@style/AppTheme" >
        <activity
            android:name=" .LocalBoundActivity"
            android:label="@string/app_name" >
            <intent-filter>
                <action android:name="android.intent.action.MAIN" />

                <category
android:name="android.intent.category.LAUNCHER" />
            </intent-filter>
        </activity>

        <service
    android:name=".BoundService"
            android:enabled="true"
            android:exported="true" >
        </service>
    </application>
```

```
</manifest>
```

The next phase is to implement the necessary code within the activity to bind to the service and call the *getCurrentTime()* method.

38.6 **Binding the Client to the Service**

For the purposes of this tutorial, the client is the *LocalBoundActivity* instance of the running application. As previously noted, in order to successfully bind to a service and receive the IBinder object returned by the service's *onBind()* method, it is necessary to create a ServiceConnection subclass and implement *onServiceConnected()* and *onServiceDisconnected()* callback methods. Edit the *LocalBoundActivity.java* file and modify it as follows:

```
package com.ebookfrenzy.localbound;

import android.support.v7.app.ActionBarActivity;
import android.os.Bundle;
import android.view.Menu;
import android.view.MenuItem;
import android.os.IBinder;
import android.content.Context;
import android.content.Intent;
import android.content.ComponentName;
import android.content.ServiceConnection;
import com.ebookfrenzy.localbound.BoundService.MyLocalBinder;

public class LocalBoundActivity extends ActionBarActivity {

    BoundService myService;
    boolean isBound = false;

    @Override
    protected void onCreate(Bundle savedInstanceState) {
        super.onCreate(savedInstanceState);
        setContentView(R.layout.activity_local_bound);
    }

    private ServiceConnection myConnection = new ServiceConnection()
    {

        public void onServiceConnected(ComponentName className,
                                       IBinder service) {
            MyLocalBinder binder = (MyLocalBinder) service;
```

```
            myService = binder.getService();
            isBound = true;
        }

        public void onServiceDisconnected(ComponentName arg0) {
            isBound = false;
        }
    };
    .
    .
}
```

The *onServiceConnected()* method will be called when the client binds successfully to the service. The method is passed as an argument the IBinder object returned by the *onBind()* method of the service. This argument is cast to an object of type MyLocalBinder and then the *getService()* method of the binder object is called to obtain a reference to the service instance, which, in turn, is assigned to *myService.* A Boolean flag is used to indicate that the connection has been successfully established.

The *onServiceDisconnected()* method is called when the connection ends and simply sets the Boolean flag to false.

Having established the connection, the next step is to modify the activity to bind to the service. This involves the creation of an intent and a call to the *bindService()* method, which can be performed in the *onCreate()* method of the activity:

```
@Override
    public void onCreate(Bundle savedInstanceState) {
        super.onCreate(savedInstanceState);
        setContentView(R.layout.activity_local_bound);
        Intent intent = new Intent(this, BoundService.class);
        bindService(intent, myConnection, Context.BIND_AUTO_CREATE);
}
```

38.7 Completing the Example

All that remains is to implement a mechanism for calling the *getCurrentTime()* method and displaying the result to the user. As is now customary, Android Studio will have created a template *activity_local_bound.xml* file for the activity containing only a TextView. Load this file into the Designer tool using Design mode, double-click on the TextView component and change the ID to *myTextView.* Move the TextView to the center of the display canvas, add a Button view beneath the TextView and change the text on the button to read "Show Time", extracting the text to a string resource named *button_string.* On completion of these changes, the layout should resemble that illustrated in Figure 38-1:

Figure 38-1

Next, switch Designer into Text mode and modify the button element to declare an *onClick* property configured to call a method named *showTime*:

```
<RelativeLayout
xmlns:android="http://schemas.android.com/apk/res/android"
    xmlns:tools="http://schemas.android.com/tools"
    android:layout_width="match_parent"
    android:layout_height="match_parent"
    android:paddingLeft="@dimen/activity_horizontal_margin"
    android:paddingRight="@dimen/activity_horizontal_margin"
    android:paddingTop="@dimen/activity_vertical_margin"
    android:paddingBottom="@dimen/activity_vertical_margin"
    tools:context=".LocalBoundActivity">

    <TextView
        android:text="@string/hello_world"
        android:layout_width="wrap_content"
```

```
            android:layout_height="wrap_content"
            android:layout_centerVertical="true"
            android:layout_centerHorizontal="true"
            android:id="@+id/myTextView" />

    <Button
            android:layout_width="wrap_content"
            android:layout_height="wrap_content"
            android:text="@string/button_string"
            android:id="@+id/button"
            android:layout_below="@+id/myTextView"
            android:layout_centerHorizontal="true"
            android:onClick="showTime"
            android:layout_marginTop="44dp" />

</RelativeLayout>
```

Finally, edit the code in the *LocalBoundActivity.java* file to implement the *showTime()* method. This method simply calls the *getCurrentTime()* method of the service (which, thanks to the *onServiceConnected()* method, is now available from within the activity via the *myService* reference) and assigns the resulting string to the TextView:

```
package com.ebookfrenzy.localbound;

import android.support.v7.app.ActionBarActivity;
import android.os.Bundle;
import android.view.Menu;
import android.view.MenuItem;
import android.os.IBinder;
import android.content.Context;
import android.content.Intent;
import android.content.ComponentName;
import android.content.ServiceConnection;
import com.ebookfrenzy.localbound.BoundService.MyLocalBinder;
import android.view.View;
import android.widget.TextView;

public class LocalBoundActivity extends ActionBarActivity {

    BoundService myService;
    boolean isBound = false;

    public void showTime(View view)
```

```
{
        String currentTime = myService.getCurrentTime();
        TextView myTextView =
                (TextView)findViewById(R.id.myTextView);
        myTextView.setText(currentTime);
    }
    .
    .
    .
}
```

38.8 Testing the Application

With the code changes complete, perform a test run of the application. Once visible, touch the button and note that the text view changes to display the current date and time. The example has successfully started and bound to a service and then called a method of that service to cause a task to be performed and results returned to the activity.

38.9 Summary

When a bound service is local and private to an application, components within that application can interact with the service without the need to resort to inter-process communication (IPC). In general terms, the service's *onBind()* method returns an IBinder object containing a reference to the instance of the running service. The client component implements a ServiceConnection subclass containing callback methods that are called when the service is connected and disconnected. The former method is passed the IBinder object returned by the *onBind()* method allowing public methods within the service to be called.

Having covered the implementation of local bound services, the next chapter will focus on using IPC to interact with remote bound services.

Chapter 39

39. Android Remote Bound Services – A Worked Example

In this, the final chapter dedicated to Android services, an example application will be developed to demonstrate the use of a messenger and handler configuration to facilitate interaction between a client and remote bound service.

39.1 Client to Remote Service Communication

As outlined in the previous chapter, interaction between a client and a local service can be implemented by returning to the client an IBinder object containing a reference to the service object. In the case of remote services, however, this approach does not work because the remote service is running in a different process and, as such, cannot be reached directly from the client.

In the case of remote services, a Messenger and Handler configuration must be created that allows messages to be passed across process boundaries between client and service.

Specifically, the service creates a Handler instance that will be called when a message is received from the client. In terms of initialization, it is the job of the Handler to create a Messenger object which, in turn, creates an IBinder object to be returned to the client in the *onBind()* method. This IBinder object is used by the client to create an instance of the Messenger object and, subsequently, to send messages to the service handler. Each time a message is sent by the client, the *handleMessage()* method of the handler is called, passing through the message object.

The simple example created in this chapter will consist of an activity and a bound service running in separate processes. The Messenger/Handler mechanism will be used to send a string to the service, which will then display that string in a Toast message.

39.2 Creating the Example Application

Launch Android Studio and follow the steps to create a new project, entering *RemoteBound* into the Application name field and *ebookfrenzy.com* as the Company Domain setting before clicking on the *Next* button.

On the form factors screen, enable the *Phone and Tablet* option and set the minimum SDK setting to API 8: Android 2.2 (Froyo). Continue to proceed through the screens, requesting the creation of a blank activity named *RemoteBoundActivity* with corresponding layout and menu resource files named *activity_remote_bound* and *menu_remote_bound.*

39.3 **Designing the User Interface**

Locate the *activity_remote_bound.xml* file in the Project tool window and double click on it to load it into the Designer tool. With the Designer tool in Design mode, delete the default TextView instance and drag and drop a Button widget from the palette so that it is positioned in the center of the layout. Double click on the button and change the text property to read "Send Message". Extract the string using the light bulb menu to a new string resource named *button_text.*

Next, switch Designer to Text mode and modify the Button element to declare an *onClick* property:

```
<RelativeLayout
xmlns:android="http://schemas.android.com/apk/res/android"
    xmlns:tools="http://schemas.android.com/tools"
    android:layout_width="match_parent"
    android:layout_height="match_parent"
    android:paddingLeft="@dimen/activity_horizontal_margin"
    android:paddingRight="@dimen/activity_horizontal_margin"
    android:paddingTop="@dimen/activity_vertical_margin"
    android:paddingBottom="@dimen/activity_vertical_margin"
tools:context="com.ebookfrenzy.remotebound.remotebound.RemoteBoundActi
vity">

    <Button
        android:layout_width="wrap_content"
        android:layout_height="wrap_content"
        android:text="@string/button_string"
        android:id="@+id/button"
        android:layout_centerVertical="true"
        android:layout_centerHorizontal="true"
        android:onClick="sendMessage" />
</RelativeLayout>
```

39.4 **Implementing the Remote Bound Service**

In order to implement the remote bound service for this example, add a new class to the project by right-clicking on the package name (located under *app -> java*) within the Project tool window and select the *New -> Service -> Service* menu option. Specify *RemoteService* as the class name and make sure that both the *Exported* and *Enabled* options are selected before clicking on *Finish* to create the class.

The next step is to implement the handler class for the new service. This is achieved by extending the Handler class and implementing the *handleMessage()* method. This method will be called when a message is received from the client. It will be passed as an argument a Message object containing any data that the client needs to pass to the service. In this instance, this will be a Bundle object containing a string to be displayed to the user. The modified class in the *RemoteService.java* file should read as follows once this has been implemented:

```java
package com.ebookfrenzy.remotebound;

import android.app.Service;
import android.content.Intent;
import android.os.IBinder;
import android.os.Bundle;
import android.os.Handler;
import android.os.Message;
import android.widget.Toast;
import android.os.Messenger;


public class RemoteService extends Service {

    public RemoteService() {
    }


    class IncomingHandler extends Handler {
        @Override
        public void handleMessage(Message msg) {

            Bundle data = msg.getData();
            String dataString = data.getString("MyString");
            Toast.makeText(getApplicationContext(),
                    dataString, Toast.LENGTH_SHORT).show();

        }
    }


    @Override
    public IBinder onBind(Intent intent) {
        // TODO: Return the communication channel to the service.
        throw new UnsupportedOperationException("Not yet
implemented");
    }
```

```
}
```

With the handler implemented, the only remaining task in terms of the service code is to modify the *onBind()* method such that it returns an IBinder object containing a Messenger object which, in turn, contains a reference to the handler:

```
final Messenger myMessenger = new Messenger(new IncomingHandler());

@Override
public IBinder onBind(Intent intent) {
        return myMessenger.getBinder();
}
```

The first line of the above code fragment creates a new instance of our handler class and passes it through to the constructor of a new Messenger object. Within the *onBind()* method, the *getBinder()* method of the messenger object is called to return the messenger's IBinder object.

39.5 Configuring a Remote Service in the Manifest File

In order to portray the communication between a client and remote service accurately, it will be necessary to configure the service to run in a separate process from the rest of the application. This is achieved by adding an *android:process* property within the <service> tag for the service in the manifest file. In order to launch a remote service it is also necessary to provide an intent filter for the service. To implement these changes, modify the *AndroidManifest.xml* file to add the required entries:

```
<?xml version="1.0" encoding="utf-8"?>
<manifest xmlns:android="http://schemas.android.com/apk/res/android"
    package="com.ebookfrenzy.remotebound" >

    <application
        android:allowBackup="true"
        android:icon="@mipmap/ic_launcher"
        android:label="@string/app_name"
        android:theme="@style/AppTheme" >
        <activity
            android:name=".RemoteBoundActivity"
            android:label="@string/app_name" >
            <intent-filter>
                <action android:name="android.intent.action.MAIN" />

                <category
android:name="android.intent.category.LAUNCHER" />
            </intent-filter>
```

```
            </activity>

            <service
                android:name=".RemoteService"
                android:enabled="true"
                android:exported="true"
                android:process=":my_process" >
            </service>
        </service>
        </application>

</manifest>
```

39.6 Launching and Binding to the Remote Service

As with a local bound service, the client component needs to implement an instance of the ServiceConnection class with *onServiceConnected()* and *onServiceDisconnected()* methods. Also in common with local services, the *onServiceConnected()* method will be passed the IBinder object returned by the *onBind()* method of the remote service which will be used to send messages to the server handler. In the case of this example, the client is *RemoteBoundActivity*, the code for which is located in *RemoteBoundActivity.java*. Load this file and modify it to add the ServiceConnection class and a variable to store a reference to the received Messenger object together with a Boolean flag to indicate whether or not the connection is established:

```
package com.ebookfrenzy.remotebound;

import android.support.v7.app.ActionBarActivity;
import android.os.Bundle;
import android.view.Menu;
import android.view.MenuItem;
import android.os.IBinder;
import android.os.Message;
import android.os.Messenger;
import android.os.RemoteException;
import android.content.ComponentName;
import android.content.Context;
import android.content.Intent;
import android.content.ServiceConnection;
import android.view.View;

public class RemoteBoundActivity extends ActionBarActivity {

    Messenger myService = null;
```

```
    boolean isBound;

    @Override
    protected void onCreate(Bundle savedInstanceState) {
        super.onCreate(savedInstanceState);
        setContentView(R.layout.activity_remote_bound);
    }

    private ServiceConnection myConnection =
            new ServiceConnection() {
                public void onServiceConnected(ComponentName
className,
                                               IBinder service) {
                    myService = new Messenger(service);
                    isBound = true;
                }

                public void onServiceDisconnected(ComponentName
className) {
                    myService = null;
                    isBound = false;
                }
            };
    .
    .
    .
}
```

Next, some code needs to be added to bind to the remote service. This involves creating an intent that matches the intent filter for the service as declared in the manifest file and then making a call to the *bindService()* method, providing the intent and a reference to the ServiceConnection instance as arguments. For the purposes of this example, this code will be implemented in the activity's *onCreate()* method:

```
@Override
protected void onCreate(Bundle savedInstanceState) {
        super.onCreate(savedInstanceState);
        setContentView(R.layout.activity_remote_bound);

        Intent intent = new Intent(getApplicationContext(),
                        RemoteService.class);

        bindService(intent, myConnection, Context.BIND_AUTO_CREATE);
```

```
}
```

39.7 Sending a Message to the Remote Service

All that remains before testing the application is to implement the *sendMessage()* method in the *RemoteBoundActivity* class which is configured to be called when the button in the user interface is touched by the user. This method needs to check that the service is connected, create a bundle object containing the string to be displayed by the server, add it to a Message object and send it to the server:

```java
public void sendMessage(View view)
{
        if (!isBound) return;

        Message msg = Message.obtain();

        Bundle bundle = new Bundle();
        bundle.putString("MyString", "Message Received");

        msg.setData(bundle);

        try {
            myService.send(msg);
        } catch (RemoteException e) {
            e.printStackTrace();
        }
}
```

With the code changes complete, compile and run the application. Once loaded, touch the button in the user interface, at which point a Toast message should appear that reads "Message Received".

39.8 Summary

In order to implement interaction between a client and remote bound service it is necessary to implement a handler/message communication framework. The basic concepts behind this technique have been covered in this chapter together with the implementation of an example application designed to demonstrate communication between a client and a bound service, each running in a separate process.

40. An Overview of Android SQLite Databases

Mobile applications that do not need to store at least some amount of persistent data are few and far between. The use of databases is an essential aspect of most applications, ranging from applications that are almost entirely data driven, to those that simply need to store small amounts of data such as the prevailing score of a game.

The importance of persistent data storage becomes even more evident when taking into consideration the somewhat transient lifecycle of the typical Android application. With the ever-present risk that the Android runtime system will terminate an application component to free up resources, a comprehensive data storage strategy to avoid data loss is a key factor in the design and implementation of any application development strategy.

This chapter will provide an overview of the SQLite database management system bundled with the Android operating system, together with an outline of the Android SDK classes that are provided to facilitate persistent SQLite based database storage from within an Android application. Before delving into the specifics of SQLite in the context of Android development, however, a brief overview of databases and SQL will be covered.

40.1 Understanding Database Tables

Database *Tables* provide the most basic level of data structure in a database. Each database can contain multiple tables and each table is designed to hold information of a specific type. For example, a database may contain a *customer* table that contains the name, address and telephone number for all the customers of a particular business. The same database may also include a *products* table used to store the product descriptions with associated product codes for the items sold by the business.

Each table in a database is assigned a name that must be unique within that particular database. A table name, once assigned to a table in one database, may only be re-used within the context of a different database.

40.2 **Introducing Database Schema**

Database Schema define the characteristics of the data stored in a database table. For example, the table schema for a customer database table might define that the customer name is a string of no more than 20 characters in length, and that the customer phone number is a numerical data field of a certain format.

Schema are also used to define the structure of entire databases and the relationship between the various tables contained in each database.

40.3 **Columns and Data Types**

It is helpful at this stage to begin to view a database table as being similar to a spreadsheet where data is stored in rows and columns.

Each column represents a data field in the corresponding table. For example, the name, address and telephone data fields of a table are all *columns*.

Each column, in turn, is defined to contain a certain *datatype* which dictates the type of data the column can contain. A column designed to store numbers would, therefore, be defined as a numerical datatype.

40.4 **Database Rows**

Each new record that is saved to a table is stored in a row. Each row, in turn, consists of the columns of data associated with the saved record.

Once again, consider the spreadsheet analogy described earlier in this chapter. Each entry in a customer table is equivalent to a row in a spreadsheet and each column contains the data for each customer (name, address, telephone etc). When a new customer is added to the table, a new row is created and the data for that customer stored in the corresponding columns of the new row.

Rows are also sometimes referred to as *records* or *entries* and these terms can generally be used interchangeably.

40.5 **Introducing Primary Keys**

Each database table must contain one or more columns that can be used to identify each row in the table uniquely. This is known in database terminology as the *Primary Key*. For example, a table may use a bank account number column as the primary key. Alternatively, a customer table may use the customer's social security number as the primary key.

Primary keys allow the database management system to identify a specific row in a table uniquely. Without a primary key it would not be possible to retrieve or delete a specific row in a table because there can be no certainty that the correct row has been selected. For example, suppose a table existed where the customer's last name had been defined as the primary key. Imagine then the problem that might arise if more than one customer named "Smith" were recorded in the database. Without some guaranteed way to identify a specific row uniquely, it would be impossible to ensure the correct data was being accessed at any given time.

Primary keys can comprise a single column or multiple columns in a table. To qualify as a single column primary key, no two rows can contain matching primary key values. When using multiple columns to construct a primary key, individual column values do not need to be unique, but all the columns combined *must be unique*.

40.6 **What is SQLite?**

SQLite is an embedded, relational database management system (RDBMS). Most relational databases (Oracle and MySQL being prime examples) are standalone server processes that run independently, and in cooperation with, applications that require database access. SQLite is referred to as *embedded* because it is provided in the form of a library that is linked into applications. As such, there is no standalone database server running in the background. All database operations are handled internally within the application through calls to functions contained in the SQLite library.

The developers of SQLite have placed the technology into the public domain with the result that it is now a widely deployed database solution.

SQLite is written in the C programming language and as such, the Android SDK provides a Java based "wrapper" around the underlying database interface. This essentially consists of a set of classes that may be utilized within the Java code of an application to create and manage SQLite based databases.

For additional information about SQLite refer to *http://www.sqlite.org*.

40.7 **Structured Query Language (SQL)**

Data is accessed in SQLite databases using a high-level language known as Structured Query Language. This is usually abbreviated to SQL and pronounced *sequel*. SQL is a standard language used by most relational database management systems. SQLite conforms mostly to the SQL-92 standard.

SQL is essentially a very simple and easy to use language designed specifically to enable the reading and writing of database data. Because SQL contains a small set of keywords, it can be learned quickly. In addition, SQL syntax is more or less identical between most DBMS implementations, so having learned SQL for one system, it is likely that your skills will transfer to other database management systems.

Whilst some basic SQL statements will be used within this chapter, a detailed overview of SQL is beyond the scope of this book. There are, however, many other resources that provide a far better overview of SQL than we could ever hope to provide in a single chapter here.

40.8 **Trying SQLite on an Android Virtual Device (AVD)**

For readers unfamiliar with databases in general and SQLite in particular, diving right into creating an Android application that uses SQLite may seem a little intimidating. Fortunately, Android is shipped with SQLite pre-installed, including an interactive environment for issuing SQL commands from within an *adb shell* session connected to a running Android AVD emulator instance. This is both a useful way to learn about SQLite and SQL, and also an invaluable tool for identifying problems with databases created by applications running in an emulator.

To launch an interactive SQLite session, begin by running an AVD session. This can be achieved from within Android Studio by launching the Android Virtual Device Manager (*Tools -> Android -> AVD Manager*), selecting a previously configured AVD and clicking on *Start*.

Once the AVD is up and running, open a Terminal or Command-Prompt window and connect to the emulator using the *adb* command-line tool as follows (note that the –e flag directs the tool to look for an emulator with which to connect, rather than a physical device):

```
adb -e shell
```

Once connected, the shell environment will provide a command prompt at which commands may be entered:

```
root@android:/ #
```

Data stored in SQLite databases are actually stored in database files on the file system of the Android device on which the application is running. By default, the file system path for these database files is as follows:

```
/data/data/<package name>/databases/<database filename>.db
```

For example, if an application with the package name *com.example.MyDBApp* creates a database named *mydatabase.db*, the path to the file on the device would read as follows:

```
/data/data/com.example.MyDBApp/databases/mydatabase.db
```

For the purposes of this exercise, therefore, change directory to /data/data within the adb shell and create a sub-directory hierarchy suitable for some SQLite experimentation:

```
cd /data/data
```

```
mkdir com.example.dbexample
cd com.example.dbexample
mkdir databases
cd databases
```

With a suitable location created for the database file, launch the interactive SQLite tool as follows:

```
root@android:/data/data/databases # sqlite3 ./mydatabase.db
sqlite3 ./mydatabase.db
SQLite version 3.7.4
Enter ".help" for instructions
Enter SQL statements terminated with a ";"
sqlite>
```

At the *sqlite>* prompt, commands may be entered to perform tasks such as creating tables and inserting and retrieving data. For example, to create a new table in our database with fields to hold ID, name, address and phone number fields the following statement is required:

```
create table contacts (_id integer primary key autoincrement, name
text, address text, phone text);
```

Note that each row in a table must have a *primary key* that is unique to that row. In the above example, we have designated the ID field as the primary key, declared it as being of type *integer* and asked SQLite to increment automatically the number each time a row is added. This is a common way to make sure that each row has a unique primary key. On most other platforms, the choice of name for the primary key is arbitrary. In the case of Android, however, it is essential that the key be named _id in order for the database to be fully accessible using all of the Android database related classes. The remaining fields are each declared as being of type *text.*

To list the tables in the currently selected database, use the *.tables* statement:

```
sqlite> .tables
contacts
```

To insert records into the table:

```
sqlite> insert into contacts (name, address, phone) values ("Bill
Smith", "123 Main Street, California", "123-555-2323");
sqlite> insert into contacts (name, address, phone) values ("Mike
Parks", "10 Upping Street, Idaho", "444-444-1212");
```

To retrieve all rows from a table:

```
sqlite> select * from contacts;
```

```
1|Bill Smith|123 Main Street, California|123-555-2323
2|Mike Parks|10 Upping Street, Idaho|444-444-1212
```

To extract a row that meets specific criteria:

```
sqlite> select * from contacts where name="Mike Parks";
2|Mike Parks|10 Upping Street, Idaho|444-444-1212
```

To exit from the sqlite3 interactive environment:

```
sqlite> .exit
```

When running an Android application in the emulator environment, any database files will be created on the file system of the emulator using the previously discussed path convention. This has the advantage that you can connect with adb, navigate to the location of the database file, load it into the sqlite3 interactive tool and perform tasks on the data to identify possible problems occurring in the application code.

It is also important to note that, whilst it is possible to connect with an adb shell to a physical Android device, the shell is not granted sufficient privileges by default to create and manage SQLite databases. Debugging of database problems is, therefore, best performed using an AVD session.

40.9 Android SQLite Java Classes

SQLite is, as previously mentioned, written in the C programming language whilst Android applications are primarily developed using Java. To bridge this "language gap", the Android SDK includes a set of classes that provide a Java layer on top of the SQLite database management system. The remainder of this chapter will provide a basic overview of each of the major classes within this category. More details on each class can be found in the online Android documentation.

40.9.1 Cursor

A class provided specifically to provide access to the results of a database query. For example, a SQL SELECT operation performed on a database will potentially return multiple matching rows from the database. A Cursor instance can be used to step through these results, which may then be accessed from within the application code using a variety of methods. Some key methods of this class are as follows:

- **close()** – Releases all resources used by the cursor and closes it.
- **getCount()** – Returns the number of rows contained within the result set.
- **moveToFirst()** – Moves to the first row within the result set.
- **moveToLast()** – Moves to the last row in the result set.
- **moveToNext()** – Moves to the next row in the result set.

- **move()** – Moves by a specified offset from the current position in the result set.
- **get<*type*>()** – Returns the value of the specified <*type*> contained at the specified column index of the row at the current cursor position (variations consist of *getString()*, *getInt()*, *getShort()*, *getFloat()* and *getDouble()*).

40.9.2 SQLiteDatabase

This class provides the primary interface between the application code and underlying SQLite databases including the ability to create, delete and perform SQL based operations on databases. Some key methods of this class are as follows:

- **insert()** – Inserts a new row into a database table.
- **delete()** – Deletes rows from a database table.
- **query()** – Performs a specified database query and returns matching results via a Cursor object.
- **execSQL()** – Executes a single SQL statement that does not return result data.
- **rawQuery()** – Executes an SQL query statement and returns matching results in the form of a Cursor object.

40.9.3 SQLiteOpenHelper

A helper class designed to make it easier to create and update databases. This class must be subclassed within the code of the application seeking database access and the following callback methods implemented within that subclass:

- **onCreate()** – Called when the database is created for the first time. This method is passed as an argument the SQLiteDatabase object for the newly created database. This is the ideal location to initialize the database in terms of creating a table and inserting any initial data rows.
- **onUpgrade()** – Called in the event that the application code contains a more recent database version number reference. This is typically used when an application is updated on the device and requires that the database schema also be updated to handle storage of additional data.

In addition to the above mandatory callback methods, the *onOpen()* method, called when the database is opened, may also be implemented within the subclass.

The constructor for the subclass must also be implemented to call the super class, passing through the application context, the name of the database and the database version.

Notable methods of the SQLiteOpenHelper class include:

- **getWritableDatabase()** – Opens or creates a database for reading and writing. Returns a reference to the database in the form of a SQLiteDatabase object.
- **getReadableDatabase()** – Creates or opens a database for reading only. Returns a reference to the database in the form of a SQLiteDatabase object.

- **close**() – Closes the database.

40.9.4 ContentValues

ContentValues is a convenience class that allows key/value pairs to be declared consisting of table column identifiers and the values to be stored in each column. This class is of particular use when inserting or updating entries in a database table.

40.10 **Summary**

SQLite is a lightweight, embedded relational database management system that is included as part of the Android framework and provides a mechanism for implementing organized persistent data storage for Android applications. In addition to the SQLite database, the Android framework also includes a range of Java classes that may be used to create and manage SQLite based databases and tables.

The goal of this chapter has been to provide an overview of databases in general and SQLite in particular within the context of Android application development. The next chapters will work through the creation of an example application intended to put this theory into practice in the form of a step-by-step tutorial. Since the user interface for the example application will require a forms based layout, the first chapter, entitled *An Android TableLayout and TableRow Tutorial*, will detour slightly from the core topic by introducing the basics of the TableLayout and TableRow views.

41. An Android TableLayout and TableRow Tutorial

When the work began on the next chapter of this book (*An Android SQLite Database Tutorial*) it was originally intended that it would include the steps to design the user interface layout for the database example application. It quickly became evident, however, that the best way to implement the user interface was to make use of the Android TableLayout and TableRow views and that this topic area deserved a self-contained chapter. As a result, this chapter will focus solely on the user interface design of the database application completed in the next chapter, and in doing so, take some time to introduce the basic concepts of table layouts in Android Studio.

41.1 The TableLayout and TableRow Layout Views

The purpose of the TableLayout container view is to allow user interface elements to be organized on the screen in a table format consisting of rows and columns. Each row within a TableLayout is occupied by a TableRow instance, which, in turn, is divided into cells, with each cell containing a single child view (which may itself be a container with multiple view children).

The number of columns in a table is dictated by the row with the most columns and, by default, the width of each column is defined by the widest cell in that column. Columns may be configured to be shrinkable or stretchable (or both) such that they change in size relative to the parent TableLayout. In addition, a single cell may be configured to span multiple columns.

Consider the user interface layout shown in Figure 41-1:

Figure 41-1

From the visual appearance of the layout, it is difficult to identify the TableLayout structure used to design the interface. The hierarchical tree illustrated in Figure 41-2, however, makes the structure a little easier to understand:

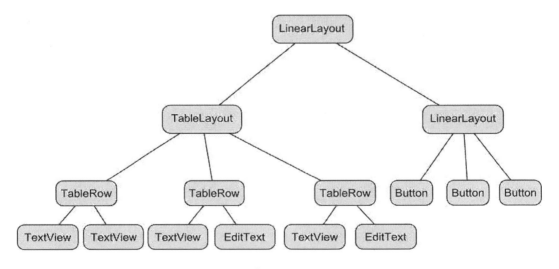

Figure 41-2

Clearly, the layout consists of a parent LinearLayout view with TableLayout and LinearLayout children. The TableLayout contains three TableRow children representing three rows in the table. The TableRows contain two child views, with each child representing the contents of a column cell. The LinearLayout child view contains three Button children.

The layout shown in Figure 41-2 is the exact layout that is required for the database example that will be completed in the next chapter. The remainder of this chapter, therefore, will be used to work step by step through the design of this user interface using the Android Studio Designer tool.

41.2 Creating the Database Project

Start Android Studio and create a new project, entering *Database* into the Application name field and *ebookfrenzy.com* as the Company Domain setting before clicking on the *Next* button.

On the form factors screen, enable the *Phone and Tablet* option and set the minimum SDK setting to API 8: Android 2.2 (Froyo). Continue to proceed through the screens, requesting the creation of a blank activity named *DatabaseActivity* with corresponding layout and menu resource files named *activity_database* and *menu_database* respectively.

41.3 Adding the TableLayout to the User Interface

Locate the *activity_database.xml* file in the Project tool window (*app -> res -> layout*) and double click on it to load it into the Designer tool. By default, Android Studio has used a RelativeLayout as the root layout element in the user interface. This needs to be replaced by a vertically oriented LinearLayout. With the Designer tool in Text mode, replace the XML with the following:

```
<LinearLayout
    android:orientation="vertical"
    android:layout_width="fill_parent"
    android:layout_height="fill_parent"
    xmlns:android="http://schemas.android.com/apk/res/android">


</LinearLayout>
```

Switch to Design mode and, referring to the *Layouts* section of the Palette, drag and drop a TableLayout view so that it is positioned at the top of the LinearLayout canvas area as illustrated in Figure 41-3:

Figure 41-3

Once these initial steps are complete, the Component Tree for the layout should resemble that shown in Figure 41-4:

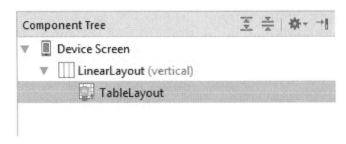

Figure 41-4

41.4 Adding and Configuring the TableRows

Now that the TableLayout has been added to the user interface layout, three TableRow instances need to be added as children. From the Designer palette, locate the *TableRow* entry listed under *Layouts* and drag and drop an instance directly onto the top of the *TableLayout* entry in the Component Tree panel. Repeat this step to add two more TableRows so that the component tree matches Figure 41-5:

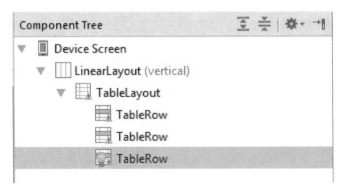

Figure 41-5

From within the *Widgets* section of the palette, drag and drop two *Large Text* TextView objects onto the uppermost TableRow entry in the Component Tree (Figure 41-6):

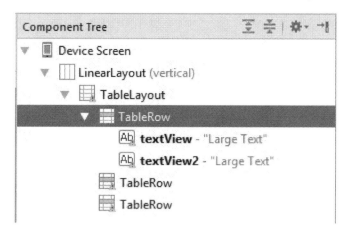

Figure 41-6

Double click on the left most TextView within the screen layout and, in the quick property settings panel, change the *text* property to "Product ID". Repeat this step for the right most TextView, this time changing the text to "Not assigned" and specifying an *id* value of *productID*. Extract the text for each TextView to new string resources using the light bulb icon displayed when the view is selected.

Drag and drop another Large Text view and a Plain Text Edit Text view from the Text Fields section of the palette onto the second TableRow entry in the Component Tree. Change the text on the TextView to *Product Name* and the ID of the EditText object to *productName*.

Drag and drop another Large Text view and a Number (Decimal) Text Field onto the third TableRow. Change the text on the TextView to *Product Quantity* and the ID of the Text Field object to *productQuantity*.

Before proceeding, be sure to extract all of the text properties added in the above steps to string resources.

41.5 Adding the Button Bar to the Layout

The next step is to add a LinearLayout (Horizontal) view to the parent LinearLayout view, positioned immediately below the TableLayout view. Drag and drop a *LinearLayout (Horizontal)* instance from the *Layouts* section of the Designer palette and drop it directly onto the *LinearLayout (Vertical)* entry in the Component Tree panel.

Drag and drop three Button objects onto the new LinearLayout and assign string resources for each button that read "Add", "Find" and "Delete" respectively.

An Android TableLayout and TableRow Tutorial

With the new horizontal Linear Layout view selected in the Component Tree, click on the Gravity button in the Designer toolbar (Figure 41-7) and select the Center gravity option so that the buttons are centered horizontally within the display:

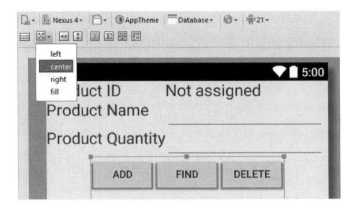

Figure 41-7

Before proceeding, also check the hierarchy of the layout in the Component Tree panel, taking extra care to ensure the view ID names match those in the following figure:

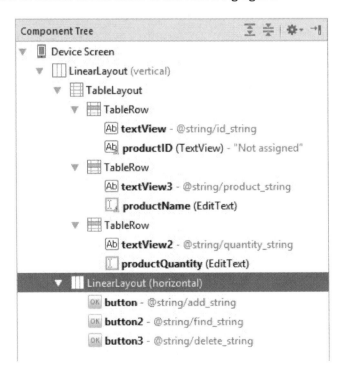

Figure 41-8

41.6 **Adjusting the Layout Margins**

All that remains is to adjust some of the layout settings. Begin by clicking on the first TableRow entry in the Component Tree panel so that it is selected. Hold down the Ctrl-key on the keyboard and click in the second and third TableRows so that all three items are selected. In the Properties panel, locate the *layout:margin* property category and, once located, unfold the category and change the *all* setting to 10dp as shown in Figure 41-9:

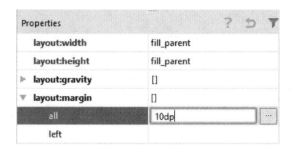

Figure 41-9

With margins set on all four sides of the three TableRows, the user interface should appear as illustrated in Figure 41-1. For the sake of completeness, and for comparison purposes in the event that your layout does not match that in Figure 41-1, the full *activity_database.xml* structure for this layout is outlined below.

```
<LinearLayout
    android:orientation="vertical"
    android:layout_width="fill_parent"
    android:layout_height="fill_parent"
    xmlns:android="http://schemas.android.com/apk/res/android">

    <TableLayout
        android:layout_width="match_parent"
        android:layout_height="wrap_content"
        android:layout_gravity="center_horizontal">

        <TableRow
            android:layout_width="fill_parent"
            android:layout_height="fill_parent"
            android:layout_margin="10dp">

            <TextView
                android:layout_width="wrap_content"
                android:layout_height="wrap_content"
                android:textAppearance="?android:attr/textAppearanceLarge"
```

```
                android:text="@string/id_string"
                android:id="@+id/textView" />

        <TextView
            android:layout_width="wrap_content"
            android:layout_height="wrap_content"
        android:textAppearance="?android:attr/textAppearanceLarge"
            android:text="Not assigned"
            android:id="@+id/productID" />
    </TableRow>

    <TableRow
        android:layout_width="fill_parent"
        android:layout_height="fill_parent"
        android:layout_margin="10dp">

        <TextView
            android:layout_width="wrap_content"
            android:layout_height="wrap_content"
        android:textAppearance="?android:attr/textAppearanceLarge"
            android:text="@string/product_string"
            android:id="@+id/textView3" />

        <EditText
            android:layout_width="wrap_content"
            android:layout_height="wrap_content"
            android:id="@+id/productName" />
    </TableRow>

    <TableRow
        android:layout_width="fill_parent"
        android:layout_height="fill_parent"
        android:layout_margin="10dp">

        <TextView
            android:layout_width="wrap_content"
            android:layout_height="wrap_content"
        android:textAppearance="?android:attr/textAppearanceLarge"
            android:text="@string/quantity_string"
            android:id="@+id/textView2" />

        <EditText
            android:layout_width="wrap_content"
```

```
            android:layout_height="wrap_content"
            android:inputType="numberDecimal"
            android:ems="10"
            android:id="@+id/productQuantity" />
    </TableRow>
</TableLayout>

<LinearLayout
    android:orientation="horizontal"
    android:layout_width="wrap_content"
    android:layout_height="fill_parent"
    android:layout_gravity="center_horizontal"
    android:layout_margin="10dp">

    <Button
        android:layout_width="wrap_content"
        android:layout_height="wrap_content"
        android:text="@string/add_string"
        android:id="@+id/button" />

    <Button
        android:layout_width="wrap_content"
        android:layout_height="wrap_content"
        android:text="@string/find_string"
        android:id="@+id/button2" />

    <Button
        android:layout_width="wrap_content"
        android:layout_height="wrap_content"
        android:text="@string/delete_string"
        android:id="@+id/button3" />
</LinearLayout>
</LinearLayout>
```

41.7 Summary

The Android TableLayout container view provides a way to arrange view components in a row and column configuration. Whilst the TableLayout view provides the overall container, each row, and the cells contained therein, are implemented via instances of the TableRow view. In this chapter, a user interface has been designed in Android Studio using the TableLayout and TableRow containers. The next chapter will add the functionality behind this user interface to implement the SQLite database capabilities.

42. An Android SQLite Database Tutorial

The chapter entitled *An Overview of Android SQLite Databases* covered the basic principles of integrating relational database storage into Android applications using the SQLite database management system. The previous chapter took a minor detour into the territory of designing TableLayouts within the Android Studio Designer tool, in the course of which, the user interface for an example database application was created. In this chapter, work on the *Database* application project will be continued with the ultimate objective of completing the database example.

42.1 About the Database Example

As is probably evident from the user interface layout designed in the preceding chapter, the example project is a simple data entry and retrieval application designed to allow the user to add, query and delete database entries. The idea behind this application is to allow the tracking of product inventory.

The name of the database will be *productID.db* which, in turn, will contain a single table named *products*. Each record in the database table will contain a unique product ID, a product description and the quantity of that product item currently in stock, corresponding to column names of "productid", "productname" and "productquantity" respectively. The productid column will act as the primary key and will be automatically assigned and incremented by the database management system.

The database schema for the *products* table is outlined in Table 42-1:

Column	Data Type
productid	Integer / Primary Key/ Auto Increment
productname	Text
productquantity	Integer

Table 42-1

42.2 **Creating the Data Model**

Once completed, the application will consist of an activity and a database handler class. The database handler will be a subclass of SQLiteOpenHelper and will provide an abstract layer between the underlying SQLite database and the activity class, with the activity calling on the database handler to interact with the database (adding, removing and querying database entries). In order to implement this interaction in a structured way, a third class will need to be implemented to hold the database entry data as it is passed between the activity and the handler. This is actually a very simple class capable of holding product ID, product name and product quantity values, together with getter and setter methods for accessing these values. Instances of this class can then be created within the activity and database handler and passed back and forth as needed. Essentially, this class can be thought of as representing the database model.

Within Android Studio, navigate within the Project tool window to *app -> java* and right-click on the package name. From the popup menu, choose the *New -> Java Class* option and, in the *Create New Class* dialog, name the class *Product* before clicking on the *OK* button.

Once created the *Product.java* source file will automatically load into the Android Studio editor. Once loaded, modify the code to add the appropriate data members and methods:

```java
package com.ebookfrenzy.database;

public class Product {

    private int _id;
    private String _productname;
    private int _quantity;

    public Product() {

    }

    public Product(int id, String productname, int quantity) {
        this._id = id;
        this._productname = productname;
        this._quantity = quantity;
    }

    public Product(String productname, int quantity) {
        this._productname = productname;
        this._quantity = quantity;
    }
```

```
    public void setID(int id) {
        this._id = id;
    }

    public int getID() {
        return this._id;
    }

    public void setProductName(String productname) {
        this._productname = productname;
    }

    public String getProductName() {
        return this._productname;
    }

    public void setQuantity(int quantity) {
        this._quantity = quantity;
    }

    public int getQuantity() {
        return this._quantity;
    }
}
```

The completed class contains private data members for the internal storage of data columns from database entries and a set of methods to get and set those values.

42.3 Implementing the Data Handler

The data handler will be implemented by subclassing from the Android SQLiteOpenHelper class and, as outlined in *An Overview of Android SQLite Databases*, adding the constructor, *onCreate()* and *onUpgrade()* methods. Since the handler will be required to add, query and delete data on behalf of the activity component, corresponding methods will also need to be added to the class.

Begin by adding a second new class to the project to act as the handler, this time named *MyDBHandler*. Once the new class has been created, modify it so that it reads as follows:

```
package com.ebookfrenzy.database;

import android.database.sqlite.SQLiteDatabase;
import android.database.sqlite.SQLiteOpenHelper;

public class MyDBHandler extends SQLiteOpenHelper {
```

```
    @Override
    public void onCreate(SQLiteDatabase db) {


    }

    @Override
    public void onUpgrade(SQLiteDatabase db, int oldVersion,
                            int newVersion) {


    }

}
```

Having now pre-populated the source file with template *onCreate()* and *onUpgrade()* methods the next task is to add a constructor method. Modify the code to declare constants for the database name, table name, table columns and database version and to add the constructor method as follows:

```
package com.ebookfrenzy.database;

import android.database.sqlite.SQLiteDatabase;
import android.database.sqlite.SQLiteOpenHelper;
import android.content.Context;
import android.content.ContentValues;
import android.database.Cursor;

public class MyDBHandler extends SQLiteOpenHelper {

    private static final int DATABASE_VERSION = 1;
    private static final String DATABASE_NAME = "productDB.db";
    public static final String TABLE_PRODUCTS = "products";

    public static final String COLUMN_ID = "_id";
    public static final String COLUMN_PRODUCTNAME = "productname";
    public static final String COLUMN_QUANTITY = "quantity";

    public MyDBHandler(Context context, String name,
        SQLiteDatabase.CursorFactory factory, int version) {
            super(context, DATABASE_NAME, factory, DATABASE_VERSION);
    }

    @Override
    public void onCreate(SQLiteDatabase db) {
```

```
    }

    @Override
    public void onUpgrade(SQLiteDatabase db, int oldVersion,
            int newVersion) {

    }
}
```

Next, the *onCreate()* method needs to be implemented so that the *products* table is created when the database is first initialized. This involves constructing a SQL CREATE statement containing instructions to create a new table with the appropriate columns and then passing that through to the *execSQL()* method of the SQLiteDatabase object passed as an argument to *onCreate()*:

```
@Override
public void onCreate(SQLiteDatabase db) {
        String CREATE_PRODUCTS_TABLE = "CREATE TABLE " +
                TABLE_PRODUCTS + "("
                + COLUMN_ID + " INTEGER PRIMARY KEY," +
COLUMN_PRODUCTNAME
                + " TEXT," + COLUMN_QUANTITY + " INTEGER" + ")";
        db.execSQL(CREATE_PRODUCTS_TABLE);
}
```

The *onUpgrade()* method is called when the handler is invoked with a greater database version number from the one previously used. The exact steps to be performed in this instance will be application specific, so for the purposes of this example we will simply remove the old database and create a new one:

```
@Override
public void onUpgrade(SQLiteDatabase db, int oldVersion,
                        int newVersion) {
        db.execSQL("DROP TABLE IF EXISTS " + TABLE_PRODUCTS);
        onCreate(db);
}
```

All that now remains to be implemented in the *MyDBHandler.java* handler class are the methods to add, query and remove database table entries.

42.3.1 The Add Handler Method

The method to insert database records will be named *addProduct()* and will take as an argument an instance of our Product data model class. A ContentValues object will be created in the body of the method and primed with key-value pairs for the data columns extracted from the Product object. Next, a reference to the database will be obtained via a call to *getWritableDatabase()* followed by a call to the *insert()* method of the returned database object. Finally, once the insertion has been performed, the database needs to be closed:

```
public void addProduct (Product product) {

        ContentValues values = new ContentValues();
        values.put(COLUMN_PRODUCTNAME, product.getProductName());
        values.put(COLUMN_QUANTITY, product.getQuantity());

        SQLiteDatabase db = this.getWritableDatabase();

        db.insert(TABLE_PRODUCTS, null, values);
        db.close();
}
```

42.3.2 The Query Handler Method

The method to query the database will be named *findProduct()* and will take as an argument a String object containing the name of the product to be located. Using this string, a SQL SELECT statement will be constructed to find all matching records in the table. For the purposes of this example, only the first match will then be returned, contained within a new instance of our Product data model class:

```
public Product findProduct (String productname) {
        String query = "Select * FROM " + TABLE_PRODUCTS + " WHERE " +
COLUMN_PRODUCTNAME + " =  \"" + productname + "\"";

        SQLiteDatabase db = this.getWritableDatabase();

        Cursor cursor = db.rawQuery(query, null);

        Product product = new Product();

        if (cursor.moveToFirst()) {
                cursor.moveToFirst();
                product.setID(Integer.parseInt(cursor.getString(0)));
                product.setProductName(cursor.getString(1));

        product.setQuantity(Integer.parseInt(cursor.getString(2)));
```

```
            cursor.close();
        } else {
            product = null;
        }
        db.close();
        return product;
}
```

42.3.3 The Delete Handler Method

The deletion method will be named *deleteProduct()* and will accept as an argument the entry to be deleted in the form of a Product object. The method will use a SQL SELECT statement to search for the entry based on the product name and, if located, delete it from the table. The success or otherwise of the deletion will be reflected in a Boolean return value:

```
public boolean deleteProduct(String productname) {

    boolean result = false;

    String query = "Select * FROM " + TABLE_PRODUCTS + " WHERE " +
COLUMN_PRODUCTNAME + " =  \"" + productname + "\"";

    SQLiteDatabase db = this.getWritableDatabase();

    Cursor cursor = db.rawQuery(query, null);

    Product product = new Product();

    if (cursor.moveToFirst()) {
            product.setID(Integer.parseInt(cursor.getString(0)));
            db.delete(TABLE_PRODUCTS, COLUMN_ID + " = ?",
                new String[] { String.valueOf(product.getID()) });
            cursor.close();
            result = true;
    }
    db.close();
    return result;
}
```

42.4 Implementing the Activity Event Methods

The final task prior to testing the application is to wire up *onClick* event handlers on the three buttons in the user interface and to implement corresponding methods for those events. Locate and load the *activity_database.xml* file into the Designer tool, switch to Text mode and locate and modify the three button elements to add *onClick* properties:

```
<Button
    android:layout_width="wrap_content"
    android:layout_height="wrap_content"
    android:text="@string/add_string"
    android:id="@+id/button"
    android:onClick="newProduct" />

<Button
    android:layout_width="wrap_content"
    android:layout_height="wrap_content"
    android:text="@string/find_string"
    android:id="@+id/button2"
    android:onClick="lookupProduct" />

<Button
    android:layout_width="wrap_content"
    android:layout_height="wrap_content"
    android:text="@string/delete_string"
    android:id="@+id/button3"
    android:onClick="removeProduct" />
```

Load the *DatabaseActivity.java* source file into the editor and implement the code to identify the views in the user interface and to implement the three "onClick" target methods:

```
package com.ebookfrenzy.database;

import android.support.v7.app.ActionBarActivity;
import android.os.Bundle;
import android.view.Menu;
import android.view.MenuItem;
import android.view.View;
import android.widget.EditText;
import android.widget.TextView;

public class DatabaseActivity extends ActionBarActivity {

    TextView idView;
    EditText productBox;
    EditText quantityBox;

    @Override
```

```java
protected void onCreate(Bundle savedInstanceState) {
    super.onCreate(savedInstanceState);
    setContentView(R.layout.activity_database);

    idView = (TextView) findViewById(R.id.productID);
    productBox = (EditText) findViewById(R.id.productName);
    quantityBox =
            (EditText) findViewById(R.id.productQuantity);
}

public void newProduct (View view) {
    MyDBHandler dbHandler = new MyDBHandler(this, null, null, 1);

    int quantity =
            Integer.parseInt(quantityBox.getText().toString());

    Product product =
            new Product(productBox.getText().toString(),
quantity);

    dbHandler.addProduct(product);
    productBox.setText("");
    quantityBox.setText("");
}

public void lookupProduct (View view) {
    MyDBHandler dbHandler = new MyDBHandler(this, null, null, 1);

    Product product =

dbHandler.findProduct(productBox.getText().toString());

    if (product != null) {
        idView.setText(String.valueOf(product.getID()));


quantityBox.setText(String.valueOf(product.getQuantity()));
    } else {
        idView.setText("No Match Found");
    }
}

public void removeProduct (View view) {
```

```
        MyDBHandler dbHandler = new MyDBHandler(this, null,
                null, 1);

        boolean result = dbHandler.deleteProduct(
                productBox.getText().toString());

        if (result)
        {
            idView.setText("Record Deleted");
            productBox.setText("");
            quantityBox.setText("");
        }
        else
            idView.setText("No Match Found");
    }
    .
    .
    .
}
```

42.5 Testing the Application

With the coding changes completed, compile and run the application either in an AVD session or on a physical Android device. Once the application is running, enter a product name and quantity value into the user interface form and touch the *Add* button. Once the record has been added the text boxes will clear. Repeat these steps to add a second product to the database. Next, enter the name of one of the newly added products into the product name field and touch the *Find* button. The form should update with the product ID and quantity for the selected product. Touch the *Delete* button to delete the selected record. A subsequent search by product name should indicate that the record no longer exists.

42.6 Summary

The purpose of this chapter has been to work step by step through a practical application of SQLite based database storage in Android applications. As an exercise to develop your new database skill set further, consider extending the example to include the ability to update existing records in the database table.

43. Understanding Android Content Providers

The previous chapter worked through the creation of an example application designed to store data using a SQLite database. When implemented in this way, the data is private to the application and, as such, inaccessible to other applications running on the same device. Whilst this may be the desired behavior for many types of application, situations will inevitably arise whereby the data stored on behalf of an application could be of benefit to other applications. A prime example of this is the data stored by the built-in Contacts application on an Android device. Whilst the Contacts application is primarily responsible for the management of the user's address book details, this data is also made accessible to any other applications that might need access to this data. This sharing of data between Android applications is achieved through the implementation of *content providers*.

43.1 What is a Content Provider?

A content provider provides access to structured data between different Android applications. This data is exposed to applications either as tables of data (in much the same way as a SQLite database) or as a handle to a file. This essentially involves the implementation of a client/server arrangement whereby the application seeking access to the data is the client and the content provider is the server, performing actions and returning results on behalf of the client.

A successful content provider implementation involves a number of different elements, each of which will be covered in detail in the remainder of this chapter.

43.2 The Content Provider

A content provider is created as a subclass of the *android.content.ContentProvider* class. Typically, the application responsible for managing the data to be shared will implement a content provider to facilitate the sharing of that data with other applications.

The creation of a content provider involves the implementation of a set of methods to manage the data on behalf of other, client applications. These methods are as follows:

43.2.1 onCreate()

This method is called when the content provider is first created and should be used to perform any initialization tasks required by the content provider.

43.2.2 query()

This method will be called when a client requests that data be retrieved from the content provider. It is the responsibility of this method to identify the data to be retrieved (either single or multiple rows), perform the data extraction and return the results wrapped in a Cursor object.

43.2.3 insert()

This method is called when a new row needs to be inserted into the provider database. This method must identify the destination for the data, perform the insertion and return the full URI of the newly added row.

43.2.4 update()

The method called when existing rows need to be updated on behalf of the client. The method uses the arguments passed through to update the appropriate table rows and return the number of rows updated as a result of the operation.

43.2.5 delete()

Called when rows are to be deleted from a table. This method deletes the designated rows and returns a count of the number of rows deleted.

43.2.6 getType()

Returns the MIME type of the data stored by the content provider.

It is important when implementing these methods in a content provider to keep in mind that, with the exception of the *onCreate()* method, they can be called from many processes simultaneously and must, therefore, be thread safe.

Once a content provider has been implemented, the issue that then arises is how the provider is identified within the Android system. This is where the *content URI* comes into play.

43.3 The Content URI

An Android device will potentially contain a number of content providers. The system must, therefore, provide some way of identifying one provider from another. Similarly, a single content provider may provide access to multiple forms of content (typically in the form of database tables). Client applications, therefore, need a way to specify the underlying data for which access is required. This is achieved through the use of content URIs.

The content URI is essentially used to identify specific data within a specific content provider. The *Authority* section of the URI identifies the content provider and usually takes the form of the package name of the content provider. For example:

```
com.example.mydbapp.myprovider
```

A specific database table within the provider data structure may be referenced by appending the table name to the authority. For example, the following URI references a table named *products* within the content provider:

```
com.example.mydbapp.myprovider/products
```

Similarly, a specific row within the specified table may be referenced by appending the row ID to the URI. The following URI, for example, references the row in the products table in which the value stored in the _ID column equals 3:

```
com.example.mydbapp.myprovider/products/3
```

When implementing the insert, query, update and delete methods in the content provider, it will be the responsibility of these methods to identify whether the incoming URI is targeting a specific row in a table, or references multiple rows and act accordingly. This can potentially be a complex task given that a URI can extend to multiple levels. This process can, however, be eased significantly by making use of the *UriMatcher* class as will be outlined in the next chapter.

43.4 **The Content Resolver**

Access to a content provider is achieved via a ContentResolver object. An application can obtain a reference to its content resolver by making a call to the *getContentResolver()* method of the application context.

The content resolver object contains a set of methods that mirror those of the content provider (insert, query, delete etc). The application simply makes calls to the methods, specifying the URI of the content on which the operation is to be performed. The content resolver and content provider objects then communicate to perform the requested task on behalf of the application.

43.5 **The <provider> Manifest Element**

In order for a content provider to be visible within an Android system, it must be declared within the Android manifest file for the application in which it resides. This is achieved using the *<provider>* element, which must contain the following items:

- **android:authority** – The full authority URI of the content provider. For example com.example.mydbapp.mydbapp.myprovider.

- **android:name** – The name of the class that implements the content provider. In most cases, this will use the same value as the authority.

Similarly, the <provider> element may be used to define the permissions that must be held by client applications in order to qualify for access to the underlying data. If no permissions are declared, the default behavior is for permission to be allowed for all applications.

Permissions can be set to cover the entire content provider, or limited to specific tables and records.

43.6 **Summary**

The data belonging to an application is typically private to the application and inaccessible to other applications. In situations where the data needs to be shared, it is necessary to set up a content provider. This chapter has covered the basic elements that combine to enable data sharing between applications and outlined the concepts of the content provider, content URI and content resolver.

In the next chapter, the Android Studio Database example application created previously will be extended to make the underlying product data available via a content provider.

44. Implementing an Android Content Provider in Android Studio

As outlined in the previous chapter, content providers provide a mechanism through which the data stored by one Android application can be made accessible to other applications. Having provided a theoretical overview of content providers, this chapter will continue the coverage of content providers by extending the Database project created in the chapter entitled *An Android SQLite Database Tutorial* to implement content provider based access to the database.

44.1 Copying the Database Project

In order to keep the original Database project intact, we will make a backup copy of the project before modifying it to implement content provider support for the application. If the Database project is currently open within Android Studio, close it using the *File -> Close Project* menu option.

Using the file system explorer for your operating system type, navigate to the directory containing your Android Studio projects (typically this will be a folder named *AndroidStudioProjects* located in your home directory). Within this folder, copy the Database project folder to a new folder named *DatabaseOriginal.*

Within the Android Studio welcome screen, select the *Open an existing Android Studio project* option from the Quick Start list and navigate to and select the original *Database* project so that it loads into the main window.

44.2 Adding the Content Provider Package

The next step is to add a new package to the Database project into which the content provider class will be created. Add this new package by navigating within the Project tool window to *app -> java*, right-clicking on the *java* entry and selecting the *New -> Package* menu option. When the *Choose Destination Directory* dialog appears, select the *..\app\src\main\java* option from the *Directory Structure* panel and click on OK.

In the *New Package* dialog, enter the following package name into the name field before clicking on the *OK* button:

```
com.ebookfrenzy.database.provider
```

The new package should now be listed within the Project tool window as illustrated in Figure 44-1:

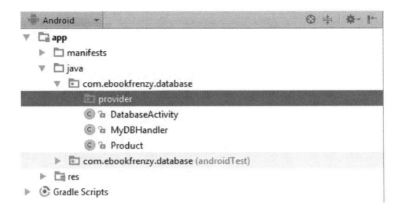

Figure 44-1

44.3 Creating the Content Provider Class

As discussed in *Understanding Android Content Providers*, content providers are created by subclassing the *android.content.ContentProvider* class. Consequently, the next step is to add a class to the new *provider* package to serve as the content provider for this application. Locate the new package in the Project tool window, right-click on it and select the *New -> Other -> Content Provider* menu option. In the *New Content Provider* dialog, enter *MyContentProvider* into the *Class Name* field and the following into the *URI Authorities* field:

```
com.ebookfrenzy.database.provider.MyContentProvider
```

Make sure that the new content provider class is both exported and enabled before clicking on *Finish* to create the new class.

Once the new class has been created, the *MyContentProvider.java* file should be listed beneath the *provider* package in the Project tool window and automatically loaded into the editor where it should appear as outlined in the following listing:

```
package com.ebookfrenzy.database.provider;

import android.content.ContentProvider;
import android.content.ContentValues;
import android.database.Cursor;
import android.net.Uri;
```

```
public class MyContentProvider extends ContentProvider {
    public MyContentProvider() {
    }


    @Override
    public int delete(Uri uri, String selection, String[]
selectionArgs) {
        // Implement this to handle requests to delete one or more
rows.
        throw new UnsupportedOperationException("Not yet
implemented");
    }

    @Override
    public String getType(Uri uri) {
        // TODO: Implement this to handle requests for the MIME type
of the data
        // at the given URI.
        throw new UnsupportedOperationException("Not yet
implemented");
    }

    @Override
    public Uri insert(Uri uri, ContentValues values) {
        // TODO: Implement this to handle requests to insert a new
row.
        throw new UnsupportedOperationException("Not yet
implemented");
    }

    @Override
    public boolean onCreate() {
        // TODO: Implement this to initialize your content provider on
startup.
        return false;
    }

    @Override
    public Cursor query(Uri uri, String[] projection, String
selection,
            String[] selectionArgs, String sortOrder) {
        // TODO: Implement this to handle query requests from clients.
```

```
            throw new UnsupportedOperationException("Not yet
implemented");
    }


    @Override
    public int update(Uri uri, ContentValues values, String selection,
            String[] selectionArgs) {
        // TODO: Implement this to handle requests to update one or
more rows.
        throw new UnsupportedOperationException("Not yet
implemented");
    }
}
```

As is evident from a quick review of the code in this file, Android Studio has already populated the class with stubs for each of the methods that a subclass of ContentProvider is required to implement. It will soon be necessary to begin implementing these methods, but first some constants relating to the provider's content authority and URI need to be declared.

44.4 Constructing the Authority and Content URI

As outlined in the previous chapter, all content providers must have associated with them an *authority* and a *content uri*. In practice, the authority is typically the full package name of the content provider class itself, in this case *com.ebookfrenzy.database.database.provider.MyContentProvider* as declared when the new Content Provider class was created in the previous section.

The content URI will vary depending on application requirements, but for the purposes of this example will comprise the authority with the name of the database table appended at the end. Within the *MyContentProvider.java* file, make the following modifications:

```
package com.ebookfrenzy.database.provider;

import android.content.ContentProvider;
import android.content.ContentValues;
import android.database.Cursor;
import android.net.Uri;
import android.content.UriMatcher;

public class MyContentProvider extends ContentProvider {

    private static final String AUTHORITY =
        "com.ebookfrenzy.database.provider.MyContentProvider";
    private static final String PRODUCTS_TABLE = "products";
```

```
    public static final Uri CONTENT_URI =
            Uri.parse("content://" + AUTHORITY + "/" +
PRODUCTS_TABLE);

    public MyContentProvider() {
    }
.
.
.
}
```

The above statements begin by creating a new String object named *AUTHORITY* and assigning the authority string to it. Similarly, a second String object named *PRODUCTS_TABLE* is created and initialized with the name of our database table (products).

Finally, these two string elements are combined, prefixed with *content://* and converted to a Uri object using the *parse()* method of the Uri class. The result is assigned to a variable named *CONTENT_URI.*

44.5 **Implementing URI Matching in the Content Provider**

When the methods of the content provider are called, they will be passed as an argument a URI indicating the data on which the operation is to be performed. This URI may take the form of a reference to a specific row in a specific table. It is also possible that the URI will be more general, for example specifying only the database table. It is the responsibility of each method to identify the *Uri type* and to act accordingly. This task can be eased considerably by making use of a UriMatcher instance. Once a UriMatcher instance has been created, it can be configured to return a specific integer value corresponding to the type of URI it detects when asked to do so. For the purposes of this tutorial, we will be configuring our UriMatcher instance to return a value of 1 when the URI references the entire products table, and a value of 2 when the URI references the ID of a specific row in the products table. Before working on creating the URIMatcher instance, we will first create two integer variables to represent the two URI types:

```
package com.ebookfrenzy.database.provider;

import android.content.ContentProvider;
import android.content.ContentValues;
import android.database.Cursor;
import android.net.Uri;
import android.content.UriMatcher;

public class MyContentProvider extends ContentProvider {

    private static final String AUTHORITY =
```

```
          "com.ebookfrenzy.database.provider.MyContentProvider";
      private static final String PRODUCTS_TABLE = "products";
      public static final Uri CONTENT_URI =
              Uri.parse("content://" + AUTHORITY + "/" +
PRODUCTS_TABLE);

      public static final int PRODUCTS = 1;
      public static final int PRODUCTS_ID = 2;
      .
      .
}
```

With the Uri type variables declared, it is now time to add code to create a UriMatcher instance and configure it to return the appropriate variables:

```
public class MyContentProvider extends ContentProvider {

      private static final String AUTHORITY =
        "com.ebookfrenzy.database.provider.MyContentProvider";
      private static final String PRODUCTS_TABLE = "products";
      public static final Uri CONTENT_URI =
              Uri.parse("content://" + AUTHORITY + "/" +
PRODUCTS_TABLE);

      public static final int PRODUCTS = 1;
      public static final int PRODUCTS_ID = 2;

      private static final UriMatcher sURIMatcher =
                              new UriMatcher(UriMatcher.NO_MATCH);

      static {
              sURIMatcher.addURI(AUTHORITY, PRODUCTS_TABLE, PRODUCTS);
              sURIMatcher.addURI(AUTHORITY, PRODUCTS_TABLE + "/#",
                                      PRODUCTS_ID);
      }
      .
      .
}
```

The UriMatcher instance (named sURIMatcher) is now primed to return the value of PRODUCTS when just the products table is referenced in a URI, and PRODUCTS_ID when the URI includes the ID of a specific row in the table.

44.6 **Implementing the Content Provider onCreate() Method**

When the content provider class is created and initialized, a call will be made to the *onCreate()* method of the class. It is within this method that any initialization tasks for the class need to be performed. For the purposes of this example, all that needs to be performed is for an instance of the MyDBHandler class implemented in *An Android SQLite Database Tutorial* to be created. Once this instance has been created, it will need to be accessible from the other methods in the class, so a declaration for the database handler also needs to be declared, resulting in the following code changes to the *MyContentProvider.java* file:

```
package com.ebookfrenzy.database.provider;

import com.ebookfrenzy.database.MyDBHandler;

import android.content.ContentProvider;
import android.content.ContentValues;
import android.database.Cursor;
import android.net.Uri;
import android.content.UriMatcher;
import android.database.sqlite.SQLiteDatabase;
import android.database.sqlite.SQLiteQueryBuilder;
import android.text.TextUtils;

public class MyContentProvider extends ContentProvider {

        private MyDBHandler myDB;
.
.
.

        @Override
        public boolean onCreate() {
                myDB = new MyDBHandler(getContext(), null, null, 1);
                return false;
        }
}
```

44.7 **Implementing the Content Provider insert() Method**

When a client application or activity requests that data be inserted into the underlying database, the *insert()* method of the content provider class will be called. At this point, however, all that exists in the *MyContentProvider.java* file of the project is a stub method, which reads as follows:

```
@Override
```

```
public Uri insert(Uri uri, ContentValues values) {
    // TODO: Implement this to handle requests to insert a new row.
    throw new UnsupportedOperationException("Not yet implemented");
}
```

Passed as arguments to the method are a URI specifying the destination of the insertion and a ContentValues object containing the data to be inserted.

This method now needs to be modified to perform the following tasks:

- Use the sUriMatcher to identify the URI type.
- Throw an exception if the URI is not valid.
- Obtain a reference to a writable instance of the underlying SQLite database.
- Perform a SQL insert operation to insert the data into the database table.
- Notify the corresponding content resolver that the database has been modified.
- Return the URI of the newly added table row.

Bringing these requirements together results in a modified *insert()* method, which reads as follows:

```
@Override
public Uri insert(Uri uri, ContentValues values) {

    int uriType = sURIMatcher.match(uri);

    SQLiteDatabase sqlDB = myDB.getWritableDatabase();

    long id = 0;
    switch (uriType) {
        case PRODUCTS:
            id = sqlDB.insert(MyDBHandler.TABLE_PRODUCTS,
                    null, values);
            break;
        default:
            throw new IllegalArgumentException("Unknown URI: "
                    + uri);
    }
    getContext().getContentResolver().notifyChange(uri, null);
    return Uri.parse(PRODUCTS_TABLE + "/" + id);
}
```

44.8 Implementing the Content Provider query() Method

When a content provider is called upon to return data, the *query()* method of the provider class will be called. When called, this method is passed some or all of the following arguments:

- **URI** – The URI specifying the data source on which the query is to be performed. This can take the form of a general query with multiple results, or a specific query targeting the ID of a single table row.
- **Projection** – A row within a database table can comprise multiple columns of data. In the case of this application, for example, these correspond to the ID, product name and product quantity. The projection argument is simply a String array containing the name for each of the columns that is to be returned in the result data set.
- **Selection** – The "where" element of the selection to be performed as part of the query. This argument controls which rows are selected from the specified database. For example, if the query was required to select only products named "Cat Food" then the selection string passed to the query() method would read *productname = "Cat Food"*.
- **Selection Args** – Any additional arguments that need to be passed to the SQL query operation to perform the selection.
- **Sort Order** – The sort order for the selected rows.

When called, the *query()* method is required to perform the following operations:

- Use the sUriMatcher to identify the Uri type.
- Throw an exception if the URI is not valid.
- Construct a SQL query based on the criteria passed to the method. For convenience, the SQLiteQueryBuilder class can be used in construction of the query.
- Execute the query operation on the database.
- Notify the content resolver of the operation.
- Return a Cursor object containing the results of the query.

With these requirements in mind, the code for the *query()* method in the *MyContentProvider.java* file should now read as outlined in the following listing:

```
@Override
public Cursor query(Uri uri, String[] projection, String selection,
        String[] selectionArgs, String sortOrder) {

    SQLiteQueryBuilder queryBuilder = new SQLiteQueryBuilder();
    queryBuilder.setTables(MyDBHandler.TABLE_PRODUCTS);

    int uriType = sURIMatcher.match(uri);

    switch (uriType) {
        case PRODUCTS_ID:
            queryBuilder.appendWhere(MyDBHandler.COLUMN_ID + "="
                    + uri.getLastPathSegment());
            break;
```

```
        case PRODUCTS:
            break;
        default:
            throw new IllegalArgumentException("Unknown URI");
    }

    Cursor cursor = queryBuilder.query(myDB.getReadableDatabase(),
                projection, selection, selectionArgs, null, null,
                sortOrder);
    cursor.setNotificationUri(getContext().getContentResolver(),
                uri);
    return cursor;

}
```

44.9 Implementing the Content Provider update() Method

The *update()* method of the content provider is called when changes are being requested to existing database table rows. The method is passed a URI, the new values in the form of a ContentValues object and the usual selection argument strings.

When called, the *update()* method would typically perform the following steps:

- Use the sUriMatcher to identify the URI type.
- Throw an exception if the URI is not valid.
- Obtain a reference to a writable instance of the underlying SQLite database.
- Perform the appropriate update operation on the database depending on the selection criteria and the URI type.
- Notify the content resolver of the database change.
- Return a count of the number of rows that were changed as a result of the update operation.

A general-purpose *update()* method, and the one we will use for this project, would read as follows:

```
@Override
public int update(Uri uri, ContentValues values, String selection,
            String[] selectionArgs) {

            int uriType = sURIMatcher.match(uri);
            SQLiteDatabase sqlDB = myDB.getWritableDatabase();
            int rowsUpdated = 0;

            switch (uriType) {
              case PRODUCTS:
```

```
                    rowsUpdated =
                        sqlDB.update(MyDBHandler.TABLE_PRODUCTS,
                        values,
                        selection,
                        selectionArgs);
                break;
            case PRODUCTS_ID:
                String id = uri.getLastPathSegment();
                if (TextUtils.isEmpty(selection)) {
                    rowsUpdated =
                        sqlDB.update(MyDBHandler.TABLE_PRODUCTS,
                            values,
                            MyDBHandler.COLUMN_ID + "=" + id,
                            null);
                } else {
                    rowsUpdated =
                        sqlDB.update(MyDBHandler.TABLE_PRODUCTS,
                            values,
                            MyDBHandler.COLUMN_ID + "=" + id
                            + " and "
                            + selection,
                            selectionArgs);
                }
                break;
            default:
                throw new IllegalArgumentException("Unknown URI: "
                    + uri);
            }
        getContext().getContentResolver().notifyChange(uri,
                                                        null);

        return rowsUpdated;
    }
}
```

44.10 Implementing the Content Provider delete() Method

In common with a number of other content provider methods, the *delete()* method is passed a URI, a selection string and an optional set of selection arguments. A typical *delete()* method will also perform the following, and by now largely familiar, tasks when called:

- Use the sUriMatcher to identify the URI type.
- Throw an exception if the URI is not valid.
- Obtain a reference to a writable instance of the underlying SQLite database.

- Perform the appropriate delete operation on the database depending on the selection criteria and the Uri type.
- Notify the content resolver of the database change.
- Return the number of rows deleted as a result of the operation.

A typical *delete()* method is, in many ways, very similar to the *update()* method and may be implemented as follows:

```
@Override
public int delete(Uri uri, String selection, String[] selectionArgs)
{
        int uriType = sURIMatcher.match(uri);
        SQLiteDatabase sqlDB = myDB.getWritableDatabase();
        int rowsDeleted = 0;

        switch (uriType) {
            case PRODUCTS:
                rowsDeleted = sqlDB.delete(MyDBHandler.TABLE_PRODUCTS,
                  selection,
                   selectionArgs);
                   break;

            case PRODUCTS_ID:
                String id = uri.getLastPathSegment();
                if (TextUtils.isEmpty(selection)) {
                  rowsDeleted = sqlDB.delete(MyDBHandler.TABLE_PRODUCTS,
                            MyDBHandler.COLUMN_ID + "=" + id,
                    null);
                } else {
                  rowsDeleted = sqlDB.delete(MyDBHandler.TABLE_PRODUCTS,
                            MyDBHandler.COLUMN_ID + "=" + id
                    + " and " + selection,
                    selectionArgs);
                }
                break;
            default:
                throw new IllegalArgumentException("Unknown URI: " +
 uri);
        }
        getContext().getContentResolver().notifyChange(uri, null);
        return rowsDeleted;
}
```

With these methods implemented, the content provider class, in terms of the requirements for this example at least, is complete. The next step is to make sure that the content provider is declared in the project manifest file so that it is visible to any content resolvers seeking access to it.

44.11 **Declaring the Content Provider in the Manifest File**

Unless a content provider is declared in the manifest file of the application to which it belongs, it will not be possible for a content resolver to locate and access it. As outlined, content providers are declared using the <provider> tag and the manifest entry must correctly reference the content provider authority and content URI.

For the purposes of this project, therefore, locate the *AndroidManifest.xml* file for the DatabaseProvider project within the Project tool window and double click on it to load it into the editing panel. Within the editing panel, make sure that the content provider declaration has already been added by Android Studio when the MyContentProvider class was added to the project:

```xml
<?xml version="1.0" encoding="utf-8"?>
<manifest xmlns:android="http://schemas.android.com/apk/res/android"
    package="com.ebookfrenzy.database" >

    <application
        android:allowBackup="true"
        android:icon="@mipmap/ic_launcher"
        android:label="@string/app_name"
        android:theme="@style/AppTheme" >
        <activity
            android:name=".DatabaseActivity"
            android:label="@string/app_name" >
            <intent-filter>
                <action android:name="android.intent.action.MAIN" />

                <category
android:name="android.intent.category.LAUNCHER" />
            </intent-filter>
        </activity>

        <provider android:name=".provider.MyContentProvider"
            android:authorities=
    "com.ebookfrenzy.database.provider.MyContentProvider"
            android:enabled="true"
            android:exported="true" >
        </provider>
    </application>
```

```
</manifest>
```

All that remains before testing the application is to modify the database handler class to use the content provider instead of directly accessing the database.

44.12 Modifying the Database Handler

When this application was originally created, it was designed to use a database handler to access the underlying database directly. Now that a content provider has been implemented, the database handler needs to be modified so that all database operations are performed using the content provider via a content resolver.

The first step is to modify the *MyDBHandler.java* class so that it obtains a reference to a ContentResolver instance. This can be achieved in the constructor method of the class:

```java
package com.ebookfrenzy.database;

import com.ebookfrenzy.database.provider.MyContentProvider;

import android.database.sqlite.SQLiteDatabase;
import android.database.sqlite.SQLiteOpenHelper;
import android.content.Context;
import android.content.ContentValues;
import android.database.Cursor;
import android.content.ContentResolver;

public class MyDBHandler extends SQLiteOpenHelper {

    private ContentResolver myCR;

    private static final int DATABASE_VERSION = 1;
    private static final String DATABASE_NAME = "productDB.db";
    public static final String TABLE_PRODUCTS = "products";

    public static final String COLUMN_ID = "_id";
    public static final String COLUMN_PRODUCTNAME = "productname";
    public static final String COLUMN_QUANTITY = "quantity";

    public MyDBHandler(Context context, String name,
                SQLiteDatabase.CursorFactory factory, int version) {
        super(context, DATABASE_NAME, factory, DATABASE_VERSION);
        myCR = context.getContentResolver();
    }
```

```
        .
        .
        .
}
```

Next, the *addProduct()*, *findProduct()* and *removeProduct()* methods need to be re-written to use the content resolver and content provider for data management purposes:

```java
public void addProduct(Product product) {

        ContentValues values = new ContentValues();
        values.put(COLUMN_PRODUCTNAME, product.getProductName());
        values.put(COLUMN_QUANTITY, product.getQuantity());

        myCR.insert(MyContentProvider.CONTENT_URI, values);
}

public Product findProduct(String productname) {
        String[] projection = {COLUMN_ID,
           COLUMN_PRODUCTNAME, COLUMN_QUANTITY };

        String selection = "productname = \"" + productname + "\"";

        Cursor cursor = myCR.query(MyContentProvider.CONTENT_URI,
                projection, selection, null,
                 null);

        Product product = new Product();

        if (cursor.moveToFirst()) {
                cursor.moveToFirst();
                product.setID(Integer.parseInt(cursor.getString(0)));
                product.setProductName(cursor.getString(1));

        product.setQuantity(Integer.parseInt(cursor.getString(2)));
                cursor.close();
        } else {
                product = null;
        }
        return product;
}

public boolean deleteProduct(String productname) {
```

```
        boolean result = false;

        String selection = "productname = \"" + productname + "\"";

        int rowsDeleted = myCR.delete(MyContentProvider.CONTENT_URI,
                selection, null);

        if (rowsDeleted > 0)
                result = true;

        return result;
}
```

With the database handler class updated to use a content resolver and content provider, the application is now ready to be tested. Compile and run the application and perform some operations to add, find and remove product entries. In terms of operation and functionality, the application should behave exactly as it did when directly accessing the database, except that it is now using the content provider.

With the content provider now implemented and declared in the manifest file, any other applications can potentially access that data (since no permissions were declared the default full access is in effect). The only information that the other applications need to know to gain access is the content URI and the names of the columns in the products table.

44.13 Summary

The goal of this chapter has been to provide a more detailed overview of the exact steps involved in implementing an Android content provider with a particular emphasis on the structure and implementation of the query, insert, delete and update methods of the content provider class. Practical use of the content resolver class to access data in the content provider was also covered, and the Database project created in the SQLite tutorial modified to make use of both a content provider and content resolver.

45. Accessing Cloud Storage using the Android Storage Access Framework

Recent years have seen the wide adoption of remote storage services (otherwise known as "cloud storage") to store user files and data. Driving this growth are two key factors. One is that most mobile devices now provide continuous, high speed internet connectivity, thereby making the transfer of data fast and affordable. The second factor is that, relative to traditional computer systems (such as desktops and laptops), these mobile devices are constrained in terms of internal storage resources. A high specification Android tablet today, for example, typically comes with 64Gb of storage capacity. When compared with a mid-range laptop system with a 750Gb disk drive, the need for the seamless remote storage of files is a key requirement for many mobile applications today.

In recognition of this fact, Google introduced the Storage Access Framework as part of the Android 4.4 SDK. This chapter will provide a high level overview of the storage access framework in preparation for the more detail oriented tutorial contained in the next chapter, entitled *An Android Storage Access Framework Example*.

45.1 The Storage Access Framework

From the perspective of the user, the Storage Access Framework provides an easy to use user interface that allows the user to browse, select, delete and create files hosted by storage services (also referred to as *document providers*) from within Android applications. Using this browsing interface (also referred to as the *picker*), users can, for example, browse through the files (such as documents, audio, images and videos) hosted by their chosen document providers. Figure 45-1, for example, shows the picker user interface in action displaying a collection of files hosted by a document provider service:

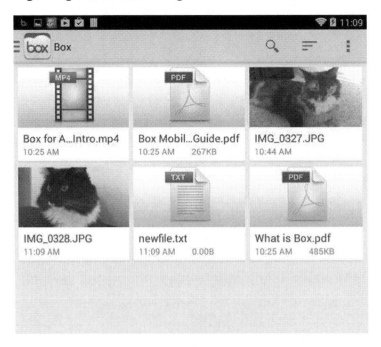

Figure 45-1

In terms of document providers, these can range from cloud-based services to local document providers running on the same device as the client application. At the time of writing, the most prominent document providers compatible with the Storage Access Framework are Box and, unsurprisingly, Google Drive. It is highly likely that other cloud storage providers and application developers will soon also provide services that conform to the Android Storage Access Framework. Figure 45-2, for example, illustrates some document provider options listed by the picker interface:

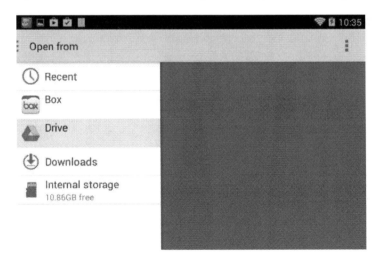

Figure 45-2

As shown in the above figure, in addition to cloud based document providers the picker also provides access to internal storage on the device providing a range of file storage options to the application user.

Through a set of Intents included with Android 4.4, Android application developers can incorporate these storage capabilities into applications with just a few lines of code. A particularly compelling aspect of the Storage Access Framework from the point of view of the developer is that the underlying document provider selected by the user is completely transparent to the application. Once the storage functionality has been implemented using the framework within an application, it will work with all document providers without any code modifications.

45.2 **Working with the Storage Access Framework**

Android 4.4 introduced a new set of Intents designed to integrate the features of the Storage Access Framework into Android applications. These intents display the Storage Access Framework picker user interface to the user and return the results of the interaction to the application via a call to the *onActivityResult()* method of the activity that launched the intent. When the *onActivityResult()* method is called, it is passed the Uri of the selected file together with a value indicating the success or otherwise of the operation.

The Storage Access Framework intents can be summarized as follows:

- **ACTION_OPEN_DOCUMENT** – Provides the user with access to the picker user interface so that files may be selected from the document providers configured on the device. Selected files are passed back to the application in the form of Uri objects.
- **ACTION_CREATE_DOCUMENT** – Allows the user to select a document provider, a location on that provider's storage and a file name for a new file. Once selected, the file is created by the Storage Access Framework and the Uri of that file returned to the application for further processing.

45.3 **Filtering Picker File Listings**

The files listed within the picker user interface when an intent is started may be filtered using a variety of options. Consider, for example, the following code to start an ACTION_OPEN_DOCUMENT intent:

```
private static final int OPEN_REQUEST_CODE = 41;

Intent intent = new Intent(Intent.ACTION_OPEN_DOCUMENT);
startActivityForResult(intent, OPEN_REQUEST_CODE);
```

When executed, the above code will cause the picker user interface to be displayed, allowing the user to browse and select any files hosted by available document providers. Once a file has been selected by the user, a reference to that file will be provided to the application in the form of a Uri object. The application can then open the file using the *openFileDescriptor(Uri, String)* method. There is some risk, however, that not all files listed by a document provider can be opened in this way. The exclusion of such files within the picker can be achieved by modifying the intent using the *CATEGORY_OPENABLE* option. For example:

```
private static final int OPEN_REQUEST_CODE = 41;

Intent intent = new Intent(Intent.ACTION_OPEN_DOCUMENT);
intent.addCategory(Intent.CATEGORY_OPENABLE);
startActivityForResult(intent, OPEN_REQUEST_CODE);
```

When the picker is now displayed, files which cannot be opened using the *openFileDescriptor()* method will be listed but not selectable by the user.

Another useful approach to filtering allows the files available for selection to be restricted by file type. This involves specifying the types of the files the application is able to handle. An image editing application might, for example, only want to provide the user with the option of selecting image files from the document providers. This is achieved by configuring the intent object with the MIME types of the files that are to be selectable by the user. The following code, for example, specifies that only image files are suitable for selection in the picker:

```
Intent intent = new Intent(Intent.ACTION_OPEN_DOCUMENT);

intent.addCategory(Intent.CATEGORY_OPENABLE);
intent.setType("image/*");
startActivityForResult(intent, OPEN_REQUEST_CODE);
```

This could be further refined to limit selection to JPEG images:

```
intent.setType("image/jpeg");
```

Alternatively, an audio player app might only be able to handle audio files:

```
intent.setType("audio/*");
```

The audio app might be limited even further in only supporting the playback of MP4 based audio files:

```
intent.setType("audio/mp4");
```

A wide range of MIME type settings are available for use when working with the Storage Access Framework, the more common of which can be found listed online at:

http://en.wikipedia.org/wiki/Internet_media_type#List_of_common_media_types

45.4 **Handling Intent Results**

When an intent returns control to the application, it does so by calling the *onActivityResult()* method of the activity which started the intent. This method is passed the request code that was handed to the intent at launch time, a result code indicating whether or not the intent was successful and a result data object containing the Uri of the selected file. The following code, for example, might be used as the basis for handling the results from the ACTION_OPEN_DOCUMENT intent outlined in the previous section:

```
public void onActivityResult(int requestCode, int resultCode,
        Intent resultData) {

    Uri currentUri = null;

    if (resultCode == Activity.RESULT_OK)
    {
            if (requestCode == OPEN_REQUEST_CODE)
            {
                    if (resultData != null) {
                            currentUri = resultData.getData();
                            readFileContent(currentUri);
                    }
            }
    }
}
```

The above method verifies that the intent was successful, checks that the request code matches that for a file open request and then extracts the Uri from the intent data. The Uri can then be used to read the content of the file.

45.5 **Reading the Content of a File**

The exact steps required to read the content of a file hosted by a document provider will depend to a large extent on the type of the file. The steps to read lines from a text file, for example, differ from those for image or audio files.

An image file can be assigned to a Bitmap object by extracting the file descriptor from the Uri object and then decoding the image into a BitmapFactory instance. For example:

```
ParcelFileDescriptor pFileDescriptor =
        getContentResolver().openFileDescriptor(uri, "r");

FileDescriptor fileDescriptor =
        pFileDescriptor.getFileDescriptor();
```

```
Bitmap image = BitmapFactory.decodeFileDescriptor(fileDescriptor);

pFileDescriptor.close();

myImageView.setImageBitmap(image);
```

Note that the file descriptor is opened in "r" mode. This indicates that the file is to be opened for reading. Other options are "w" for write access and "rwt" for read and write access where existing content in the file is truncated by the new content.

Reading the content of a text file requires slightly more work and the use of an InputStream object. The following code, for example, reads the lines from a text file:

```
InputStream inputStream = getContentResolver().openInputStream(uri);

BufferedReader reader = new BufferedReader(new InputStreamReader(
                        inputStream));
String readline;

while ((readline = reader.readLine()) != null) {
        // Do something with each line in the file
}
inputStream.close();
```

45.6 Writing Content to a File

Writing to an open file hosted by a document provider is similar to reading with the exception that an output stream is used instead of an input stream. The following code, for example, writes text to the output stream of the storage based file referenced by the specified Uri:

```
try{
        ParcelFileDescriptor pFileDescriptor =
this.getContentResolver().
                openFileDescriptor(uri, "w");

        FileOutputStream fileOutputStream =
                new
FileOutputStream(pFileDescriptor.getFileDescriptor());

        String textContent = "Some sample text";
        fileOutputStream.write(textContent.getBytes());
        fileOutputStream.close();
        pFileDescriptor.close();
```

```
}  catch  (FileNotFoundException  e)  {
      e.printStackTrace();
}  catch  (IOException  e)  {
      e.printStackTrace();
}
```

First, the file descriptor is extracted from the Uri, this time requesting write permission to the target file. The file descriptor is subsequently used to obtain a reference to the file's output stream. The content (in this example some text) is then written to the output stream before the file descriptor and output stream are closed.

45.7 Deleting a File

Whether a file can be deleted from storage depends on whether or not the file's document provider supports deletion of the file. Assuming deletion is permitted, it may be performed on a designated Uri as follows:

```
if  (DocumentsContract.deleteDocument(getContentResolver(),  uri))
      // Deletion was successful
else
      // Deletion failed
```

45.8 Gaining Persistent Access to a File

When an application gains access to a file via the Storage Access Framework, the access will remain valid until the Android device on which the application is running is restarted. Persistent access to a specific file can be obtained by "taking" the necessary permissions for the Uri. The following code, for example, persists read and write permissions for the file referenced by the *fileUri* Uri instance:

```
final int takeFlags = intent.getFlags()
            & (Intent.FLAG_GRANT_READ_URI_PERMISSION
            | Intent.FLAG_GRANT_WRITE_URI_PERMISSION);

getContentResolver().takePersistableUriPermission(fileUri, takeFlags);
```

Once the permissions for the file have been taken by the application, and assuming the Uri has been saved by the application, the user should be able to continue accessing the file after a device restart without the user having to reselect the file from the picker interface.

If, at any time, the persistent permissions are no longer required, they can be released via a call to the *releasePersistableUriPermission()* method of the content resolver:

```
final int releaseFlags = intent.getFlags()
            & (Intent.FLAG_GRANT_READ_URI_PERMISSION
```

```
                | Intent.FLAG_GRANT_WRITE_URI_PERMISSION);

getContentResolver().releasePersistableUriPermission(fileUri,
releaseFlags);
```

45.9 Summary

It is interesting to consider how perceptions of storage have changed in recent years. Once synonymous with high capacity internal hard disk drives, the term "storage" is now just as likely to refer to storage space hosted remotely in the cloud and accessed over an internet connection. This is increasingly the case with the wide adoption of resource constrained, "always-connected" mobile devices with minimal internal storage capacity.

The Android Storage Access Framework provides a simple mechanism for both users and application developers to seamlessly gain access to files stored in the cloud. Through the use of a set of intents introduced into Android 4.4 and a built-in user interface for selecting document providers and files, comprehensive cloud based storage can now be integrated into Android applications with a minimal amount of coding.

46. An Android Storage Access Framework Example

As previously discussed, the Storage Access Framework considerably eases the process of integrating cloud based storage access into Android applications. Consisting of a picker user interface and a set of new intents, access to files stored on document providers such as Google Drive and Box can now be built into Android applications with relative ease. With the basics of the Android Storage Access Framework covered in the preceding chapter, this chapter will work through the creation of an example application which uses the Storage Access Framework to store and manage files.

46.1 About the Storage Access Framework Example

The Android application created in this chapter will take the form of a rudimentary text editor designed to create and store text files remotely onto a cloud based storage service. In practice, the example will work with any cloud based document storage provider that is compatible with the Storage Access Framework, though for the purpose of this example the use of Google Drive is assumed.

In functional terms, the application will present the user with a multi-line text view into which text may be entered and edited, together with a set of buttons allowing storage based text files to be created, opened and saved.

46.2 Creating the Storage Access Framework Example

Create a new project in Android Studio, entering *StorageDemo* into the Application name field and *ebookfrenzy.com* as the Company Domain setting before clicking on the *Next* button.

On the form factors screen, enable the *Phone and Tablet* option and set the minimum SDK setting to API 19: Android 4.4 (KitKat). Continue to proceed through the screens, requesting the creation of a blank activity named *StorageDemoActivity* with a corresponding layout named *activity_storage_demo* and a menu resource file named *menu_storage_demo.*

46.3 Designing the User Interface

The user interface will need to be comprised of three Button views and a single EditText view. Within the Project tool window, navigate to the *activity_storage_demo.xml* layout file located in *app -> res -> layout* and double click on it to load it into the Designer tool. With the tool in Design mode, select and delete the *Hello World!* TextView object.

Switch the Designer tool to Text mode and remove the padding elements from the file so that it now reads as outlined in the following listing:

```
<RelativeLayout
xmlns:android="http://schemas.android.com/apk/res/android"
    xmlns:tools="http://schemas.android.com/tools"
    android:layout_width="match_parent"
    android:layout_height="match_parent"
    android:paddingLeft="@dimen/activity_horizontal_margin"
    android:paddingRight="@dimen/activity_horizontal_margin"
    android:paddingTop="@dimen/activity_vertical_margin"
    android:paddingBottom="@dimen/activity_vertical_margin"
tools:context=".StorageDemoActivity">
```

Return to Design mode and drag and drop three Button objects onto the layout canvas. Position the Button views and change the text properties to "New", "Open" and "Save" so that the user interface layout matches that shown in Figure 46-1:

Figure 46-1

Switch back to Text mode and directly modify the layout to add onClick handlers to the buttons and a multiline EditText view with vertical scrolling enabled:

```
<RelativeLayout
xmlns:android="http://schemas.android.com/apk/res/android"
    xmlns:tools="http://schemas.android.com/tools"
    android:layout_width="match_parent"
    android:layout_height="match_parent"
tools:context=".StorageDemoActivity">

    <Button
        android:layout_width="wrap_content"
        android:layout_height="wrap_content"
        android:text="@string/new_string"
        android:id="@+id/button"
        android:layout_alignParentTop="true"
        android:layout_alignParentStart="true"
        android:onClick="newFile" />

    <Button
        android:layout_width="wrap_content"
        android:layout_height="wrap_content"
        android:text="@string/open_string"
        android:id="@+id/button2"
        android:layout_alignBottom="@+id/button"
        android:layout_toRightOf="@+id/button"
        android:onClick="openFile" />

    <Button
        android:layout_width="wrap_content"
        android:layout_height="wrap_content"
        android:text="@string/save_string"
        android:id="@+id/button3"
        android:layout_alignParentTop="true"
        android:layout_toRightOf="@+id/button2"
        android:onClick="saveFile" />

    <EditText
        android:id="@+id/fileText"
        android:layout_width="match_parent"
        android:layout_height="wrap_content"
        android:layout_alignParentLeft="true"
        android:layout_below="@+id/button"
```

```
            android:inputType="textMultiLine"
            android:scrollbars="vertical" />

</RelativeLayout>
```

46.4 Declaring Request Codes

Working with files in the Storage Access Framework involves triggering a variety of intents depending on the specific action to be performed. Invariably this will result in the framework displaying the storage picker user interface so that the user can specify the storage location (such as a directory on Google Drive and the name of a file). When the work of the intent is complete, the application will be notified by a call to a method named *onActivityResult()*.

Since all intents from a single activity will result in a call to the same *onActivityResult()* method, a mechanism is required to identify which intent triggered the call. This can be achieved by passing a request code through to the intent when it is launched. This code is then passed on to the *onActivityResult()* method by the intents enabling the method to identify which action has been requested by the user. Before implementing the onClick handlers to create, save and open files, the first step is to declare some request codes for these three actions.

Locate and load the *StorageDemoActivity.java* file into the editor and declare constant values for the three actions to be performed by the application. Also add some code to obtain a reference to the multiline EditText object which will be referenced in later methods:

```
package com.ebookfrenzy.storagedemo;

import android.app.Activity;
import android.os.Bundle;
import android.view.Menu;
import android.view.MenuItem;
import android.widget.EditText;

public class StorageDemoActivity extends Activity {

    private static EditText textView;

    private static final int CREATE_REQUEST_CODE = 40;
    private static final int OPEN_REQUEST_CODE = 41;
    private static final int SAVE_REQUEST_CODE = 42;

    @Override
    protected void onCreate(Bundle savedInstanceState) {
        super.onCreate(savedInstanceState);
```

```
        setContentView(R.layout.activity_storage_demo);

        textView = (EditText) findViewById(R.id.fileText);
    }
    .
    .
    .
}
```

46.5 Creating a New Storage File

When the New button is selected, the application will need to trigger an *ACTION_CREATE_DOCUMENT* intent configured to create a file with a plain text MIME type. When the user interface was designed, the New button was configured to call a method named *newFile()*. It is within this method that the appropriate intent needs to be launched.

Remaining in the *StorageDemoActivity.java* file, implement this method as follows:

```
package com.ebookfrenzy.storagedemo;

import android.app.Activity;
import android.os.Bundle;
import android.view.Menu;
import android.view.MenuItem;
import android.widget.EditText;
import android.content.Intent;
import android.view.View;

public class StorageDemoActivity extends Activity {

    private static EditText textView;

    private static final int CREATE_REQUEST_CODE = 40;
    private static final int OPEN_REQUEST_CODE = 41;
    private static final int SAVE_REQUEST_CODE = 42;
    .
    .
    .
    public void newFile(View view)
    {
        Intent intent = new Intent(Intent.ACTION_CREATE_DOCUMENT);

        intent.addCategory(Intent.CATEGORY_OPENABLE);
        intent.setType("text/plain");
```

```
              intent.putExtra(Intent.EXTRA_TITLE, "newfile.txt");

              startActivityForResult(intent, CREATE_REQUEST_CODE);
       }
   .
   .
   .
}
```

This code creates a new ACTION_CREATE_INTENT Intent object. This intent is then configured so that only files that can be opened with a file descriptor are returned (via the Intent.CATEGORY_OPENABLE category setting).

Next the code specifies that the file to be opened is to have a plain text MIME type and a placeholder filename is provided (which can be changed by the user in the picker interface). Finally, the intent is started, passing through the previously declared *CREATE_REQUEST_CODE*.

When this method is executed and the intent has completed the assigned task, a call will be made to the application's *onActivityResult()* method and passed, amongst other arguments, the Uri of the newly created document and the request code that was used when the intent was started. Now is an ideal opportunity to begin to implement this method.

46.6 The onActivityResult() Method

The *onActivityResult()* method will be shared by all of the intents that will be called during the lifecycle of the application. In each case the method will be passed a request code, a result code and a set of result data which contains the Uri of the storage file. The method will need to be implemented such that it checks for the success or otherwise of the intent action, identifies the type of action performed and extracts the file Uri from the results data. At this point in the tutorial, the method only needs to handle the creation of a new file on the selected document provider, so modify the *StorageDemoActivity.java* file to add this method as follows:

```
public void onActivityResult(int requestCode, int resultCode,
        Intent resultData) {

    if (resultCode == Activity.RESULT_OK)
    {
            if (requestCode == CREATE_REQUEST_CODE)
            {
                    if (resultData != null) {
                            textView.setText("");
                    }
            }
```

```
        }
}
```

The code in this method is largely straightforward. The result of the activity is checked and, if successful, the request code is compared to the CREATE_REQUEST_CODE value to verify that the user is creating a new file. That being the case, the edit text view is cleared of any previous text to signify the creation of a new file.

Compile and run the application and select the New button. The Storage Access Framework should subsequently display the "Save to" storage picker user interface as illustrated in Figure 46-2.

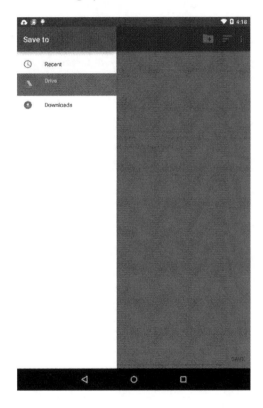

Figure 46-2

From this menu select the *Drive* option followed by *My Drive* and navigate to a suitable location on your Google Drive storage into which to save the file. In the text field at the bottom of the picker interface change the name from "newfile.txt" to a suitable name (but keeping the *.txt* extension) before selecting the *Save* option.

Once the new file has been created, the app should return to the main activity and a notification will appear within the notifications panel which reads "1 file uploaded"

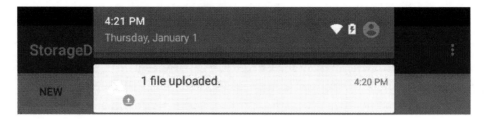

Figure 46-3

At this point it should be possible to log into your Google Drive account in a browser window and find the newly created file in the requested location (in the event that the file is missing, make sure that the Android device on which the application is running has an active internet connection). Access to Google Drive on the device may also be verified by running the Google *Drive* app which is installed by default on many Android devices and available for download from the Google Play store.

46.7 Saving to a Storage File

Now that the application is able to create new storage based files, the next step is to add the ability to save any text entered by the user to a file. The user interface is configured to call the *saveFile()* method when the Save button is selected by the user. This method will be responsible for starting a new intent of type *ACTION_OPEN_DOCUMENT* which will result in the picker user interface appearing so that the user can choose the file to which the text is to be stored. Since we are only working with plain text files, the intent needs to be configured to restrict the user's selection options to existing files that match the text/plain MIME type. Having identified the actions to be performed by the *saveFile()* method, this can now be added to the *StorageDemoActivity.java* class file as follows:

```
public void saveFile(View view)
{
        Intent intent = new Intent(Intent.ACTION_OPEN_DOCUMENT);
        intent.addCategory(Intent.CATEGORY_OPENABLE);
        intent.setType("text/plain");

        startActivityForResult(intent, SAVE_REQUEST_CODE);
}
```

Since the SAVE_REQUEST_CODE was passed through to the intent, the *onActivityResult()* method must now be extended to handle save actions:

```
package com.ebookfrenzy.storagedemo;

import android.app.Activity;
import android.os.Bundle;
import android.view.Menu;
```

```java
import android.view.MenuItem;
import android.widget.EditText;
import android.content.Intent;
import android.view.View;
import android.net.Uri;

public class StorageDemoActivity extends Activity {
.
.

        public void onActivityResult(int requestCode, int resultCode,
                Intent resultData) {

            Uri currentUri = null;

            if (resultCode == Activity.RESULT_OK)
            {
                    if (requestCode == CREATE_REQUEST_CODE)
                    {
                            if (resultData != null) {
                                textView.setText("");
                            }
                    } else if (requestCode == SAVE_REQUEST_CODE) {

                            if (resultData != null) {
                                currentUri =
resultData.getData();

                                writeFileContent(currentUri);
                            }
                    }
            }
        }
.
.
.
}
```

The method now checks for the save request code, extracts the Uri of the file selected by the user in the storage picker and calls a method named *writeFileContent()*, passing through the Uri of the file to which the text is to be written. Remaining in the *StorageDemoActivity.java* file, implement this method now so that it reads as follows:

```java
package com.ebookfrenzy.storagedemo;

import java.io.FileNotFoundException;
```

```java
import java.io.FileOutputStream;
import java.io.IOException;

import android.app.Activity;
import android.os.Bundle;
import android.view.Menu;
import android.view.MenuItem;
import android.widget.EditText;
import android.content.Intent;
import android.view.View;
import android.net.Uri;
import android.os.ParcelFileDescriptor;

public class StorageDemoActivity extends Activity {
.
.

    private void writeFileContent(Uri uri)
    {
            try{
                    ParcelFileDescriptor pfd =
                            this.getContentResolver().
                            openFileDescriptor(uri, "w");

                    FileOutputStream fileOutputStream =
                        new
FileOutputStream(pfd.getFileDescriptor());

                    String textContent =
                            textView.getText().toString();

                    fileOutputStream.write(textContent.getBytes());

                    fileOutputStream.close();
                    pfd.close();
            } catch (FileNotFoundException e) {
                    e.printStackTrace();
            } catch (IOException e) {
                    e.printStackTrace();
            }
    }
.
.
}
```

The method begins by obtaining and opening the file descriptor from the Uri of the file selected by the user. Since the code will need to write to the file, the descriptor is opened in write mode ("w"). The file descriptor is then used as the basis for creating an output stream that will enable the application to write to the file.

The text entered by the user is extracted from the edit text object and written to the output stream before both the file descriptor and stream are closed. Code is also added to handle any IO exceptions encountered during the file writing process.

With the new method added, compile and run the application, enter some text into the text area and select the *Save* button. From the picker interface, locate the previously created file from the Google Drive storage to save the text to that file. Return to your Google Drive account in a browser window and select the text file to display the contents. The file should now contain the text entered within the StorageDemo application on the Android device.

46.8 Opening and Reading a Storage File

Having written the code to create and save text files, the final task is to add some functionality to open and read a file from the storage. This will involve writing the *openFile()* onClick event handler method and implementing it so that it starts an ACTION_OPEN_DOCUMENT intent:

```
public void openFile(View view)
{
        Intent intent = new Intent(Intent.ACTION_OPEN_DOCUMENT);
        intent.addCategory(Intent.CATEGORY_OPENABLE);
        intent.setType("text/plain");
        startActivityForResult(intent, OPEN_REQUEST_CODE);
}
```

In this code, the intent is configured to filter selection to files which can be opened by the application. When the activity is started it is passed the open request code constant which will now need to be handled within the *onActivityResult()* method:

```
public void onActivityResult(int requestCode, int resultCode,
        Intent resultData) {

    Uri currentUri = null;

    if (resultCode == Activity.RESULT_OK)
    {

            if (requestCode == CREATE_REQUEST_CODE)
            {
```

```
                    if (resultData != null) {
                        textView.setText("");
                    }
            } else if (requestCode == SAVE_REQUEST_CODE) {

                if (resultData != null) {
                    currentUri = resultData.getData();
                    writeFileContent(currentUri);
                }
            } else if (requestCode == OPEN_REQUEST_CODE) {

                if (resultData != null) {
                    currentUri = resultData.getData();

                    try {
                        String content =
                                readFileContent(currentUri);
                        textView.setText(content);
                    } catch (IOException e) {
                        // Handle error here
                    }
                }
            }
        }
    }
}
```

The new code added above to handle the open request obtains the Uri of the file selected by the user from the picker user interface and passes it through to a method named *readFileContent()* which is expected to return the content of the selected file in the form of a String object. The resulting string is then assigned to the text property of the edit text view. Clearly, the next task is to implement the *readFileContent()* method:

```
package com.ebookfrenzy.storagedemo;

import java.io.FileNotFoundException;
import java.io.FileOutputStream;
import java.io.IOException;
import java.io.BufferedReader;
import java.io.InputStream;
import java.io.InputStreamReader;

import android.app.Activity;
import android.os.Bundle;
```

```
import android.view.Menu;
import android.view.MenuItem;
import android.widget.EditText;
import android.content.Intent;
import android.view.View;
import android.net.Uri;
import android.os.ParcelFileDescriptor;

public class StorageDemoActivity extends Activity {.
    .
    .
        private String readFileContent(Uri uri) throws IOException {

            InputStream inputStream =
                    getContentResolver().openInputStream(uri);
            BufferedReader reader =
                    new BufferedReader(new InputStreamReader(
                        inputStream));
            StringBuilder stringBuilder = new StringBuilder();
            String currentline;
            while ((currentline = reader.readLine()) != null) {
                    stringBuilder.append(currentline + "\n");
            }
            inputStream.close();
            return stringBuilder.toString();
    }
    .
    .
}
```

This method begins by extracting the file descriptor for the selected text file and opening it for reading. The input stream associated with the Uri is then opened and used as the input source for a BufferedReader instance. Each line within the file is then read and stored in a StringBuilder object. Once all the lines have been read, the input stream and file descriptor are both closed and the file content is returned as a String object.

46.9 Testing the Storage Access Application

With the coding phase complete the application is now ready to be fully tested. Begin by launching the application on a physical Android device and selecting the "New" button. Within the resulting storage picker interface, select a Google Drive location and name the text file *storagedemo.txt* before selecting the Save option located to the right of the file name field.

When control returns to your application look for the file uploading notification, then enter some text into the text area before selecting the "Save" button. Select the previously created *storagedemo.txt* file from the picker to save the content to the file. On returning to the application, delete the text and select the "Open" button, once again choosing the *storagedemo.txt* file. When control is returned to the application, the text view should have been populated with the content of the text file.

It is important to note that the Storage Access Framework will cache storage files locally in the event that the Android device lacks an active internet connection. Once connectivity is re-established, however, any cached data will be synchronized with the remote storage service. As a final test of the application, therefore, log into your Google Drive account in a browser window, navigate to the *storagedemo.txt* file and click on it to view the content which should, all being well, contain the text saved by the application.

46.10 **Summary**

This chapter has worked through the creation of an example Android Studio application in the form of a very rudimentary text editor designed to use cloud based storage to create, save and open files using the Android Storage Access Framework.

47. Implementing Video Playback on Android using the VideoView and MediaController Classes

One of the primary uses for smartphones and tablets is to enable the user to access and consume content. One key form of content widely used, especially in the case of tablet devices, is video.

The Android SDK includes two classes that make the implementation of video playback on Android devices extremely easy to implement when developing applications. This chapter will provide an overview of these two classes, VideoView and MediaController, before working through the creation of a simple video playback application.

47.1 Introducing the Android VideoView Class

By far the simplest way to display video within an Android application is to use the VideoView class. This is a visual component which, when added to the layout of an activity, provides a surface onto which a video may be played. Android currently supports the following video formats:

- H.263
- H.264 AVC
- MPEG-4 SP
- VP8

The VideoView class has a wide range of methods that may be called in order to manage the playback of video. Some of the more commonly used methods are as follows:

- **setVideoPath(String path)** – Specifies the path (as a string) of the video media to be played. This can be either the URL of a remote video file or a video file local to the device.
- **setVideoUri(Uri uri)** – Performs the same task as the setVideoPath() method but takes a Uri object as an argument instead of a string.
- **start()** – Starts video playback.
- **stopPlayback()** – Stops the video playback.
- **pause()** – Pauses video playback.

- **isPlaying()** – Returns a Boolean value indicating whether a video is currently playing.
- **setOnPreparedListener(MediaPlayer.OnPreparedListener)** – Allows a callback method to be called when the video is ready to play.
- **setOnErrorListener(MediaPlayer.OnErrorListener)** - Allows a callback method to be called when an error occurs during the video playback.
- **setOnCompletionListener(MediaPlayer.OnCompletionListener)** - Allows a callback method to be called when the end of the video is reached.
- **getDuration()** – Returns the duration of the video. Will typically return -1 unless called from within the OnPreparedListener() callback method.
- **getCurrentPosition()** – Returns an integer value indicating the current position of playback.
- **setMediaController(MediaController)** – Designates a MediaController instance allowing playback controls to be displayed to the user.

47.2 Introducing the Android MediaController Class

If a video is simply played using the VideoView class, the user will not be given any control over the playback, which will run until the end of the video is reached. This issue can be addressed by attaching an instance of the MediaController class to the VideoView instance. The MediaController will then provide a set of controls allowing the user to manage the playback (such as pausing and seeking backwards/forwards in the video timeline).

The position of the controls is designated by anchoring the controller instance to a specific view in the user interface layout. Once attached and anchored, the controls will appear briefly when playback starts and may subsequently be restored at any point by the user tapping on the view to which the instance is anchored.

Some of the key methods of this class are as follows:

- **setAnchorView(View view)** – Designates the view to which the controller is to be anchored. This controls the location of the controls on the screen.
- **show()** – Displays the controls.
- **show(int timeout)** – Controls are displayed for the designated duration (in milliseconds).
- **hide()** – Hides the controller from the user.
- **isShowing()** – Returns a Boolean value indicating whether the controls are currently visible to the user.

47.3 Testing Video Playback

At the time of writing, it is not possible to test video playback when using the Android AVD emulators. To test the video playback functionality of an application it will be necessary to deploy it onto a physical device.

47.4 **Creating the Video Playback Example**

The remainder of this chapter is dedicated to working through an example application intended to use the VideoView and MediaController classes to play a web based MPEG-4 video file.

Create a new project in Android Studio, entering *VideoPlayer* into the Application name field and *ebookfrenzy.com* as the Company Domain setting before clicking on the *Next* button.

On the form factors screen, enable the *Phone and Tablet* option and set the minimum SDK setting to API 8: Android 2.2 (Froyo). Continue to proceed through the screens, requesting the creation of a blank activity named *VideoPlayerActivity* with a corresponding layout named *activity_video_player* and a menu resource file named *menu_video_player.*

47.5 **Designing the VideoPlayer Layout**

The user interface for the main activity will simply consist solely of an instance of the VideoView class. Use the Project tool window to locate the *VideoPlayer -> app -> res -> layout -> activity_video_player.xml* file, double click on it and switch the Designer tool to Design mode. Delete the "Hello world!" TextView, switch to Text mode and remove the padding properties from the layout so that the XML reads as follows:

```
<RelativeLayout
xmlns:android="http://schemas.android.com/apk/res/android"
    xmlns:tools="http://schemas.android.com/tools"
    android:layout_width="match_parent"
    android:layout_height="match_parent"
    android:paddingLeft="@dimen/activity_horizontal_margin"
    android:paddingRight="@dimen/activity_horizontal_margin"
    android:paddingTop="@dimen/activity_vertical_margin"
    android:paddingBottom="@dimen/activity_vertical_margin"
tools:context=".VideoPlayerActivity">

</RelativeLayout>
```

Switch back to Design mode and, from the *Containers* section of the Palette panel, drag and drop a VideoView instance onto the center point of the layout so that the user interface resembles that of Figure 47-1:

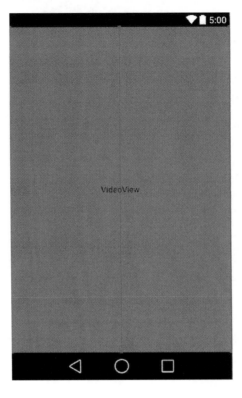

Figure 47-1

Double click on the VideoView instance in the device screen layout and change the ID of the component to *videoView1*. Finally, either edit the XML or use the Designer toolbar buttons to change the layout_width and layout_height properties for the VideoView instance to *match_parent*.

47.6 Configuring the VideoView

The next step is to configure the VideoView with the path of the video to be played and then start the playback. This will be performed when the main activity has initialized, so load the *VideoPlayerActivity.java* file into the editor and modify the *OnCreate()* method as outlined in the following listing:

```
package com.ebookfrenzy.videoplayer;

import android.support.v7.app.ActionBarActivity;
import android.os.Bundle;
import android.view.Menu;
import android.view.MenuItem;
import android.widget.VideoView;

public class VideoPlayerActivity extends ActionBarActivity {
```

```
    @Override
    protected void onCreate(Bundle savedInstanceState) {
        super.onCreate(savedInstanceState);
        setContentView(R.layout.activity_video_player);

        final VideoView videoView =
                (VideoView) findViewById(R.id.videoView1);

        videoView.setVideoPath(
                "http://www.ebookfrenzy.com/android_book/movie.mp4");

        videoView.start();
    }
.
.
.
}
```

All that this code does is obtain a reference to the VideoView instance in the layout, set the video path on it to point to an MPEG-4 file hosted on a web site and then start the video playing.

47.7 **Adding Internet Permission**

An attempt to run the application at this point would result in the application failing to launch with an error dialog appearing on the Android device that reads "Unable to Play Video. Sorry, this video cannot be played". This is not because of an error in the code or an incorrect video file format. The issue would be that the application is attempting to access a file over the internet, but has failed to request appropriate permissions to do so. To resolve this, edit the *AndroidManifest.xml* file for the project and add a line to request internet access:

```
<?xml version="1.0" encoding="utf-8"?>
<manifest xmlns:android="http://schemas.android.com/apk/res/android"
    package="com.ebookfrenzy.videoplayer.videoplayer" >

    <uses-permission android:name="android.permission.INTERNET" />

    <application
        android:allowBackup="true"
        android:icon="@mipmap/ic_launcher"
        android:label="@string/app_name"
        android:theme="@style/AppTheme" >
```

```
    .
    .
</manifest>
```

Test the application by running it on a physical Android device. After the application launches there may be a short delay while video content is buffered before the playback begins (Figure 47-2).

Figure 47-2

This provides an indication of how easy it can be to integrate video playback into an Android application. Everything so far in this example has been achieved using a VideoView instance and three lines of code.

47.8 Adding the MediaController to the Video View

As the VideoPlayer application currently stands, there is no way for the user to control playback. As previously outlined, this can be achieved using the MediaController class. To add a controller to the VideoView, modify the *onCreate()* method once again:

```
package com.ebookfrenzy.videoplayer;

import android.support.v7.app.ActionBarActivity;
import android.os.Bundle;
import android.view.Menu;
```

```
import android.view.MenuItem;
import android.widget.VideoView;
import android.widget.MediaController;

public class VideoPlayerActivity extends Activity {

    @Override
    protected void onCreate(Bundle savedInstanceState) {
        super.onCreate(savedInstanceState);
        setContentView(R.layout.activity_video_player);

        final VideoView videoView = (VideoView)
                    findViewById(R.id.videoView1);

        videoView.setVideoPath(
            "http://www.ebookfrenzy.com/android_book/movie.mp4");

        MediaController mediaController = new
                MediaController(this);
        mediaController.setAnchorView(videoView);
        videoView.setMediaController(mediaController);

        videoView.start();
    }
    .
    .
    .
}
```

When the application is launched with these changes implemented, the media controls will appear over the video playback for a few seconds at the start of playback. These controls should include a seekbar, volume control and a play/pause button. After the controls recede from view, they can be restored by tapping on the VideoView canvas. With just three more lines of code, our video player application now has media controls as shown in Figure 47-3:

Figure 47-3

47.9 **Setting up the onPreparedListener**

As a final example of working with video based media, the *onCreate()* method will now be extended further to demonstrate the mechanism for configuring a listener. In this case, a listener will be implemented that is intended to output the duration of the video as a message in the Android Studio LogCat panel:

```java
package com.ebookfrenzy.videoplayer;

import android.support.v7.app.ActionBarActivity;
import android.os.Bundle;
import android.view.Menu;
import android.view.MenuItem;
import android.widget.VideoView;
import android.widget.MediaController;
import android.util.Log;
import android.media.MediaPlayer;

public class VideoPlayerActivity extends ActionBarActivity {

    String TAG = "VideoPlayer";

    @Override
    protected void onCreate(Bundle savedInstanceState) {
        super.onCreate(savedInstanceState);
        setContentView(R.layout.activity_video_player);

        final VideoView videoView =
                (VideoView) findViewById(R.id.videoView1);

        videoView.setVideoPath(
                "http://www.ebookfrenzy.com/android_book/movie.mp4");

        MediaController mediaController = new
                MediaController(this);
        mediaController.setAnchorView(videoView);
        videoView.setMediaController(mediaController);

        videoView.setOnPreparedListener(new
                MediaPlayer.OnPreparedListener()   {
                    @Override
                    public void onPrepared(MediaPlayer mp) {
                        Log.i(TAG, "Duration = " +
```

```
                                           videoView.getDuration());
                    }
         });

         videoView.start();


    }
    .
    .
    .
}
```

Now just before the video playback begins, a message will appear in the Android Studio LogCat panel that reads along the lines of:

```
05-30 13:13:33.955   30044-
30044/com.ebookfrenzy.videoplayer.videoplayer I/VideoPlayer : Duration
= 6874
```

47.10 Summary

Tablet based Android devices make excellent platforms for the delivery of content to users, particularly in the form of video media. As outlined in this chapter, the Android SDK provides two classes, namely VideoView and MediaController, which combine to make the integration of video playback into Android applications quick and easy, often involving just a few lines of Java code.

48. Video Recording and Image Capture on Android using Camera Intents

Many Android devices are equipped with at least one camera. There are a number of ways to allow the user to record video from within an Android application via these built-in cameras, but by far the easiest approach is to make use of a camera intent included with the Android operating system. This allows an application to invoke the standard Android video recording interface. When the user has finished recording, the intent will return to the application, passing through a reference to the media file containing the recorded video.

As will be demonstrated in this chapter, this approach allows video recording capabilities to be added to applications with just a few lines of code.

48.1 Checking for Camera Support

Before attempting to access the camera on an Android device, it is essential that defensive code be implemented to verify the presence of camera hardware. This is of particular importance since not all Android devices include a camera.

The presence or otherwise of a camera can be identified via a call to the *PackageManager.hasSystemFeature()* method. In order to check for the presence of a front-facing camera, the code needs to check for the presence of the *PackageManager.FEATURE_CAMERA_FRONT* feature. This can be encapsulated into the following convenience method:

```
private boolean hasCamera() {
    if (getPackageManager().hasSystemFeature(
        PackageManager.FEATURE_CAMERA_FRONT)){
            return true;
    } else {
            return false;
    }
}
```

The presence of a camera facing away from the device screen can be similarly verified using the *PackageManager.FEATURE_CAMERA* constant. A test for whether a device has any camera can be performed by referencing *PackageManager.FEATURE_CAMERA_ANY*.

48.2 Calling the Video Capture Intent

Use of the video capture intent involves, at a minimum, the implementation of code to call the intent activity and a method to handle the return from the activity. The Android built-in video recording intent is represented by *MediaStore.ACTION_VIDEO_CAPTURE* and may be launched as follows:

```
private static final int VIDEO_CAPTURE = 101;

Intent intent = new Intent(MediaStore.ACTION_VIDEO_CAPTURE);
startActivityForResult(intent, VIDEO_CAPTURE);
```

When invoked in this way, the intent will place the recorded video into a file using a default location and file name. A specific location for the media file may be specified using the *putExtra()* method of the intent, referencing the *MediaStore.EXTRA_OUTPUT* key constant to pass through the target URI value. The following code, for example, specifies that the video should be stored on the SD card in a file named *myvideo.mp4*:

```
File mediaFile =
    new
File(Environment.getExternalStorageDirectory().getAbsolutePath()
        + "/myvideo.mp4");

Intent intent = new Intent(MediaStore.ACTION_VIDEO_CAPTURE);

Uri videoUri = Uri.fromFile(mediaFile);

intent.putExtra(MediaStore.EXTRA_OUTPUT, videoUri);
startActivityForResult(intent, VIDEO_CAPTURE);
```

When the user either completes or cancels the video recording session, the *onActivityResult()* method of the calling activity will be called. This method needs to check that the request code passed through as an argument matches that specified when the intent was launched, verify that the recording session was successful and extract the path of the video media file. The corresponding *onActivityResult()* method for the above intent launch code might, therefore, be implemented as follows:

```
protected void onActivityResult(int requestCode, int resultCode,
Intent data) {
    if (requestCode == VIDEO_CAPTURE) {
        if (resultCode == RESULT_OK) {
```

```
            Toast.makeText(this, "Video saved to:\n" +
                    videoUri, Toast.LENGTH_LONG).show();
        } else if (resultCode == RESULT_CANCELED) {
            Toast.makeText(this, "Video recording cancelled.",
                    Toast.LENGTH_LONG).show();
        } else {
            Toast.makeText(this, "Failed to record video",
                    Toast.LENGTH_LONG).show();
        }
    }
}
```

The above code example simply displays a toast message indicating the success or otherwise of the recording intent session. In the event of a successful recording, the path to the stored video file is displayed.

When executed, the video capture intent (Figure 48-1) will launch and provide the user the opportunity to record video.

Figure 48-1

48.3 Calling the Image Capture Intent

In addition to the video capture intent, Android also includes an intent designed for taking still photos using the built-in camera. This intent is launched by referencing *MediaStore.ACTION_IMAGE_CAPTURE*:

```
private static final int IMAGE_CAPTURE = 102;

Intent intent = new Intent(MediaStore.ACTION_IMAGE_CAPTURE);
startActivityForResult(intent, IMAGE_CAPTURE);
```

As with video capture, the intent may be passed the location and file name into which the image is to be stored, or left to use the default location and naming convention.

48.4 **Creating an Android Studio Video Recording Project**

In the remainder of this chapter, a very simple application will be created to demonstrate the use of the video capture intent. The application will consist of a single button which, when touched by the user, will launch the video capture intent. Once video has been recorded and the video capture intent dismissed, the application will simply display the path to the video file as a Toast message. The VideoPlayer application created in the previous chapter may then be modified to play back the recorded video.

Create a new project in Android Studio, entering *CameraApp* into the Application name field and *ebookfrenzy.com* as the Company Domain setting before clicking on the *Next* button.

On the form factors screen, enable the *Phone and Tablet* option and set the minimum SDK setting to API 8: Android 2.2 (Froyo). Continue to proceed through the screens, requesting the creation of a blank activity named *CameraAppActivity* with layout and menu resource files named *activity_camera_app* and *menu_camera_app.*

48.5 **Designing the User Interface Layout**

Navigate to *app -> res -> layout* and double click on the *activity_camera_app.xml* layout file to load it into the Designer tool. With the Designer tool in Design mode, delete the default "Hello world!" text view and replace it with a Button view positioned in the center of the display canvas. Change the text on the button to read "Record Video" and assign an *onClick* property to the button so that it calls a method named *startRecording* when selected by the user:

Figure 48-2

Finally, double click on the button and change the ID to *recordButton.* The corresponding XML in the *activity_camera_app.xml* file should approximately resemble the following listing:

```xml
<RelativeLayout
xmlns:android="http://schemas.android.com/apk/res/android"
    xmlns:tools="http://schemas.android.com/tools"
    android:layout_width="match_parent"
    android:layout_height="match_parent"
    android:paddingLeft="@dimen/activity_horizontal_margin"
    android:paddingRight="@dimen/activity_horizontal_margin"
    android:paddingTop="@dimen/activity_vertical_margin"
    android:paddingBottom="@dimen/activity_vertical_margin"
tools:context=".CameraAppActivity">

    <Button
        android:layout_width="wrap_content"
        android:layout_height="wrap_content"
        android:text="@string/record_string"
        android:id="@+id/recordButton"
        android:layout_centerVertical="true"
        android:layout_centerHorizontal="true"
        android:onClick="startRecording" />

</RelativeLayout>
```

48.6 Checking for the Camera

Before attempting to launch the video capture intent, the application first needs to verify that the device on which it is running actually has a camera. For the purposes of this example, we will simply make use of the previously outlined *hasCamera()* method, this time checking for any camera type. In the event that a camera is not present, the Record Video button will be disabled.

Edit the *CameraAppActivity.java* file and modify it as follows:

```java
package com.ebookfrenzy.cameraapp;

import android.support.v7.app.ActionBarActivity;
import android.os.Bundle;
import android.view.Menu;
import android.view.MenuItem;
import android.content.pm.PackageManager;
import android.widget.Button;

public class CameraAppActivity extends ActionBarActivity {
```

```
        @Override
        protected void onCreate(Bundle savedInstanceState) {
                super.onCreate(savedInstanceState);
                setContentView(R.layout.activity_camera_app);

                Button recordButton =
                    (Button) findViewById(R.id.recordButton);

                if (!hasCamera())
                        recordButton.setEnabled(false);
        }

        private boolean hasCamera() {
            if (getPackageManager().hasSystemFeature(
                        PackageManager.FEATURE_CAMERA_ANY)){
                return true;
            } else {
                return false;
            }
        }
    }
    .
    .
    .
}
```

48.7 Launching the Video Capture Intent

The objective is for the video capture intent to launch when the user selects the *Record Video* button. Since this is now configured to call a method named *startRecording()*, the next logical step is to implement this method within the *CameraAppActivity.java* source file:

```
package com.ebookfrenzy.cameraapp;

import java.io.File;

import android.support.v7.app.ActionBarActivity;
import android.os.Bundle;
import android.view.Menu;
import android.view.MenuItem;
import android.content.pm.PackageManager;
import android.widget.Button;
import android.net.Uri;
import android.os.Environment;
```

```
import android.provider.MediaStore;
import android.content.Intent;
import android.view.View;

public class CameraAppActivity extends ActionBarActivity {

    private static final int VIDEO_CAPTURE = 101;
    private Uri fileUri;

    public void startRecording(View view)
    {
        File mediaFile = new

File(Environment.getExternalStorageDirectory().getAbsolutePath()
                + "/myvideo.mp4");

        Intent intent = new Intent(MediaStore.ACTION_VIDEO_CAPTURE);
        fileUri = Uri.fromFile(mediaFile);

        intent.putExtra(MediaStore.EXTRA_OUTPUT, fileUri);
        startActivityForResult(intent, VIDEO_CAPTURE);
    }
    .
    .
    .
}
```

48.8 Handling the Intent Return

When control returns back from the intent to the application's main activity the *onActivityResult()* method will be called. All that this method needs to do for this example is verify the success or otherwise of the video capture and display the path of the file into which the video has been stored:

```
package com.ebookfrenzy.cameraapp;

import java.io.File;

import android.support.v7.app.ActionBarActivity;
import android.os.Bundle;
import android.view.Menu;
import android.view.MenuItem;
import android.content.pm.PackageManager;
import android.widget.Button;
import android.net.Uri;
```

```
import android.os.Environment;
import android.provider.MediaStore;
import android.content.Intent;
import android.view.View;
import android.widget.Toast;

public class CameraAppActivity extends ActionBarActivity {
.
.
.

    protected void onActivityResult(int requestCode,
            int resultCode, Intent data) {

        if (requestCode == VIDEO_CAPTURE) {
            if (resultCode == RESULT_OK) {
                Toast.makeText(this, "Video has been saved to:\n" +
                        fileUri, Toast.LENGTH_LONG).show();
            } else if (resultCode == RESULT_CANCELED) {
                Toast.makeText(this, "Video recording cancelled.",
                        Toast.LENGTH_LONG).show();
            } else {
                Toast.makeText(this, "Failed to record video",
                        Toast.LENGTH_LONG).show();
            }
        }
    }
.
.
.
}
```

48.9 Testing the Application

Compile and run the application on a physical Android device, touch the record button and use the video capture intent to record some video. Once completed, stop the video recording. Play back the recording by selecting the play button on the screen. Finally, touch the *Done* (sometimes represented by a check mark) button on the screen to return to the CameraApp application. On returning, a Toast message should appear stating that the video has been stored in a specific location on the device (the exact location will differ from one device type to another).

From the Android Studio welcome screen, locate the VideoPlayer project created in the previous chapter, navigate to the *VideoPlayerActivity.java* file and modify the *setVideoPath()* method call to reference the newly recorded video file path.

Running the modified VideoPlayer application on the Android device should result in the previously recorded video being played back.

48.10 Summary

Most Android tablet and smartphone devices include a camera that can be accessed by applications. Whilst there are a number of different approaches to adding camera support to applications, the Android video and image capture intents provide a simple and easy solution to capturing video and images.

49. Android Audio Recording and Playback using MediaPlayer and MediaRecorder

This chapter will provide an overview of the MediaRecorder class and explain the basics of how this class can be used to record audio or video. The use of the MediaPlayer class to play back audio will also be covered. Having covered the basics, an example application will be created to demonstrate these techniques in action. In addition to looking at audio and video handling, this chapter will also touch on the subjects of saving files to the SD card and the steps involved in detecting whether or not a device has a microphone or camera.

49.1 Playing Audio

In terms of audio playback, most implementations of Android support AAC LC/LTP, HE-AACv1 (AAC+), HE-AACv2 (enhanced AAC+), AMR-NB, AMR-WB, MP3, MIDI, Ogg Vorbis, and PCM/WAVE formats.

Audio playback can be performed using either the MediaPlayer or the AudioTrack classes. AudioTrack is a more advanced option that uses streaming audio buffers and provides greater control over the audio. The MediaPlayer class, on the other hand, provides an easier programming interface for implementing audio playback and will meet the needs of most audio requirements.

The MediaPlayer class has associated with it a range of methods that can be called by an application to perform certain tasks. A subset of some of the key methods of this class is as follows:

- **create()** – Called to create a new instance of the class, passing through the Uri of the audio to be played.
- **setDataSource()** – Sets the source from which the audio is to play.
- **prepare()** – Instructs the player to prepare to begin playback.
- **start()** – Starts the playback.
- **pause()** – Pauses the playback. Playback may be resumed via a call to the *resume()* method.
- **stop()** – Stops playback.

- **setVolume()** – Takes two floating-point arguments specifying the playback volume for the left and right channels.
- **resume()** – Resumes a previously paused playback session.
- **reset()** – Resets the state of the media player instance. Essentially sets the instance back to the uninitialized state. At a minimum, a reset player will need to have the data source set again and the *prepare()* method called.
- **release()** – To be called when the player instance is no longer needed. This method ensures that any resources held by the player are released.

In a typical implementation, an application will instantiate an instance of the MediaPlayer class, set the source of the audio to be played and then call *prepare()* followed by *start()*. For example:

```
MediaPlayer mediaPlayer = new MediaPlayer();

mediaPlayer.setDataSource("http://www.ebookfrenzy.com/myaudio.mp3");
mediaPlayer.prepare();
mediaPlayer.start();
```

49.2 Recording Audio and Video using the MediaRecorder Class

As with audio playback, recording can be performed using a number of different techniques. One option is to use the MediaRecorder class, which, as with the MediaPlayer class, provides a number of methods that are used to record audio:

- **setAudioSource()** – Specifies the source of the audio to be recorded (typically this will be MediaRecorder.AudioSource.MIC for the device microphone).
- **setVideoSource()** – Specifies the source of the video to be recorded (for example MediaRecorder.VideoSource.CAMERA).
- **setOutputFormat()** – Specifies the format into which the recorded audio or video is to be stored (for example MediaRecorder.OutputFormat.AAC_ADTS).
- **setAudioEncoder()** – Specifies the audio encoder to be used for the recorded audio (for example MediaRecorder.AudioEncoder.AAC).
- **setOutputFile()** – Configures the path to the file into which the recorded audio or video is to be stored.
- **prepare()** – Prepares the MediaRecorder instance to begin recording.
- **start()** - Begins the recording process.
- **stop()** – Stops the recording process. Once a recorder has been stopped, it will need to be completely reconfigured and prepared before being restarted.
- **reset()** – Resets the recorder. The instance will need to be completely reconfigured and prepared before being restarted.

- **release()** – Should be called when the recorder instance is no longer needed. This method ensures all resources held by the instance are released.

A typical implementation using this class will set the source, output and encoding format and output file. Calls will then be made to the *prepare()* and *start()* methods. The *stop()* method will then be called when recording is to end followed by the *reset()* method. When the application no longer needs the recorder instance a call to the *release()* method is recommended:

```
MediaRecorder mediaRecorder = new MediaRecorder();

mediaRecorder.setAudioSource(MediaRecorder.AudioSource.MIC);
mediaRecorder.setOutputFormat(MediaRecorder.OutputFormat.AAC_ADTS);
mediaRecorder.setAudioEncoder(MediaRecorder.AudioEncoder.AAC);
mediaRecorder.setOutputFile(audioFilePath);

mediaRecorder.prepare();
mediaRecorder.start();
.
.
.
mediaRecorder.stop()
mediaRecorder.reset()
mediaRecorder.release()
```

In order to record audio, the manifest file for the application must include the android.permission.RECORD_AUDIO permission:

```
<uses-permission android:name="android.permission.RECORD_AUDIO" />
```

49.3 **About the Example Project**

The remainder of this chapter will work through the creation of an example application intended to demonstrate the use of the MediaPlayer and MediaRecorder classes to implement the recording and playback of audio on an Android device.

When developing applications that make use of specific hardware features, the microphone being a case in point, it is important to check the availability of the feature before attempting to access it in the application code. The application created in this chapter will, therefore, also demonstrate the steps involved in detecting the presence or otherwise of a microphone on the device.

Once completed, this application will provide a very simple interface intended to allow the user to record and playback audio. The recorded audio will need to be stored within an audio file on the device. That being the case, this tutorial will also briefly explore the mechanism for using SD Card storage.

49.4 **Creating the AudioApp Project**

Create a new project in Android Studio, entering *AudioApp* into the Application name field and *ebookfrenzy.com* as the Company Domain setting before clicking on the *Next* button.

On the form factors screen, enable the *Phone and Tablet* option and set the minimum SDK setting to API 8: Android 2.2 (Froyo). Continue to proceed through the screens, requesting the creation of a blank activity named *AudioAppActivity* with corresponding layout and menu resource files named *activity_audio_app* and *menu_audio_app* respectively.

49.5 **Designing the User Interface**

Once the new project has been created, select the *activity_audio_app.xml* file from the Project tool window and, with the Designer tool in Design mode, select the "Hello world!" TextView and delete it from the layout. Drag and drop three Button views onto the layout. The positioning of the buttons is not of paramount importance to this example, though Figure 49-1 shows a suggested layout.

Configure the buttons to display string resources that read *Play, Record* and *Stop* and give them view IDs of *recordButton, playButton,* and *stopButton* respectively.

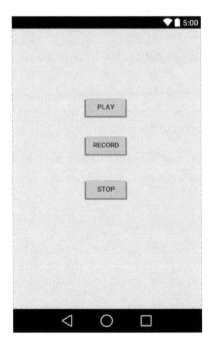

Figure 49-1

Select the Play button and, within the Properties panel, configure the *OnClick* property to call a method named *playAudio* when selected by the user. Repeat these steps to configure the remaining buttons to call methods named *recordAudio* and *stopAudio* respectively.

49.6 **Checking for Microphone Availability**

Attempting to record audio on a device without a microphone will cause the Android system to throw an exception. It is vital, therefore, that the code check for the presence of a microphone before making such an attempt. There are a number of ways of doing this including checking for the physical presence of the device. An easier approach, and one that is more likely to work on different Android devices, is to ask the Android system if it has a package installed for a particular *feature*. This involves creating an instance of the Android PackageManager class and then making a call to the object's *hasSystemFeature()* method. In this case, the feature of interest is *PackageManager.FEATURE_MICROPHONE*.

For the purposes of this example, we will create a method named *hasMicrophone()* that may be called upon to check for the presence of a microphone. Within the Project tool window, locate and double click on the *AudioAppActivity.java* file and modify it to add this method:

```
package com.ebookfrenzy.audioapp;

import android.support.v7.app.ActionBarActivity;
import android.os.Bundle;
import android.view.Menu;
import android.view.MenuItem;
import android.content.pm.PackageManager;

public class AudioAppActivity extends ActionBarActivity {

    @Override
    protected void onCreate(Bundle savedInstanceState) {
        super.onCreate(savedInstanceState);
        setContentView(R.layout.activity_audio_app);
    }

    protected boolean hasMicrophone() {
        PackageManager pmanager = this.getPackageManager();
        return pmanager.hasSystemFeature(
                PackageManager.FEATURE_MICROPHONE);
    }
.
.
}
```

49.7 **Performing the Activity Initialization**

The next step is to modify the *onCreate()* method of the activity to perform a number of initialization tasks. Remaining within the *AudioAppActivity.java* file, modify the method as follows:

```java
package com.ebookfrenzy.audioapp;

import java.io.IOException;

import android.support.v7.app.ActionBarActivity;
import android.os.Bundle;
import android.view.Menu;
import android.view.MenuItem;
import android.content.pm.PackageManager;
import android.media.MediaRecorder;
import android.os.Environment;
import android.widget.Button;
import android.view.View;
import android.media.MediaPlayer;

public class AudioAppActivity extends ActionBarActivity {

        private static MediaRecorder mediaRecorder;
        private static MediaPlayer mediaPlayer;

        private static String audioFilePath;
        private static Button stopButton;
        private static Button playButton;
        private static Button recordButton;

        private boolean isRecording = false;

        @Override
        protected void onCreate(Bundle savedInstanceState) {
                super.onCreate(savedInstanceState);
                setContentView(R.layout.activity_audio_app);

            recordButton = (Button)
 findViewById(R.id.recordButton);
                playButton = (Button) findViewById(R.id.playButton);
                stopButton = (Button) findViewById(R.id.stopButton);

                if (!hasMicrophone())
                {
```

```
                    stopButton.setEnabled(false);
                    playButton.setEnabled(false);
                    recordButton.setEnabled(false);
            } else {
                    playButton.setEnabled(false);
                    stopButton.setEnabled(false);
            }

            audioFilePath =

Environment.getExternalStorageDirectory().getAbsolutePath()
                    + "/myaudio.3gp";
        }
    .
    .
}
```

The added code begins by obtaining references to the three button views in the user interface. Next, the previously implemented *hasMicrophone()* method is called to ascertain whether the device includes a microphone. If it does not, all the buttons are disabled, otherwise only the Stop and Play buttons are disabled.

The next line of code needs a little more explanation:

```
audioFilePath =
        Environment.getExternalStorageDirectory().getAbsolutePath()
            + "/myaudio.3gp";
```

The purpose of this code is to identify the location of the SD card storage on the device and to use that to create a path to a file named *myaudio.acc* into which the audio recording will be stored. The path of the SD card (which is referred to as external storage even though it is internal to the device on many Android devices) is obtained via a call to the *getExternalStorageDirectory()* method of the Android Environment class.

When working with external storage it is important to be aware that such activity by an application requires permission to be requested in the application manifest file. For example:

```
<uses-permission
android:name="android.permission.WRITE_EXTERNAL_STORAGE" />
```

49.8 Implementing the recordAudio() Method

When the user touches the Record button, the *recordAudio()* method will be called. This method will need to enable and disable the appropriate buttons, configure the MediaRecorder instance with information about the source of the audio, the output format and encoding and the location of the file into which the audio is to be stored. Finally, the *prepare()* and *start()* methods of the MediaRecorder object will need to be called. Combined, these requirements result in the following method implementation in the *AudioAppActivity.java* file:

```java
public void recordAudio (View view) throws IOException
{
    isRecording = true;
    stopButton.setEnabled(true);
    playButton.setEnabled(false);
    recordButton.setEnabled(false);

    try {
        mediaRecorder = new MediaRecorder();
        mediaRecorder.setAudioSource(MediaRecorder.AudioSource.MIC);

mediaRecorder.setOutputFormat(MediaRecorder.OutputFormat.THREE_GPP);
        mediaRecorder.setOutputFile(audioFilePath);
        mediaRecorder.setAudioEncoder(MediaRecorder.AudioEncoder.AMR_NB);
        mediaRecorder.prepare();
    } catch (Exception e) {
            e.printStackTrace();
    }

    mediaRecorder.start();
}
```

49.9 Implementing the stopAudio() Method

The *stopAudio()* method is responsible for enabling the Play button, disabling the Stop button and then stopping and resetting the MediaRecorder instance. The code to achieve this reads as outlined in the following listing and should be added to the *AudioAppAcitivy.java* file:

```java
public void stopAudio (View view)
{

        stopButton.setEnabled(false);
        playButton.setEnabled(true);

        if (isRecording)
        {
                recordButton.setEnabled(false);
                mediaRecorder.stop();
```

```
            mediaRecorder.release();
            mediaRecorder = null;
            isRecording = false;
    } else {
            mediaPlayer.release();
            mediaPlayer = null;
            recordButton.setEnabled(true);
    }
}
```

49.10 Implementing the playAudio() method

The *playAudio()* method will simply create a new MediaPlayer instance, assign the audio file located on the SD card as the data source and then prepare and start the playback:

```
public void playAudio (View view) throws IOException
{
    playButton.setEnabled(false);
    recordButton.setEnabled(false);
    stopButton.setEnabled(true);

    mediaPlayer = new MediaPlayer();
    mediaPlayer.setDataSource(audioFilePath);
    mediaPlayer.prepare();
    mediaPlayer.start();
}
```

49.11 Configuring Permissions in the Manifest File

Before testing the application, it is essential that the appropriate permissions be requested within the manifest file for the application. Specifically, the application will require permission to record audio and to access the external storage (SD card). Within the Project tool window, locate and double click on the *AndroidManifest.xml* file to load it into the editor and modify the XML to add the two permission tags:

```
<?xml version="1.0" encoding="utf-8"?>
<manifest xmlns:android="http://schemas.android.com/apk/res/android"
    package="com.ebookfrenzy.audioapp" >

    <uses-permission android:name=
                "android.permission.WRITE_EXTERNAL_STORAGE" />
    <uses-permission android:name="android.permission.RECORD_AUDIO" />

    <application
```

```
            android:allowBackup="true"
            android:icon="@mipmap/ic_launcher"
            android:label="@string/app_name"
            android:theme="@style/AppTheme" >
            <activity android:name=".AudioAppActivity"
                android:label="@string/app_name" >
                <intent-filter>
                    <action android:name="android.intent.action.MAIN" />

                    <category android:name=
                        "android.intent.category.LAUNCHER" />
                </intent-filter>
            </activity>
        </application>

</manifest>
```

49.12 Testing the Application

Compile and run the application on an Android device containing a microphone and touch the Record button. After recording, touch Stop followed by Play, at which point the recorded audio should play back through the device speakers.

49.13 Summary

The Android SDK provides a number of mechanisms for the implementation of audio recording and playback. This chapter has looked at two of these in the form of the MediaPlayer and MediaRecorder classes. Having covered the theory of using these techniques, this chapter worked through the creation of an example application designed to record and then play back audio. In the course of working with audio in Android, this chapter also looked at the steps involved in ensuring that the device on which the application is running has a microphone before attempting to record audio. The use of external storage in the form of an SD card was also covered.

50. Working with the Google Maps Android API in Android Studio

When Google decided to introduce a map service many years ago, it is hard to say whether or not they ever anticipated having a version available for integration into mobile applications. When the first web based version of what would eventually be called Google Maps was introduced in 2005, the iPhone had yet to ignite the smartphone revolution and the company that was developing the Android operating system would not be acquired by Google for another six months. Whatever aspirations Google had for the future of Google Maps, it is remarkable to consider that all of the power of Google Maps can now be accessed directly via Android applications using the Google Maps Android API.

This chapter is intended to provide an overview of the Google Maps system and Google Maps Android API. The chapter will provide an overview of the different elements that make up the API, detail the steps necessary to configure a development environment to work with Google Maps and then work through some code examples demonstrating some of the basics of Google Maps Android integration.

50.1 The Elements of the Google Maps Android API

The Google Maps Android API consists of a core set of classes that combine to provide mapping capabilities in Android applications. The key elements of a map are as follows:

- **GoogleMap** – The main class of the Google Maps Android API. This class is responsible for downloading and displaying map tiles and for displaying and responding to map controls. The GoogleMap object is not created directly by the application but is instead created when MapView or MapFragment instances are created. A reference to the GoogleMap object can be obtained within application code via a call to the *getMap()* method of a MapView, MapFragment or SupportMapFragment instance.
- **MapView** - A subclass of the View class, this class provides the view canvas onto which the map is drawn by the GoogleMap object, allowing a map to be placed in the user interface layout of an activity.
- **SupportMapFragment** – A subclass of the Fragment class, this class allows a map to be placed within a Fragment in an Android layout.

- **Marker** – The purpose of the Marker class is to allow locations to be marked on a map. Markers are added to a map by obtaining a reference to the GoogleMap object associated with a map and then making a call to the *addMarker()* method of that object instance. The position of a marker is defined via Longitude and Latitude. Markers can be configured in a number of ways, including specifying a title, text and an icon. Markers may also be made to be "draggable", allowing the user to move the marker to different positions on a map.
- **Shapes** – The drawing of lines and shapes on a map is achieved through the use of the *Polyline*, *Polygon* and *Circle* classes.
- **UiSettings** – The UiSettings class provides a level of control from within an application of which user interface controls appear on a map. Using this class, for example, the application can control whether or not the zoom, current location and compass controls appear on a map. This class can also be used to configure which touch screen gestures are recognized by the map.
- **My Location Layer** – When enabled, the My Location Layer displays a button on the map which, when selected by the user, centers the map on the user's current geographical location. If the user is stationary, this location is represented on the map by a blue marker. If the user is in motion the location is represented by a chevron indicating the user's direction of travel.

The best way to gain familiarity with the Google Maps Android API is to work through an example. The remainder of this chapter will create a simple Google Maps based application while highlighting the key areas of the API.

50.2 Creating the Google Maps Project

Create a new project in Android Studio, entering *MapDemo* into the Application name field and *com.ebookfrenzy* as the Company Domain setting before clicking on the *Next* button.

On the form factors screen, enable the *Phone and Tablet* option and set the minimum SDK setting to API 19: Android 4.4 (KitKat). Continue to proceed through the screens, requesting the creation of a *Google Maps Activity* named *MapDemoActivity* with a corresponding layout named *activity_map_demo*.

50.3 Obtaining Your Developer Signature

Before an application can make use of the Google Maps Android API, it must first be registered within the Google APIs Console. Before an application can be registered, however, the developer signature (also referred to as the SHA-1 fingerprint) associated with your development environment must be identified. This is contained in a keystore file located in the *.android* subdirectory of your home directory and may be obtained using the *keytool* utility provided as part of the Java SDK as outlined below. In order to make the process easier, however, Android Studio adds some additional files to the project when the *Google Maps Activity* option is selected during the project creation process. One of these files is named *google_maps_api.xml* and is located in the *app -> res -> values* folder of the project.

Contained within the *google_maps_api.xml* file is a link to the Google Developer console. Copy and paste this link into a browser window. Once loaded, a page similar to the following will appear:

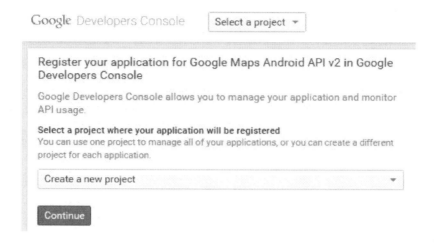

Figure 50-1

Change the setting of the *Select a project* menu to *Create a new project* before clicking on the *Continue* button. Once the API has been enabled, click on the *Go to Credentials* button. After a short delay, the new project will be created and a panel will appear (Figure 50-2) providing the option to create an Android key for the application.

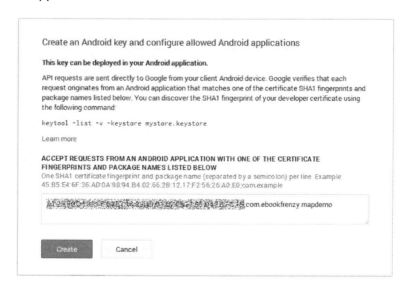

Figure 50-2

Check that the SHA-1 fingerprint and application package name match those listed in the *google_maps_api.xml* file and click on the *Create* button to generate the API key for your application.

The Google Developer Console will update and display the Credentials screen, including a section entitled *Key for Android applications*. Within this section of the page, highlight and copy the *API KEY* value as shown in Figure 50-3:

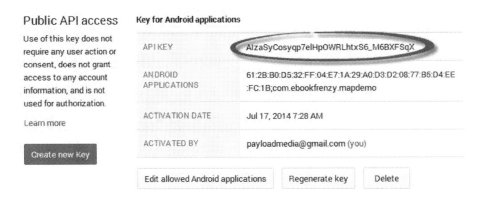

Figure 50-3

Return to Android Studio and paste the API key into the *YOUR_KEY_HERE* section of the file:

```
<string name="google_maps_key"
templateMergeStrategy="preserve">YOUR_KEY_HERE</string>
```

50.4 **Testing the Application**

Perform a test run of the application to verify that the API key is correctly configured. Assuming that the configuration is correct, the application will run and display a map on the screen.

In the event that a map is not displayed, check the following areas:

- If the application is running on an emulator, make sure that the emulator is running a version of Android that includes the Google APIs. The current operating system can be changed for an AVD configuration by selecting the *Tools -> Android -> AVD Manager* menu option, clicking on the pencil icon in the *Actions* column of the AVD followed by the *Change...* button next to the current Android version. Within the system image dialog, select a target which includes the Google APIs.
- Check the LogCat output for any areas relating to authentication problems with regard to the Google Maps API. This usually means the API key was entered incorrectly or that the application package name does not match that specified when the API key was generated.
- Verify within the Google API Console that the *Google Maps Android API* has been enabled in the Services panel.

50.5 Understanding Geocoding and Reverse Geocoding

It is impossible to talk about maps and geographical locations without first covering the subject of Geocoding. Geocoding can best be described as the process of converting a textual based geographical location (such as a street address) into geographical coordinates expressed in terms of longitude and latitude.

Geocoding can be achieved using the Android Geocoder class. An instance of the Geocoder class can, for example, be passed a string representing a location such as a city name, street address or airport code. The Geocoder will attempt to find a match for the location and return a list of Address objects that potentially match the location string, ranked in order with the closest match at position 0 in the list. A variety of information can then be extracted from the Address objects, including the longitude and latitude of the potential matches.

The following code, for example, requests the location of the National Air and Space Museum in Washington, D.C.:

```
import java.io.IOException;
import java.util.List;

import android.location.Address;
import android.location.Geocoder;
.
.
.
double latitude;
double longitude;

List<Address> geocodeMatches = null;

try {
    geocodeMatches =
        new Geocoder(this).getFromLocationName(
            "600 Independence Ave SW, Washington, DC 20560", 1);
    } catch (IOException e) {
        // TODO Auto-generated catch block
        e.printStackTrace();
}

if (!geocodeMatches.isEmpty())
{
        latitude = geocodeMatches.get(0).getLatitude();
        longitude = geocodeMatches.get(0).getLongitude();
```

```
}
```

Note that the value of 1 is passed through as the second argument to the *getFromLocationName()* method. This simply tells the Geocoder to return only one result in the array. Given the specific nature of the address provided, there should only be one potential match. For more vague location names, however, it may be necessary to request more potential matches and allow the user to choose the correct one.

The above code is an example of *forward-geocoding* in that coordinates are calculated based on a text location description. *Reverse-geocoding*, as the name suggests, involves the translation of geographical coordinates into a human readable address string. Consider, for example, the following code:

```
import java.io.IOException;
import java.util.List;

import android.location.Address;
import android.location.Geocoder;
.
.
.
List<Address> geocodeMatches = null;
String Address1;
String Address2;
String State;
String Zipcode;
String Country;

try {
        geocodeMatches =
            new Geocoder(this).getFromLocation(38.8874245, -77.0200729,
1);
} catch (IOException e) {
        // TODO Auto-generated catch block
        e.printStackTrace();
}

if (!geocodeMatches.isEmpty())
{
        Address1 = geocodeMatches.get(0).getAddressLine(0);
        Address2 = geocodeMatches.get(0).getAddressLine(1);
        State = geocodeMatches.get(0).getAdminArea();
        Zipcode = geocodeMatches.get(0).getPostalCode();
```

```
        Country = geocodeMatches.get(0).getCountryName();
}
```

In this case the Geocoder object is initialized with latitude and longitude values via the *getFromLocation()* method. Once again, only a single matching result is requested. The text based address information is then extracted from the resulting Address object.

It should be noted that the geocoding is not actually performed on the Android device, but rather on a server to which the device connects when a translation is required and the results subsequently returned when the translation is complete. As such, geocoding can only take place when the device has an active internet connection.

50.6 Adding a Map to an Application

The simplest way to add a map to an application is to specify it in the user interface layout XML file for an activity. The following example layout file shows the SupportMapFragment instance added to the *activity_map_demo.xml* file created by Android Studio:

```
<fragment xmlns:android="http://schemas.android.com/apk/res/android"
    xmlns:tools="http://schemas.android.com/tools"
    android:layout_width="match_parent"
    android:layout_height="match_parent"
    android:id="@+id/map"
    tools:context=".MapDemoActivity"
    android:name="com.google.android.gms.maps.SupportMapFragment"/>
```

50.7 Displaying the User's Current Location

The user's current location may be displayed on the map by obtaining a reference to the GoogleMap object associated with the displayed map and calling the *setMyLocationEnabled()* method of that instance, passing through a value of *true*. Edit the *onCreate()* method in the *MapDemoActivty.java* file to enable display of the user's current location:

```
package com.ebookfrenzy.mapdemo;

import android.support.v4.app.FragmentActivity;
import android.os.Bundle;

import com.google.android.gms.maps.GoogleMap;
import com.google.android.gms.maps.SupportMapFragment;
import com.google.android.gms.maps.model.LatLng;
import com.google.android.gms.maps.model.MarkerOptions;
```

```
public class MapDemoActivity extends FragmentActivity {

    private GoogleMap mMap; // Might be null if Google Play services
APK is not available.

    @Override
    protected void onCreate(Bundle savedInstanceState) {
        super.onCreate(savedInstanceState);
        setContentView(R.layout.activity_map_demo);
        setUpMapIfNeeded();

        if (mMap != null) {
            mMap.setMyLocationEnabled(true);
        }
    }
    .
    .
    .
}
```

50.8 Changing the Map Type

The type of map displayed can be modified dynamically by making a call to the *setMapType()* method of the corresponding GoogleMap object, passing through one of the following values:

- **GoogleMap.MAP_TYPE_NONE** – An empty grid with no mapping tiles displayed.
- **GoogleMap.MAP_TYPE_NORMAL** – The standard view consisting of the classic road map.
- **GoogleMap.MAP_TYPE_SATELLITE** – Displays the satellite imagery of the map region.
- **GoogleMap.MAP_TYPE_HYBRID** – Displays satellite imagery with the road maps superimposed.
- **GoogleMap.MAP_TYPE_TERRAIN** – Displays topographical information such as contour lines and colors.

The following code change to the *onCreate()* method, for example, switches a map to Terrain mode:

```
    @Override
    protected void onCreate(Bundle savedInstanceState) {
        super.onCreate(savedInstanceState);
        setContentView(R.layout.activity_map_demo);
        setUpMapIfNeeded();

        if (mMap != null) {
            mMap.setMyLocationEnabled(true);
            mMap.setMapType(GoogleMap.MAP_TYPE_TERRAIN);
```

```
            }

      }
```

Alternatively, the map type may be specified in the XML layout file in which the map is embedded using the *map:mapType* property together with a value of *none*, *normal*, *hybrid*, *satellite* or *terrain*. In order to be able to use this directive, however, it is first necessary to add the *map* namespace to the XML resource file in which the directives are being used:

```
xmlns:map="http://schemas.android.com/apk/res-auto"
```

For example:

```
<?xml version="1.0" encoding="utf-8"?>
<fragment xmlns:android="http://schemas.android.com/apk/res/android"
          xmlns:map="http://schemas.android.com/apk/res-auto"
          android:id="@+id/map"
          android:layout_width="match_parent"
          android:layout_height="match_parent"
          map:mapType="hybrid"

android:name="com.google.android.gms.maps.SupportMapFragment"/>
```

50.9 Displaying Map Controls to the User

The Google Maps Android API provides a number of controls that may be optionally displayed to the user consisting of zoom in and out buttons, a "my location" button and a compass.

Whether or not the zoom and compass controls are displayed may be controlled either programmatically or within the map element in XML layout resources. In order to configure the controls programmatically, a reference to the UiSettings object associated with the GoogleMap object must be obtained:

```
import com.google.android.gms.maps.UiSettings;
.
.
.
UiSettings mapSettings;
mapSettings = mMap.getUiSettings();
```

The zoom controls are enabled and disabled via calls to the *setZoomControlsEnabled()* method of the UiSettings object. For example:

```
mapSettings.setZoomControlsEnabled(true);
```

Alternatively, the *map:uiZoomControls* property may be set within the map element of the XML resource file:

```
map:uiZoomControls="false"
```

The compass may be displayed either via a call to the *setCompassEnabled()* method of the UiSettings instance, or through XML resources using the *map:uiCompass* property.

The "My Location" button will only appear when *My Location* mode is enabled as outlined earlier in this chapter. The button may be prevented from appearing even when in this mode via a call to the *setMyLocationButtonEnabled()* method of the UiSettings instance.

50.10 Handling Map Gesture Interaction

The Google Maps Android API is capable of responding to a number of different user interactions. These interactions can be used to change the area of the map displayed, the zoom level and even the angle of view (such that a 3D representation of the map area is displayed for certain cities).

50.10.1 Map Zooming Gestures

Support for gestures relating to zooming in and out of a map may be enabled or disabled using the *setZoomControlsEnabled()* method of the UiSettings object associated with the GoogleMap instance. For example, the following code enables zoom gestures for our example map:

```
UiSettings mapSettings;
mapSettings = map.getUiSettings();
mapSettings.setZoomGesturesEnabled(true);
```

The same result can be achieved within an XML resource file by setting the *map:uiZoomGestures* property to true or false.

When enabled, zooming will occur when the user makes pinching gestures on the screen. Similarly, a double tap will zoom in whilst a two finger tap will zoom out. One finger zooming gestures, on the other hand, are performed by tapping twice but not releasing the second tap and then sliding the finger up and down on the screen to zoom in and out respectively.

50.10.2 Map Scrolling/Panning Gestures

A scrolling, or panning gesture allows the user to move around the map by dragging the map around the screen with a single finger motion. Scrolling gestures may be enabled within code via a call to the *setScrollGesturesEnabled()* method of the UiSettings instance:

```
UiSettings mapSettings;
mapSettings = mMap.getUiSettings();
```

```
mapSettings.setScrollGesturesEnabled(true);
```

Alternatively, scrolling on a map instance may be enabled in an XML resource layout file using the *map:uiScrollGestures* property.

50.10.3 Map Tilt Gestures

Tilt gestures allow the user to tilt the angle of projection of the map by placing two fingers on the screen and moving them up and down to adjust the tilt angle. Tilt gestures may be enabled or disabled via a call to the *setTiltGesturesEnabled()* method of the UiSettings instance, for example:

```
UiSettings mapSettings;
mapSettings = mMap.getUiSettings();
mapSettings.setTiltGesturesEnabled(true);
```

Tilt gestures may also be enabled and disabled using the *map:uiTiltGestures* property in an XML layout resource file.

50.10.4 Map Rotation Gestures

By placing two fingers on the screen and rotating them in a circular motion, the user may rotate the orientation of a map when map rotation gestures are enabled. This gesture support is enabled and disabled in code via a call to the *setRotateGesturesEnabled()* method of the UiSettings instance, for example:

```
UiSettings mapSettings;
mapSettings = mMap.getUiSettings();
mapSettings.setRotateGesturesEnabled(true);
```

Rotation gestures may also be enabled or disabled using the *map:uiRotateGestures* property in an XML layout resource file.

50.11 Creating Map Markers

Markers are used to notify the user of locations on a map and take the form of either a standard or custom icon. Markers may also include a title and optional text (referred to as a snippet) and may be configured such that they can be dragged to different locations on the map by the user. When tapped by the user an *info window* will appear displaying additional information about the marker location.

Markers are represented by instances of the Marker class and are added to a map via a call to the *addMarker()* method of the corresponding GoogleMap object. Passed through as an argument to this method is a MarkerOptions class instance containing the various options required for the marker such as the title and snippet text. The location of a marker is defined by specifying latitude and longitude values, also included as part of the MarkerOptions instance. For example, the following code adds a marker including a title, snippet and a position to a specific location on the map:

```
import com.google.android.gms.maps.model.Marker;
import com.google.android.gms.maps.model.LatLng;
import com.google.android.gms.maps.model.MarkerOptions;
.
.
.
LatLng MUSEUM = new LatLng(38.8874245, -77.0200729);
Marker museum = mMap.addMarker(new MarkerOptions()
                    .position(MUSEUM)
                    .title("Museum")
                    .snippet("National Air and Space Museum"));
```

When executed, the above code will mark the location specified which, when tapped, will display an info window containing the title and snippet as shown in Figure 50-4:

Figure 50-4

50.12 Controlling the Map Camera

Because Android device screens are flat and the world is a sphere, the Google Maps Android API uses the Mercator projection to represent the earth on a flat surface. The default view of the map is presented to the user as though through a *camera* suspended above the map and pointing directly down at the map. The Google Maps Android API allows the *target, zoom, bearing* and *tilt* of this camera to be changed in real-time from within the application:

- **Target** – The location of the center of the map within the device display specified in terms of longitude and latitude.
- **Zoom** – The zoom level of the camera specified in levels. Increasing the zoom level by 1.0 doubles the width of the amount of the map displayed.
- **Tilt** – The viewing angle of the camera specified as a position on an arc spanning directly over the center of the viewable map area measured in degrees from the top of the arc (this being the nadir of the arc where the camera points directly down to the map).
- **Bearing** – The orientation of the map in degrees measured in a clockwise direction from North.

Camera changes are made by creating an instance of the CameraUpdate class with the appropriate settings. CameraUpdate instances are created by making method calls to the *CameraUpdateFactory* class. Once a CameraUpdate instance has been created, it is applied to the map via a call to the *moveCamera()* method of the GoogleMap instance. To obtain a smooth animated effect as the camera changes, the *animateCamera()* method may be called instead of *moveCamera()*.

A summary of CameraUpdateFactory methods is as follows:

- **CameraUpdateFactory.zoomIn()** – Provides a CameraUpdate instance zoomed in by one level.
- **CameraUpdateFactory.zoomOut()** - Provides a CameraUpdate instance zoomed out by one level.
- **CameraUpdateFactory.zoomTo(float)** - Generates a CameraUpdate instance that changes the zoom level to the specified value.
- **CameraUpdateFactory.zoomBy(float)** – Provides a CameraUpdate instance with a zoom level increased or decreased by the specified amount.
- **CameraUpdateFactory.zoomBy(float, Point)** - Creates a CameraUpdate instance that increases or decreases the zoom level by the specified value.
- **CameraUpdateFactory.newLatLng(LatLng)** - Creates a CameraUpdate instance that changes the camera's target latitude and longitude.
- **CameraUpdateFactory.newLatLngZoom(LatLng, float)** - Generates a CameraUpdate instance that changes the camera's latitude, longitude and zoom.
- **CameraUpdateFactory.newCameraPosition(CameraPosition)** - Returns a CameraUpdate instance that moves the camera to the specified position. A CameraPosition instance can be obtained using CameraPosition.Builder().

The following code, for example, zooms in the camera by one level using animation:

```
mMap.animateCamera(CameraUpdateFactory.zoomIn());
```

The following code, on the other hand, moves the camera to a new location and adjusts the zoom level to 10 without animation:

```
private static final LatLng MUSEUM =
```

```
        new LatLng(38.8874245, -77.0200729);

mMap.moveCamera(CameraUpdateFactory.newLatLngZoom(MUSEUM, 10));
```

Finally, the next code example uses CameraPosition.Builder() to create a CameraPosition object with changes to the target, zoom, bearing and tilt. This change is then applied to the camera using animation:

```
CameraPosition cameraPosition = new CameraPosition.Builder()
     .target(MUSEUM)
     .zoom(10)
     .bearing(70)
     .tilt(25)
     .build();
map.animateCamera(CameraUpdateFactory.newCameraPosition(cameraPosition
));
```

50.13 Summary

This chapter has provided an overview of the key classes and methods that make up the Google Maps Android API and outlined the steps involved in preparing both the development environment and an application project to make use of the API.

51. Printing with the Android Printing Framework

With the introduction of the Android 4.4 KitKat release, it is now possible to print content from within Android applications. Whilst subsequent chapters will explore in more detail the options for adding printing support to your own applications, this chapter will focus on the various printing options now available in Android and the steps involved in enabling those options. Having covered these initial topics, the chapter will then provide an overview of the various printing features that are available to Android developers in terms of building printing support into applications.

51.1 The Android Printing Architecture

Printing in Android 4.4 and later is provided by the Printing framework. In basic terms, this framework consists of a Print Manager and a number of print service plugins. It is the responsibility of the Print Manager to handle the print requests from applications on the device and to interact with the print service plugins that are installed on the device, thereby ensuring that print requests are fulfilled. By default, many Android devices have print service plugins installed to enable printing using the Google Cloud Print and Google Drive services. Print Services Plugin for other printer types, if not already installed, may also be obtained from the Google Play store. Print Service Plugins are currently available for HP, Epson and Canon printers and plugins from other printer manufactures will most likely be released in the near future though the Google Cloud Print service plugin can also be used to print from an Android device to just about any printer type and model. For the purposes of this book, we will use the HP Print Services Plugin as a reference example.

51.2 The HP Print Services Plugin

The HP Print Services Plugin is installed by default on most devices running Android 4.4 or later. The purpose of this plugin is to enable applications to print to compatible HP printers that are visible to the Android device via a local area wireless network.

The presence of the HP Print Services Plugin on an Android device can be verified by loading the Google Play app and performing a search for "HP Print Services Plugin". Once the plugin is listed in the Play Store, and in the event that the plugin is not already installed, it can be installed by selecting the *Install* button.

Figure 51-1

To check whether your HP printer is supported by the HP Print Services Plugin, visit the following HP web page for a list of supported printer models:

http://h10025.www1.hp.com/ewfrf/wc/document?cc=us&lc=en&docname=c03722645#

The HP Print Services Plugin will automatically detect compatible HP printers on the network to which the Android device is currently connected and list them as options when printing from an application.

51.3 Google Cloud Print

Google Cloud Print is a service provided by Google that enables you to print content onto your own printer over the web from anywhere with internet connectivity. Google Cloud Print supports a wide range of devices and printer models in the form of both *Cloud Ready* and *Classic* printers. A Cloud Ready printer has technology built-in that enables printing via the web. Manufacturers that provide cloud ready printers include Brother, Canon, Dell, Epson, HP, Kodak and Samsung. To identify if your printer is both cloud ready and supported by Google Cloud Print, review the list of printers at the following URL:

https://www.google.com/cloudprint/learn/printers.html

In the case of classic, non-Cloud Ready printers, Google Cloud Print provides support for cloud printing through the installation of software on the computer system to which the classic printer is connected (either directly or over a home or office network).

To set up Google Cloud Print, visit the following web page and login using the same Google account ID that you use when logging in to your Android devices:

https://www.google.com/cloudprint/learn/index.html

Once printers have been added to your Google Cloud Print account, they will be listed as printer destination options when you print from within Android applications on your devices.

51.4 **Printing to Google Drive**

In addition to supporting physical printers, it is also possible to save printed output to your Google Drive account. When printing from a device, select the *Save to Google Drive* option in the printing panel. The content to be printed will then be converted to a PDF file and saved to the Google Drive cloud-based storage associated with the currently active Google Account ID on the device.

51.5 **Save as PDF**

The final printing option provided by Android allows the printed content to be saved locally as a PDF file on the Android device. Once selected, this option will request a name for the PDF file and a location on the device into which the document is to be saved.

Both the Save as PDF and Google Drive options can be invaluable in terms of saving paper when testing the printing functionality of your own Android applications.

51.6 **Printing from Android Devices**

Google recommends that applications which provide the ability to print content do so by placing the print option in the Overflow menu (a topic covered in some detail in the chapter entitled *Creating and Managing Overflow Menus on Android*). A number of applications bundled with Android now include "Print..." menu options. Figure 51-2, for example, shows the Print option in the Overflow menu of the Chrome browser application:

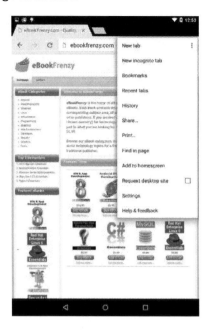

Figure 51-2

Once the print option has been selected from within an application, the standard Android print screen will appear showing a preview of the content to be printed as illustrated in Figure 51-3:

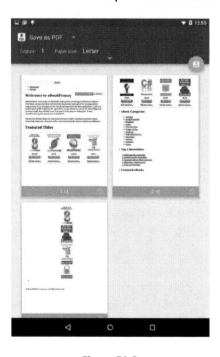

Figure 51-3

Tapping the panel along the top of the screen will display the full range of printing options:

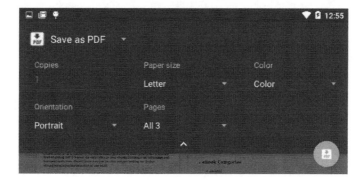

Figure 51-4

The Android print panel provides the usual printing options such as paper size, color, orientation and number of copies. Other print destination options may be accessed by tapping on the current printer or PDF output selection.

51.7 Options for Building Print Support into Android Apps

The Printing framework introduced into the Android 4.4 SDK provides a number of options for incorporating print support into Android applications. These options can be categorized as follows:

51.7.1 Image Printing

As the name suggests, this option allows image printing to be incorporated into Android applications. When adding this feature to an application, the first step is to create a new instance of the PrintHelper class:

```
PrintHelper imagePrinter = new PrintHelper(context);
```

Next, the scale mode for the printed image may be specified via a call to the *setScaleMode()* method of the PrintHelper instance. Options are as follows:

- **SCALE_MODE_FIT** – The image will be scaled to fit within the paper size without any cropping or changes to aspect ratio. This will typically result in white space appearing in one dimension.
- **SCALE_MODE_FILL** – The image will be scaled to fill the paper size with cropping performed where necessary to avoid the appearance of white space in the printed output.

In the absence of a scale mode setting, the system will default to SCALE_MODE_FILL. The following code, for example, sets scale to fit mode on the previously declared PrintHelper instance:

```
imagePrinter.setScaleMode(PrintHelper.SCALE_MODE_FIT);
```

Similarly, the color mode may also be configured to indicate whether the print output is to be in color or black and white. This is achieved by passing one of the following options through to the *setColorMode()* method of the PrintHelper instance:

- **COLOR_MODE_COLOR** – Indicates that the image is to be printed in color.
- **COLOR_MODE_MONOCHROME** – Indicates that the image is to be printed in black and white.

The printing framework will default to color printing unless the monochrome option is specified as follows:

```
imagePrinter.setColorMode(PrintHelper.COLOR_MODE_MONOCHROME);
```

All that is required to complete the printing operation is an image to be printed and a call to the *printBitmap()* method of the PrintHelper instance, passing through a string representing the name to be assigned to the print job and a reference to the image (in the form of either a Bitmap object or a Uri reference to the image):

```
Bitmap bitmap = BitmapFactory.decodeResource(getResources(),
            R.drawable.oceanscene);
imagePrinter.printBitmap("My Test Print Job", bitmap);
```

Once the print job has been started, the Printing framework will display the print dialog and handle both the subsequent interaction with the user and the printing of the image on the user selected print destination.

51.7.2 Creating and Printing HTML Content

The Android Printing framework also provides an easy way to print HTML based content from within an application. This content can either be in the form of HTML content referenced by the URL of a page hosted on a web site, or HTML content that is dynamically created within the application.

To enable HTML printing, the WebView class has been extended in Android 4.4 to include support for printing with minimal coding requirements.

When dynamically creating HTML content (as opposed to loading and printing an existing web page) the process involves the creation of a WebView object and associating with it a WebViewClient instance. The web view client is then configured to start a print job when the HTML has finished being loaded into the WebView. With the web view client configured, the HTML is then loaded into the WebView, at which point the print process is triggered.

Consider, for example, the following code:

```
private WebView myWebView;
```

```
public void printContent(View view)
{
        WebView webView = new WebView(this);
        webView.setWebViewClient(new WebViewClient() {

                public boolean shouldOverrideUrlLoading(WebView view,
                        String url)
                {
                        return false;
                }

                @Override
                    public void onPageFinished(WebView view, String url) {
                        createWebPrintJob(view);
                        myWebView = null;
                    }
        });

        String htmlDocument =
                "<html><body><h1>Android Print Test</h1><p>"
            + "This is some sample content.</p></body></html>";


        webView.loadDataWithBaseURL(null, htmlDocument,
                "text/HTML", "UTF-8", null);

        myWebView = webView;
}
```

The code in this method begins by declaring a variable named *myWebView* in which will be stored a reference to the WebView instance created in the method. Within the *printContent()* method, an instance of the WebView class is created to which a WebViewClient instance is then assigned.

The WebViewClient assigned to the web view object is configured to indicate that loading of the HTML content is to be handled by the WebView instance (by returning *false* from the *shouldOverrideUrlLoading()*) method. More importantly, an *onPageFinished()* handler method is declared and implemented to call a method named *createWebPrintJob()*. The *onPageFinished()* callback method will be called automatically when all of the HTML content has been loaded into the web view. This ensures that the print job is not started until the content is ready, thereby ensuring that all of the content is printed.

Next, a string is created containing some HTML to serve as the content. This is then loaded into the web view. Once the HTML is loaded, the *onPageFinished()* method will trigger. Finally, the method stores a reference to the web view object. Without this vital step, there is a significant risk that the Java runtime system will assume that the application no longer needs the web view object and will discard it to free up memory (a concept referred to in Java terminology as *garbage collection*) resulting in the print job terminating prior to completion.

All that remains in this example is to implement the *createWebPrintJob()* method as follows:

```
private void createWebPrintJob(WebView webView) {

        PrintManager printManager = (PrintManager) this
                    .getSystemService(Context.PRINT_SERVICE);

        PrintDocumentAdapter printAdapter =
                    webView.createPrintDocumentAdapter("MyDocument");
        String jobName = getString(R.string.app_name) + " Document";

        PrintJob printJob = printManager.print(jobName, printAdapter,
                new PrintAttributes.Builder().build());
}
```

This method simply obtains a reference to the PrintManager service and instructs the web view instance to create a print adapter. A new string is created to store the name of the print job (in this case based on the name of the application and the word "Document").

Finally, the print job is started by calling the *print()* method of the print manager, passing through the job name, print adapter and a set of default print attributes. If required, the print attributes could be customized to specify resolution (dots per inch), margin and color options.

51.7.3 Printing a Web Page

The steps involved in printing a web page are similar to those outlined above, with the exception that the web view is passed the URL of the web page to be printed in place of the dynamically created HTML, for example:

```
webView.loadUrl("http://developer.android.com/google/index.html");
```

It is also important to note that the WebViewClient configuration is only necessary if a web page is to automatically print as soon as it has loaded. If the printing is to be initiated by the user selecting a menu option after the page has loaded, only the code in the *createWebPrintJob()* method outlined above need be included in the application code. The next chapter, entitled *An Android HTML and Web Content Printing Example*, will demonstrate just such a scenario.

51.7.4 Printing a Custom Document

Whilst the HTML and web printing features introduced by the Printing framework provide an easy path to printing content from within an Android application, it is clear that these options will be overly simplistic for more advanced printing requirements. For more complex printing tasks, the Printing framework also provides custom document printing support. This allows content in the form of text and graphics to be drawn onto a canvas and then printed.

Unlike HTML and image printing, which can be implemented with relative ease, custom document printing is a more complex, multi-stage process which will be outlined in the *A Guide to Android Custom Document Printing* chapter of this book. These steps can be summarized as follows:

- Connect to the Android Print Manager
- Create a Custom Print Adapter sub-classed from the PrintDocumentAdapter class
- Create a PdfDocument instance to represent the document pages
- Obtain a reference to the pages of the PdfDocument instance, each of which has associated with it a Canvas instance
- Draw the content on the page canvases
- Notify the print framework that the document is ready to print

The custom print adapter outlined in the above steps needs to implement a number of methods which will be called upon by the Android system to perform specific tasks during the printing process. The most important of these are the *onLayout()* method which is responsible for re-arranging the document layout in response to the user changing settings such as paper size or page orientation, and the *onWrite()* method which is responsible for rendering the pages to be printed. This topic will be covered in detail in the chapter entitled *A Guide to Android Custom Document Printing*.

51.8 Summary

The Android 4.4 KitKat release introduced the ability to print content from Android devices. Print output can be directed to suitably configured printers, a local PDF file or to the cloud via Google Drive. From the perspective of the Android application developer, these capabilities are available for use in applications by making use of the Printing framework. By far the easiest printing options to implement are those involving content in the form of images and HTML. More advanced printing may, however, be implemented using the custom document printing features of the framework.

52. An Android HTML and Web Content Printing Example

As outlined in the previous chapter, entitled *Printing with the Android Printing Framework*, the Android Printing framework can be used to print both web pages and dynamically created HTML content. Whilst there is much similarity in these two approaches to printing, there are also some subtle differences that need to be taken into consideration. This chapter will work through the creation of two example applications in order to bring some clarity to these two printing options.

52.1 Creating the HTML Printing Example Application

Begin this example by launching the Android Studio environment and creating a new project, entering *HTMLPrint* into the Application name field and *ebookfrenzy.com* as the Company Domain setting before clicking on the *Next* button.

On the form factors screen, enable the *Phone and Tablet* option and set the minimum SDK setting to API 21: Android 5.0 (Lollipop). Continue to proceed through the screens, requesting the creation of a blank activity named *HTMLPrintActivity* with a corresponding layout named *activity_html_print* and menu resource file named *menu_html_print*.

52.2 Printing Dynamic HTML Content

The first stage of this tutorial is to add code to the project to create some HTML content and send it to the Printing framework in the form of a print job.

Begin by locating the *HTMLPrintActivity.java* file (located in the Project tool window under *app -> java -> com.ebookfrenzy.com -> htmlprint*) and loading it into the editing panel. Once loaded, modify the code so that it reads as outlined in the following listing:

```
package com.ebookfrenzy.htmlprint;

import android.app.Activity;
import android.os.Bundle;
import android.view.Menu;
import android.view.MenuItem;
```

```
import android.webkit.WebView;
import android.webkit.WebViewClient;
import android.print.PrintAttributes;
import android.print.PrintDocumentAdapter;
import android.print.PrintManager;
import android.content.Context;

public class HTMLPrintActivity extends Activity {

    private WebView myWebView;

    @Override
    protected void onCreate(Bundle savedInstanceState) {
        super.onCreate(savedInstanceState);
        setContentView(R.layout.activity_html_print);

        WebView webView = new WebView(this);
        webView.setWebViewClient(new WebViewClient() {

            public boolean shouldOverrideUrlLoading(WebView view,
                                                    String url)
            {
                return false;
            }

            @Override
            public void onPageFinished(WebView view, String url)
            {
                createWebPrintJob(view);
                myWebView = null;
            }
        });

        String htmlDocument =
            "<html><body><h1>Android Print Test</h1><p>"
            + "This is some sample content.</p></body></html>";

        webView.loadDataWithBaseURL(null, htmlDocument,
                "text/HTML", "UTF-8", null);

        myWebView = webView;
    }
```

```
    .
    .
    }
```

The code changes begin by declaring a variable named *myWebView* in which will be stored a reference to the WebView instance used for the printing operation. Within the *onCreate()* method, an instance of the WebView class is created to which a WebViewClient instance is then assigned.

The WebViewClient assigned to the web view object is configured to indicate that loading of the HTML content is to be handled by the WebView instance (by returning *false* from the *shouldOverrideUrlLoading()* method). More importantly, an *onPageFinished()* handler method is declared and implemented to call a method named *createWebPrintJob()*. The *onPageFinished()* method will be called automatically when all of the HTML content has been loaded into the web view. As outlined in the previous chapter, this step is necessary when printing dynamically created HTML content to ensure that the print job is not started until the content has fully loaded into the WebView.

Next, a String object is created containing some HTML to serve as the content and subsequently loaded into the web view. Once the HTML is loaded, the *onPageFinished()* callback method will trigger. Finally, the method stores a reference to the web view object in the previously declared *myWebView* variable. Without this vital step, there is a significant risk that the Java runtime system will assume that the application no longer needs the web view object and will discard it to free up memory resulting in the print job terminating before completion.

All that remains in this example is to implement the *createWebPrintJob()* method which is currently configured to be called by the *onPageFinished()* callback method. Remaining within the *HTMLPrintActivity.java* file, therefore, implement this method so that it reads as follows:

```java
private void createWebPrintJob(WebView webView) {

        PrintManager printManager = (PrintManager) this
                .getSystemService(Context.PRINT_SERVICE);

        PrintDocumentAdapter printAdapter =
                webView.createPrintDocumentAdapter("MyDocument");

        String jobName = getString(R.string.app_name) + " Print Test";

        printManager.print(jobName, printAdapter,
                new PrintAttributes.Builder().build());
}
```

An Android HTML and Web Content Printing Example

This method obtains a reference to the PrintManager service and instructs the web view instance to create a print adapter. A new string is created to store the name of the print job (in this case based on the name of the application and the word "Print Test").

Finally, the print job is started by calling the *print()* method of the print manager, passing through the job name, print adapter and a set of default print attributes.

Compile and run the application on a device running Android 5.0 or later. Once launched, the standard Android printing page should appear as illustrated in Figure 52-1.

Figure 52-1

Print to a physical printer if you have one configured, save to Google Drive or, alternatively, select the option to save to a PDF file. Once the print job has been initiated, check the generated output on your chosen destination. Note that when using the Save to PDF option, the system will request a name and location for the PDF file. The *Downloads* folder makes a good option, the contents of which can be viewed by selecting the *Downloads* icon located amongst the other app icons on the device. Figure 52-2, for example, shows the PDF output generated by the Save to PDF option viewed on an Android device:

Figure 52-2

52.3 Creating the Web Page Printing Example

The second example application to be created in this chapter will provide the user with an Overflow menu option to print the web page currently displayed within a WebView instance. Create a new project in Android Studio, entering *WebPrint* into the Application name field and *ebookfrenzy.com* as the Company Domain setting before clicking on the *Next* button.

On the form factors screen, enable the *Phone and Tablet* option and set the minimum SDK setting to API 21: Android 5.0 (Lollipop). Continue to proceed through the screens, requesting the creation of a blank activity named *WebPrintActivity* with the remaining properties set to the default values.

52.4 Designing the User Interface Layout

Load the *activity_web_print.xml* layout resource file into the Designer tool if it has not already been loaded and, in Design mode, select and delete the "Hello World!" TextView object.

Switch to the XML view by clicking on the *Text* tab located along the lower edge of the Designer panel and remove the padding properties from the file so that the WebView will extend to the edges of the display when added to the layout:

```
<RelativeLayout
xmlns:android="http://schemas.android.com/apk/res/android"
```

```
    xmlns:tools="http://schemas.android.com/tools"
    android:layout_width="match_parent"
    android:layout_height="match_parent"
    android:paddingLeft="@dimen/activity_horizontal_margin"
    android:paddingRight="@dimen/activity_horizontal_margin"
    android:paddingTop="@dimen/activity_vertical_margin"
    android:paddingBottom="@dimen/activity_vertical_margin"
    tools:context=".WebPrintActivity">

</RelativeLayout>
```

Switch back to Design mode and, from the *Widgets* section of the palette, drag and drop a WebView object onto the center of the device screen layout. Using either the Properties panel or the Designer toolbar buttons, change the *layout_width* and *layout_height* properties of the WebView to *match_parent* so that it fills the entire layout canvas as outlined in Figure 52-3:

Figure 52-3

Double-click on the newly added WebView instance, and change the ID of the view to *myWebView*.

Before proceeding to the next step of this tutorial, an additional permission needs to be added to the project to enable the WebView object to access the internet and download a web page for printing.

Add this permission by locating the *AndroidManifest.xml* file in the Project tool window and double clicking on it to load it into the editing panel. Once loaded, edit the XML content to add the appropriate permission line as shown in the following listing:

```xml
<?xml version="1.0" encoding="utf-8"?>
<manifest xmlns:android="http://schemas.android.com/apk/res/android"
    package="com.ebookfrenzy.webprint" >

    <uses-permission android:name="android.permission.INTERNET" />

    <application
        android:allowBackup="true"
        android:icon="@mipmap/ic_launcher"
        android:label="@string/app_name"
        android:theme="@style/AppTheme" >
        <activity
            android:name=".WebPrintActivity"
            android:label="@string/app_name" >
            <intent-filter>
                <action android:name="android.intent.action.MAIN" />

                <category android:name=
                        "android.intent.category.LAUNCHER" />
            </intent-filter>
        </activity>
    </application>

</manifest>
```

52.5 Loading the Web Page into the WebView

Before the web page can be printed it needs to be loaded into the WebView instance. For the purposes of this tutorial, this will be performed by a call to the *loadUrl()* method of the WebView instance which will be placed in the *onCreate()* method of the WebPrintActivity class. Edit the *WebPrintActivity.java* file, therefore, and modify it as follows:

```java
package com.ebookfrenzy.webprint;

import android.app.Activity;
import android.os.Bundle;
import android.view.Menu;
import android.view.MenuItem;
import android.webkit.WebView;
```

```
public class WebPrintActivity extends Activity {

    private WebView myWebView;

    @Override
    protected void onCreate(Bundle savedInstanceState) {
        super.onCreate(savedInstanceState);
        setContentView(R.layout.activity_web_print);

        myWebView = (WebView) findViewById(R.id.myWebView);

        myWebView.loadUrl(
                "http://developer.android.com/google/index.html");
    }
    .

    .

}
```

52.6 Adding the Print Menu Option

The option to print the web page will now be added to the Overflow menu using the techniques outlined in the chapter entitled *Creating and Managing Overflow Menus on Android*.

The first requirement is a string resource with which to label the menu option. Within the Project tool window, locate the *app -> res -> values -> strings.xml* file, double click on it to load it into the editor and modify it to add a new string resource:

```
<?xml version="1.0" encoding="utf-8"?>
<resources>

    <string name="app_name">WebPrint</string>
    <string name="action_settings">Settings</string>
    <string name="hello_world">Hello world!</string>
    <string name="print_string">Print</string>

</resources>
```

Next, locate and edit the *app -> res -> menu -> menu_web_print.xml* file and replace the *Settings* menu option with the print option:

```
<menu xmlns:android="http://schemas.android.com/apk/res/android"
    xmlns:tools="http://schemas.android.com/tools"
    tools:context=".WebPrintActivity" >
```

```
    <item android:id="@+id/action_settings"
        android:title="@string/action_settings"
        android:orderInCategory="100"
        android:showAsAction="never" />

    <item
        android:id="@+id/action_print"
        android:orderInCategory="100"
        android:showAsAction="never"
        android:title="@string/print_string"/>

</menu>
```

All that remains in terms of configuring the menu option is to modify the *onOptionsItemSelected()* handler method within the *WebPrintActivity.java* file:

```java
@Override
public boolean onOptionsItemSelected(MenuItem item) {
    int id = item.getItemId();
    if (id == R.id.action_print) {
        createWebPrintJob(myWebView);
        return true;
    }
    return super.onOptionsItemSelected(item);
}
```

With the *onOptionsItemSelected()* method implemented, the activity will call a method named *createWebPrintJob()* when the print menu option is selected from the overflow menu. The implementation of this method is identical to that used in the previous HTMLPrint project and may now be added to the *WebPrintActivity.java* file such that it reads as follows:

```java
package com.ebookfrenzy.webprint;

import android.app.Activity;
import android.os.Bundle;
import android.view.Menu;
import android.view.MenuItem;
import android.webkit.WebView;
import android.print.PrintAttributes;
import android.print.PrintDocumentAdapter;
import android.print.PrintManager;
import android.content.Context;

public class WebPrintActivity extends Activity {
```

```java
private WebView myWebView;

@Override
protected void onCreate(Bundle savedInstanceState) {
    super.onCreate(savedInstanceState);
    setContentView(R.layout.activity_web_print);

    myWebView = (WebView) findViewById(R.id.myWebView);

    myWebView.loadUrl(
            "http://developer.android.com/google/index.html");
}

private void createWebPrintJob(WebView webView) {

    PrintManager printManager = (PrintManager) this
            .getSystemService(Context.PRINT_SERVICE);

    PrintDocumentAdapter printAdapter =
            webView.createPrintDocumentAdapter("MyDocument");

    String jobName = getString(R.string.app_name) +
            " Print Test";

    printManager.print(jobName, printAdapter,
            new PrintAttributes.Builder().build());
}
    .
    .
}
```

With the code changes complete, run the application on a physical Android device running Android version 5.0 or later. Once successfully launched, the WebView should be visible with the designated web page loaded. Once the page has loaded, select the Print option from the Overflow menu (Figure 52-4) and use the resulting print panel to print the web page to a suitable destination.

Figure 52-4

52.7 Summary

The Android Printing framework includes extensions to the WebView class that make it possible to print HTML based content from within an Android application. This content can be in the form of HTML created dynamically within the application at runtime, or a pre-existing web page loaded into a WebView instance. In the case of dynamically created HTML, it is important to use a WebViewClient instance to ensure that printing does not start until the HTML has been fully loaded into the WebView.

53. A Guide to Android Custom Document Printing

As we have seen in the preceding chapters, the Android Printing framework makes it relatively easy to build printing support into applications as long as the content is in the form of an image or HTML markup. More advanced printing requirements can be met by making use of the custom document printing feature of the Printing framework.

53.1 An Overview of Android Custom Document Printing

In simplistic terms, custom document printing uses canvases to represent the pages of the document to be printed. The application draws the content to be printed onto these canvases in the form of shapes, colors, text and images. In actual fact, the canvases are represented by instances of the Android Canvas class, thereby providing access to a rich selection of drawing options. Once all the pages have been drawn the document is then printed.

Whilst this sounds simple enough, there are actually a number of steps that need to be performed to make this happen, each of which can be summarized as follows:

- Implement a custom print adapter sub-classed from the PrintDocumentAdapter class
- Obtain a reference to the Print Manager Service
- Create an instance of the PdfDocument class in which to store the document pages
- Add pages to the PdfDocument in the form of PdfDocument.Page instances
- Obtain references to the Canvas objects associated with the document pages
- Draw content onto the canvases
- Write the PDF document to a destination output stream provided by the Printing framework
- Notify the Printing framework that the document is ready to print

In this chapter, an overview of these steps will be provided followed by a detailed tutorial designed to demonstrate the implementation of custom document printing within Android applications.

53.1.1 Custom Print Adapters

The role of the print adapter is to provide the Printing framework with the content to be printed, and to ensure that it is formatted correctly for the user's chosen preferences (taking into consideration factors such as paper size and page orientation).

When printing HTML and images, much of this work is performed by the print adapters provided as part of the Android Printing framework and designed for these specific printing tasks. When printing a web page, for example, a print adapter is created for us when a call is made to the *createPrintDocumentAdapter()* method of an instance of the WebView class.

In the case of custom document printing, however, it is the responsibility of the application developer to design the print adapter and implement the code to draw and format the content in preparation for printing.

Custom print adapters are created by sub-classing the PrintDocumentAdapter class and overriding a set of callback methods within that class which will be called by the Printing framework at various stages in the print process. These callback methods can be summarized as follows:

- **onStart()** – This method is called when the printing process begins and is provided so that the application code has an opportunity to perform any necessary tasks in preparation for creating the print job. Implementation of this method within the PrintDocumentAdapter sub-class is optional.
- **onLayout()** – This callback method is called after the call to the *onStart()* method and then again each time the user makes changes to the print settings (such as changing the orientation, paper size or color settings). This method should adapt the content and layout where necessary to accommodate these changes. Once these changes are completed, the method must return a count of the number of pages to be printed. Implementation of the *onLayout()* method within the PrintDocumentAdapter sub-class is mandatory.
- **onWrite()** – This method is called after each call to *onLayout()* and is responsible for rendering the content on the canvases of the pages to be printed. Amongst other arguments, this method is passed a file descriptor to which the resulting PDF document must be written once rendering is complete. A call is then made to the *onWriteFinished()* callback method passing through an argument containing information about the page ranges to be printed. Implementation of the *onWrite()* method within the PrintDocumentAdapter sub-class is mandatory.
- **onFinish()** – An optional method which, if implemented, is called once by the Printing framework when the printing process is completed, thereby providing the application the opportunity to perform any clean-up operations that may be necessary.

53.2 **Preparing the Custom Document Printing Project**

Launch the Android Studio environment and create a new project, entering *CustomPrint* into the Application name field and *ebookfrenzy.com* as the Company Domain setting before clicking on the *Next* button.

On the form factors screen, enable the *Phone and Tablet* option and set the minimum SDK setting to API 21: Android 5.0 (Lollipop). Continue to proceed through the screens, requesting the creation of a blank activity named *CustomPrintActivity* with corresponding layout and menu resource files named *activity_custom_print* and *menu_custom_print* respectively.

Load the *activity_custom_print.xml* layout file into the Designer tool and, in Design mode, select and delete the "Hello World!" TextView object. Drag and drop a Button view from the Form Widgets section of the palette and position it in the center of the layout view. Double click on the Button view, and change the text displayed to "Print Document". Extract the string to a new string resource named *print_string*. On completion, the user interface layout should match that shown in Figure 53-1:

Figure 53-1

When the button is selected within the application it will be required to call a method to initiate the document printing process. Switch Designer to Text mode and add an *onClick* property to the button configured to call a method named *printDocument*. Assuming that the layout has been configured correctly, the completed XML should now read as follows:

```xml
<RelativeLayout
xmlns:android="http://schemas.android.com/apk/res/android"
    xmlns:tools="http://schemas.android.com/tools"
    android:layout_width="match_parent"
    android:layout_height="match_parent"
    android:paddingLeft="@dimen/activity_horizontal_margin"
    android:paddingRight="@dimen/activity_horizontal_margin"
    android:paddingTop="@dimen/activity_vertical_margin"
    android:paddingBottom="@dimen/activity_vertical_margin"
    tools:context=".CustomPrintActivity">

    <Button
        android:layout_width="wrap_content"
        android:layout_height="wrap_content"
        android:text="@string/print_string"
        android:id="@+id/button"
        android:layout_centerVertical="true"
        android:layout_centerHorizontal="true"
        android:onClick="printDocument" />
</RelativeLayout>
```

53.3 Creating the Custom Print Adapter

Most of the work involved in printing a custom document from within an Android application involves the implementation of the custom print adapter. This example will require a print adapter with the *onLayout()* and *onWrite()* callback methods implemented. Within the *CustomPrintActivity.java* file, add the template for this new class so that it reads as follows:

```java
package com.ebookfrenzy.customprint;

import android.app.Activity;
import android.os.Bundle;
import android.view.Menu;
import android.view.MenuItem;
import android.os.CancellationSignal;
import android.os.ParcelFileDescriptor;
import android.print.PageRange;
import android.print.PrintAttributes;
import android.print.PrintDocumentAdapter;
import android.content.Context;

public class CustomPrintActivity extends Activity {

    public class MyPrintDocumentAdapter extends PrintDocumentAdapter
```

```
{
    Context context;

    public MyPrintDocumentAdapter(Context context)
    {
        this.context = context;
    }

    @Override
    public void onLayout(PrintAttributes oldAttributes,
                        PrintAttributes newAttributes,
                        CancellationSignal cancellationSignal,
                        LayoutResultCallback callback,
                        Bundle metadata) {

    }


    @Override
    public void onWrite(final PageRange[] pageRanges,
                        final ParcelFileDescriptor destination,
                        final CancellationSignal
                            cancellationSignal,
                        final WriteResultCallback callback) {

    }

}
.
.
.
}
```

As the new class currently stands, it contains a constructor method which will be called when a new instance of the class is created. The constructor takes as an argument the context of the calling activity which is then stored so that it can be referenced later in the two callback methods.

With the outline of the class established, the next step is to begin implementing the two callback methods, beginning with *onLayout()*.

53.4 **Implementing the onLayout() Callback Method**

Remaining within the *CustomPrintActivity.java* file, begin by adding some import directives that will be required by the code in the *onLayout()* method:

```
package com.ebookfrenzy.customprint;
```

```
import android.app.Activity;
import android.os.Bundle;
import android.view.Menu;
import android.view.MenuItem;
import android.os.CancellationSignal;
import android.os.ParcelFileDescriptor;
import android.print.PageRange;
import android.print.PrintAttributes;
import android.print.PrintDocumentAdapter;
import android.content.Context;
import android.print.PrintDocumentInfo;
import android.print.pdf.PrintedPdfDocument;
import android.graphics.pdf.PdfDocument;

public class CustomPrintActivity extends Activity {.
    .
    .
}
```

Next, modify the MyPrintDocumentAdapter class to declare variables to be used within the *onLayout()* method:

```
public class MyPrintDocumentAdapter extends PrintDocumentAdapter
{
        Context context;
        private int pageHeight;
        private int pageWidth;
        public PdfDocument myPdfDocument;
        public int totalpages = 4;
    .
    .
}
```

Note that for the purposes of this example, a four page document is going to be printed. In more complex situations, the application will most likely need to dynamically calculate the number of pages to be printed based on the quantity and layout of the content in relation to the user's paper size and page orientation selections.

With the variables declared, implement the *onLayout()* method as outlined in the following code listing:

```
@Override
public void onLayout (PrintAttributes oldAttributes,
```

```
                            PrintAttributes newAttributes,
                            CancellationSignal cancellationSignal,
                            LayoutResultCallback callback,
                            Bundle metadata) {

        myPdfDocument = new PrintedPdfDocument(context, newAttributes);

        pageHeight =
                newAttributes.getMediaSize().getHeightMils()/1000 *
72;
        pageWidth =
                newAttributes.getMediaSize().getWidthMils()/1000 * 72;

        if (cancellationSignal.isCanceled() ) {
                callback.onLayoutCancelled();
                return;
        }

        if (totalpages > 0) {
            PrintDocumentInfo.Builder builder = new PrintDocumentInfo
                    .Builder("print_output.pdf")

 .setContentType(PrintDocumentInfo.CONTENT_TYPE_DOCUMENT)
                    .setPageCount(totalpages);

            PrintDocumentInfo info = builder.build();
            callback.onLayoutFinished(info, true);
        } else {
            callback.onLayoutFailed("Page count is zero.");
        }
}
```

Clearly this method is performing quite a few tasks, each of which requires some detailed explanation.

To begin with, a new PDF document is created in the form of a PdfDocument class instance. One of the arguments passed into the *onLayout()* method when it is called by the Printing framework is an object of type PrintAttributes containing details about the paper size, resolution and color settings selected by the user for the print output. These settings are used when creating the PDF document, along with the context of the activity previously stored for us by our constructor method:

```
myPdfDocument = new PrintedPdfDocument(context, newAttributes);
```

The method then uses the PrintAttributes object to extract the height and width values for the document pages. These dimensions are stored in the object in the form of thousandths of an inch.

Since the methods that will use these values later in this example work in units of 1/72 of an inch these numbers are converted before they are stored:

```
pageHeight = newAttributes.getMediaSize().getHeightMils()/1000 * 72;
pageWidth = newAttributes.getMediaSize().getWidthMils()/1000 * 72;
```

Although this example does not make use of the user's color selection, this property can be obtained via a call to the *getColorMode()* method of the PrintAttributes object which will return a value of either COLOR_MODE_COLOR or COLOR_MODE_MONOCHROME.

When the *onLayout()* method is called, it is passed an object of type *LayoutResultCallback*. This object provides a way for the method to communicate status information back to the Printing framework via a set of methods. The *onLayout()* method, for example, will be called in the event that the user cancels the print process. The fact that the process has been cancelled is indicated via a setting within the CancellationSignal argument. In the event that a cancellation is detected, the *onLayout()* method must call the *onLayoutCancelled()* method of the *LayoutResultCallback* object to notify the Print framework that the cancellation request was received and that the layout task has been cancelled:

```
if (cancellationSignal.isCanceled() ) {
        callback.onLayoutCancelled();
        return;
}
```

When the layout work is complete, the method is required to call the *onLayoutFinished()* method of the *LayoutResultCallback* object, passing through two arguments. The first argument takes the form of a PrintDocumentInfo object containing information about the document to be printed. This information consists of the name to be used for the PDF document, the type of content (in this case a document rather than an image) and the page count. The second argument is a Boolean value indicating whether or not the layout has changed since the last call made to the *onLayout()* method:

```
if (totalpages > 0) {
        PrintDocumentInfo.Builder builder = new PrintDocumentInfo
                .Builder("print_output.pdf")

 .setContentType(PrintDocumentInfo.CONTENT_TYPE_DOCUMENT)
                .setPageCount(totalpages);

        PrintDocumentInfo info = builder.build();

        callback.onLayoutFinished(info, true);
} else {
        callback.onLayoutFailed("Page count is zero.");
```

```
}
```

In the event that the page count is zero, the code reports this failure to the Printing framework via a call to the *onLayoutFailed()* method of the *LayoutResultCallback* object.

The call to the *onLayoutFinished()* method notifies the Printing framework that the layout work is complete, thereby triggering a call to the *onWrite()* method.

53.5 Implementing the onWrite() Callback Method

The *onWrite()* callback method is responsible for rendering the pages of the document and then notifying the Printing framework that the document is ready to be printed. When completed, the *onWrite()* method reads as follows:

```
package com.ebookfrenzy.customprint;

import java.io.FileOutputStream;
import java.io.IOException;

import android.app.Activity;
import android.os.Bundle;
import android.view.Menu;
import android.view.MenuItem;
import android.os.CancellationSignal;
import android.os.ParcelFileDescriptor;
import android.print.PageRange;
import android.print.PrintAttributes;
import android.print.PrintDocumentAdapter;
import android.content.Context;
import android.print.PrintDocumentInfo;
import android.print.pdf.PrintedPdfDocument;
import android.graphics.pdf.PdfDocument;
import android.graphics.pdf.PdfDocument.PageInfo;
.
.
.
.
@Override
public void onWrite(final PageRange[] pageRanges,
                    final ParcelFileDescriptor destination,
                    final CancellationSignal cancellationSignal,
                    final WriteResultCallback callback) {

    for (int i = 0; i < totalpages; i++) {
```

```
            if (pageInRange(pageRanges, i))
            {
                    PageInfo newPage = new PageInfo.Builder(pageWidth,
                            pageHeight, i).create();

                    PdfDocument.Page page =
                            myPdfDocument.startPage(newPage);

                    if (cancellationSignal.isCanceled()) {
                        callback.onWriteCancelled();
                        myPdfDocument.close();
                        myPdfDocument = null;
                        return;
                    }
                    drawPage(page, i);
                    myPdfDocument.finishPage(page);
            }
    }

    try {
            myPdfDocument.writeTo(new FileOutputStream(
                        destination.getFileDescriptor()));
    } catch (IOException e) {
            callback.onWriteFailed(e.toString());
            return;
    } finally {
            myPdfDocument.close();
            myPdfDocument = null;
    }

    callback.onWriteFinished(pageRanges);
}
```

The *onWrite()* method starts by looping through each of the pages in the document. It is important to take into consideration, however, that the user may not have requested that all of the pages that make up the document be printed. In actual fact, the Printing framework user interface panel provides the option to specify that specific pages, or ranges of pages be printed. Figure 53-2, for example, shows the print panel configured to print pages 1-4, pages 8 and 9 and pages 11-13 of a document.

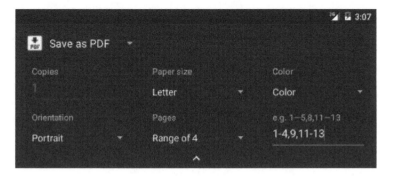

Figure 53-2

When writing the pages to the PDF document, the *onWrite()* method must take steps to ensure that only those pages specified by the user are printed. To make this possible, the Printing framework passes through as an argument an array of PageRange objects indicating the ranges of pages to be printed. In the above *onWrite()* implementation, a method named *pagesInRange()* is called for each page to verify that the page is within the specified ranges. The code for the *pagesInRange()* method will be implemented later in this chapter.

```
for (int i = 0; i < totalpages; i++) {
    if (pageInRange(pageRanges, i))
    {
```

For each page that is within any specified ranges, a new PdfDocument.Page object is created. When creating a new page, the height and width values previously stored by the *onLayout()* method are passed through as arguments so that the page size matches the print options selected by the user:

```
PageInfo newPage = new PageInfo.Builder(pageWidth,
                        pageHeight, i).create();

PdfDocument.Page page = myPdfDocument.startPage(newPage);
```

As with the *onLayout()* method, the *onWrite()* method is required to respond to cancellation requests. In this case, the code notifies the Printing framework that the cancellation has been performed before closing and de-referencing the myPdfDocument variable:

```
if (cancellationSignal.isCanceled()) {
    callback.onWriteCancelled();
    myPdfDocument.close();
    myPdfDocument = null;
    return;
}
```

As long as the print process has not been cancelled, the method then calls a method to draw the content on the current page before calling the *finishedPage()* method on the myPdfDocument object.

```
drawPage(page, i);
myPdfDocument.finishPage(page);
```

The *drawPage()* method will be responsible for drawing the content onto the page and will be implemented once the *onWrite()* method is complete.

When the required number of pages have been added to the PDF document, the document is then written to the *destination* stream using the file descriptor which was passed through as an argument to the *onWrite()* method. If, for any reason, the write operation fails, the method notifies the framework by calling the *onWriteFailed()* method of the *WriteResultCallback* object (also passed as an argument to the *onWrite()* method).

```
try {
        myPdfDocument.writeTo(new FileOutputStream(
                destination.getFileDescriptor()));
} catch (IOException e) {
                callback.onWriteFailed(e.toString());
                return;
} finally {
                myPdfDocument.close();
                myPdfDocument = null;
}
```

Finally, the *onWriteFinish()* method of the *WriteResultsCallback* object is called to notify the Printing framework that the document is ready to be printed.

53.6 Checking a Page is in Range

As previously outlined, when the *onWrite()* method is called it is passed an array of PageRange objects indicating the ranges of pages within the document that are to be printed. The PageRange class is designed to store the start and end pages of a page range which, in turn, may be accessed via the *getStart()* and *getEnd()* methods of the class.

When the *onWrite()* method was implemented in the previous section, a call was made to a method named *pageInRange()*, which takes as arguments an array of PageRange objects and a page number. The role of the *pageInRange()* method is to identify whether the specified page number is within the ranges specified and may be implemented within the MyPrintDocumentAdapter class in the *CustomPrintActivity.java* class as follows:

```
public class MyPrintDocumentAdapter extends PrintDocumentAdapter
```

```
{
    .
    .
    .

    private boolean pageInRange(PageRange[] pageRanges, int page)
    {
        for (int i = 0; i<pageRanges.length; i++)
        {
            if ((page >= pageRanges[i].getStart()) &&
                    (page <= pageRanges[i].getEnd()))
                return true;
        }
        return false;
    }
    .
    .
    .
}
```

53.7 Drawing the Content on the Page Canvas

We have now reached the point where some code needs to be written to draw the content on the pages so that they are ready for printing. The content that gets drawn is completely application specific and limited only by what can be achieved using the Android Canvas class. For the purposes of this example, however, some simple text and graphics will be drawn on the canvas.

The *onWrite()* method has been designed to call a method named *drawPage()* which takes as arguments the PdfDocument.Page object representing the current page and an integer representing the page number. Within the *CustomPrintActivity.java* file this method should now be implemented as follows:

```
package com.ebookfrenzy.customprint;

import java.io.FileOutputStream;
import java.io.IOException;

import android.app.Activity;
import android.os.Bundle;
import android.view.Menu;
import android.view.MenuItem;
import android.os.CancellationSignal;
import android.os.ParcelFileDescriptor;
import android.print.PageRange;
import android.print.PrintAttributes;
```

```
import android.print.PrintDocumentAdapter;
import android.content.Context;
import android.print.PrintDocumentInfo;
import android.print.pdf.PrintedPdfDocument;
import android.graphics.pdf.PdfDocument;
import android.graphics.pdf.PdfDocument.PageInfo;
import android.graphics.Canvas;
import android.graphics.Color;
import android.graphics.Paint;

public class CustomPrintActivity extends Activity {
.
.

    public class MyPrintDocumentAdapter extends
PrintDocumentAdapter
    {
.
.

            private void drawPage(PdfDocument.Page page,
                        int pagenumber) {
                Canvas canvas = page.getCanvas();

                pagenumber++; // Make sure page numbers start at 1

                int titleBaseLine = 72;
                int leftMargin = 54;

                Paint paint = new Paint();
                paint.setColor(Color.BLACK);
                paint.setTextSize(40);
                canvas.drawText(
                    "Test Print Document Page " + pagenumber,
                                        leftMargin,
                                        titleBaseLine,
                                        paint);

                paint.setTextSize(14);
                canvas.drawText("This is some test content to
verify that custom document printing works", leftMargin, titleBaseLine
+ 35, paint);

                if (pagenumber % 2 == 0)
                        paint.setColor(Color.RED);
```

```
                    else
                        paint.setColor(Color.GREEN);

                    PageInfo pageInfo = page.getInfo();


                    canvas.drawCircle(pageInfo.getPageWidth()/2,
                                      pageInfo.getPageHeight()/2,
                                      150,
                                      paint);
            }
        .
        .
}
```

Page numbering within the code starts at 0. Since documents traditionally start at page 1, the method begins by incrementing the stored page number. A reference to the Canvas object associated with the page is then obtained and some margin and baseline values declared:

```
Canvas canvas = page.getCanvas();

pagenumber++;

int titleBaseLine = 72;
int leftMargin = 54;
```

Next, the code creates Paint and Color objects to be used for drawing, sets a text size and draws the page title text, including the current page number:

```
Paint paint = new Paint();

paint.setColor(Color.BLACK);
paint.setTextSize(40);

canvas.drawText("Test Print Document Page " + pagenumber,
                                      leftMargin,
                                      titleBaseLine,
                                      paint);
```

The text size is then reduced and some body text drawn beneath the title:

```
paint.setTextSize(14);
```

```
canvas.drawText("This is some test content to verify that custom
document printing works", leftMargin, titleBaseLine + 35, paint);
```

The last task performed by this method involves drawing a circle (red on even numbered pages and green on odd). Having ascertained whether the page is odd or even, the method obtains the height and width of the page before using this information to position the circle in the center of the page:

```
if (pagenumber % 2 == 0)
        paint.setColor(Color.RED);
else
        paint.setColor(Color.GREEN);

PageInfo pageInfo = page.getInfo();

canvas.drawCircle(pageInfo.getPageWidth()/2,
                  pageInfo.getPageHeight()/2,
                  150, paint);
```

Having drawn on the canvas, the method returns control to the *onWrite()* method.

With the completion of the *drawPage()* method, the MyPrintDocumentAdapter class is now finished.

53.8 **Starting the Print Job**

When the "Print Document" button is touched by the user, the *printDocument()* onClick event handler method will be called. All that now remains before testing can commence, therefore, is to add this method to the *CustomPrintActivity.java* file, taking particular care to ensure that it is placed outside of the MyPrintDocumentAdapter class:

```
package com.ebookfrenzy.customprint;

import java.io.FileOutputStream;
import java.io.IOException;

import android.app.Activity;
import android.os.Bundle;
import android.view.Menu;
import android.view.MenuItem;
import android.os.CancellationSignal;
import android.os.ParcelFileDescriptor;
import android.print.PageRange;
import android.print.PrintAttributes;
import android.print.PrintDocumentAdapter;
import android.content.Context;
```

```
import android.print.PrintDocumentInfo;
import android.print.pdf.PrintedPdfDocument;
import android.graphics.pdf.PdfDocument;
import android.graphics.pdf.PdfDocument.PageInfo;
import android.graphics.Canvas;
import android.graphics.Color;
import android.graphics.Paint;
import android.print.PrintManager;
import android.view.View;

public class CustomPrintActivity extends Activity {

    public void printDocument(View view)
    {
        PrintManager printManager = (PrintManager) this
                .getSystemService(Context.PRINT_SERVICE);

        String jobName = this.getString(R.string.app_name) +
                " Document";

        printManager.print(jobName, new
                MyPrintDocumentAdapter(this),
                null);
    }
    .
    .
    .
}
```

This method obtains a reference to the Print Manager service running on the device before creating a new String object to serve as the job name for the print task. Finally the *print()* method of the Print Manager is called to start the print job, passing through the job name and an instance of our custom print document adapter class.

53.9 Testing the Application

Compile and run the application on a physical Android device that is running Android 4.4 or later. When the application has loaded, touch the "Print Document" button to initiate the print job and select a suitable target for the output (the Save to PDF option is a useful option for avoiding wasting paper and printer ink).

Check the printed output which should consist of 4 pages including text and graphics. Figure 53-3, for example, shows the four pages of the document viewed as a PDF file ready to be saved on the device:

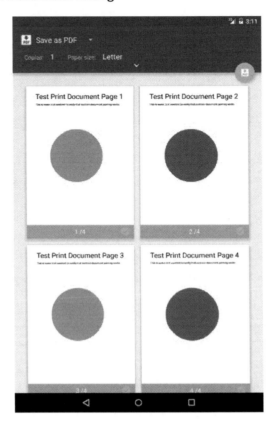

Figure 53-3

Experiment with other print configuration options such as changing the paper size, orientation and pages settings within the print panel. Each setting change should be reflected in the printed output, indicating that the custom print document adapter is functioning correctly.

53.10 Summary

Although more complex to implement than the Android Printing framework HTML and image printing options, custom document printing provides considerable flexibility in terms of printing complex content from within an Android application. The majority of the work involved in implementing custom document printing involves the creation of a custom Print Adapter class such that it not only draws the content on the document pages, but also responds correctly as changes are made by the user to print settings such as the page size and range of pages to be printed.

54. Handling Different Android Devices and Displays

Before being made available for purchase on the Google Play App Store, an application must first be submitted to the portal for review and approval. One of the most important steps to take before submitting an application is to decide which Android device models the application is intended to support and, more importantly, that the application runs without issue on those devices.

This chapter will cover some of the areas to consider when making sure that an application runs on the widest possible range of Android devices.

54.1 Handling Different Device Displays

Android devices come in a variety of different screen sizes and resolutions. The ideal solution is to design the user interface of your application so that it appears correctly on the widest possible range of devices. The best way to achieve this is to design the user interface using layout managers that do not rely on absolute positioning (in other words specific X and Y coordinates) such as the RelativeLayout so that views are positioned relative to both the size of the display and each other.

Similarly, avoid using specific width and height properties wherever possible. When such properties are unavoidable, always use *density-independent (dp)* values as these are automatically scaled to match the device display at application runtime.

Having designed the user interface, be sure to test it on each device on which it is intended to be supported. In the absence of the physical device hardware, use the emulator templates wherever possible to test on the widest possible range of devices.

In the event that it is not possible to design the user interface such that a single design will work on all Android devices, another option is to provide a different layout for each display.

54.2 Creating a Layout for each Display Size

The ideal solution to the multiple display problem is to design user interface layouts that adapt to the display size of the device on which the application is running. This, for example, has the advantage of having only one layout to manage when modifying the application. Inevitably, however, there will be situations where this ideal is unachievable given the vast difference in screen size between a phone and a tablet. Another option is to provide different layouts, each tailored for a specific display category. This involves identifying the *smallest width* qualifier value of each display and creating an XML layout file for each one. The smallest width value of a display indicates the minimum width of that display measured in dp units.

Display-specific layouts are implemented by creating additional sub-directories under the *res* directory of a project. The naming convention for these folders is:

layout-<*smallest-width*>

For example, layout resource folders for a range of devices might be configured as follows:

- *res/layout* – The default layout file
- *res/layout-sw200dp*
- *res/layout-sw600dp*
- *res/layout-sw800dp*

Alternatively, more general categories can be created by targeting *small*, *normal*, *large* and *xlarge* displays:

- *res/layout* – The default layout file
- *res/layout-small*
- *res/layout-normal*
- *res/layout-large*
- *res/layout-xlarge*

Each folder must, in turn, contain a copy of the layout XML file adapted for the corresponding display, all of which must have matching file names. Once implemented, the Android runtime system will automatically select the correct layout file to display to the user to match the device display.

54.3 Providing Different Images

User interface layouts are not the only area of concern when adapting an application for different screen densities, dimensions and aspect ratios. Another area to pay attention to is that of images. An image that appears correctly scaled on a large tablet screen, for example, might not appear correctly scaled on a smaller phone based device. As with layouts, however, multiple sets of images can be bundled with the application, each tailored for a specific display. This can once again be achieved by referencing the smallest width value. In this case, *drawable* folders need to be created in the *res* directory. For example:

- *res/drawable* – The default image folder
- *res/drawable-sw200dp*

- *res/drawable-sw600dp*
- *res/drawable-sw800dp*

Having created the folders, simply place the display specific versions of the images into the corresponding folder, using the same name for each of the images.

Alternatively, the images may be categorized into broader display densities using the following directories based on the pixel density of the display:

- *res/drawable-ldpi* - Images for low density screens (approx. 120 dpi)
- *res/drawable-mdpi* – Images for medium-density screens (approx. 160 dpi)
- *res/drawable-hdpi* – Images for high-density screens (approx. 240 dpi)
- *res/drawable-xhdpi* – Images for extra high-density screens (approx. 320 dpi)
- *res/drawable-*tvdpi – Images for displays between medium and high density (approx. 213 dpi)
- *res/drawable-nodpi* – Images that must not be scaled by the system

54.4 **Checking for Hardware Support**

By now, it should be apparent that not all Android devices were created equal. An application that makes use of specific hardware features (such as a microphone or camera) should include code to gracefully handle the absence of that hardware. This typically involves performing a check to find out if the hardware feature is missing, and subsequently reporting to the user that the corresponding application functionality will not be available.

The following method can be used to check for the presence of a microphone:

```
protected boolean hasMicrophone() {
    PackageManager pmanager = this.getPackageManager();
    return pmanager.hasSystemFeature(
        PackageManager.FEATURE_MICROPHONE);
}
```

Similarly, the following method is useful for checking for the presence of a front facing camera:

```
private boolean hasCamera() {
    if (getPackageManager().hasSystemFeature(
        PackageManager.FEATURE_CAMERA_FRONT)){
            return true;
    } else {
            return false;
    }
}
```

54.5 **Providing Device Specific Application Binaries**

Even with the best of intentions, there will inevitably be situations where it is not possible to target all Android devices within a single application (though Google certainly encourages developers to target as many devices as possible within a single application binary package). In this situation, the application submission process allows multiple application binaries to be uploaded for a single application. Each binary is then configured to indicate to Google the devices with which the binary is configured to work. When a user subsequently purchases the application, Google ensures that the correct binary is downloaded for the user's device.

It is also important to be aware that it may not always make sense to try to provide support for every Android device model. There is little point, for example, in making an application that relies heavily on a specific hardware feature available on devices that lack that specific hardware. These requirements can be defined using Google Play Filters as outlined at:

http://developer.android.com/google/play/filters.html

54.6 **Summary**

There is more to completing an Android application than making sure it works on a single device model. Before an application is submitted to the Google Play Developer Console, it should first be tested on as wide a range of display sizes as possible. This includes making sure that the user interface layouts and images scale correctly for each display variation and taking steps to ensure that the application gracefully handles the absence of certain hardware features. It is also possible to submit to the developer console a different application binary for specific Android models, or to state that a particular application simply does not support certain Android devices.

55. Signing and Preparing an Android Application for Release

Once the development work on an Android application is complete and it has been tested on a wide range of Android devices, the next step is to prepare the application for submission to the Google Play App Store. Before submission can take place, however, the application must be packaged for release and signed with a private key. This chapter will work through the steps involved in obtaining a private key and preparing the application package for release.

55.1 The Release Preparation Process

Up until this point in the book we have been building application projects in a mode suitable for testing and debugging. Building an application package for release to customers via the Google Play store, on the other hand, requires that some additional steps be taken. The first requirement is that the application be compiled in *release mode* instead of *debug mode.* Secondly, the application must be signed with a private key that uniquely identifies you as the application's developer. Finally, the application package must be *aligned*. This is simply a process by which some data files in the application package are formatted with a certain byte alignment to improve performance.

Whilst each of these tasks can be performed outside of the Android Studio environment, the procedures can more easily be performed using the Android Studio build mechanism as outlined in the remainder of this chapter.

55.2 Changing the Build Variant

The first step in the process of generating a signed application APK file involves changing the build variant for the project from debug to release. This is achieved using the *Build Variants* tool window which can be accessed from the tool window quick access menu (located in the bottom left hand corner of the Android Studio main window as shown in Figure 55-1).

Figure 55-1

Once the Build Variants tool window is displayed, change the Build Variant settings for all the modules listed from *debug* to *release*:

Figure 55-2

The project is now configured to build in release mode. The next step is to configure signing key information for use when generating the signed application package.

55.3 Enabling ProGuard

When generating an application package, the option is available to use ProGuard during the package creation process. ProGuard performs a series of optimization and verification tasks that result in smaller and more efficient byte code. In order to use ProGuard, it is necessary to enable this feature within the Project Structure settings prior to generating the APK file.

The steps to enable ProGuard in Android Studio 1.2 are as follows:

1. Display the Project Structure dialog (*File -> Project Structure*).
2. Select the "app" module in the far left panel and the "release" entry from the middle panel.

3. Select the "Build Types" tab in the main panel.

4. Change the "Minify Enabled" option from "false" to "true" and click on *OK*.

5. Follow the steps to create a keystore file and build the release APK file.

55.4 **Creating a Keystore File**

To create a keystore file, select the *Build -> Generate Signed APK...* menu option to display the Generate Signed APK Wizard dialog as shown in Figure 55-3:

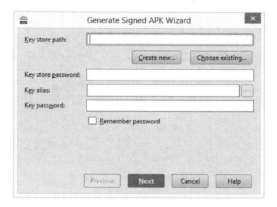

Figure 55-3

In the event that you have an existing release keystore file, click on the *Choose existing...* button and navigate to and select the file. In the event that you have yet to create a keystore file, click on the *Create new...* button to display the *New Key Store* dialog (Figure 55-4). Click on the button to the right of the Key store path field and navigate to a suitable location on your file system, enter a name for the keystore file (for example *release.keystore.jks*) and click on the OK button.

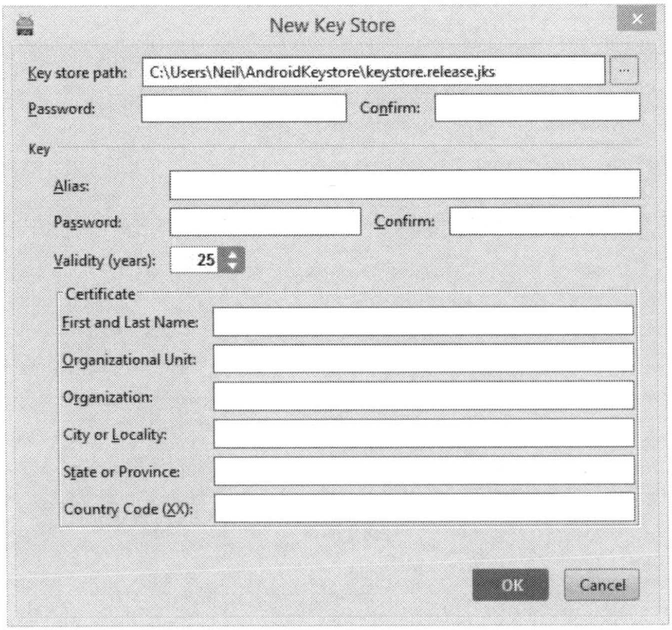

Figure 55-4

The New Key Store dialog is now divided into two sections. The top section relates to the keystore file. In this section, enter a strong password with which to protect the keystore file into both the *Password* and *Confirm* fields. The lower section of the dialog relates to the release key that will be stored in the key store file.

55.5 Generating a Private Key

The next step is to generate a new private key which will be used to sign the application package. Within the *Key* section of the New Key Store dialog, enter the following details:

- An alias by which the key will be referenced. This can be any sequence of characters, though only the first 8 are used by the system.
- A suitably strong password to protect the key.
- The number of years for which the key is to be valid (Google recommends a duration in excess of 27 years).

In addition, information must be provided for at least one of the remaining fields (for example your first and last name or organization name).

Figure 55-5

Once the information has been entered, click on the *Next* button to proceed with the package creation.

55.6 Creating the Application APK File

The next task to be performed is to instruct Android Studio to build the application APK package file in release mode and then sign it with the newly created private key. At this point the *Generate Signed APK Wizard* dialog should still be displayed with the keystore path, passwords and key alias fields populated with information:

Figure 55-6

Assuming that the settings are correct, click on the *Next* button to proceed to the APK generation screen (Figure 55-7). Within this screen, review the *Destination APK path:* setting to verify that the location into which the APK file will be generated is acceptable. In the event that another location is preferred, click on the button to the right of the text field and navigate to the desired file system location and click *Finish*.

Figure 55-7

The Gradle system will now compile the application in release mode. Once the build is complete, a dialog will appear providing the option to open the folder containing the APK file in an explorer window:

Figure 55-8

At this point the application is ready to be submitted to the Google Play store.

The private key generated as part of this process should be used when signing and releasing future applications and, as such, should be kept in a safe place and securely backed up.

The final step in the process of bringing an Android application to market involves submitting it to the Google Play Developer Console. Once submitted, the application will be available for download from the Google Play App Store.

55.7 Register for a Google Play Developer Console Account

The first step in the application submission process is to create a Google Play Developer Console account. To do so, navigate to *https://play.google.com/apps/publish/signup/* and follow the instructions to complete the registration process. Note that there is a one-time $25 fee to register. Once an application goes on sale, Google will keep 30% of all revenues associated with the application.

Once the account has been created, the next step is to gather together information about the application. In order to bring your application to market, the following information will be required:

- **Title** – The title of the application.
- **Description** – Up to 4000 words describing the application.
- **Screenshots** – Up to 8 screenshots of your application running (a minimum of two is required). Google recommends submitted screenshots of the application running on a 7" or 10" tablet.
- **Language** – The language of the application (the default is US English).
- **Promotional Text** – The text that will be used when your application appears in special promotional features within the Google Play environment.
- **Application Type** – Whether your application is considered to be a *game* or an *application*.
- **Category** – The category that best describes your application (for example finance, health and fitness, education, sports etc.).
- **Locations** – The geographical locations into which you wish your application to be made available for purchase.

- **Contact Information** – Methods by which users may contact you for support relating to the application. Options include web, email and phone.
- **Pricing & Distribution** – Information about the price of the application and the geographical locations where it is to be marketed and sold.

Having collected the above information and prepared the application package file for release, simply follow the steps in the Google Play Developer Console to submit the application for testing and sale.

55.8 Uploading New APK Versions to the Google Play Developer Console

The first APK file uploaded for your application will invariably have a version code of 1. If an attempt is made to upload another APK file with the same version code number, the console will reject the file with the following error:

```
You need to use a different version code for your APK because you
already have one with version code 1.
```

To resolve this problem, the version code embedded into the APK needs to be increased. This is performed in the *module* level build.gradle file of the project, shown highlighted in Figure 55-9. It is important to note that this is not the *top* level build.gradle file positioned lower in the project hierarchy listing:

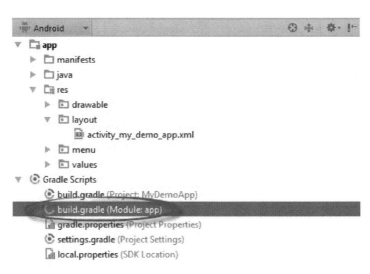

Figure 55-9

By default, this file will typically read as follows:

```
apply plugin: 'com.android.application'

android {
```

```
    compileSdkVersion 21
    buildToolsVersion "21.1.2"

    defaultConfig {
        applicationId "com.ebookfrenzy.mydemoapp"
        minSdkVersion 21
        targetSdkVersion 21
        versionCode 1
        versionName "1.0"
    }
    buildTypes {
        release {
            minifyEnabled false
            proguardFiles getDefaultProguardFile('proguard-
android.txt'), 'proguard-rules.pro'
        }
    }
}

dependencies {
    compile fileTree(dir: 'libs', include: ['*.jar'])
}
```

To change the version code, simply change the number declared next to *versionCode*. To also change the version number displayed to users of your application, change the *versionName* string. For example:

```
versionCode 2
versionName "2.0"
```

Having made these changes, rebuild the APK file and perform the upload again.

55.9 **Summary**

Before an application can be submitted to the Google Play store, it must first be built in release mode, signed with a private certificate and the resulting APK package file subjected to a process referred to as *alignment*. As outlined in this chapter, all of these steps can be performed with relative ease through the use of the Android Studio build system.

Chapter 56

56. Integrating Google Play In-app Billing into an Android Application

In the early days of mobile applications for operating systems such as Android and iOS, the most common method for earning revenue was to charge an upfront fee to download and install the application. Another revenue opportunity was soon introduced in the form of embedding advertising within applications. Perhaps the most common and lucrative option is now to charge the user for purchasing items from within the application after it has been installed. This typically takes the form of access to a higher level in a game, acquiring virtual goods or currency, or subscribing to the digital edition of a magazine or newspaper.

Google provides support for the integration of in app purchasing through the Google Play In-App Billing API. The purpose of this chapter is to work through a tutorial that demonstrates the steps involved in implementing basic Google Play based in-app billing within an Android application.

56.1 Installing the Google Play Billing Library

A prerequisite to implementing Google Play In-app Billing is that the Google Play Billing Library be installed on the development system. Check whether or not the library is installed by launching the Android SDK Manager by selecting *Configure -> SDK Manager* from the Android Studio welcome screen, or via the *Tools -> Android -> SDK Manager* menu of the main window. Once the SDK Manager has loaded, scroll down to the *Extras* section and check the *Status* column next to the Google Play Billing Library entry as shown in Figure 56-1:

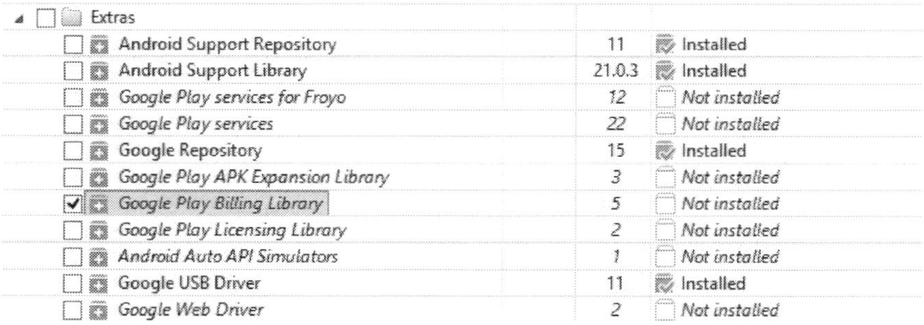

Extras		
Android Support Repository	11	Installed
Android Support Library	21.0.3	Installed
Google Play services for Froyo	12	Not installed
Google Play services	22	Not installed
Google Repository	15	Installed
Google Play APK Expansion Library	3	Not installed
Google Play Billing Library	5	Not installed
Google Play Licensing Library	2	Not installed
Android Auto API Simulators	1	Not installed
Google USB Driver	11	Installed
Google Web Driver	2	Not installed

Figure 56-1

If the library's status is listed as *Not Installed*, select the check box next to the library and click on the *Install packages...* button. Once the download has completed, the SDK will have been installed into the *sdk/extras/google/play_billing* subfolder of the Android Studio installation directory (the location of which can be found in the *SDK Path* field at the top of the Android SDK Manager window).

Within the above SDK subfolder resides a file named *IInAppBillingService.aidl* which will need to be included with any projects that require Google Play billing support. The folder also includes a sample application (contained within the *samples* sub-directory) named *TrivialDrive*. Part of this sample application is a package containing a set of convenience classes that significantly ease the process of integrating billing into an application. Later in this tutorial, these classes will be imported into our own application project and used to implement in-app billing.

56.2 Creating the Example In-app Billing Project

The objective of this tutorial is to create a simple application that uses the Google in-app billing system to allow consumable purchases to be made. The application will consist of two buttons, one of which will be disabled by default. In order to enable the button so that it can be clicked, the user must purchase a "button click" item by clicking on the second button and completing a purchase. The first button will then be enabled for a single click before being disabled again until the user makes another purchase.

Create a new project in Android Studio, entering *InAppBilling* into the Application name field and *ebookfrenzy.com* as the Company Domain setting before clicking on the *Next* button.

On the form factors screen, enable the *Phone and Tablet* option and set the minimum SDK setting to API 19: Android 4.4 (KitKat). Continue to proceed through the screens, requesting the creation of a blank activity named *InAppBillingActivity* with corresponding layout and menu resource files named *activity_in_app_billing* and *menu_in_app_billing*.

Click on *Finish* to initiate the project creation process.

56.3 Adding Billing Permission to the Manifest File

Before an application can support in-app billing, a new permission line must be added to the project's *AndroidManifest.xml* file. Within the Project tool window, therefore, locate and load the *AndroidManifest.xml* file for the newly created InAppBilling project and modify it to add the billing permission as follows:

```
<?xml version="1.0" encoding="utf-8"?>
<manifest xmlns:android="http://schemas.android.com/apk/res/android"
    package="com.ebookfrenzy.inappbilling" >
```

```
<uses-permission android:name="com.android.vending.BILLING" />

<application
    android:allowBackup="true"
    android:icon="@mipmap/ic_launcher"
    android:label="@string/app_name"
    android:theme="@style/AppTheme" >
    <activity
        android:name=".InAppBillingActivity"
        android:label="@string/app_name" >
        <intent-filter>
            <action android:name="android.intent.action.MAIN" />

            <category android:name=
                "android.intent.category.LAUNCHER" />
        </intent-filter>
    </activity>
</application>

</manifest>
```

56.4 Adding the IInAppBillingService.aidl File to the Project

The *IInAppBillingService.aidl* file included as part of the Google Play Billing Library should now be added to the project. This file must be added such that it is contained in a package named *com.android.vending.billing* located in the *app -> aidl* folder of the InAppBilling project module.

To create the aidl directory, right-click on the *app* node in the project tool window, selecting the *New -> Folder -> AIDL Folder* menu option as shown in Figure 56-2:

Figure 56-2

In the resulting options dialog, accept the defaults by clicking on the *Finish* button.

Within the Project tool window the aidl folder should now be listed. The next step is to create the *com.android.vending.billing* package. Right-click on the aidl folder and select the *New -> Package* menu item. In the resulting dialog, enter *com.android.vending.billing* into the text field and click on *OK*.

Using the explorer or finder tool for your operating system, navigate to the *<sdk path>/sdk/extras/google/play_billing* where *<sdk path>* is replaced by the path into which you installed the Android SDK. From this location, copy the *IInAppBillingService.aidl* file, return to Android Studio and paste the file onto the *com.android.vending.billing* package in the Project tool window. In the Copy dialog, accept the default settings and click on the *OK* button. At this point the relevant sections of the Project tool window should be organized to match that of Figure 56-3:

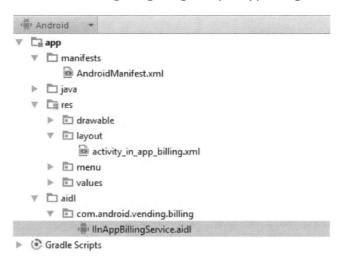

Figure 56-3

With the library file installed, the next step is to import the utility classes from the TrivialDrive sample into the project so that these can be utilized within the application code.

56.5 Adding the Utility Classes to the Project

The TrivialDrive sample project that was installed into the SDK as part of the Google Play Billing library includes a set of classes intended specifically to make the task of implementing in-app billing easier. Although bundled as part of the TrivialDrive project, these classes are general purpose in nature and are applicable to most application billing requirements. For the purposes of this example, we will create a new package named *com.ebookfrenzy.inappbilling.util* within our project.

To create this package, right-click on the *app -> java* folder in the Project tool window and select the *New -> Package* menu option. In the resulting dialog, select *..\app\src\main\java* from the *Directory Structure* panel and click on OK. In the next dialog name the package *com.ebookfrenzy.inappbilling.util* and click on *Finish*.

The next step is to import the TrivialDrive utility class files into the Android Studio project. Returning to the file system explorer window (and assuming it is still positioned in the *<sdk path>/sdk/extras/google/play_billing* directory), navigate further into the file system hierarchy to the following directory:

```
samples/TrivialDrive/src/com/example/android/trivialdrivesample/util
```

Select all nine files in this folder and copy them. Return to Android Studio and paste the files onto the *com.example.inappbilling.inappbilling.util* package in the Project tool window. Verify that the project hierarchy now matches Figure 56-4:

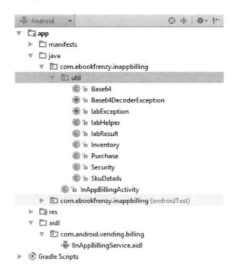

Figure 56-4

56.6 Designing the User Interface

The user interface, as previously outlined, is going to consist of two buttons, the first of which can only be clicked after a purchase has been made via a click performed on the second button. Double-click on the *app -> res -> layout -> activity_in_app_billing.xml* file to load it into the Designer tool and design the user interface so that it resembles that of Figure 56-5:

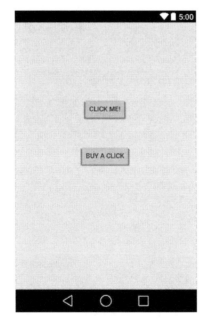

Figure 56-5

Extract the button text strings to string resources named *click_string* and *buy_string* and, with the user interface layout designed, switch the Designer tool to Text mode and name the buttons *clickButton* and *buyButton* respectively. Also, set *onClick* properties to configure the buttons to call methods named *buttonClicked* and *buyClick* such that the completed XML layout file reads as follows:

```
<RelativeLayout
xmlns:android="http://schemas.android.com/apk/res/android"
    xmlns:tools="http://schemas.android.com/tools"
    android:layout_width="match_parent"
    android:layout_height="match_parent"
    android:paddingLeft="@dimen/activity_horizontal_margin"
    android:paddingRight="@dimen/activity_horizontal_margin"
    android:paddingTop="@dimen/activity_vertical_margin"
    android:paddingBottom="@dimen/activity_vertical_margin"
    tools:context=".InAppBillingActivity">

    <Button
        android:layout_width="wrap_content"
        android:layout_height="wrap_content"
        android:text="@string/buy_string"
        android:id="@+id/buyButton"
        android:layout_centerVertical="true"
        android:layout_centerHorizontal="true"
        android:onClick="buyClick" />

    <Button
        android:layout_width="wrap_content"
        android:layout_height="wrap_content"
        android:text="@string/click_string"
        android:id="@+id/clickButton"
        android:layout_above="@+id/buyButton"
        android:layout_centerHorizontal="true"
        android:layout_marginBottom="83dp"
        android:onClick="buttonClicked"/>
</RelativeLayout>
```

With the user interface design complete, it is time to start writing some Java code to handle the purchasing and consumption of clicks.

56.7 **Implementing the "Click Me" Button**

When the application is initially launched, the "Click Me!" button will be disabled. To make sure that this happens, load the *InAppBillingActivity.java* file into the editor and modify the *onCreate* method to obtain a reference to both buttons and then disable the clickButton:

```
package com.ebookfrenzy.inappbilling;

import android.app.Activity;
import android.os.Bundle;
import android.view.Menu;
import android.view.MenuItem;
import android.widget.Button;

public class InAppBillingActivity extends Activity {

    private Button clickButton;
    private Button buyButton;

    @Override
    protected void onCreate(Bundle savedInstanceState) {
        super.onCreate(savedInstanceState);
        setContentView(R.layout.activity_in_app_billing);

        buyButton = (Button)findViewById(R.id.buyButton);
        clickButton = (Button)findViewById(R.id.clickButton);
        clickButton.setEnabled(false);
    }
    .
    .
    .
}
```

The *buttonClicked* method that will be called when the button is clicked by the user now also needs to be implemented. All this method needs to do is to disable the button once again so that the button cannot be clicked until another purchase is made and to enable the buy button so that another click can be purchased. Remaining within the *InAppBillingActivity.java* file, implement this method as follows:

```
package com.ebookfrenzy.inappbilling;

import android.app.Activity;
import android.os.Bundle;
```

```
import android.view.Menu;
import android.view.MenuItem;
import android.widget.Button;
import android.view.View;

public class InAppBillingActivity extends Activity {
  .
  .
  .
    public void buttonClicked (View view)
    {
        clickButton.setEnabled(false);
        buyButton.setEnabled(true);
    }
  .
  .
}
```

Work on the functionality of the first button is now complete. The next steps are to begin implementing the in-app billing functionality.

56.8 Google Play Developer Console and Google Wallet Accounts

Application developers making use of Google Play billing must be identified by a unique public license key. The only way to obtain a public license key is to register an application within the Google Play Developer Console. If you do not already have a Google Play Developer Console account, go to *http://play.google.com/apps/publish* and follow the steps to register as outlined in the chapter entitled *Signing and Preparing an Android Application for Release*.

Once you are logged in, click on the Settings option (represented by the cog icon on the left hand edge of the web page) and, on the *Account details* page, scroll down to the *Merchant Account* section. In order to use in-app billing, your Google Play Developer Console account must have a Google Wallet Merchant account associated with it. If a Google Wallet merchant account is not set up, create a merchant account and register it with your Google Developer Console account before proceeding.

56.9 Obtaining the Public License Key for the Application

From the home page of the Google Play Developer Console, click on the *Add new application* button, specifying the default language and a title of *InAppBilling*. Once this information has been entered, click on the *Upload APK* button:

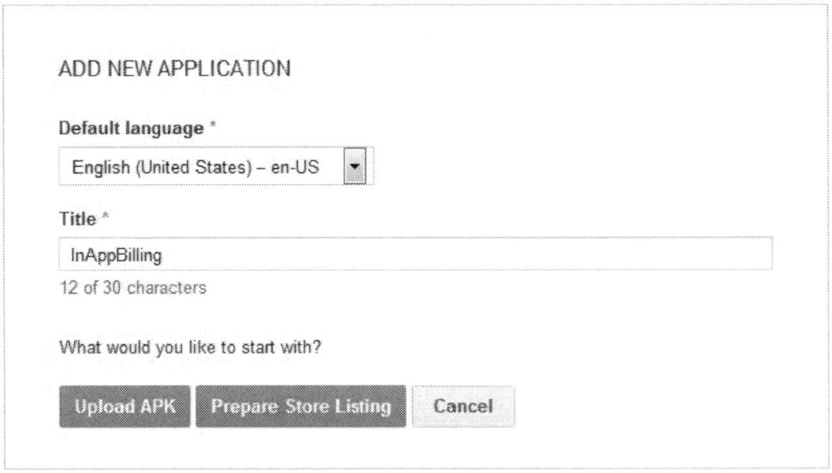

ADD NEW APPLICATION

Default language *

English (United States) – en-US

Title *

InAppBilling

12 of 30 characters

What would you like to start with?

Upload APK   Prepare Store Listing   Cancel

Figure 56-6

It is not necessary to upload the APK file at this point, so once the application has been registered, click on the *Services & APIs* option to display the Base64-encoded RSA public key for the application as shown in Figure 56-7:

Figure 56-7

Keep this Browser window open for now as this key will need to be included in the application code in the next step of this tutorial.

56.10 Setting Up Google Play Billing in the Application

With the public key generated, it is now time to use that key to initialize billing within the application code. For the InAppBilling example project this will be performed in the *onCreate* method of the *InAppBillingActivity.java* file and will make use of the IabHelper class from the utilities classes previously added to the project as follows. Note that *<your license key here>* should be replaced by your own license key generated in the previous section:

```java
package com.ebookfrenzy.inappbilling;

import com.ebookfrenzy.inappbilling.util.IabHelper;
import com.ebookfrenzy.inappbilling.util.IabResult;
import com.ebookfrenzy.inappbilling.util.Inventory;
import com.ebookfrenzy.inappbilling.util.Purchase;

import android.app.Activity;
import android.os.Bundle;
import android.view.Menu;
import android.view.MenuItem;
import android.widget.Button;
import android.view.View;
import android.content.Intent;
import android.util.Log;

public class InAppBillingActivity extends Activity {

    private static final String TAG =
                "InAppBilling";
    IabHelper mHelper;

    private Button clickButton;
    private Button buyButton;

    @Override
    protected void onCreate(Bundle savedInstanceState) {
        super.onCreate(savedInstanceState);
        setContentView(R.layout.activity_in_app_billing);

        buyButton = (Button)findViewById(R.id.buyButton);
        clickButton = (Button)findViewById(R.id.clickButton);
        clickButton.setEnabled(false);

        String base64EncodedPublicKey =
                            "<your license key here>";

        mHelper = new IabHelper(this, base64EncodedPublicKey);

        mHelper.startSetup(new
```

```
                            IabHelper.OnIabSetupFinishedListener() {
                            public void onIabSetupFinished(IabResult
result)
                            {
                                if (!result.isSuccess()) {
                                    Log.d(TAG, "In-app Billing setup failed: "
+
                                            result);
                                } else {
                                    Log.d(TAG, "In-app Billing is set up OK");
                                }
                            }
                        });
        }
        .
        .
        .
}
```

After implementing the above changes, compile and run the application on a physical Android device (Google Play Billing cannot be tested within an emulator session) and make sure that the "In-app Billing is set up OK" message appears in the LogCat output panel.

56.11 Initiating a Google Play In-app Billing Purchase

With access to the billing system initialized, we can now turn our attention to initiating a purchase when the user touches the *Buy Click* button in the user interface. This was previously configured to trigger a call to a method named *buyClick* which now needs to be implemented in the *InAppBillingActivity.java* file. In addition to initiating the purchase process in this method, it will be necessary to implement an *onActivityResult* method and also a listener method to be called when the purchase has completed.

Begin by editing the *InAppBillingActivity.java* file and adding the code for the *buyClick* method so that it reads as follows:

```
.
.
.
public class InAppBillingActivity extends Activity {

        private static final String TAG = "InAppBilling";
        IabHelper mHelper;
        static final String ITEM_SKU = "android.test.purchased";
```

```
        .
        .
        .

        public void buyClick(View view) {
            mHelper.launchPurchaseFlow(this, ITEM_SKU, 10001,
                        mPurchaseFinishedListener,
"mypurchasetoken");
        }

        .
        .
        .
}
```

Clearly, all this method needs to do is make a call to the *launchPurchaseFlow* method of our mHelper instance. The arguments passed through to the method are as follows:

- A reference to the enclosing Activity instance from which the method is being called.
- The SKU that identifies the product that is being purchased. In this instance we are going to use a standard SKU provided by Google for testing purposes. This SKU, referred to as a static response SKU, will always result in a successful purchase. Other testing SKUs available for use when testing purchasing functionality without making real purchases are *android.test.cancelled*, *android.test.refunded* and *android.test.item_unavailable*.
- The request code which can be any positive integer value. When the purchase has completed, the *onActivityResult* method will be called and passed this integer along with the purchase response. This allows the method to identify which purchase process is returning and can be useful when the method needs to be able to handle purchasing for different items.
- The listener method to be called when the purchase is complete.
- The developer payload token string. This can be any string value and is used to identify the purchase. For the purposes of this example, this is set to "mypurchasetoken".

56.12 Implementing the onActivityResult Method

When the purchasing process returns, it will call a method on the calling activity named *onActivityResult*, passing through as arguments the request code passed through to the *launchPurchaseFlow* method, a result code and intent data containing the purchase response.

This method needs to identify if it was called as a result of an in-app purchase request or some request unrelated to in-app billing. It does this by calling the *handleActivityResult* method of the mHelper instance and passing through the incoming arguments. If this is a purchase request the mHelper will handle it and return a *true* value. If this is not the result of a purchase, then the method needs to pass it up to the superclass to be handled. Bringing this together results in the following code:

```
@Override
protected void onActivityResult(int requestCode, int resultCode,
      Intent data)
{

      if (!mHelper.handleActivityResult(requestCode,
            resultCode, data)) {
            super.onActivityResult(requestCode, resultCode, data);
      }

}
```

In the event that the onActivityResult method was called in response to an in-app billing purchase, a call will then be made to the listener method referenced in the call to the *launchPurchaseFlow* method (in this case a method named *mPurchaseFinishedListener*). The next task, therefore, is to implement this method.

56.13 **Implementing the Purchase Finished Listener**

The "purchase finished" listener must perform a number of different tasks. In the first instance, it must check to ensure that the purchase was successful. It then needs to check the SKU of the purchased item to make sure it matches the one specified in the purchase request. In the event of a successful purchase, the method will need to *consume* the purchase so that the user can purchase it again when another one is needed. If the purchase is not consumed, future attempts to purchase the item will fail stating that the item has already been purchased. Whilst this would be desired behavior if the user only needed to purchase the item once, clearly this is not the behavior required for consumable purchases. Finally, the method needs to enable the "Click Me!" button so that the user can perform the button click that was purchased.

Within the *InAppBillingActivity.java* file, implement this method as follows:

```
IabHelper.OnIabPurchaseFinishedListener mPurchaseFinishedListener
      = new IabHelper.OnIabPurchaseFinishedListener() {
      public void onIabPurchaseFinished(IabResult result,
                  Purchase purchase)
      {
          if (result.isFailure()) {
              // Handle error
              return;
          }
          else if (purchase.getSku().equals(ITEM_SKU)) {
              consumeItem();
              buyButton.setEnabled(false);
          }
```

```
        }
};
```

As can be seen from the above code fragment, in the event that the purchase was successful, a method named *consumeItem()* will be called. Clearly, the next step is to implement this method.

56.14 **Consuming the Purchased Item**

In the documentation for Google Play In-app Billing, Google recommends that consumable items be consumed before providing the user with access to the purchased item. So far in this tutorial we have performed the purchase of the item but not yet consumed it. In the event of a successful purchase, the *mPurchaseFinishedListener* implementation has been configured to call a method named *consumeItem()*. It will be the responsibility of this method to query the billing system to make sure that the purchase has been made. This involves making a call to the *queryInventoryAsync()* method of the mHelper object. This task is performed asynchronously from the application's main thread and a listener method called when the task is complete. If the item has been purchased, the listener will consume the item via a call to the *consumeAsync()* method of the *mHelper* object. Bringing these requirements together results in the following additions to the *InAppBillingActivity.java* file:

```
public void consumeItem() {
        mHelper.queryInventoryAsync(mReceivedInventoryListener);
}

IabHelper.QueryInventoryFinishedListener mReceivedInventoryListener
    = new IabHelper.QueryInventoryFinishedListener() {
        public void onQueryInventoryFinished(IabResult result,
            Inventory inventory) {

            if (result.isFailure()) {
                // Handle failure
            } else {
                mHelper.consumeAsync(inventory.getPurchase(ITEM_SKU),
                    mConsumeFinishedListener);
            }

        }
};
```

As with the query, the consumption task is also performed asynchronously and, in this case, is configured to call a listener named *mConsumeFinishedListener* when completed. This listener now needs to be implemented such that it enables the "Click Me!" button after the item has been consumed in the billing system:

```
IabHelper.OnConsumeFinishedListener mConsumeFinishedListener =
```

```
               new IabHelper.OnConsumeFinishedListener() {
                public void onConsumeFinished(Purchase purchase,
                    IabResult result) {

            if (result.isSuccess()) {
                    clickButton.setEnabled(true);
            } else {
                    // handle error
            }

        }
};
```

56.15 **Releasing the IabHelper Instance**

Throughout this tutorial, much of the work has been performed by calling methods on an instance of the IabHelper utility class named *mHelper*. Now that the code to handle purchasing and subsequent consumption of a virtual item is complete, the last task is to make sure this object is released when the activity is destroyed. Remaining in the *InAppBillingActivity.java* file, override the *onDestroy()* activity lifecycle method as follows:

```
@Override
public void onDestroy() {
        super.onDestroy();
        if (mHelper != null) mHelper.dispose();
        mHelper = null;
}
```

56.16 **Modifying the Security.java File**

When an application is compiled and installed on a device from within Android Studio, it is built and executed in *debug mode*. When the application is complete it is then built in *release mode* and uploaded to the Google Play App Store as described in the chapter entitled *Signing and Preparing an Android Application for Release*.

As the InAppBilling application is currently configured, purchases are being made using the *android.test.purchased* static response SKU code. It is important to be aware that static response SKUs can only be used when running an application in debug mode. As will be outlined later, new in-app products must be created within the Google Play Developer Console before full testing can be performed in release mode.

The current version of the utility classes provided with the TrivialDrive example application include an added level of security that prevents purchases from being made without a valid signature key being returned from the Google Play billing server. A side effect of this change is that it prevents the code from functioning when using the static response SKU values. Before testing the application in debug mode, therefore, a few extra lines of code need to be added to the *verifyPurchase()* method in the *Security.java* file. Within the Android Studio Project tool window, select the *Security.java* file located in the *app -> java -> <package name> -> util* folder of the project to load it into the editor. Once loaded, locate and modify the *verifyPurchase()* method so that it reads as follows:

```java
package com.ebookfrenzy.inappbilling.util;

import android.text.TextUtils;
import android.util.Log;

import org.json.JSONException;
import org.json.JSONObject;

import com.ebookfrenzy.inappbilling.BuildConfig;

import java.security.InvalidKeyException;
import java.security.KeyFactory;
import java.security.NoSuchAlgorithmException;
import java.security.PublicKey;
import java.security.Signature;
import java.security.SignatureException;
import java.security.spec.InvalidKeySpecException;
import java.security.spec.X509EncodedKeySpec;
.
.
.
    public static boolean verifyPurchase(String base64PublicKey,
            String signedData, String signature) {
        if (TextUtils.isEmpty(signedData) ||
                TextUtils.isEmpty(base64PublicKey) ||
                TextUtils.isEmpty(signature)) {
            Log.e(TAG, "Purchase verification failed: missing data.");
            if (BuildConfig.DEBUG) {
                return true;
            }
            return false;
        }

        PublicKey key = Security.generatePublicKey(base64PublicKey);
        return Security.verify(key, signedData, signature);
    }
```

This will ensure that when the application is running in *debug mode* the method does not report an error if the signature is missing when a static response SKU purchase is verified. By checking for debug mode in this code, we ensure that this security check will function as intended when the application is built in release mode.

56.17 **Testing the In-app Billing Application**

Compile and run the application on a physical Android device with Google Play support and click on the "Buy a Click" button. This should cause the Google Play purchase dialog to appear listing the test item as illustrated in Figure 56-8:

Figure 56-8

Click on the *Buy* button to simulate a purchase at which point a Payment Successful message (Figure 56-9) should appear after which it should be possible to click on the "Click Me!" button once.

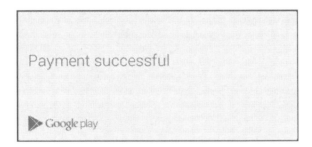

Figure 56-9

Having consumed the click, it will be necessary to purchase another click in order to once again enable the button.

56.18 **Building a Release APK**

Up until this point the example application created in this chapter has used a static response testing SKU provided by Google for early stage testing of in-app billing. The next step is to create a real in-app billing product SKU code for a virtual item and use this when testing the application. Before creating an in-app billing product, however, the application code needs to be changed slightly so that it uses a real SKU instead of the static response SKU. The product SKU that will be used in the remainder of this chapter will be named *com.example.buttonclick*, so edit the *InAppBillingActivity.java* file and modify the SKU reference accordingly:

```
public class InAppBillingActivity extends Activity {

        private static final String TAG =
                "InAppBilling";
        IabHelper mHelper;
        static final String ITEM_SKU = "android.test.purchased";
        static final String ITEM_SKU = "com.example.buttonclick";

        private Button clickButton;
        private Button buyButton;
        .
        .
        .
```

Before any products can be created, a release APK file for the application must first be uploaded to the developer console. In order to prepare this release APK file for the InAppBilling application, follow the steps outlined in the chapter entitled *Signing and Preparing an Android Application for Release*. Once the APK file has been created, select the previously registered application from the list of applications in the Google Play Developer Console and, from the resulting screen, click on the *APK* link in the left hand panel. When prompted, upload the release APK file to the console.

56.19 Creating a New In-app Product

Once the APK file has been uploaded, select the *In-app Products* menu item from the left hand panel of the developer console to display the screen shown in Figure 56-10:

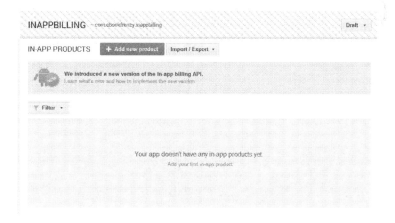

Figure 56-10

To add a new product, click on the *Add new product* button and, in the resulting panel, set the product type to *Managed product* and enter a Product ID (in this case *com.example.buttonclick*). Click on *Continue* and in the second screen enter a title, description and price for the item. Change the menu at the top of the page to *Activate*.

On returning to the In-app Products home screen, the new product should now be listed:

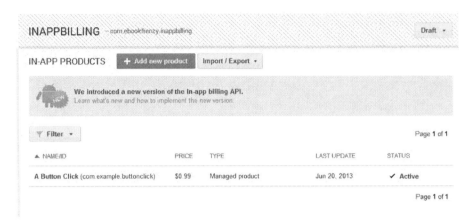

Figure 56-11

56.20 **Publishing the Application to the Alpha Distribution Channel**

The application APK file is currently stored within the Google Play Developer Console in *Draft* mode. Before it can be used for further testing using real in-app products, the application must be published to either the Alpha or Beta testing distribution channels. These channels make the application available for testing by designated groups of users.

Before an application APK can be submitted to either of the testing channels, the store listing, pricing and distribution information for the application must be completed. To meet this requirement, select the application from the Google Play Developer Console and click on the *Store Listing* link in the left hand navigation panel. From within this screen, fill out the mandatory information (those areas marked with an asterisk) and upload the necessary images. Once the form is complete, click on the *Save* button located at the top of the page. To configure the pricing and distribution information, select the *Pricing & Distribution* option from the side panel and complete the necessary fields.

When the required information has been provided, the application is eligible to be published in the testing distribution channels. Once all the information has been saved, the button in the top right hand corner of the screen should have changed from *Draft* to *Ready to Publish*. If the button still reads *Draft*, click on it and select "Why can't I publish?" from the menu. This option will list any issues that need to be resolved before the application can be published.

Once any issues have been addressed, click on the *Ready to Publish* button and select *Publish this app* from the menu. Note that it can take several hours before the application is actually published to the channel and available to respond to in-app purchase request made by testers.

56.21 Adding In-app Billing Test Accounts

Unfortunately, Google will not allow developers to make test purchases using real product SKUs from their own Google accounts. In order to test in-app billing from this point on, it will be necessary to setup other Google accounts as testing accounts. The users of these accounts must load your application onto their devices and make test purchases. To add individual test user accounts, click on the *Settings* icon located on the left hand side of your Google Play Developer Console home screen and on the account details screen scroll down to the *License Testing* section. In the corresponding text box, enter the Gmail accounts for the users who will be performing the in-app testing on your behalf before saving the changes.

In the absence of real users willing to test your application, it is also possible to set up a new Google account for testing purposes. Simply create a new Gmail account that is not connected in any way with your existing Google account identity. Once the account has been created and added as a test account in the Google Play Developer Console, open the Settings application on the physical Android device, select Users from the list of options and, on the Users screen, click on the *ADD USER* button at the top of the screen. Enter the new Gmail account and password information to create the new user on the device. Return to the device lock screen and log into the device as the test user by selecting the appropriate icon at the bottom of the screen. Note that during the test purchase, it will be necessary to enter credit card information for the new user in order to be able to fully test the in-app billing implementation.

Once the user has been added as a test account, the next step is to load the previously generated release APK file onto the device. Begin by enabling the device for USB debugging by following the steps in the chapter entitled *Testing Android Studio Apps on a Physical Android Device*. Once enabled, attach the device to the development system and remove any previous versions of the application from the device by running the following in a terminal or command prompt window, where <package name> is the full package name of the application (for example *<your domain>*.inappbilling):

```
adb uninstall <package name>
```

Next, upload the release APK created earlier in this chapter by running the following command:

```
adb -d install /path/to/release/apkfile.apk
```

Once the application is installed, locate it among the applications on the device and launch it. As long as the application remains in testing status within the Google Play Developer console no charges will be incurred by the user whilst testing the in-app billing functionality of the application. Note that the

Google Play dialog (Figure 56-12) now lists the product title and price as declared for the product in the Google Play Developer Console:

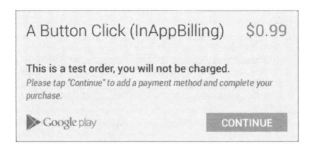

Figure 56-12

Any test purchases made in this way will be listed within the developer's Google Wallet account but will not be billed to the user performing the testing. Any transactions not cancelled manually within Google Wallet will be cancelled automatically after 14 days.

56.22 Configuring Group Testing

Testing can be expanded beyond the limits of a single test account, thereby allowing larger groups to be involved in the testing of a new application. The only restriction is that the users to be designated as testers be members of a Google Group or Google+ Community to be eligible for inclusion in the testing. To configure such a group, access the application settings within the Google Play Developer Console and select the *APK* item in the left hand navigation panel. Select either the beta or alpha testing tab (depending on which testing distribution channel you are currently using) and select the *Manage list of testers* link as highlighted in Figure 56-13:

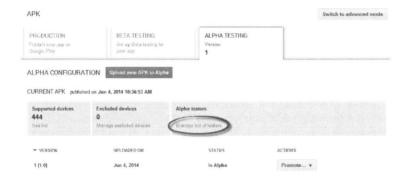

Figure 56-13

Within the resulting dialog (Figure 56-14), enter the email address of a Google Group or the URL of a Google+ Community that is ready to perform the testing. The dialog also includes the URL of the application within the Google Play store which will need to be sent to your testers so that they can download and install the application.

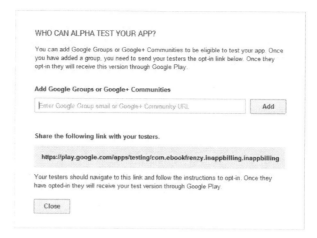

Figure 56-14

56.23 Resolving Problems with In-App Purchasing

Implementation of Google Play in-app purchasing is a multi-step process where even the simplest of mistakes can lead to unsuccessful and confusing results. There are, however, a number of steps that can be taken to identify and resolve issues. It is important to note that Google occasionally changes the mechanism for implementing and testing in-app purchasing. Before spending too much debugging time it is always worth checking the Announcements section in the Google Play Developer Console to see if anything has changed since this book was written.

If in-app purchasing is still not working, the next step is to ensure that the license key in the Google Play developer console matches that contained in the application code. If the key is not an exact match, purchase attempts will fail. Also keep in mind that it can take a few hours after an application has been published to a testing distribution channel before it will be available for testing purposes.

When testing, it is also important to keep in mind that static response SKU codes only work when the application is running in debug mode. Similarly, real SKU product codes created in the developer console can only be purchased from within a release version of the application running under an account that has been authorized from within the developer console. This account must not be the same as that of the application developer registered with the Google Play developer console.

If problems persist, check the output on the Android Studio LogCat panel while the application is running in debug mode. The in-app purchase utility classes provide useful feedback in most failure situations. The level of diagnostic detail can be increased by adding the following line of code to the in-app billing initialization sequence:

```
mHelper.enableDebugLogging(true, TAG);
```

For example:

```
mHelper.startSetup(new
        IabHelper.OnIabSetupFinishedListener() {
        public void onIabSetupFinished(IabResult result)
        {
            if (!result.isSuccess()) {
                Log.d(TAG, "In-app Billing setup failed: " +
                        result);
            } else {
                Log.d(TAG, "In-app Billing is set up OK");
                mHelper.enableDebugLogging(true, TAG);
            }
        }
    });
}
```

Finally, it is not unusual for the developer to find that code that worked in debug mode using static responses fails when in release mode with real SKU values. In this situation, the LogCat output from the running release mode application can be viewed in real-time by connecting the device to the development computer and running the following adb command in a terminal or command prompt window:

```
adb logcat
```

Generally, the diagnostic messages will provide a good starting point to identify potential causes of most failures.

56.24 **Summary**

The Google Play In-app Billing API provides a mechanism by which users can be charged for virtual goods or services from within applications. In-app products can be configured to be subscription based, one-time purchase only, or consumable (in that the item needs to re-purchased after it is used within the application).

This chapter worked through the steps involved in preparing for and implementing Google Play in-app billing within an Android application

57. An Overview of Gradle in Android Studio

U p until this point it has, for the most part, been taken for granted that Android Studio will take the necessary steps to compile and run the application projects that have been created. Android Studio has been achieving this in the background using a system known as *Gradle*.

It is now time to look at how Gradle is used to compile and package together the various elements of an application project and to begin exploring how to configure this system when more advanced requirements are needed in terms of building projects in Android Studio.

57.1 An Overview of Gradle

Gradle is an automated build toolkit that allows the way in which projects are built to be configured and managed through a set of build configuration files. This includes defining how a project is to be built, what dependencies need to be fulfilled for the project to build successfully and what the end result (or results) of the build process should be.

The strength of Gradle lies in the flexibility that it provides to the developer. The Gradle system is a self-contained, command-line based environment that can be integrated into other environments through the use of plug-ins. In the case of Android Studio, Gradle integration is provided through the appropriately named Android Studio Plug-in.

Although the Android Studio Plug-in allows Gradle tasks to be initiated and managed from within Android Studio, the Gradle command-line wrapper can still be used to build Android Studio based projects, including on systems on which Android Studio is not installed.

The configuration rules to build a project are declared in Gradle build files and scripts based on the Groovy programming language.

57.2 Gradle and Android Studio

Gradle brings a number of powerful features to building Android application projects. Some of the key features are as follows:

57.2.1 Sensible Defaults

Gradle implements a concept referred to as *convention over configuration*. This simply means that Gradle has a pre-defined set of sensible default configuration settings that will be used unless they are overridden by settings in the build files. This means that builds can be performed with the minimum of configuration required by the developer. Changes to the build files are only needed when the default configuration does not meet your build needs.

57.2.2 Dependencies

Another key area of Gradle functionality is that of dependencies. Consider, for example, a module within an Android Studio project which triggers an intent to load another module in the project. The first module has, in effect, a dependency on the second module since the application will fail to build if the second module cannot be located and launched at runtime. This dependency can be declared in the Gradle build file for the first module so that the second module is included in the application build, or an error flagged in the event the second module cannot be found or built. Other examples of dependencies are libraries and JAR files on which the project depends in order to compile and run.

Gradle dependencies can be categorized as *local* or *remote.* A local dependency references an item that is present on the local file system of the computer system on which the build is being performed. A remote dependency refers to an item that is present on a remote server (typically referred to as a *repository*).

Remote dependencies are handled for Android Studio projects using another project management tool named *Maven*. If a remote dependency is declared in a Gradle build file using Maven syntax then the dependency will be downloaded automatically from the designated repository and included in the build process. The following dependency declaration, for example, causes the Google Play Services library to be added to the project from the Google repository:

```
compile 'com.google.android.gms:play-services:+'
```

57.2.3 Build Variants

In addition to dependencies, Gradle also provides *build variant* support for Android Studio projects. This allows multiple variations of an application to be built from a single project. Android runs on many different devices encompassing a range of processor types and screen sizes. In order to target as wide a range of device types and sizes as possible it will often be necessary to build a number of different variants of an application (for example, one with a user interface for phones and another for tablet sized screens). Through the use of Gradle, this is now possible in Android Studio.

57.2.4 Manifest Entries

Each Android Studio project has associated with it an AndroidManifest.xml file containing configuration details about the application. A number of manifest entries can be specified in Gradle build files which are then auto-generated into the manifest file when the project is built. This capability is complementary to the build variants feature, allowing elements such as the application version number, application id and SDK version information to be configured differently for each build variant.

57.2.5 APK Signing

The chapter entitled *Signing and Preparing an Android Application for Release* covered the creation of a signed release APK file using the Android Studio environment. It is also possible to include the signing information entered through the Android Studio user interface within a Gradle build file so that signed APK files can be generated from the command-line.

57.2.6 ProGuard Support

ProGuard is a tool included with Android Studio that optimizes, shrinks and obfuscates Java byte code to make it more efficient and harder to reverse engineer (the method by which the logic of an application can be identified by others through analysis of the compiled Java byte code). The Gradle build files provide the ability to control whether or not ProGuard is run on your application when it is built.

57.3 The Top-level Gradle Build File

A completed Android Studio project contains everything needed to build an Android application and consists of modules, libraries, manifest files and Gradle build files.

Each project contains one top-level Gradle build file. This file is listed as *build.gradle (Project: <project name>)* and can be found in the project tool window as highlighted in Figure 57-1:

Figure 57-1

By default, the contents of the top level Gradle build file read as follows:

```
// Top-level build file where you can add configuration options common
to all sub-projects/modules.

buildscript {
    repositories {
        jcenter()
    }
    dependencies {
        classpath 'com.android.tools.build:gradle:1.0.0'

        // NOTE: Do not place your application dependencies here; they
belong
        // in the individual module build.gradle files
    }
}

allprojects {
    repositories {
        jcenter()
    }
}
```

As it stands all the file does is declare that remote libraries are to be obtained using the jcenter repository and that builds are dependent on the Android plugin for Gradle. In most situations it is not necessary to make any changes to this build file.

57.4 Module Level Gradle Build Files

An Android Studio application project is made up of one or more modules. Take, for example, a hypothetical application project named GradleDemo which contains two modules named Module1 and Module2 respectively. In this scenario, each of the modules will require its own Gradle build file. In terms of the project structure, these would be located as follows:

- Module1/build.gradle
- Module2/build.gradle

By default, the Module1 build.gradle file would resemble that of the following listing:

```
apply plugin: 'com.android.application'

android {
    compileSdkVersion 21
    buildToolsVersion "21.1.2"

    defaultConfig {
        applicationId "com.ebookfrenzy.gradledemo.module1"
        minSdkVersion 19
        targetSdkVersion 21
        versionCode 1
        versionName "1.0"
    }
    buildTypes {
        release {
            minifyEnabled false
            proguardFiles getDefaultProguardFile('proguard-
android.txt'), 'proguard-rules.pro'
        }
    }
}

dependencies {
    compile fileTree(dir: 'libs', include: ['*.jar'])
    compile 'com.android.support:appcompat-v7:21.0.3'
}
```

As is evident from the file content, the build file begins by declaring the use of the Gradle Android plug-in:

```
apply plugin: 'com.android.application'
```

The *android* section of the file then states the version of both the SDK and the Android Build Tools that are to be used when building Module1.

```
android {
    compileSdkVersion 21
    buildToolsVersion "21.1.2"
```

The items declared in the defaultConfig section define elements that are to be generated into the module's *AndroidManifest.xml* file during the build. These settings, which may be modified in the build file, are taken from the settings entered within Android Studio when the module was first created:

```
defaultConfig {
    applicationId "com.ebookfrenzy.gradledemo.module1"
    minSdkVersion 19
    targetSdkVersion 21
    versionCode 1
    versionName "1.0"
}
```

The buildTypes section contains instructions on whether and how to run ProGuard on the APK file when a release version of the application is built:

```
buildTypes {
    release {
        runProguard false
        proguardFiles getDefaultProguardFile('proguard-android.txt'),
                    'proguard-rules.pro'
    }
}
```

As currently configured, ProGuard will not be run when Module1 is built. To enable ProGuard, the *runProguard* entry needs to be changed from *false* to *true*. The *proguard-rules.pro* file can be found in the module directory of the project. Changes made to this file override the default settings in the *proguard-android.txt* file which is located on the Android SDK installation directory under *sdk/tools/proguard*.

Since no debug buildType is declared in this file, the defaults will be used (built without ProGuard, signed with a debug key and with debug symbols enabled).

An additional section, entitled *productFlavors* may also be included in the module build file to enable multiple build variants to be created. This topic will be covered in the next chapter entitled *An Android Studio Gradle Build Variants Example*.

Finally, the dependencies section lists any local and remote dependencies on which the module is dependent. The first dependency reads as follows:

```
compile fileTree(dir: 'libs', include: ['*.jar'])
```

This is a standard line that tells the Gradle system that any JAR file located in the module's lib subdirectory is to be included in the project build. If, for example, a JAR file named myclasses.jar was present in the GradleDemo/Module1/lib folder of the project, that JAR file would be treated as a module dependency and included in the build process.

A dependency on other modules within the same application project may also be declared within the build file. If, for example, Module1 has a dependency on Module2, the following line would need to be added to the dependencies section of the Module1 *build.gradle* file:

```
compile project(":Module2")
```

The last dependency line in the above example file uses Maven syntax to designate that the Android Support library needs to be included from the Android Repository:

```
compile 'com.android.support:appcompat-v7:19.+'
```

Another common repository requirement is the Google Play Services library, a dependency which can be declared as follows:

```
compile 'com.google.android.gms:play-services:+'
```

Note that the dependency declaration can include an optional version number to indicate which version of the library should be included. Version 19.0 or later is mandated for the support library whereas no particular version is specified for the play services (resulting in the most recent version being obtained from the repository).

57.5 Configuring Signing Settings in the Build File

The *Signing and Preparing an Android Application for Release* chapter of this book covered the steps involved in setting up keys and generating a signed release APK file using the Android Studio user interface. These settings may also be declared within a *signingSettings* section of the build.gradle file. For example:

```
apply plugin: 'android'
```

```
android {
    compileSdkVersion 21
    buildToolsVersion "21.1.2"

    defaultConfig {
        applicationId "com.ebookfrenzy.gradledemo.module1"
        minSdkVersion 9
        targetSdkVersion 19
        versionCode 1
        versionName "1.0"
    }

    signingConfigs {
        release {
            storeFile file("keystore.release")
            storePassword "your keystore password here"
            keyAlias "your key alias here"
            keyPassword "your key password here"
        }
    }
    buildTypes {

        .

        .

        .
}
```

The above example embeds the key password information directly into the build file. Alternatives to this approach are to extract these values from system environment variables:

```
signingConfigs {
    release {
        storeFile file("keystore.release")
        storePassword System.getenv("KEYSTOREPASSWD")
        keyAlias "your key alias here"
        keyPassword System.getenv("KEYPASSWD")
    }
}
```

Yet another approach is to configure the build file so that Gradle prompts for the passwords to be entered during the build process:

```
signingConfigs {
    release {
```

```
            storeFile file("keystore.release")
            storePassword System.console().readLine
                    ("\nEnter Keystore password: ")
            keyAlias "your key alias here"
            keyPassword System.console().readLIne("\nEnter Key password:
")
        }
    }
}
```

57.6 Running Gradle Tasks from the Command-line

Each Android Studio project contains a Gradle wrapper tool for the purpose of allowing Gradle tasks to be invoked from the command line. This tool is located in the root directory of each project folder. While this wrapper is executable on Windows systems, it needs to have execute permission enabled on Linux and Mac OS X before it can be used. To enable execute permission, open a terminal window, change directory to the project folder for which the wrapper is needed and execute the following command:

```
chmod +x gradlew
```

Once the file has execute permissions, the location of the file will either need to be added to your $PATH environment variable, or the name prefixed by ./ in order to run. For example:

```
./gradlew tasks
```

Gradle views project building in terms of number of different tasks. A full listing of tasks that are available for the current project can be obtained by running the following command from within the project directory (remembering to prefix the command with a ./ if running in Mac OS X or Linux):

```
gradlew tasks
```

It is also worth noting that this list is also available from the Gradle tool window in Android Studio as shown in Figure 57-2:

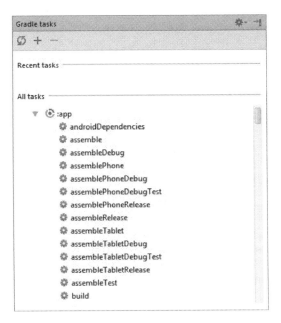

Figure 57-2

Double clicking on any task within the tool window will launch that build task.

To build a debug release of the project suitable for device or emulator testing, use the assembleDebug option:

```
gradlew assembleDebug
```

Alternatively, to build a release version of the application:

```
gradlew assembleRelease
```

57.7 Summary

For the most part, Android Studio performs application builds in the background without any intervention from the developer. This build process is handled using the Gradle system, an automated build toolkit designed to allow the ways in which projects are built to be configured and managed through a set of build configuration files. Whilst the default behavior of Gradle is adequate for many basic project build requirements, the need to configure the build process is inevitable with more complex projects. This chapter has provided an overview of the Gradle build system and configuration files within the context of an Android Studio project. The next chapter, entitled *An Android Studio Gradle Build Variants Example* will take this a step further in the form of using Gradle to build different versions of the same application project.

58. An Android Studio Gradle Build Variants Example

The goal of this chapter is to use the build variants feature of Android Studio to create a project which can be built in two flavors designed to target phone and tablet devices respectively. The build environment will be configured such that each flavor can be built using either a release or debug build type. The end result, therefore, will be four build variant options available for selection within Android Studio:

- phoneDebug
- phoneRelease
- tabletDebug
- tabletRelease

This raises the question as to the difference between a build type and a build flavor. In general, a build type defines *how* a module is built (for example whether or not ProGuard is run, how the resulting application package is signed and whether debug symbols are to be included).

The build flavor, on the other hand, typically defines *what* is built (such as which resource and source code files are to be included in the build) for each variant of the module.

Initially the two flavors will be configured such that they differ only visually in terms of the resources that are used for each target such as layouts and string values. The project will then be further extended to provide an example of how each flavor might make use of different source code bases in order to provide differing application behavior.

58.1 Creating the Build Variant Example Project

Create a new project in Android Studio, entering *BuildExample* into the Application name field and ebookfrenzy.com as the Company Domain setting before clicking on the *Next* button.

On the form factors screen, enable the *Phone and Tablet* option and set the minimum SDK setting to API 19: Android 4.4 (KitKat). Continue to proceed through the screens, requesting the creation of a blank activity named *BuildExampleActivity* with the remaining fields set to the default values.

58.2 **Adding the Build Flavors to the Module Build File**

With the initial project created, the next step is to configure the module level *build.gradle* file to add the two build flavor configurations. Within the Android Studio Project tool window, navigate to the *build.gradle* file listed as *app -> Gradle Scripts -> build.gradle (Module: app)* (Figure 58-1) and double click on it to load it into the editor:

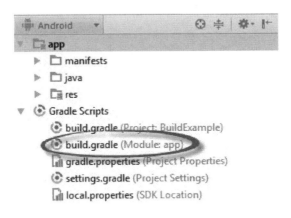

Figure 58-1

Once loaded into the editor, the build file should resemble the following listing:

```
apply plugin: 'com.android.application'

android {
    compileSdkVersion 21
    buildToolsVersion "21.1.2"

    defaultConfig {
        applicationId "com.ebookfrenzy.buildexample"
        minSdkVersion 19
        targetSdkVersion 21
        versionCode 1
        versionName "1.0"
    }
    buildTypes {
        release {
            minifyEnabled false
            proguardFiles getDefaultProguardFile('proguard-
android.txt'), 'proguard-rules.pro'
        }
    }
}
```

```
dependencies {
    compile fileTree(dir: 'libs', include: ['*.jar'])
    compile 'com.android.support:appcompat-v7:21.0.3'
}
```

As previously outlined, the project is going to consist of two build types (release and debug) together with two flavors (phone and tablet). As is evident from the build file, the release build type is already declared in the file so this does not need to be added. In practice, Gradle is also using sensible default settings for the debug build so this type also does not need to be added to the file. All this leaves is the requirement to declare the two build flavors as follows:

```
apply plugin: 'com.android.application'

android {
    compileSdkVersion 19
    buildToolsVersion "19.1.0"

    defaultConfig {
        applicationId "com.ebookfrenzy.buildexample"
        minSdkVersion 15
        targetSdkVersion 19
        versionCode 1
        versionName "1.0"
    }
    buildTypes {
        release {
            runProguard false
            proguardFiles getDefaultProguardFile('proguard-
android.txt'), 'proguard-rules.pro'
        }
    }
    productFlavors {
        phone {
            applicationId
            "com.ebookfrenzy.buildexample.app.phone"
            versionName "1.0-phone"
        }
        tablet {
            applicationId
            "com.ebookfrenzy.buildexample.app.tablet"
            versionName "1.0-tablet"
        }
```

```
        }
}

dependencies {
    compile fileTree(dir: 'libs', include: ['*.jar'])
}
```

Once the changes have been made, a yellow warning bar will appear across the top of the editor indicating that the changes to the Gradle build file need to be synchronized with the rest of the project. Click on the *Sync Now* link located in the warning panel to perform the synchronization.

Before proceeding to the next step, open the Build Variants tool window either using the quick access menu located in the status bar in the bottom left hand corner of the Android Studio main window or using the *Build Variant* tool window bar. Once loaded, clicking in the Build Variant cell for the app module should now list the four build variants:

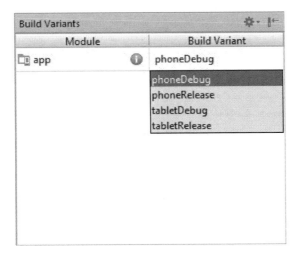

Figure 58-2

Now that the build flavors have been added to the project the project structure needs to be extended to provide support for these two new flavors.

58.3 Adding the Flavors to the Project Structure

So far in this book we have been using the Android Studio Project tool window in *Android* mode. This mode presents a less cluttered view of the directory structure of a project. When working with build variants, however, it will be necessary to switch the window into *Project* mode so that we can gain access to all of the directory levels in the project. To switch mode, click on the *Android* menu at the top of the Project tool window and select *Project* from the list of options as outlined in Figure 58-3:

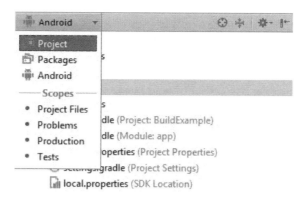

Figure 58-3

Within the Project tool window, right-click on the *BuildExample -> app -> src* directory and select the *New -> Directory* menu option and create a new directory named *phone/res/layout*. Right-click once again on the src directory, this time adding a new directory named *phone/res/values*.

Repeat these steps, this time naming the new directories *tablet/res/layout* and *tablet/res/values*. Once complete, the module section of the project structure should resemble that of Figure 58-4:

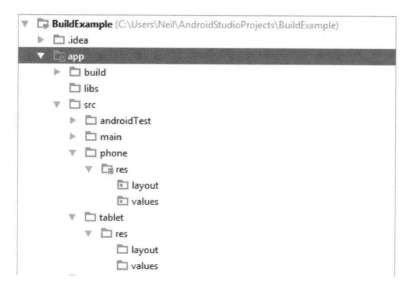

Figure 58-4

58.4 Adding Resource Files to the Flavors

Each flavor is going to need to contain a copy of the activity's *activity_build_example.xml* and *strings.xml* resource files. Each copy will then be modified to meet the requirements of the respective flavor.

An Android Studio Gradle Build Variants Example

Within the Project tool window, navigate to the *app -> src -> main -> res -> layout -> activity_build_example.xml* file and double click on it to load it into the Designer tool. With the tool in Design mode, double click on the background of the screen layout and specify *layout* as the id of the relative layout view.

In the Project tool window, right-click on the *activity_build_example.xml* file and select the *Copy* menu option. With the file copied, right-click on the *src -> phone -> res -> layout* folder and select the *Paste* menu option to add a copy of the file to the folder. Within the *Copy* dialog click on *OK* to accept the defaults.

Using the same technique, add a copy of the *src -> main -> res -> values –> strings.xml* file to the *src -> phone -> res -> values* folder.

Once the resource files have been added, edit the *strings.xml* file in the phone flavor to change the *hello_world* string resource as follows:

```xml
<?xml version="1.0" encoding="utf-8"?>
<resources>

    <string name="app_name">BuildExample</string>
    <string name="hello_world">This is the phone flavor</string>
    <string name="action_settings">Settings</string>

</resources>
```

Change the Build Variant setting to *tabletDebug* and copy and paste the phone *activity_build_example.xml* and *strings.xml* files to the corresponding locations in the tablet *res -> layout* and *res -> values* folders respectively.

Edit the tablet flavor *strings.xml* file so that the *hello_world* string resource reads "This is the tablet flavor" and modify the layout in the *activity_build_example.xml* layout file so that the TextView is positioned in the center of the display.

With the changes made, the flavor section of the project structure should now match that of Figure 58-5:

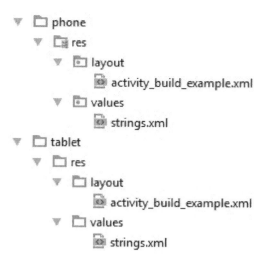

Figure 58-5

58.5 Testing the Build Flavors

At this point two flavors have been configured, each with different string and layout resources. Before moving on to the next step, it is important to check that the two build variants work as expected.

Within the Build Variants tool window, change the Build Variant setting for the *app* module to *phoneDebug* before running the application on a device or emulator. Once running, the phone flavor of the user interface should be displayed with the "This is the phone flavor" message displayed on the TextView object.

Change the build variant to *tabletDebug* and re-run the application once again, noting that this time the tablet flavor has been built with the "This is the tablet flavor" message positioned in the center of the display.

58.6 Build Variants and Class Files

As the project currently stands, the two flavors of the application share the main BuildExample activity class and all of the flavor changes have been made through resource files. Whilst much can be achieved through resource file modifications, it is inevitable that in many instances changes in the source code will be necessary from one flavor to the next. In the remainder of this chapter the main Activity class will be moved into the flavor variants so that different code bases can be used for each flavor.

58.7 Adding Packages to the Build Flavors

From this point on, each of the build flavors will have its own activity class file which can be customized to meet the requirements of the two different build targets.

Within the Build Variants tool window, begin by selecting the *phoneDebug* variant. Move to the Project tool window, right-click on the *phone* entry and select the *New -> Directory* menu option. Name the new directory *java* before clicking on the *OK* button.

Right-click on the new *java* directory, this time selecting the *New -> Package* menu option and naming the new package *com.ebookfrenzy.buildexample*.

Finally, find the *BuildExampleActivity* class which is located in the *src -> main -> java -> com.ebookfrenzy.buildexample* folder, right-click on it and select the *Copy* menu option. Right-click on the new package added to the phone variant and select the *Paste* menu option to copy the Activity source file into the package. In the resulting Copy Class dialog click on the *OK* button to accept the default settings.

The phone variant now has its own version of the activity class. Using the Build Variants tool window, change the build variant to *tabletDebug* and repeat the above steps to add instances of the package and Activity class file to the tablet flavor of the build.

At this point, Android Studio will most likely have started to complain about duplicate instances of the BuildExampleActivity class. This is because in addition to having the class declared within the flavor variants, the original instance still exists within the main build folder. Locate, therefore, and delete the *BuildExampleActivity* entry listed under *src -> main -> java -> com.ebookfrenzy.buildexample.*

58.8 Customizing the Activity Classes

With *phoneDebug* selected in the Build Variants tool window, load the *phone -> java -> com.ebookfrenzy.buildexample -> BuildExampleActivity* class file into the editing window and modify the *onCreate* method to change the background color of the RelativeLayout to red:

```
package com.ebookfrenzy.buildexample;

import android.support.v7.app.ActionBarActivity;
import android.graphics.Color;
import android.os.Bundle;
import android.view.Menu;
import android.view.MenuItem;
import android.widget.RelativeLayout;

public class BuildExampleActivity extends Activity {

    @Override
    protected void onCreate(Bundle savedInstanceState) {
        super.onCreate(savedInstanceState);
        setContentView(R.layout.activity_build_example);
```

```
            RelativeLayout myLayout =
                    (RelativeLayout) findViewById(R.id.layout);
            myLayout.setBackgroundColor(Color.RED);
    }
    .
    .
    .
}
```

Change the build variant to tabletDebug and modify the *tablet* -> *java* -> *com.ebookfrenzy.buildexample* -> *BuildExampleActivity* class file to change the background color of the layout to green:

```
package com.ebookfrenzy.buildexample;

import android.support.v7.app.ActionBarActivity;
import android.graphics.Color;
import android.os.Bundle;
import android.view.Menu;
import android.view.MenuItem;
import android.widget.RelativeLayout;

public class BuildExampleActivity extends Activity {

    @Override
    protected void onCreate(Bundle savedInstanceState) {
        super.onCreate(savedInstanceState);
        setContentView(R.layout.activity_build_example);
        RelativeLayout myLayout =
                (RelativeLayout) findViewById(R.id.layout);
        myLayout.setBackgroundColor(Color.GREEN);
    }
    .
    .
    .
}
```

Compile and run the application using each variant and note that the background color changes to indicate that each flavor is using its own activity class file in addition to different resource files.

58.9 **Summary**

The Android market now comprises a diverse range of devices all of which have different hardware capabilities and screen sizes. While there is much that can be achieved with careful use of layout managers such as the RelativeLayout and defensive coding, there will inevitably be situations where some target devices will need a separate application package to be built. In recognition of this fact, Android Studio introduces the concept of build variants and flavors designed specifically to make the task of building multiple variations of an application project easier to manage.

Index

Index

I

J

K

L

M

Index

Q

R

S

Index